BY EMILY NUSSBAUM

I Like to Watch: Arguing My Way Through the TV Revolution

Cue the Sun!: The Invention of Reality TV

CUE
THE
SUN!

CUE
THE
SUN!

THE INVENTION OF REALITY TV

EMILY NUSSBAUM

RANDOM HOUSE

New York

Published in the United States by Random House, an imprint and
division of Penguin Random House LLC, New York.

RANDOM HOUSE and the HOUSE colophon are registered trademarks of
Penguin Random House LLC.

Library of Congress Cataloging-in-Publication Data
Names: Nussbaum, Emily, author.
Title: Cue the sun : the invention of reality TV / Emily Nussbaum.
Description: New York : Random House, 2024. | Includes index.
Identifiers: LCCN 2023045197 (print) | LCCN 2023045198 (ebook) |
ISBN 9780525508991 (hardcover) | ISBN 9780525509004 (ebook)
Subjects: LCSH: Reality television programs—United States—History
and criticism.
Classification: LCC PN1992.8.R43 N87 2024 (print) |
LCC PN1992.8.R43 (ebook) | DDC 791.45/6—dc23/eng/20240116
LC record available at https://lccn.loc.gov/2023045197
LC ebook record available at https://lccn.loc.gov/2023045198

Printed in the United States of America on acid-free paper

randomhousebooks.com

9 8 7 6 5 4 3 2 1

First Edition

Book design by Debbie Glasserman

To Clive, with chains of love

When you invent the ship, you also invent the shipwreck.

—Paul Virilio

They bought their tickets, they knew what they were getting into. I say, let 'em crash.

—Airplane!

CONTENTS

Introduction: Better Write That One Fast xiii

SPAGHETTI AGAINST THE WALL: 1947–1989 1

1. **The Reveal:** *Queen for a Day* and *Candid Camera* 3

2. **The Gong:** The Filthy, Farkakte Chuck Barris 1970s 29

3. **The Betrayal:** *An American Family* 49

4. **The Clip:** *America's Funniest Home Videos* and *Cops* 85

THE REV UP: 1990–2000 111

5. **The House:** *The Real World* 113

6. **The Con:** The Nihilistic Fox '90s 147

7. **The Game:** The Invention of *Survivor* (and Mark Burnett) 171

8. **The Island:** *Survivor: Borneo* 193

9. **The Feed:** *Big Brother* 234

CUE THE SUN!: 2001–2007(ish) 265

10. **The Explosion:** Reality Blows Up—and Becomes an Industry 267

11. **The Rose:** *The Bachelor* and *Joe Millionaire* 304

12. **The Wink:** Bravo and the Gentrification of Reality TV 333

13. **The Job:** *The Apprentice* and the End of Reality Innocence 360

Epilogue: Fake It Till You Make It 388

Acknowledgments 395

Bibliography 399

Index 421

INTRODUCTION
Better Write That One Fast

ONE WARM SPRING NIGHT, BACK IN 2003, I MET UP WITH TWO FELlow freelance journalists at a bar in Boston. We were planning to talk about potential book ideas, a nerve-racking exercise, since none of us had written any actual books. Two bourbons in, I made my pitch: I wanted to write a book about a hot new pop-culture genre, "reality television."

That year, reality shows seemed to be everywhere, mushrooming across the TV schedule, an inescapable topic of debate. Three years earlier, CBS had struck ratings gold with *Survivor,* a controversial game show in which regular people ate live, squirming grubs on an island in Borneo. Now ABC had *The Bachelor,* on which twenty-five women competed for one man; Fox's *American Idol* was minting new pop stars; and I'd been secretly binge-watching an even more perverse project online—a voyeuristic hotbox called *Big Brother,* which had a newfangled live "streaming" component. Reality stars were bumping actors from the covers of magazines. Every week something weirder (*Man vs. Beast? Chains of Love?*) debuted. It felt like a new Wild West, full of crazy characters making big bets, an electric frenzy that resembled early Hollywood, so maybe there was a book in it?

My friend shot me a skeptical glance. "You better write *that* one fast," he said. Reality television was a fad, he told me—a bubble that would pop before I could get anything on the page.

I dropped the idea for two decades.

LUCKILY, THAT TURNED OUT TO BE THE RIGHT PLAN. OVER THE next two decades, as I worked as a freelance journalist, then a magazine editor, and eventually a TV critic for *The New Yorker,* I watched, mesmerized, as the reality genre matured—or metastasized, depending on how you looked at it—gradually soaking into every crevice of the culture. *Survivor,* a show that critics had once warned would shatter Western civilization, became a cozy pandemic favorite, whose early seasons families bonded over. Whole channels, most notably Bravo, were devoted to reality shows, while teenagers—who had never known a world *without* reality TV—uploaded thumbnail versions of these programs on TikTok, directed by and starring themselves. In the most sinister outcome, a reality star had been elected president, embraced by voters who mistook him for the masterful tycoon he played on NBC's *The Apprentice,* and then revamped the Oval Office, running it as if it were the NBC boardroom.

The scrappy, upstart genre was now a muscular industry, one whose laborers preferred not to call it "reality TV," a label no one loved in the first place. (Over the years, producers had unsuccessfully lobbied for replacement terms like "emotainment" and "dramality.") Instead, you were supposed to refer to it as "unscripted programming," an anodyne phrase designed to neutralize the taboos that still buzzed around reality shows (which is what I'm going to call them in this book), no matter how hard anyone tried to swat them away.

Still, if my friend had been wrong about a few things, so was I. Two decades earlier, I had glibly assumed that reality formats were a modern phenomenon, as much a symptom of technological change as an artistic genre—an internetty, turn-of-the-millennium, digital-culture thing, having emerged right as the Web blinked into existence and cameras burrowed into cellphones. When everything we did was recorded, a wave of narcissism had, naturally, started to rise. If reality television had any kind of history, I figured, it probably dated back to around 1992, when *The Real World* debuted on MTV.

In fact, as I discovered when I began to dig deeper, reality programming wasn't all that new—and neither was the moral outrage that inevitably accompanied it, like a clap of thunder after a bolt of lightning. Both phenomena went back more than seven decades, to the mid-1940s, shortly after World War II, in the age of radio. And as each new storm of reality experimentation emerged—starting with the jaw-dropping phenomenon of *Candid Camera,* which began as a radio show called *Candid Microphone*—the same thing happened: Critics dismissed these programs as a fad. They were cruel carnivals, which traded in humiliation. They were dumb spectacles, made on the cheap. They were shoddy imitators of better types of art: less sophisticated than cinéma vérité documentary, shallower than fiction, too crass to have any lasting value. Reality shows were strike-breakers, too—the slimy beneficiaries of anti-labor tactics, funded by executives who didn't want to pay writers and actors. Reality programming might get attention and, for a while, high ratings, but it would never last.

To audiences, however, these programs had always had an obvious allure: They offered something authentic, buried inside something fake. They stripped away the barrier between the star and the viewer. More than any other cultural product, they functioned as a mirror of the people who watched them—and if that reflection was sometimes cruel, it was also funny, riveting, outrageous, and affecting, even if—maybe especially if—you found it disturbing.

It's hard to nail down one clear definition for reality programming, but in this book I conceive of the genre as "dirty documentary": It's cinéma vérité filmmaking that has been cut with commercial contaminants, like a street drug, in order to slash the price and intensify the effect. Reality programs are shows that merge documentary techniques with some more rigid, easily repeatable approach to storytelling, like the game show or the soap opera, the talent contest or the sports competition—old-school episodic structures that were native to serialized radio and television. Cast real people, in other words—then put a tight frame around them, and squeeze.

Sometimes, the early reality shows were earnest social experiments, designed to explore human nature; other times, they were tawdry cash-grabs. But mostly, they were a bit of both. Their low cultural status was inseparable from the warning label slapped on the product—or, as critic James Poniewozik once put it wryly, "Reality TV is nonfiction television of which I personally disapprove." Even at their coarsest, though, reality shows offered up a powerful glimpse of human vulnerability, breaking taboos about what you were allowed to say or see.

The gamblers who placed their bets on the reality genre were, from the start, an intrepid crew. They were rogue documentarians and amateur sociologists, gleeful manipulators and shameless voyeurs, piratical entrepreneurs who kept a sharp eye on the bottom line. They were mostly (but not all) white men, something that was true of the majority of the people who had the power to produce television, until recently. Some of them, like *Gong Show* host Chuck Barris and Fox impresario Mike Darnell, were distinguished by their P. T. Barnum–like enthusiasm—a gift for humbug (Barnum for "bullshit") and a warm, seductive salesmanship. Others, like *Candid Camera* creator Allen Funt, had a Warholian coldness, a craving to observe and control. A few women—particularly *Real World* cocreator Mary-Ellis Bunim and the Prada-wearing trickster Lisa Levenson—helped shaped crucial elements of the genre. And a striking slice, from the 1990s onward, were gay men, like *Real World* cocreator Jon Murray, who had a deep understanding of behavior as performance.

Whatever their motives, this cadre grasped one thing: If you could knock your subjects off balance, they'd reveal a moment so shocking and, sometimes, so tender or surprising, that it would shatter viewer skepticism. It was the quality that Allen Funt liked to describe as being "caught in the act of being yourself," the fuel that fed the reality engine, at both its loftiest moments and its lowest. Capturing that fuel required a new kind of artistic engineering—and a new kind of collaboration between cast and crew.

This meant a new kind of reality laborer, a group of workers who, during the early years of the genre, had to invent their own jobs from scratch. There were field producers who created an intimate bond with cast members; skilled editors who figured out how to cut a thrilling story from real life, by any means necessary; and "preditors," the alarming term of art for people who did both. There were casting directors who could see the star quality (or the necessary instability) in amateurs, writers who knew how to brainstorm clever challenges, and camera operators and audio technicians who could hover invisibly in regular people's lives. There was also a brilliant (and largely unknown) universe of puzzle-building producers who invented reality formats that transformed the culture, like the ingenious format for *Survivor*.

Mostly, though, the industry required a new mindset: an ability to tolerate moral ambiguity, creating strange, temporary, but intense professional relationships whose residue would be edited into (and, in a sense, become) the show itself. Working behind the scenes as a reality laborer wasn't easy, early on or more recently: Without union protection, struggling in the margins of Hollywood, crew members were often flinty-eyed scrappers, who became numb to, and also proud of, their ability to endure terrible work conditions. But for the people at the top, the job could be an intoxicant: It gave you the god-like power to create stories from the lives of ordinary human beings.

That theme is central to Peter Weir's darkly prescient 1998 movie *The Truman Show,* which debuted just before the reality explosion at the turn of the millennium, inspired by early reality hits including MTV's *The Real World* and the Fox show *Cops.* In *The Truman Show,* Jim Carrey plays Truman Burbank, a man who suspects that he's trapped inside a soap opera. Truman's friends and family are actors, smiling like sharks; his kitchen is full of products paid for by the show's sponsors. The seemingly wholesome '50s-style town he grew up in is full of hidden cameras—and an invisible audience has been watching him when he sleeps. When Truman escapes in the middle of the night, the program's showrunner, Christof, played by Ed Harris with a sphinxlike hauteur and an auteur's beret, is determined to hunt him down: Truman's hidden by the darkness, so Christof commands, "Cue the sun!," flooding the world with sunlight.

Truman sprints toward the horizon. Desperate, he boards a ship, sailing through a wild, artificially induced storm. And then, with a jolt, the prow of his ship punctures the edge of the world, which is also the edge of an enormous Hollywood set. Just as he pushes open a door that reads EXIT, he hears a voice from above. It's Christof, who is hidden behind the clouds. He needs to stop Truman from leaving the show and ending their relationship.

"I am the creator," explains Christof gently. And then, after an infinitesimal pause, "of a television show that gives hope and joy and inspiration to millions."

Truman asks, "Then who am I?," the question that lies at the heart of reality television and also many other forms of art.

"You're the *star*."

I BEGAN THIS BOOK EXCITED TO DIG INTO THE LIVELY, OUTRA-geous origins of the reality genre, but the deeper I dug, the darker things got. There are people whose lives were wrecked by reality TV; there are methods of production so ugly they're hard to look at; and reality programs, like any kind of television, reflect the limits, and the bigotries, of their creators. Early reality production was utterly reliant on the innocence of its stars, their inability to understand what they were consenting to: That was the genre's secret sauce, its original sin.

But if this is a story that's impossible to tell without some pain, there is also a lot of glory and beauty in it. Reality shows threatened the economics of television, but they also made it bigger—bolder, broader, stranger. They made visible the sort of people that the medium had historically ignored, from the working-class single moms on *Queen for a Day* to Cuban American activist Pedro Zamora, a young gay man with AIDS who turned into a national star on *The Real World*. These shows cracked open forbidden topics like homosexuality and divorce, making private subjects public ones. And despite the genre's reputation for crudeness, reality production added sophistication to the television medium. Adventure shows like *Survivor* spearheaded unusual new methods of filming action; many of the tools of modern TV comedy—the shaky-cam, the confessional, the insta-flashback—were adapted from reality shows, often in the guise of satirizing their excesses. Without the reality TV boom, there's no *The Office*.

For critics, writing about the reality genre has always been a trap. If you clutch your pearls—if you can't see the fun in it, if you won't stop yammering about Baudrillard—you turn into a scold. But if you treat reality too lightly, dismissing it as a frothy nothing, you've missed the point, too. This book is an attempt to take a different approach: to describe the reality genre through the voices of the people who built it, step by step, experiment by experiment, a series of failures that alternated with (and sometimes doubled as) breakthroughs. It's an attempt to see it as they saw it, as well as seeing it from the audience's point of view.

Like other "lowbrow" art forms—comic books, horror films, pornography—reality has often been treated as a substance sold under the counter, less an art form than a drug, powerful because it was forbidden. As Marshall McLuhan once put it, art is anything you can get away with. But the discomfort that has always radiated around these shows—their nosiness, their brutality—isn't an argument for looking away from them. It's a reason to look closer.

SPAGHETTI
AGAINST
THE WALL

||||||||||||||||||||||||||||||||||||||||||||||||

1947–1989

1

||||||||

THE REVEAL

Queen for a Day and *Candid Camera*

DIRTY DOCUMENTARY SET OFF ITS FIRST MORAL PANIC IN 1947, just after World War II. Radio still ruled the roost back then, as it had since the 1920s, broadcasting opera, jazz and news, comedy and Shakespeare, all of it live—a cozy console the whole family could huddle around. Now and then, there was a prestige blockbuster like Orson Welles's *War of the Worlds*—a scripted sci-fi drama so realistic, listeners freaked out, convinced that aliens were invading the Earth, for real. If you were a radio writer or actor, you could make a nice living. If you were a star, you could make a killing.

Still, even in the early days, ordinary people sometimes stumbled onto the airwaves—and around the 1930s, disc jockeys began taking phone calls from listeners. These unknowns did something the pros had never done: They confessed their secrets to the world, liberated by the sensation of strangers listening in. It was the beginning of talk radio—the first strand of the "audience participation" trend, a fad that would jump to television in the late 1940s, like a tapped cigarette ash starting a forest fire. Pundits hated the audience participation shows from the start, a response that was saturated with class revulsion: These were vulgar programs, created by vulgar people, for vulgar people, *about* vulgar people. Worst of all, they were insanely popular.

One of the earliest of these DJ-pioneers was Lester Kroll, a former cab driver from New York City and the son of an immigrant lacemaker. In 1929, Kroll went through an ugly divorce, and then, after he refused to pay child support, got tossed into "alimony jail." His months in the clink appear to have radicalized Kroll: He became an anti-alimony activist—and then a self-appointed expert on marriage itself. According to *It Sounds Impossible,* a dishy 1963 history of early radio written by former CBS executives Sam J. Slate and Joe Cook, the self-promoting Kroll, a wannabe playwright and an amateur lecturer on the Times Square "flea-circus belt," found his way into radio through the Depression-era WPA, then shrewdly re-branded. By 1932, he was no longer a high school dropout: Instead, he was thought leader "John J. Anthony," the highly educated founder of a "Marital Relations Institute." He offered advice on the tiny Long Island station WMRJ, and soon, across the nation. "Never was a program concept uglier—or a show more fun to listen to than *The Original Good Will Hour,*" wrote Slate and Cook.

Each week, Anthony invited fifteen to twenty guests, chosen based on their letters, to come to his studio, then "eat their hearts out over who did what to whom at home." The radio host's visitors confessed to everything under the sun, from cheating to (on at least one occasion) murder. Critics sometimes suspected Anthony of using actors, but no fakery was required, according to Slate and Cook: A cadre of listeners stepped up right away, eager to "broadcast [their] troubles, anonymously or otherwise." The show became a smash hit, particularly with women, who ate up the host's confident, supremely smarmy advice, which often boiled down to "stop nagging." By 1939, the show was airing on more than seven hundred stations and Anthony had become a tycoon, the Dr. Phil of his era—and also a juicy target for satirists, who mocked him as a maudlin phony.

The Good Will Hour got canceled, then re-upped, a few times, but by the time it ended in 1953, it had plenty of company on the dial, as radio producers encouraged regular people to step in front of the mic, for cash or kicks—and, often, for both. Some of these programs were traditional quiz shows, like *Dr. I.Q.* or *Name That Tune,* a tradition that went back to the 1923 man-on-the-street program *Brooklyn Eagle Quiz on Current Events.* But more anarchic formats bubbled up as well, relying less on skill than on their guests' willingness to uncork and let loose. On *People Are Funny,* contestants took wacky dares, like checking a seal in to The Knickerbocker Hotel. On *Welcome Travelers,* train passengers spooled out personal stories. On *Bride and Groom,* couples got married, live, decades before *The Bachelor* was a dark gleam in reality producer Mike Fleiss's eye. On *Kiss and Make Up,* Milton Berle judged marital fights, while on *Rebuttal,* media victims gave their side of the story. The most sadistic show of the bunch, *Truth or Consequences,* featured a buzzer and humiliating punishments for the losers.

For the ordinary Americans who agreed to appear on them, these programs were a lark—a quick, bracing splash of attention, with little downside. On the radio, you might become briefly famous, but it was stardom of an appealingly low-stakes type: When no one could see your face, you could be a celebrity to your neighbors while remaining anonymous in the larger world.

By the late 1940s, the audience participation formats had evolved into a robust genre, so ubiquitous that they were a threat to scripted shows and high-budget star performances. In 1948, the dryly scathing radio critic John Crosby, who wrote for the *New York Herald Tribune,* joked that there were so many audience participation shows on the air, they'd soon outnumber the fans who enjoyed them: "Eventually ALL the people will be tearing around from one radio studio to another, answering the questions and carting home the iceboxes. Nobody will have time to listen to the darn thing."

Crosby, a Yale dropout who, like Lester Kroll, had originally intended to write plays, became, instead, the shrewdest observer of the audience participation era, which exploded just as he rejoined the *Herald Tribune,* in 1946, after a stint in the military. (A crime reporter when he first got the assignment, he didn't even own a radio.) A genial literary assassin who once joked that his job was to be "literate about the illiterate, witty about the witless, and coherent about the incoherent," Crosby devoted dozens of droll columns to these protoreality shows, taking potshots at their absurdity, their frivolity, and their commercialism. He was genuinely disturbed by one trend, however—the "misery shows," in the tradition of Mr. Anthony's call-in advice show, the kind of programming that was fueled by, and also designed to produce, tears and trauma.

In 1946, Crosby wrote a scorching pan of *The Good Will Hour,* repelled by Anthony's "sanctimonious and infinitely complacent" schtick. Then, one month later, Crosby launched a full-scale attack on the audience participation genre, in a column titled "The Modern Thumb Screw." It had a banger of a lede:

> About two thousand years ago, a Roman emperor used to pitch winsome young Christian girls into his eel pond and watch with great enjoyment while they were devoured by the eels. This served two purposes. It fattened the eels for the table and it amused the emperor.
>
> This practice has been illegal for some time but the enjoyment of human suffering, otherwise known as sadism, is still buried not too deeply in all of us. Since radio is always eager to gratify our instincts, particularly our baser instincts, it has devised its own eel pond, the human misery program.

Crosby described, in furious detail, a short-lived radio show, *A. L. Alexander's Goodwill Court,* in which legal disputes were adjudicated, live, by a mediation board—a sort of great-grandfather to the 1980s small-claims court TV series *The People's Court.* In one episode of *Goodwill Court,* wrote Crosby, a birth mother and a foster mother had sobbed as they fought over custody of a child, rattled by what the critic described as "mike fright," the terror of speaking into the live microphone. The program amounted to "a peep show of the worst sort," he wrote, comparing it to superior art forms. Fiction writers had the moral bandwidth to handle this depth of human suffering, he argued; nonfiction radio shows merely exploited it. "From Mr. Alexander's program we get life in the raw without poetry, without art. The tabloid newspapers show us the undraped leg.

The human misery program offers us the undraped heart—listen to it fizz."

Other observers were more amused than outraged. The same year Crosby wrote "The Modern Thumb Screw," Associated Press writer Jean Meegan published a more playful account of the new fad, with the heading "Critics Scream, Actors Howl, but Audience Participation Shows Go On and On and On." Like Crosby, Meegan took a few shots at the new genre, quoting a psychologist who decried the hollow lives of guests, in a sniffy description that might condemn many modern podcasters: "Being 35 years old and living in Brooklyn isn't much of an achievement, but on the radio it sounds meritorious."

Still, Meegan acknowledged the true source of this boom, which was not egotism, but economics. Making scripted radio, which required writers, actors, and expensive sound effects, cost a fortune—and producers hated negotiating with unions. To stage an audience participation show, all they needed was a host and some unpaid volunteers, plus a sponsor to offer up prizes. At that price tag, even the jankiest content would turn on a fire hose of profit. Unsurprisingly, this situation posed a significant threat to the labor force, and in her article, Meegan quoted an actor who was certain that his union, the American Federation of Radio Artists, would be able to squash the audience participation craze by the fall. Then she quoted an anonymous radio executive, who had a deadpan comeback: "One recourse for an unemployed actor or writer is for him to start his own audience participation show."

The way Meegan saw it, audience participation shows might be lurid, they might be cheaply produced strikebusters, but they were also something else: originals. They were the one radio format that didn't simply imitate real-life entertainments like plays and concerts. And they had another source of appeal, as well. The voice of a regular person, quavering with amateurism, slid open what her experts described as a "psychological window," a space for authentic feeling, letting in a gust of spontaneity and helping listeners to feel less alone. Not that that feeling was always a virtuous one, she acknowledged: "You never know when someone will make a fool of himself."

III

EVEN IN THE EEL POND OF AUDIENCE PARTICIPATION, SOME SAC-rifices were tastier than others. The most notorious of these shows—and one of the biggest moneymakers—was *Queen for a Day*, which debuted as a radio show in 1945, then jumped to network TV in 1956, where it ran for eight years. A kind of upside-down beauty pageant whose winner was the woman with the ugliest life, *Queen for a Day* was hosted by the unctuous Jack Bailey, a former World's Fair barker who gazed hypnotically into the camera lens, as if he were locking eyes with a desperate housewife watching at home, then pointed his finger at her, intoning the magic words: "Would *you* like to be queen for a day?"

The format, which had been dreamed up over a boozy lunch by quiz show host Dud Williamson and ad executives Raymond R. Morgan and Robert Raisbeck, was one of several so-called "sob story" formats. On most of these shows, which had names like *Strike It Rich* (aka "The Quiz Show with a Heart"), poor contestants won prizes by answering simple questions and describing their desperate circumstances. Real philanthropies hated the trend: The New York City commissioner of welfare denounced *Strike It Rich* as "a disgusting spectacle and a national disgrace." For their critics, the issue was often less that these programs were immoral than that they were dangerously popular: Broke hopefuls were streaming into Manhattan, then ending up on government aid.

Still, *Queen for a Day* stood out from the pack in its acute focus on female suffering, offering up a unique blend of abjection and Vegas glitz, like *The Bachelor* crossed with GoFundMe. In each episode, Bailey interviewed four audience members, who filled out "wish cards" before the show. After carefully extracting a woman's tragic backstory, using a series of prying questions, Bailey would ask her to name a special gift she wanted most. "A candidate had to want something we could plug—a stove, a carpet, a plane trip, an artificial leg, a detective agency, a year's supply of baby food," wrote *Queen for a Day* producer Howard Blake, decades later, in a 1975 essay called "An Apologia from the Man Who Produced the Worst Program in TV History." "The more gifts we gave the queen, the more money we made."

The winner was determined using an "applause-o-meter," a quivering needle that measured audience enthusiasm. In the TV version, the cameras focused straight on the soon-to-be losers' faces, capturing their nervous blinking, lip-biting, and tense grins, as the results rolled in. Then Bailey would crown the winner, draping the queen in a floor-length sable robe, seating her on a throne, and handing her a scepter and roses, while "Pomp and Circumstance" played. It was a DIY twist on the British royal coronation, a ritual that was televised for the first time in 1953, and watched by, among millions of others around the globe, Mary Trump, with her six-year-old son, Donald, in her mansion in Queens, New York.

Each episode's queen got a deluge of free goods; losers got lesser gifts, like nylons or a toaster. But for the all-female audience, the true payoff was the show's emotional undertow, a pungent blend of contempt, tenderness, and pity. Some contestants wept; others were brassy or guarded. "My husband has had two heart attacks and he's not allowed to lift," a woman with an elegant bob told Bailey softly, asking for a hospital gurney for her fifteen-year-old son, confined to his bed after spinal surgery. "You've got shattered nerves," Bailey told a nervous blonde from Toledo, who twisted her handkerchief anxiously, near tears. "I lost my husband in November, in a hunting accident. . . . His buddy accidentally shot him," explained the mother of two, who asked for money to train as a beautician. In an era when women were expected to marry early and have kids, then stay tight-lipped about anything that went wrong, these agonizing public displays of suffering were at once degrading and glorifying, like sainthood. Beyond the stories themselves, the show's focus was on the gasp, the sob, the pause—the "kinetics of distress," as Marsha F. Cassidy put it in the book *What Women Watched*.

In the press, *Queen for a Day* was sometimes condemned but mostly condescended to, as icky, sticky girl stuff. In a 1960 profile of Bailey, published two years after the quiz show scandals exposed the fact that networks had fixed popular game shows like *21*, the host pushed back at the idea that his show was treacly or tedious ("I look at it like a doctor: each case is different") and also described it as "almost 100 percent deceit-proof." The TV audience, he argued, could always detect a faker—and what's more, any queen who made up her tale of misery had neighbors who would snitch on her. "We don't need a battery of investigators to know that women are telling the truth about their problems," he said.

On this issue, at least, Bailey had a point. There was in fact a more positive way to view *Queen for a Day,* as a rare outlet for a kind of prefeminist (or maybe protofeminist) candor about women's lives. The late 1940s, when television was new, had been, however briefly, a bonanza for female creators, including Gertrude Berg, a creator of the sitcom, and Irna Phillips, who invented the soap opera. Then, in 1950, the hammer fell—and during the McCarthy era, a stifling conservatism descended. The sole survivor was Lucille Ball, a brilliant performer who played Lucy Ricardo, a thirsty nobody desperate to become famous—in other words, exactly the kind of woman who might be eager to go on a show like *Queen for a Day.* For the next decade, as the media ideal narrowed, the networks rolled out sitcoms glamorizing stay-at-home mothers like Harriet Nelson on *The Adventures of Ozzie and Harriet,* happily vacuuming in pearls and heels. Other women—single or divorced, "ethnic," fat, sick, homely, or poor—were reduced to comic relief.

On *Queen for a Day,* these women had always been the stars. And if, in one sense, their suffering was packaged as entertainment for better-off Harriets, it was also true that they got to tell those stories directly, on camera, in their own voices. Beneath its layers of schmaltz, *Queen for a Day* sent an unsettling message: The nuclear family didn't guarantee your safety. "In *Queen* the concerns of working class women were front and center," the scholar Georganne Scheiner wrote in her 2003 essay "Would You Like to Be Queen for a Day?," in which she described many of the show's grittier subjects, which included physical abuse and abandonment. For all its mawkishness, *Queen for a Day* functioned as an early "consciousness raising" group, letting women bond over—and see patterns in—their shared troubles. Occasionally, a woman's distress ran too deep for the show to handle: In one case, according to Scheiner, a woman asked for $100 so that she could pursue a divorce. Her husband had tried to rape her six-year-old daughter, then stolen the car. That story never made it on the air.

Back when Southern TV stations refused to air TV shows with integrated casts, *Queen for a Day* also featured a rare racial variety of contestants. If Bailey took a smirky tone with white women, he could be even cruder with women of color, asking a Native American woman if her husband was a medicine man and telling a middle-aged African American contestant, "You've been a fine girl," as he patted her head. Even so, the show treated Black, Brown, and Jewish women as emotionally complex figures, the psychological equals of white women, wrote Scheiner. The most extreme experiences were presented side by side with more ordinary ones: One week, a contestant asked to have her concentration camp tattoo removed.

Like so much of female pop culture—from *Good Housekeeping* magazine to *The Real Housewives* a half-century later—*Queen for a Day* was full of mixed messages. It was an exposé of poverty dripping with luxury ads; it was a just-us-girls gabfest hosted by a mansplaining sexist, touting products like the perfume Fame by Corday ("Anything can happen when you wear Fame!"). If the show had a fraudulent quality, Scheiner argued, it was less about the women's stories than how they told them. You couldn't be queen if the prize was for you. It had to be for your preemie baby, your sick aunt—and the more showily self-abnegating you were, the more likely other women would let you win.

The show's effectiveness lay in the moments when this mask dropped, exposing extreme emotions that tested the limits of this saintly ideal. In one episode, the contestants included Marguerite, a widow with two disabled sons, who was grieving her parents; Kay, a stylish mother of seven who hoped to win a diaper service for triplets; and Viva, a plain-faced waitress. Viva's husband, she explained to Bailey glumly, but with a fascinating flash of frustration, was a salesman who didn't know how to sell any products. Viva herself had waited tables for twenty-five years, only to lose her job when she got leg surgery. Still, what she wanted most was the chance to fulfill a promise she'd made to her son, who was "all crippled up with cerebral palsy": He needed a special bicycle; he needed a wheelchair. As Bailey drew out each painful detail of her desperation, Viva's manner became muted, downcast.

Then she won. When the results were announced, Viva looked stunned, then let out a shy smile. When Bailey put the crown on her head, he yelled, rather goofily, "I crown you Queen Viva!" Seated on the throne, holding a spray of flowers, Viva's face shifted, unnervingly, back into something like despair, or blankness, as she was offered an absurd suite of gifts, which were described in reverent detail for five and a half minutes. On top of the bike and wheelchair, there was a Revere camera "that does all the thinking for you" (Viva nervously waved it away). Then a Westinghouse kitchen suite, an Adler sewing machine, an Imperial dishwasher, an Amana refrigerator stocked with frozen dinners, a night out at The Brown Derby, a hotel vacation, $100 for her son to buy music, and also, the chance to attend the opening night of *Spartacus*.

Viva should have been overjoyed—these products, the show kept insisting, were the tools that would fix her life. Instead, her eyes darted and she gulped, sorrowful. If everything around Viva was fake, it only made Viva's expression, from down deep inside the eel pond, feel more indelibly real.

CHAOTIC, UNPREDICTABLE EMOTIONAL RESPONSES LIKE VIVA'S— reactions that felt too potent and complex to be faked—were the ultimate prize for the audience participation viewer, a precious substance produced under pressure. Still, you could go only so far with the willing.

In the late '40s, a clever firebrand named Allen Funt crossed that line with *Candid Microphone,* a revolutionary twist on the audience participation genre. Funt's radio show—which ultimately jumped to television as *Candid Camera*—became the first prank show, recording its subjects without them knowing it. The prank show would become the second stream of the reality genre, after the game show. Later on, Funt's legacy would be remembered through a nostalgic mist, as a sweeter and more innocent project than its descendants—

rude prank shows like *Jackass* and *Punk'd;* cerebral meta-comedies by Sacha Baron Cohen and Nathan Fielder; and the legion of tricksters on YouTube and TikTok—but in its own era, Funt's show was viewed not as a cute comedy but as a deeply destabilizing experiment. It was a rude, even radical, provocation to a culture that was grounded in repression.

It had a rude, radical creator, too. A prickly workaholic, Funt understood that his critics saw him as a snoop. He preferred to think of himself as a student of human behavior—not a voyeur but an observer, and even a kind of healer and educator, putting a mirror up to human nature. To his frustration, Funt would become, instead, the first major auteur of reality television, the inventor of two crucial tools: the hidden-camera stunt and the producer-provocateur.

Funt, who was born in 1914 in Brooklyn, the son of Russian Jewish immigrants, initially hoped to be an artist. "I was the furthest from a practical joker," Funt once told an interviewer, describing himself as "serious-minded, broody, moody." He felt overshadowed by his academically brilliant older sister; he was also wounded by the death of his younger brother from leukemia. Funt graduated high school at fifteen, then studied at Pratt Institute and Cornell University, where he took a part-time job with social psychologist Kurt Lewin. By the time he graduated, in 1934, he'd lost faith in his talent as a painter. After a miserable stint in a Wall Street boiler room, Funt tried advertising ("organized lying," he called it), then got a job in radio, right at the peak of the audience participation boom.

In the early 1940s, Funt worked as a script boy for Eleanor Roosevelt's radio appearances and wrote stunts for *Truth or Consequences.* He had a gift for writing schlock, but the job bored him. He sold a scavenger hunt format called *The Funny Money Man,* a hit series he once dismissed as "the stupidest show on radio." Soon after, the Second World War started and Funt got drafted and became an officer. It was then, at twenty-seven, during the three years he spent ginning up programming for Armed Forces Radio, that Funt stumbled into the mission that would drive him all his life.

His first eureka moment was the result of a new gadget. Assigned to the Signal Corps at Camp Gruber in Oklahoma, the young officer got his hands on a wild new device, a miniaturized audio recorder. Up until then, recorders had been bulky, too heavy to lift from a desk: When you interviewed someone, they knew that they were being recorded. Now the whole world was his studio. According to Funt's 1994 memoir, *Candidly, Allen Funt: A Million Smiles Later*, he convinced a friend to pretend to dump his girlfriend while Funt hid out in the bushes, recording her reaction. The stunt misfired, badly: The woman burst into tears, then confessed that she had married someone else—and Funt's friend chased Funt around the base in a rage.

Meanwhile, at his day job for Armed Forces Radio, Funt had been honing his skills as a producer, whipping up a series of clever shows, each of them designed to raise morale. On *Behind the Dog Tag*, he fulfilled wishes for enlisted men, always adding some outrageous twist in the process, like filling a swimming pool with beer. Assigned to create a military fundraiser, Funt used a theater to stage an epic spectacle, a tearjerker in which a soldier, lit by a spotlight, walked down the center aisle toward his weeping mother, taking one precious step for each war bond bought by audience members, as the crowd roared with excitement. Funt also hosted *The Gripe Booth*, a radio show on which soldiers were encouraged to vent about their problems on the base. When the men froze with "mic fright," Funt decided to game the situation: He discreetly turned the red recording light off, so they didn't realize he was still taping.

Any one of these early productions, with their blend of pathos and slapstick, emotional manipulation and razzle-dazzle—plus devious uses of technology—might have provided a blueprint for future reality producers. Funt had a showman's impulse for turning people's taboo desires into theater, an instinct for voyeurism, a strong work ethic, and a flexible attitude toward consent. All he needed was the funding to turn those gifts into a gold mine.

AFTER FUNT GOT DISCHARGED, HE CONVINCED THE MUTUAL Broadcasting System to give him $1,500 as funding to develop a "hidden microphone" radio show. At first, he was hoping to "record the beauty of everyday conversation," he wrote in his memoir—to capture fresh insights about ordinary human behavior.

Unfortunately, that concept flopped. When Funt bugged a lunch counter soda-straw holder so he could spy on some fashion models from the Conover agency, located upstairs from his office, the women's conversations struck him as tedious, "on and on about makeup or dating, or just the trivia of everyday life." For six months, Funt kept hitting the same wall. He planted microphones all over the place—in maternity wards, on park benches and in playgrounds, even in women's bathrooms—but nothing landed. People's daily chitchat was too dull to be any kind of radio show.

Then one day Funt had a breakthrough. That day, he was in a dentist's office, attaching one of his recording devices to a drill. When a patient walked in, she assumed that Funt was the dentist and began to complain about her wisdom teeth. Funt decided to wing it. "I became bold enough to move the dentist's drill, and the microphone which hung in front of it, closer to her mouth," he wrote in his 1952 memoir, *Eavesdropper at Large*. Then he told her to "open wide"—and began to poke around with the dental instruments. Finally, Funt delivered some bad news, hoping to get a reaction: The woman *had* no wisdom teeth, he insisted.

She blew up. "Don't have any wisdom teeth?" she snapped back, enraged. According to the version from *Eavesdropper at Large* and in Funt's early interviews, the woman stormed out of the room; in another version of the story, from his 1994 memoir, the actual dentist showed up and fixed her teeth. Whatever happened that day, the experience left Funt electrified. He had realized, in a flash, what was missing from his new format.

It wasn't enough to spy on people, to tape what they were saying. You also had to puncture their sense of normality somehow—to confuse or infuriate them, to throw them off-balance. Only then would their mask slip, letting you see a burst of authentic emotion. It was an epiphany that would apply not just to *Candid Microphone* but to everything that followed it: A reality host needed to do more than simply ask questions. He (and it was always a "he," at first, with a few key exceptions) had to be a provocateur, willing to engineer situations and heighten drama. "Someone was needed to take the ordinariness of an everyday situation," Funt wrote, "and push it one step further, into a scene, and in some cases even a spectacle."

The incident in the dentist's office had offered Funt a new approach to the show, but it also taught him about his own strengths as a performer. He was unafraid to piss people off. He was good at lying and improvising, even under pressure. And, crucially, he had a chameleonlike ability to go undetected. "I was blessed with a nonprofessional Brooklyn accent and the kind of face and manner which allowed me to be a bank executive one day and a plumber the next. People trusted me. In fact, as the world would eventually discover, people trusted me too much," Funt wrote.

In 1947, *Candid Microphone* debuted on ABC radio. Early sketches were recorded in Funt's office near Grand Central Station, using a wire recorder that weighed more than one hundred pounds. (The office was shared with an accountant, who worked quietly nearby.) In one typical segment, Funt's producers chained a secretary to a desk, then called a locksmith to release her and, when he protested, explained that she was a "clock-watcher" who kept sneaking out early for lunch. "You better not get caught doing this," said the locksmith, unnerved. "That's my business," snapped Funt. (They chased the locksmith into the lobby, to make sure he didn't call the cops.)

For another early stunt, his team stuck a man in a trunk, then hired a workman to lift it, as their "hostage" moaned from inside. When his subjects cursed Funt out—and sometimes when they didn't—he'd cover their words with the gentle voice of his wife cooing "censored censored censored," making the sketches feel even more risqué.

When an affordable portable recorder—which weighed twenty-seven pounds—hit the general market, Funt began to roam around Manhattan, staging stunts, secreting the mic in a hat or an arm cast. Often, little subterfuge was required: Once, Funt just placed a layer of Kleenex over his microphone, theorizing, correctly, that no one would pick up someone else's tissue. Just as he had on *The Gripe Booth*, he'd hit record first and ask permission later, training his staff to chase

down subjects and talk them into signing releases. He paid participants $15 ($200 in today's money), to lessen the sting of being duped.
Each participant also received a medallion, which read, "You were
caught in the act of being yourself and were big enough to enjoy it."

A tiny crew worked with Funt on the early *Candid Microphone*
stunts, with an inner circle made up of Phil Pollard, Al Slep, and
Sonny Fox. It was a tough job. "Allen was a brilliant man and also a
megalomaniac," Fox told the Television Academy, describing Funt
throwing pencils in a rage. "It wasn't an accident that when we finished, one of the guys was divorced, another guy was in therapy."
The work was also physically grueling, due to the rudimentary nature of the technology. Recordings were made on a long string of
magnetic wire, since magnetic tape wasn't yet available. Each episode included six sketches, which were culled from sixty options.
And each of those three-minute stunts required up to one hundred
wire splices, which were constructed in the most metal possible manner: In order to fuse the wire, "you took a lighted end of a cigarette
and you welded it," said Fox.

Similar technical problems would haunt reality producers for decades: Until the rise of Avid machines, in the early 1990s, editing
meant sifting, blurry-eyed, through hundreds of hours of footage,
patching them together by whatever means necessary. Still, the long
hours paid off, producing a terrific array of pranks, from near-brawls
to light comedy. In a candy store, Funt asked some clerks to "squish"
the chocolates so he could find the ones with nuts. He dropped a
wallet near some repairmen, then recorded their attempts to steal it.
In one satisfyingly silly sketch, Funt got a bemused caterer to brainstorm plans for an awards dinner for cats. The best sketches were
painstakingly produced found comedy, unlike anything else on radio.

There were queasier sequences, too—among them that showdown in the dentist's chair. Funt selected it as the radio show's very
first sketch, purring in the introduction, "Now sit still, this will only
take one minute and six seconds. And it won't hurt you listeners a
bit." What followed was a shocking bit of audio, in which Funt ordered a woman to open her mouth wider as she protested, moaning,
her voice garbled by his tools. "I'm sorry, am I hurting you? Why is it

enough? I'm just getting started," Funt told her calmly. Then he left the office, ostensibly to get some Novocaine. When he was gone, the woman snapped, "If he thinks I'm opening this mouth again, he's crazy." It was presented as a punchline.

FUNT ARGUED THROUGHOUT HIS LIFE THAT HE WASN'T TRYING TO upset his listeners; his goal was merely to capture human nature, in all its variations, ugly and beautiful. In *Eavesdropper at Large,* Funt wrote that he'd originally planned to alternate the show's gentler observational bits—like a segment in which a flirtatious woman shifted her attention from man to man, like a bee buzzing among flowers—with ruder pranks. The audience was the problem, not him: They got bored by slow bits and went wild for the aggro ones. "It happened so gradually that I hardly was aware of it, but my role soon turned into that of a heckler who would tease, cajole, and shock unsuspecting people," wrote Funt.

Recordings of *Candid Microphone* suggest that this argument was somewhat disingenuous. In one remarkable segment from 1947, Funt described a letter he'd received from a listener, a savage critique that "really made our ears burn." In a classic Funtian move, the producer set out to prank the letter writer by bugging her hallway. It's a riveting sequence to listen to, even today. Funt, who was a physically imposing man in his thirties (he studied art at Cornell, but he also boxed for two years), had showed up, out of the blue, at the door of an unmarried woman who lived alone, to confront her for having criticized him. Impressively, she held her own during their conversation, calmly listing her objections to *Candid Microphone.*

"Well, I don't like it because I think it's snooping," she told Funt. In her letter, she had called the producers "dirty sneaking spies"— strong language, Funt said. Yes, the woman said, not backing down. "I also feel it's a cheap way of doing things," she added—then said that he should pay his targets, the way scripted shows paid actors. "That's one of your tactics, no doubt, you want to save. So you get these people in their home, extemporaneously answering questions, that you would probably have to pay for if they were rehearsed."

Funt responded that the show *did* pay its subjects, which the woman agreed made it less offensive. Still, she had broader objections. She had been particularly disturbed by a sketch in which Funt had recorded a man in his bedroom, to capture his sounds as he woke up. The fact that his wife had given the radio program permission to record the man's snores and moans didn't impress her; it just meant he couldn't trust his wife. Funt pressed her, asking if she found the sounds people made waking up funny. "Yes, that's funny. But it's only for *him*, though, in his own bedroom. I'm sure he doesn't enjoy having the whole world know about it," she said plaintively. "Would you? Would you?"

Finally, Funt revealed that he had been recording their conversation all along. The woman burst out laughing. "Do you think we took an unfair advantage of you?" Funt asked—and she agreed that he had, but she also told him that he had her permission to air the segment. "Yes," she said, firmly. "Of course I would. Because I want the whole world to know of my opinion on this program!" That was the end of their interaction, but when he aired it, Funt made sure to get the last word: "Most any woman would be glad to give you a piece of her mind. We had to pay $15 for that piece!"

THE SKEPTICAL LISTENER WASN'T ALONE IN HER COMPLAINTS. There were publications that were impressed by *Candid Microphone,* including the stylish New York newspaper *PM,* which reprinted transcripts of the show's sketches for readers, treating them as social commentary. Other publications, however, had strong objections: In *The Berkshire Evening Eagle,* an unsigned editorial called *Candid Microphone* an "infant monster," predicting that if the show was a hit, America would be "plagued with hidden microphones," leaving everyone helplessly paranoid about the "gruesome gadget."

John Crosby, the eagle-eyed sniper critic of mainstream radio, found *Candid Microphone* too lively to dismiss in his column—it was smarter and more daring than the regular run of programming, an edgy indie take on the audience participation vogue. In August 1947, Crosby called it "wonderful sport, like looking through keyholes but capable of infinitely greater variety," marveling at a conversation in a beauty parlor that was "as frightening and illuminating" as anything in Clare Boothe Luce's play *The Women*. A year later, however, Crosby had second thoughts. *Candid Microphone*, he wrote, was "a radio program of which I thoroughly disapprove and, impelled by morbid curiosity, listen to anyhow."

Even in that initial rave, however, Crosby had clearly sensed something unsettling about the project, predicting, with remarkable prescience, just how the dominoes might topple, when audiences needed new shocks. "The candid microphone was, I suppose, inevitable. It all started, as I see it, when the first audience participant stepped to the microphone and announced belligerently that he was from Brooklyn. It got a laugh then, and at first, that was all that was needed. But Brooklyn palled eventually and it became necessary to pelt the Brooklyn man with eggs, to put him in his wife's housedress, to send him to Alaska to search for gold. That was what you might describe as the Age of the Voluntary Amateur," Crosby wrote, summing up the recent era of confessionals, stunts, and quiz shows.

Candid Microphone marked a pivot point, he wrote. "We are at the beginning of the Age of the Involuntary Amateur, the man who doesn't know it's loaded. The possibilities are limitless; the prospect is horrifying. Wait till they get the Candid Television Camera. You won't be safe in your own bathtub."

AROUND 1948, FUNT STEPPED BEHIND THE CAMERA. AT FIRST, HE filmed a few "candid microphone" type pranks for the movies, and then he adapted *Candid Microphone* itself for television, the hot new medium. (A year later the title changed to *Candid Camera*.) It was an age of rapid change: By 1950, television consoles, once available only to the very wealthy, were about to drop in price, becoming affordable to ordinary families. Suddenly, viewers could see the faces of Funt's prank victims. They could see Funt, too.

The truth is, even when it was broadcast on the radio, Funt's program had been a niche hit, the *Nathan for You* of its genre—mesmerizing, but a bit too dark for mass embrace. The early TV version wound up struggling in the ratings, then got canceled in 1954. During the late 1950s, Funt bided his time, hoping for a comeback. He made industrial films using hidden camera techniques; he filmed a short, funny observational piece about children at the International Children's School, which aired on the prestigious arts series *Omnibus;* he did late-night spots on *The Garry Moore Show.*

Finally, in 1960, he got a second chance: a half-hour slot on prime time. To seal the deal, Funt was forced to make one concession: The popular variety performer Arthur Godfrey would be the show's co-host, an executive intervention meant to cut Funt's acid charm with some sugar. Funt and Godfrey feuded; Godfrey was ultimately replaced. But by then, *Candid Camera* had become a bona fide hit, embraced by America.

Even if fewer people were watching, those first seasons, back in the early '50s, featured some of the best *Candid Camera* sketches. There were sweet gags, like a wonderful bit in which small-town postal customers, among them a small child, politely chatted with a talkative mailbox. There were slapstick stunts, like a bowling alley whose pins shattered on impact. There were impressive feats of engineering, like a car that split in half—one of many stunts enabled by Elliot Joslin, the show's gifted engineer. Many pranks tested out social clichés, like a segment in which Funt shouted, "Follow that car!"—then couldn't get any cab driver to take him up on it.

Candid Camera had a few recurrent themes, including an attempt to wrestle with the dominant anxiety of the McCarthyist 1950s, the question of social conformity. In one of Funt's most celebrated segments, he placed his operatives in an elevator, standing near a young man in a fedora. At first, the group turned to face the back of the elevator. Then they swiveled to face forward—and then, slowly, in unison, they all removed their hats. The "mark" mirrored each of their movements, baffled but compliant.

Other pranks took aim at economic biases. In one sketch, Funt's staff offered elite high school kids career aptitude tests, then told them that they were fated to be bricklayers. Among the disappointed students was the future stand-up comedian Richard Lewis, who would return to *Candid Camera,* years later, to pull the same prank on a new batch of teens. In a 1963 sketch, the actress Fannie Flagg pretended to be the first female pilot on American Airlines, triggering bug-eyed, alarmed expressions from bystanders. "I can't believe it. I'm shaking," a stewardess told Funt, with a nervous giggle. "Will the passengers know this? I don't think you should tell them!"

The best sketches looked simple, but took days to engineer. In one sequence, the sweetly daffy Dorothy Collins drove into a series of gas stations in a car without an engine, a brutal shoot, since they only got one try at each station. In the final version, Collins glided downhill, her car pushed along by gravity; when the mechanic lifted the car's hood and sputtered in confusion, she chirped, "Don't tell my husband, he'll be so angry!"

In 1961, at the height of the Cold War, Funt pulled off a jaw-dropping feat: He filmed the show in the Soviet Union by convincing the border guards that he was a tourist, smuggling in a crew, cameras, and 90,000 feet of film. In Moscow, he managed to stage classic *Candid Camera* stunts, including the two-suitcase gag, in which a girl asked a stranger to carry her bag, which was filled with weights. Amazingly, a Russian man picked it up easily and walked off. Funt also filmed pieces that included no pranking at all, like footage of teenagers slow-dancing and shots of people eating ice cream. According to Cara Giaimo in the online encyclopedia Atlas Obscura, Funt had used a camera hidden in a cardboard box to get these shots, placing it in front of a monument and then recording Russians posing for tourist photos, "arranging their families, fixing their clothes, shooing away photobombers—and, in a true twist for *Candid Camera,* purposefully *not* smiling."

Pranks like the dentist bit were more like cringe comedy. But Funt's broader-ranging work—morally complex documentary experimentation that delved deeply into human behavior—drew intellectuals toward Funt's work, among them sociologist David Riesman, who, in his 1950 book, *The Lonely Crowd,* described Funt as "the second most ingenious sociologist in America." (His top pick: Paul Lazarsfeld, who invented influencer theory.) Cornell professor James Maas built an ongoing relationship with Funt, using *Candid Camera* sketches for decades to teach his Psychology 101 seminars.

Funt's work also attracted two more notorious social scientists: Stanley Milgram, the Yale professor who was behind the 1961 "obedience" experiment, in which volunteers gave fake electric shocks to "students," who were actually played by actors; and Philip Zimbardo, the researcher who devised the 1971 Stanford prison experiments, in which volunteers got split up into guards and prisoners. Milgram co-wrote an essay on *Candid Camera*, praising it as a mass-market experiment in social psychology; Zimbardo cited Funt's "elevator stunt" as an inspiration. But over time, each man, just like Funt, would be accused of exploiting his own subjects—and of getting insufficient consent from the people they studied.

BY THE '60S, *CANDID CAMERA* HAD BECOME A MAJOR HIT, BUT IT was still a divisive project—and even more so, in certain ways, now that the show was on television.

Part of the difficulty was that the audience could now not just hear but see Funt, with his boxer's build and mischievous charisma. The bigger problem, though, was that the show's subjects weren't anonymous anymore. When you could see people's faces, the jokes felt crueler. In a 1953 *Candid Camera* roundup of the year's best bits, there's one stunt in which a dignified man looks on, helplessly polite, as Funt breaks eggs into his expensive hat. The man's mounting distress, and his polite attempts to conceal it—the confusion and shame flickering behind his eyes—don't feel funny at all.

According to the comedian Joan Rivers, who wrote briefly for Funt in the early 1960s, even sketches that felt benign, like switching sugar for salt in a shaker, sometimes turned ugly during filming. "For every woman who went, 'What's this?,' there were ladies that just sobbed," she told the Television Academy. Everyone who appeared on the show was required to sign a legal release, but according to multiple accounts—and his own memoirs—Funt pushed back, hard, when his subjects refused to sign.

Despite, or maybe because of, the show's popular success, a few critics continued to savage *Candid Camera; The New Yorker,* in particular, loathed Funt. In 1950, the writer Philip Hamburger had written a scathing pan of *Candid Camera,* calling the show "sadistic, poisonous, anti-human, and sneaky," a series that reduced "the art, the purpose and the ethics of the documentary idea to the obscene." In 1959—when *Candid Camera* wasn't even a regular series, just a bunch of sequences on late-night talk shows!—John Lardner weighed in to condemn Funt as "nagging, suspicious, and misanthropic."

Then, in 1960, just as *Candid Camera* became a bona fide hit, *The New Yorker* gave Funt the full beatdown, in a devastating profile by J. M. Flagler. Flagler, who had embedded with Funt during production, portrayed the *Candid Camera* auteur as a self-loathing snob, a man who dismissed his time in the audience participation mines of radio as "a degrading, lackluster period of my life," but whose craving for respect was ultimately undercut by his crudity. The portrayal had a whiff of classism ("Despite his Ivy League background, his on-camera personality does include a strong element of Stanley Kowalski"), but it was a very effective takedown as, with subtle jabs, Flagler nailed Funt for hypocrisy, for blaming his sponsors for the crude gags he did *before* he had any sponsors, and for pitying himself more than he did his targets. Flagler even described an incident in which Funt convinced a nun to browbeat an elderly man, who had been a reluctant participant in a prank, into signing a legal release.

In Flagler's view, Funt was a bully-genius, a savant whose earthy gifts had turned him into a tycoon, possessing "imagination and know-how, courage and gall." A similar portrait had shown up, that same year, in Richard Stern's debut novel, *Golk,* a scathing satire of a cruel prank-show producer, clearly inspired by Funt. "Such public condemnations have left Funt edgily defensive, and even somewhat conscience-stricken, though not enough so to make him consider taking up another line of work," Flagler concluded.

FUNT RAGED AT PUT-DOWNS LIKE THIS THROUGHOUT HIS LIFE, but he also absorbed the criticism, folding it into his work—and in the process he deepened and enriched the *Candid Camera* format. He included more segments with children, with whom he had natural rapport, and whose innocence blunted the edges of meaner pranks. He cast a wide array of celebrities, who lent the show an air of glamour.

Funt's biggest innovation, however, was to introduce a crucial moment in each episode—"the reveal," which became an institution around 1962. Each *Candid Camera* segment now included not merely the setup and the prank, but also a third act, the follow-up, the big moment when Funt revealed the hidden cameras. "Can you take a little joke?" he'd ask, a question that invited his mark to become, instead, a collaborator.

Over time, Funt would hone this question into a chipper demand: "Smile! You're on *Candid Camera*!" When he said that line, he pointed to the hidden lens, which was concealed behind a hole in the wall or a screen, or sometimes camouflaged by lights. The producer even designed a special camera attachment, a "turret" with wide, medium, and close lenses, allowing the cameraman to pivot and capture the subject's expression when Funt yelled, "Smile!"

The reveal added an extra beat to the comedy. But it also provided a moral escape hatch for the viewer, a cathartic release from any lingering sense of collusion. Once the subject understood that they had been filmed, they took back a bit of agency, some dignity and control. As the sketch shifted from a prank into a collaboration between the person doing the filming and the person being filmed, the audience found themselves laughing at a different kind of joke. It was one of Funt's most brilliant insights: He needed to attend to the emotional state not only of the targets of his pranks, but of the audience at home.

He had invented the mechanism that made it okay to watch.

Once Funt's targets understood that they were being recorded, they entered a new emotional state, as well, like Viva after she was anointed Queen for a Day. Some laughed, others got angry, but most people experienced a messy, powerful blend of feelings, from confusion to a case of the giggles. Funt's targets occasionally ran away, although those moments rarely ended up on the air. Once in a while, a "no" did make it: In one clip, which Funt's family included in their family-created documentary about Funt, *Mister Candid Camera*, an adorable little girl repeatedly tells Funt she doesn't want to be on television, while Funt keeps telling her that she already is. "Well, you're not getting my permission!" the little girl says, as the studio audience laughs. This type of footage, with its eerie meta-revelations about power, reminded the viewer that they were watching a TV show being made, a drama as riveting as the prank itself.

In the 1960s, Funt added another exuberant element to the show: a bouncy song that hammered home its key theme. "When you least expect it, you're elected," sang a cheery chorus. "You're the star today. Smile! You're on *Candid Camera*!" Male voices chimed—"With a hocus-pocus, you're in focus!"—and then the women—". . . it's your lucky day." Then their voices rose, blended, in a stirring, buoyant finale, "Smile! You're on *Candid Camera*."

The next verse laid out the show's philosophy:

It's fun to laugh at yourself,
It's a tonic, tried and true.
It's fun to look at yourself, like other people do—
Have a sense of humor,
There's a rumor, laughter's on its way.
Smile! You're on Candid Camera.

The message was clear: Being pranked by Allen Funt was correctly perceived as a compliment and a thrill, not an insult. If you resisted, you were a prig, a stiff. If you didn't laugh, you needed to lighten up. But "Smile!" was also simply an irresistibly catchy ditty, a siren song to join in the fun. After you heard it, you couldn't get it out of your head.

By 1970, Funt had become an icon. He had divorced and remarried, to his glamorous former secretary Marilyn, a frequent guest on the show. He was a well-off New York City celebrity. He was also getting twitchy about the limits of his job, hemmed in by the primness of network TV. That year, Funt directed a movie called *What Do You Say to a Naked Lady?*, an X-rated variation on *Candid Camera,* which was full of lurid confessions, among them a prying interrogation of some teenage girls. Funt followed up with *Money*

Talks, in 1972, but his movie career never went anywhere. *Candid Camera*—which would run in one form or another, in fits and starts, through 2014—would become Funt's legacy.

By then, the Age of the Involuntary Amateur had dawned, just as Crosby had predicted. Cameras were everywhere. Political chaos spilled out on the TV news. Cracking a few eggs into a hat no longer felt especially transgressive—and Funt himself had evolved into something new, an avuncular and unthreatening figure, in the public imagination. By the 1980s, when the producer retired in California to live in a self-architected mansion full of Native American art, *Candid Camera* was widely perceived as old-fashioned fun.

IN 1994, FIVE YEARS BEFORE HIS DEATH, FUNT PUBLISHED *Candidly, Allen Funt,* a memoir that crackled with resentment. In it, he brooded over ancient wounds, fuming at the condescension of fancy friends like talk show host David Susskind, who had once offered to get him a less debased gig; at a trusted money manager who had robbed him blind; and at a rip-off show called *Totally Hidden Video,* which had done staged stunts, hurting his legacy. In the book, Funt also struggled, openly, with his own tricky personality, puzzling over the fits of rage and the need for control that had haunted him during his storied career.

Funt knew he had a reputation as a bully. The most well-known of his public detractors had been Joan Rivers, who wrote for the show briefly in 1960, then got fired (or possibly left for better opportunities) three weeks later. In her own memoir *Enter Talking,* she described Funt as both a comic visionary and a creep, a tyrant who fired people "in tinhorn furies" and bugged his own employees' offices, using an internal intercom. Rivers, who hardly had a gentle comic sensibility herself, was among those who found the show too mean (punching down, to use the modern expression). But her most damning accusation was that when Funt held meetings after visiting an in-office sauna, he let his robe slip, "whether by design or accident," exposing his testicles.

That story was also hinted at in *The Flying Phone Booth: My 3*

Years Behind the Candid Camera, a scathing 2011 memoir by Lou Tyrrell, who was Funt's showrunner during the same period. While Tyrrell doesn't explicitly confirm Rivers's charges (in fact, he acknowledges writing a letter backing Funt when he sued Rivers over her accusations), he describes a near-identical scene: Funt, wearing only a bathrobe, seated high up on a platform, giving harsh notes to his employees cringing far below.

In *Candidly, Allen Funt,* Funt denied that he'd flashed anyone, either on purpose or accidentally. But he owned up, with a certain bafflement, to his flaws, wondering if a dictatorial streak—an ability to manipulate, a certain workaholism—was necessary to do the work he did. Still, if he struggled to see himself the way that others saw him, Funt had no doubts about the series he'd created. *Candid Camera,* he argued, was not merely a prank show. It was ultimately a more truthful format than fiction could ever be—bolder, ruder, and far less sentimental about human nature. At its best, it was capable of healing people, not hurting them. In 1982, Funt had funded an institution called Laughter Therapy, which sent *Candid Camera* videotapes out to hospital patients. The healing power of laughter would be his ultimate contribution, he hoped.

There had always been a predatory thrum to Funt's legacy, on back to the moment he first picked up that dentist's drill. But if the producer felt comfortable, and maybe even a bit turned on, by blurring and crossing boundaries, it was difficult to separate that impulse from his gifts, the ones that had pushed television into a new stage. A better man might never have pressed record.

2

||||||

THE GONG

The Filthy, Farkakte Chuck Barris 1970s

LIKE FUNT, CHUCK BARRIS—THE MOP-TOPPED IMPRESARIO WHO launched *The Dating Game*—was a baby Barnum, a Hollywood dealmaker with a gift for humbug. He, too, enjoyed smashing taboos. But unlike his fellow reality pioneer, Barris rarely claimed to be a student of human nature, let alone any kind of healer or sociologist. Instead, he was more of a cheerful junk peddler, sexing up defunct game shows, then lobbing them like grenades into the gender wars of the late '60s and the '70s. For more than a decade, Barris reigned over L.A. as the notorious "Ayatollah of Trasherola," and then as the beloved host of *The Gong Show,* his talent contest for the talent-free. But even after his empire crumbled, as empires tend to do, Barris's influence lingered on, in a brand of bad taste that doubled, for its biggest fans, as a badge of pride.

Barris told his life story in a series of interviews, memoirs, and gonzo quasi-autobiographical novels, none of which can be fully trusted. The broad beats go something like this: Barris was born in 1929, to a status-obsessed mother and a dentist dad, who had a stroke—and later died—leaving Barris, his younger sister Riki, and his mom broke and also fascinated by the fantasy of marrying "up." His uncle was the scat singer Harry Barris. A bohemian drifter, Barris graduated from Drexel University in 1953, then veered, like a dirty sunflower, toward Manhattan and the TV industry, then in its early boom. For a while, Barris had a job as an NBC page. In the mid-1950s, he scammed his way into an elite NBC management training program, which was generally reserved for Ivy League grads, by listing RCA board members as fake references. He won a job at the network, then lost it after the department got laid off.

In 1957, when he was twenty-eight, Barris married Lyn Levy, the niece of CBS chief executive William Paley. CBS was the only television network that would never hire Barris: By the time the couple tied the knot, Levy's rich parents had cut their daughter off, convinced her fiancé was a gold-digger. (Which he was, from Barris's account—an opportunist who fell in love with his opportunity.) After a few more detours (prize-fight promotion, teleprompter sales, a failed novel), Barris stumbled into another television job, at ABC, keeping an eye on *American Bandstand* host Dick Clark, who was being investigated for a payola scandal. In 1962, while he was on the job, Barris sold a novelty song full of amusement park screams, "Palisades Park," which hit #3 on the *Billboard* Hot 100. He also applied to work for the Central Intelligence Agency, although, at least according to the CIA, they didn't hire him. (Which, to be fair, is what they'd say if they did hire him.)

For nearly a decade, he lived his life as a cynical pinball, ricocheting from gig to gig, with a raffish, schmoozy charisma but little focus. When Barris's mentor Budd Granoff, a gravel-voiced businessman he'd met on *American Bandstand,* urged him to get an executive title, Barris invented one—"Director of Daytime Television: West Coast"—only to sabotage *that* job, too. His first attempt to produce an audience participation–style television show, a series called *The People Pickers*—a snickering twist on *What's My Line?,* featuring stewardesses, policewomen, and strippers—fell apart before it ever aired.

Barris had always feared being a second-rater; now that looked like his fate. Then, in 1965, the pinball hit its target.

WHEN BARRIS SOLD *THE DATING GAME* TO ABC, HE WAS NEW TO Los Angeles, having just launched Chuck Barris Productions, using a $20,000 loan from his rich stepfather. For once, his timing was ideal. Sexually speaking, the mid-1960s were a tangle of cognitive dissonance: The Pill was legal, Helen Gurley Brown's *Sex and the Single Girl* was a bestseller—but young women were still widely expected to stay virgins until marriage. When the sitcom *That Girl* debuted, it felt like a radical feminist act just to show a single girl living alone.

In this context, *The Dating Game,* in which hot, dumb Angelenos flirted across a wall, felt like a feather-light provocation, suggesting that sex *itself* was a game, one that could be played by women as well as men. Although Barris sometimes traced his inspiration to the groovy music show *Where the Action Is, The Dating Game* was an obvious throwback to the audience participation era—and specifically, to a show called *Blind Date,* which debuted on the radio in 1943 and jumped to television in 1949.* Like *The Dating Game, Blind Date* used a wall to keep its contestants from seeing one another: on one side, six enlisted men, who were called "The Hunters," on the other side, three single women, "The Hunted." After a few rounds of banter, each of the Hunted selected a Hunter, and then the live audience picked a winning couple, who scored an evening of dining and dancing at the Stork Club, chaperoned by the show's glamorous host Arlene Francis.

Back in the 1940s, *Blind Date* was considered a touch too racy for radio: One shocked *Billboard* critic described a question about a woman's kissing style as so saucy "the control man almost threw the switch." That was too much spontaneity for a family medium, he argued: "What chance has pa or ma to stop 15-year-old sister from going downtown to find a date, when she hears it done every Thursday night over the air with the sanction of a great corporation?"

Barris took the World War II *Blind Date* setup—the wall, the hidden dates, the chaperoned night out—and updated it with a bunch

---

* Barris never mentioned *Blind Date,* but critics noticed the resemblance—and in *The Newlywed Game* host Bob Eubanks's memoir, he wrote about a rumor that Barris had paid the creators of *Blind Date* $90,000 for the rights to the format after *The Dating Game* became a hit.

of groovy Age of Aquarius design motifs, including a curvy divider and a splash of pop art daisies, and the effervescent musical stylings of Herb Alpert's "Spanish Flea." When each episode opened, the show's genial host, Jim Lange, introduced Bachelors Number One, Two, and Three to the TV audience. Once the bachelorette had been released from her "soundproof booth," she perched on a stool and asked a few flirty questions, then, eventually, picked the guy she liked best. Finally, she shook hands with her rejects—often, the show's most spontaneous moment—and then the credits rolled, as Lange blew air-kisses at the home audience. "Mwah! Mwah!"

Mike Metzger, the grandson of Eddie Cantor, got hired shortly after the first episode of *The Dating Game* was filmed, becoming the eighth employee at Chuck Barris Productions. He dug the show's concept, but the questions—"What's your ideal date?"—struck him as boring, so he took a risk, pitching his new boss on a fresh approach, inspired by "Abstracts," a party game played by his hippie aunt in Malibu, in which people responded to crazy prompts like "Describe Liz Taylor as a sandwich." Barris told Metzger to write a hundred sample questions, due the next day. "I may have smoked a joint. I didn't sleep. But I came back with this list of questions and he called me back in and said, 'Okay, I'm putting you with Jonathan Debin'"—the nineteen-year-old son of Barris's agent—"'and as long as you two don't smoke too much shit, we're putting you in an office together.'" His new job was to meet with the bachelorettes each day and brainstorm questions, the wackier the better.

Metzger's model question was "What is your favorite shape for a girl?"; his ideal answer was "a hockey puck," followed by an absurdist explanation. He urged the women to have fun and the men to get loose, creative, but the reality was that few of the show's contestants could pull off improv comedy, so the show was dominated by dorkily suggestive banter ("What would the little boy in you want to do with the little girl in me?" "Well, the big boy in me tells me not to answer you or we'd be off the air"). Still, awkwardness could be fun, too—anything that suggested a real flirtation.

The Dating Game was an instant smash hit, and Barris bragged to journalists about the novelty of his approach to daytime entertainment, with its focus on "people, as opposed to playing with words and clues." If his new blockbuster wasn't a subtle show, it nailed the contradictory mood of the era, which was post–sexual revolution but prefeminist, with both gender roles and power dynamics in flux. Abortion was illegal, a woman couldn't get a credit card without a male co-signer, and many jobs were reserved for men. Still, "free love" was in the air—and Barris's biggest complaint was that his contestants kept saying "fuck," violating FCC rules.

A year in, ABC bumped *The Dating Game* up to prime time. The ratings spiked, the budget expanded, and celebrities showed up, mixed in with the civilians. Instead of a dull dinner out in Burbank, the winners were flown to "romantic capitals" of the world (broadly defined: Karen Carpenter went to Roanoke, Virginia). Among the hot-bodied Californians, *The Dating Game* included lots of pre-fame movie stars, including Farrah Fawcett and Steve Martin.

The producers tried multiple gimmicks, like casting the Marquis Chimps as bachelors, only to have one of the trained monkeys drop a snack into his fly. In 1972, a fourteen-year-old Michael Jackson picked a date from a panel of excited little girls, selecting ten-year-old Latonya Simmons, who won dinner at Sardi's and front-row seats to a Jackson 5 concert. Sometimes, a bachelor picked from three bachelorettes. There were limits to the show's flexibility, however: Although *The Dating Game* featured all-Black dating panels, it never mixed Black and white contestants. Barris, a mouthy liberal who bragged that he'd marched at Selma, was blunt about why. "Southern stations, and for that matter stations all across the country, would drop the show," he explained to Joan Barthel in 1969 in *Life* magazine. "We're not even supposed to mix up Orientals and Puerto Ricans with whites, although we do. But when it comes right down to a Black guy with a white girl, or vice versa, it would be just suicidal. We're restricted in a purely corporate, national way—I don't know how else you would say it."

By the late 1960s, Barris was reveling in his role as a countercultural imp, strutting around Hollywood in a military helmet that read "Make Love Not War." In that glamorous *Life* profile, Chuck Barris Productions—which its employees called "The Love Company," and which had just gone public—came across as a fun, filthy pirate ship full of miniskirt-wearing crewmates, like a booze cruise blowing raspberries down Santa Monica Boulevard. At the helm was Barris himself, a CEO with an Abbie Hoffman-esque wit, a millionaire who dressed like a bum, bragging about his offices, where "everybody is equal, and nobody is automated." He shook his tambourine during rock 'n' roll jam sessions at staff meetings; he cracked jokes about vaginal cream ads. He handed out goofy awards, among them "Most Likely to Be Arrested on a Morals Charge" and "Least Jewish" (to a Black staffer). Newly separated, Barris kissed a staffer on the neck.

Barris wasn't really interested in game shows, he told Barthel. Like Funt, he wanted a jolt of authenticity, even if it required a nudge to get there. "In our shows, people have no choice but to be honest. . . . They may try to psych us out, but it doesn't work. We'll get 'em every time."

FOR ALL OF ITS SMIRKY SEX JOKES, *THE DATING GAME* WAS ACTU-ally Barris's least provocative early show: It was just a comedy show about hot people trying, and mostly failing, to be funny. *The Newly-wed Game*—which launched in 1966 and ran on and off for more than four decades—was a more transgressive project, a frothy game show designed to puncture one of America's most sentimental insti-tutions: heterosexual marriage.

The format had been devised by *Howdy Doody* veterans Robert "Nick" Nicholson and E. Roger Muir, who felt inspired by the dreamy mood of their own newly engaged children—and in its orig-inal form, *The Newlywed Game* was conceived with celebrities. Then, during an early demo taping, ABC brass found themselves mesmerized by a regular husband and wife, instead: "I couldn't take my eyes off them. They were so cute, embarrassed, naïve, sexy, funny," marveled Leonard Goldberg, then an ABC vice president. He brought the show to Barris to produce—a natural match.

Four married couples played *The Newlywed Game*, seated in small alcoves within a pastel half-moon-shaped set. During the first segment, the husbands left while host Bob Eubanks asked their wives questions, then vice versa. After that, one spouse answered the question verbally and then the other one held up a cardboard square scribbled with their answer, so the audience could see if their responses were the same. Most of this repartee was bland cocktail-party chitchat ("What's your favorite Beatles song?"), but a significant subset came from the minds of horny virgins, with repeated questions like, "How much does your wife's chest weigh?"

Eubanks himself referred to sex as "making whoopee," slang from an old Eddie Cantor song. "We couldn't say 'God,' we couldn't say 'toilet seat,' we couldn't say 'make love,' so we created our own vocabulary," Eubanks told me. His go-to question was "What's the weirdest place you've ever made whoopee?"

If a couple's answers matched, they could win a medium-sized prize, like a dishwasher. If they didn't, they'd often fight, sometimes whacking one another with their mismatched card—the ideal outcome from the perspective of Barris, who claimed that the killer question was "Which of your wife's friends would you marry?" Unlike the shiny happy Angelenos on *The Dating Game*, the newlyweds tended to be basic-issue civilians, often chubby or plain, which made the show a small-scale, achievable fantasy of fame. It even turned up in the 1971 Loretta Lynn hit "One's on the Way," as the kind of glamorous fun a pregnant Topeka housewife could only dream of.

The Newlywed Game had a sweet side, too. Couples riffed off private jokes. They surprised each other with their answers. Even smutty questions could spark emotionally layered exchanges—among them the show's most notorious moment, the one that circulated as a rumor back when I was in grade school and that you're probably thinking of, too. For years, there was a widespread rumor that one wife had responded to Eubanks's standard "making whoopee" question with a hilariously literal answer: "That'd be up the butt, Bob!"

Eubanks himself claimed the story was an urban legend, offering $10,000 to anyone who could prove him wrong—but eventually, the clip, which had never been rerun, reemerged on a 2002 bloopers special. The actual interaction, from a 1977 episode, was a little bit different from the one in the rumor: When Eubanks asked one of the wives to describe the weirdest place she had ever considered "making whoopee," the woman, Olga Perez—a sweet-faced lady with plump cheeks and a missing tooth, her eyebrows plucked thin as reeds—paused, briefly, looking uncertain about how to respond. Then she blurted out, with a nervous grin: ". . . In the ass?"

The moment would have been sordid had it not been for the reaction of her werewolf-handsome husband, Hank, who was gussied up in a maroon leisure suit and wide-collared peach shirt. He threw his head back and howled with laughter, waggling his eyebrows, not merely unembarrassed but seemingly awed by her candor. The image of the happy couple giggling cut right through the format, offering viewers a glimpse of a happy, uninhibited sex life—a joyful humanity upending a system that felt designed to humiliate them.

Not every interaction ended so well. The spotlight could work like whiskey, loosening tongues: One woman, when asked to name something her husband had asked her to keep secret, explained, earnestly, that he planned to kill her uncle for the insurance money—and then won ten points when her husband gave the same answer. Other contestants had more basic regrets. In a story Barris told again and again, a young psychiatrist accused the producer of wrecking his marriage. He had been rattled by mic fright, he'd said things that he regretted—and he blamed those mistakes on "the lights, the pressures, and the audience," he told Barris (or maybe wrote to him; Barris told the story a few different ways). The executive producer had little tolerance for such complaints: The way he saw it, aggrieved contestants were a bunch of grubby fame-seekers, who craved the spotlight but couldn't take the heat. If they had regrets, that was on them.

Eubanks, who hosted *The Newlywed Game* for four decades, was more sympathetic, looking back. In his endearingly self-flagellating memoir, *It's in the Book, Bob!*, Eubanks, a former DJ and concert promoter, wrote in thoughtful terms about how much the show's tone had shifted as the culture shifted around it. A couple of decades into *The Newlywed Game,* the couples became more affectionate, more like teammates, in the wake of feminism. They had bickered more in the late '60s—possibly, Eubanks theorized, because they were mimicking sitcoms like *The Honeymooners*. Marital meltdowns made good TV, but they depressed the host.

On the other hand, the production *itself* became significantly nastier, Eubanks wrote, as Chuck Barris Productions sailed from the innocent mid-1960s into the 1970s. By then, Barris was spinning out, losing his pirate-king mojo, saying the kinds of things he hadn't meant to say—just another victim of the lights, the pressures, and the audience.

FOR AROUND A DECADE, CHUCK BARRIS PRODUCTIONS PUT ITS stamp all over daytime television, producing short-lived spin-offs like *The Parent Game*, *The Family Game*, *The Etiquette Game*, and even *The Game Game*. In 1967, he made the sadistic *How's Your Mother-in-Law?*; in 1974, a brief revival of the old-timey music countdown *Your Hit Parade*; in 1978, a parody beauty contest, *The $1.98 Beauty Show*, hosted by Rip Taylor. If most of his shows flopped, it didn't matter much, given how little they cost. In the early '70s, when Paramount Pictures considered a merger, Barris's company turned out to have better numbers than the major studio, an embarrassing revelation.

By then, network television itself was changing. The nightly news spilled bloody footage of real-life atrocities, from the Vietnam War to the Attica Prison Rebellion, into America's living rooms. In 1973, the country watched the Watergate hearings live, riveted, as if the scandal were a sharply crafted political thriller. (Or maybe a reality show: Nixon had bugged his own White House, after all.) Meanwhile, a new set of scripted shows had begun smashing taboos—chief among them, those created by Norman Lear, whose 1971 sitcom *All in the Family* had put everyone's family fights on TV. By the mid-1970s, Lear had nearly a dozen sitcoms, featuring bold characters like the sharp-tongued feminist Maude Findlay and the preening Black tycoon George Jefferson. When activists stepped up to regulate TV, trying to clean up the new wave of sex and violence, Lear pushed back: The way he saw it, the solution was more TV, not less, opening the door to newer, more varied voices.

During the same period, Barris functioned as Lear's shadow self—the id to Lear's ego, the cynic to his idealist, the daytime to his prime time. Like Lear, he was a liberal, Jewish TV creator from the East Coast, juggling dozens of provocative shows, a freewheeling devil among the scolds. If Barris was a notch more nihilistic than Lear, he was also, like Archie Bunker's creator, a proud advocate for smashing taboos. In media interviews, he liked to joke about airing public executions. He even pitched a show called *Greed*, a format in which contestants would compete like contractors, bidding to do hideous jobs, like shooting a little boy's dog. These concepts were only dark humor, Barris inevitably clarified, although he'd add, "People would watch it, I know."

Unlike Funt's employees, the Barris workers I spoke to remembered their time at "The Love Company" with dreamy nostalgia, as a lost utopia of hedonistic liberation. Stephanie Buffington was just nineteen when Barris hired her to be a member of the Barris Bandits (originally called "The Chinese Bandits"), the scrappy, low-level team that recruited good-looking contestants to flirt with strangers, making a hundred phone calls a day. A former child actor who had dated Jim Morrison, Buffington had been a contestant on *The Dating Game* herself, then started dating Debin, the producer who cast her. Once the couple broke up, Buffington happily dipped into the same dating pool that she'd emerged from, marking the applications of sexy men with a special code. From her account, intra-office sex was "naughty," but it was also common. No one viewed that kind of thing as harassment; it was more like a perk.

Two years later, Buffington was in bed with a *Dating Game* contestant with hypnotic eyes when the phone rang, offering her the promotion she'd been jockeying for all along: the chance to chaperone *Dating Game* couples on their trips abroad. For two years, she flew around the world having X-rated adventures, but when Barris asked Buffington to write down her stories, she was savvy enough to save them. In 1976, Buffington wrote *Three on a Date* (later retitled *The Love Company*), which got adapted into a TV movie two years later.

Buffington knew her boss had a bad-boy rep. "People would go, 'Oh, you poor thing!' like he was cruel or a despot." That was not her experience. When Buffington got in a car crash, Barris showed up at her hospital bed with a pizza and a malted, then made sure her rehab was covered. She has fond memories of the company's rowdy Christmas parties, of the family-like (if R-rated) warmth of its running jokes, of the time she won Barris's chest X-ray as a prize. The 1970s were a different time, she said; she had trouble relating to how the culture had changed by the 2020s. "People are looking for the scandal, for the rotten seed," she said sadly.

Mike Metzger's wife Ellen also joined The Love Company when she was nineteen. Buffington took her out clubbing; Ellen had a tumultuous affair with Metzger, who was married at the time—and then, after his divorce, she married him and went back to work for Barris again. She, too, described Barris as a generous boss, a decent person who let her nap in the office when she was pregnant and exhausted. She had never understood the idea that Barris or his shows were sexist: "I felt the freest I've ever felt in my life because I could do whatever I wanted!"

Trixie Dejonge, who got her job through her aunt, Barris's longtime secretary, also had rosy memories. Barris had granted her that vaudeville name: She'd been Frances Kirchner ("a back-East name") when she showed up. Dejonge wrote questions for the game show contestants, chaperoned dates, and performed all sorts of odd jobs: "Chuck would put a hat on me and make me his chauffeur, then have me drive to the dentist." It wasn't lucrative work, but that didn't bother her. "I think I made $150 a week," she said, describing Barris as at once cheap and generous. For all of these Barris employees, the bonus was a sense of solidarity: It was The Love Company against the world.

Only one person had darker memories of these years: Barris himself. Some of this likely had to do with the collapse of his private life, a subject that he chewed over endlessly in his books. The sunniest such account was in his first book, the autobiographical novel *You and Me, Babe,* which became a bestseller in 1974: the story of a shambolic cynic who seduces an heiress, only to be disinherited by his heartless in-laws—and then, to his surprise, falls in love with his wife and gets rich making game shows, only to have his marriage collapse. The book shot to #7 on the *New York Times* bestseller list, likely due to the payola-ish efforts of Barris's PR team, which were investigated in *Esquire* magazine with the intensity of Woodward and Bernstein.

Barris's perspective seemed to darken, over time. Even in his glory days, critics had condemned his shows as pernicious garbage—sex-obsessed, dumb, cruel. By the mid-1970s, this chorus felt increasingly personal. In 1975, Mike Wallace ambushed Barris on *60 Minutes,* then dressed him down for humiliating contestants on a show called *The New Treasure Hunt,* a cruel format in which players seemed to win fancy prizes, only to have some of them revealed as low-priced junk, leading one woman to faint. "These people don't take participating in a game show as seriously as you think they do, Mike," Barris protested. "It's not a big sociological thing. They just want to have some fun."

By 1976, even the press release for his newest project, *The Gong Show,* inspired furious reviews, with Noel Holston publishing a fist-pounding newspaper column denouncing Barris's impact on daytime TV, "a clamorous, semilewd, sophomoric wasteland," while Gary Deeb called him "a viciously cynical man," who made a fortune by helping people "make jackasses of themselves."

It was heavy ammo, given the scale of the target: a goofy, deliberately dopey anti-talent show that was created by British-born *Laugh-In* writer Chris Bearde, inspired by a suggestion from Canadian country music legend Tommy Hunter. Howard "Sandman" Sims, the "exterminator" from the amateur night at the Apollo Theater, also claimed to have inspired the gong. To most observers, however, the show mainly looked like a remake of *Major Bowes' Original Amateur Hour,* a wildly popular audience participation classic, on both radio and television, which ran from 1934 through 1970. The *Amateur Hour* had discovered both Frank Sinatra and Maria Callas, but it was better known for mocking untalented nobodies. Early on, *The Amateur Hour* had even featured a gong, which got dumped later, when the new host, Ted Mack, decided that it was too cruel.

Barris's show revived the gong. It cranked up the humiliation. But the key ingredient was Barris himself, who stepped in to host at the last minute, replacing John Barbour, a Canadian comic who had earnest hopes of discovering the next Callas. Barris harbored no such illusions. "These are strange people. Some of them are borderline nuts. But they're not phony. They're putting it on the line. I admire their guts, because I could never do that myself. It's Iwo Jima out there and they're stark naked," he told *The Washington Post*. "People always like to see other people fed to the lions," he told *TV Guide*. "It's reassuring to find there is somebody unhappier than you are."

The result was less lion food than it was brown acid, an underground party hosted by a panel of wisecracking C-list judges, with three regulars: *M*A*S*H* star Jamie Farr, comic Arte Johnson, and the spectacular potty-mouth diva Jaye P. Morgan. During early rehearsals, Farr suggested that the panel should dress up in tatty Vegas finery, which lent *The Gong Show* a charmingly dissolute vibe, as if they were cocktail-sipping stragglers in some apocalyptic casino lounge at 5 A.M. The judges were required to watch each terrible act for at least thirty seconds, at which point they got to "gong" the performer, booting them offstage. If a contestant made it to ninety seconds, the judges graded them from 1 to 10. The winner got $516.32.

Like any talent show, *The Gong Show* was hit-or-miss, but it was also defiantly weird, and, at its high points, a camp delight that sliced through the cornball sentimentality of 1970s pop culture, parodying earnest fare like *The Lawrence Welk Show*. In one bravura episode, each act sang a different, equally terrible cover of the pop hit "Feelings," making it impossible to ever listen to that maudlin blockbuster again. Regular acts included Barris writer Murray Langston's "The Unknown Comic," who wore a paper bag over his head; Trixie Dejonge as "The Unknown Hussy," with her own paper bag and a miniskirt; and "Gene Gene the Dancing Machine," the show's stagehand, boogying ineptly as the audience threw trash.

Some genuine talents showed up, like Paul Reubens and Andrea McArdle. But the show was dominated by tone-deaf singers and clumsy jugglers, along with unclassifiable bits, like a dentist playing "The Stars and Stripes Forever" on his drill. According to Milton Delugg, Barris's music director, Hollywood Boulevard prostitutes sometimes showed up to play saxophones or twirl batons, hoping to score that sweet $516.32 (not as nutty an amount as it looks: It was reportedly the Screen Actors Guild minimum for one day's work).

Even for the 1970s, *The Gong Show* was tasteless, but the show had a liberatory quality, too—if your standards were rock-bottom, failure hurt less. Sure, the camera might linger on your face, as you gathered the tatters of your dignity. But being gonged was also an honor, like being pranked on *Candid Camera*. Do not ask for whom the gong tolls, it tolls for thee.

What kept the production spinning was Barris, whose fans nicknamed him "Chuckie Baby." Under the spotlight, the host became as manic as a Muppet, all of his nervous tics turned into trademarks. He tugged his hat down over his eyes, to avoid seeing the audience. He clapped his hands nervously, and his most inarticulate mumbles— among them, "We'll be right back with more . . . stuff"—became hip catchphrases. Like the show's bad dancers and tone-deaf singers, Barris's appeal as a host was that he seemed incompetent, which made him feel both authentic and relatable. Other hosts exuded the crisp Midwestern neutrality of TV experts, while Barris seemed as unstable as—even more unstable than—anyone he gave the gong.

For two years, *The Gong Show* was a hit, helping to revive several of Barris's canceled shows, including *The Dating Game* and *The Newlywed Game*. By then, Mike Metzger had become a skilled producer, helping the Barris lineup run like clockwork. As much as he adored his boss—Barris was like a fun big brother, said Metzger, and also a father figure, a replacement for the man who'd abandoned him—this period marked the low point in their relationship. One day, Metzger brought Barris some new questions for *The Dating Game*. "I could tell that he was displeased for the first time ever and he said, 'Mike, I don't think you got it.' And I almost puked, you know. He said, 'Mike, it's 1977, it's a different era. This is the 1965 version, it's too fucking cute, it's too sweet, it's too innocent, you've got to get with it, man.' He said, 'Where are the hookers? Where are the comics? Where's 1977?' I said, 'Ohhhhh, okay.' I got him. He said, 'Where are the girls! I'm talking about girls with giant tits! Tits and ass! Miniskirts and no underpants. We're in Shit Creek, Texas, Mike—you can do it.'"

Metzger followed Barris's orders: He cast freakier guests; he wrote seamier questions. Bob Eubanks, who was midway through his own midlife crisis and marital crack-up, didn't resist the new regime, either—and in fact, he discovered that he was raring for an outlet. "With my marriage fraying around the edges, I found the podium on *The Newlywed Game*'s stage to be the perfect sniper's perch. When life becomes overwhelming, some men abuse their spouses. I abused my guests," Eubanks wrote, with regret, in his memoir. He started pushing the participants to answer ugly, invasive questions—and then shaming them when they did.

Around 1978, the whole megillah fell apart, starting with a *Gong Show* act called "Have You Got a Nickel?" Barris sometimes claimed that he had pitched the act strategically, on the assumption that it would get cut by the standards department, only to have it slip past the network censors. The sequence was undeniably gross: Two teenage girls sat on the *Gong Show* stage, licking and sucking Popsicles in silence as the audience hooted and screamed. The faux fellatio went on for a full minute and twenty-three seconds. From the judge's podium, Jaye P. Morgan deadpanned: "Do you know that that's the way I started?" Then she rated them a 10.*

The "Popsicle Twins" aired just once, then was cut before the West Coast screening, after a furious call from the network president. By then, Barris had gone into a tailspin. He was having panic attacks onstage. Strangers recognized him in the street, sometimes harassing and mocking him, sometimes stalking him obsessively. One contestant who got gonged got angry, then broke into the Barris Productions offices and lit them on fire. Worst of all, Barris's teenage

---

* Later that year, the redoubtable Morgan would get fired for flashing her breasts at the camera, an incident that NBC aired with a big "OOPS" over her chest.

daughter, Della, who had often introduced him on *The Gong Show*, had begun a brutal descent into drug addiction. Their many estrangements and reconciliations—and Barris's failed attempt at "tough love," which he came to regret—would haunt the producer for the rest of his life.

The growing darkness was reflected on the air. Despite the chaperones on *The Dating Game*, the show had no background checks, even to make sure people were single. In 1978, this hands-off approach led to a disaster when one of the show's winners, Rodney Alcala, turned out to be a serial killer. Jim Lange had introduced Alcala, who had lank hair down to his shoulders, as "a successful photographer who got his start when his father found him in the darkroom at the age of thirteen, fully developed." Asked what time of day he preferred, Alcala murmured, "Nighttime, that's the only time there is." His bachelorette was so unnerved after they met that she wisely refused to go out on their tennis date.

Alcala turned out to be a convicted sex offender, paroled twice—and at the time he filmed his segment, in the midst of a murder spree. A year later, he was arrested and nicknamed "The Dating Game Killer" in the press. His crimes were legitimately hideous, among them the rape of an eight-year-old girl. His trials, on the other hand, were often ridiculous: At one juncture, Alcala acted as his own attorney, interrogating himself on the stand for five hours, using a deeper voice whenever he spoke as the lawyer and playing the song "Alice's Restaurant" during his closing argument. He aired clips of his appearance on *The Dating Game*; Bachelor Number Two testified for the prosecution. Alcala was ultimately sentenced to death, then died in prison in 2021. It wasn't the last time a reality contestant would have a criminal record, but it was probably the most extreme.

By the late '70s, Barris was spinning out, destabilized by the spotlight he'd stepped into, after so many years pointing it at other people. Later, Barris would express bafflement at his own behavior while hosting *The Gong Show*: Whatever viewers had imagined, he wasn't high or drunk. "If I would never dance with a bowl on my head in front of my family, why did I dance that way before millions of strangers; perform in such a demented manner that I was never able to watch myself on television, then or now?" he wrote in his book *The Game Show King*.

In July 1978, *The Gong Show* was axed by the network's new boss, Fred Silverman. In the finale, Barris played "Take This Job and Shove It," and gave NBC the finger (which aired with an "OOPS!" sign superimposed). Then, he got gonged.

THE *GONG SHOW* CANCELLATION DIDN'T KILL BARRIS PRODUCtions. The final blow was another show: *3's a Crowd*, which ran for five disastrous months beginning in 1979.

3's a Crowd was basically *The Newlywed Game* for cheaters: A man's wife and his secretary competed over who knew him best, scribbling their answers on cardboard squares. It wasn't a new concept for Barris, who had been bragging about this format in the press since the 1960s, always insisting that it was too hot for his network bosses. By the time he actually produced it, however, the culture had grown less tolerant of snickering misogyny. *3's a Crowd* was protested from every possible angle: by the National Organization for Women, the United Auto Workers, the Homemakers' Equal Rights Association, and the National Secretaries Association. When it was pulled off the air in Detroit, Barris's partner Budd Granoff compared the boycott to a "book burning," warning that feminists would soon take down *Charlie's Angels*. The show's creator, Jess Oppenheimer— the former head writer for *I Love Lucy*—had his name taken off the credits. Metzger, still working hard to fulfill his boss's vision, found himself having nightmares about the contestants, "just looking at these poor people who we were going to turn against each other and thinking, 'We can't do it.'"

3's a Crowd also managed to attract the attention of one unusual critic: George W. S. Trow, a *New Yorker* contributor who was writing an anti-television manifesto called "Within the Context of No-Context." Published in 1980, "Within the Context of No-Context" took aim at television's moral vacuity and its focus on demographics. In the essay's key section, Trow tore into a show that he never named, although it's pretty clearly Barris's *3's a Crowd*. Aghast,

Trow described the series only—in his patter-poetic style—as "a little slice of time during which a man and his wife and a woman who works for him sit together behind a little desk-like thing. So shoddy, the little desk like thing. Like a bit of contempt molded into a kind of cage." This awful TV show debased its participants, Trow wrote, describing their faces shimmering "with doubt and embarrassment." These contestants struck the critic as a novel type of human being, a breed invented by television: "a new aristocracy of people who have had the imagination to have an intention to wound themselves."

For literary snobs who hated television, a small but powerful demographic, Trow's essay would become a go-to text, reprinted twice in book form, first in 1981, then in the late 1990s. The manifesto employed a few questionable rhetorical tactics—among them, using Chuck Barris's biggest flop as a metonym for the entire medium—but Trow had a prescient sense of this "new aristocracy" of unknowns, the ensemble of reality stars and influencers who would seize center stage in the culture at the turn of the millennium.

Ultimately, 3's a Crowd dragged Barris's business down, as each affiliate pulled the plug. In 1980, Barris made one last attempt to salvage his brand when he released The Gong Show Movie, a scripted comedy co-created with the avant-garde filmmaker Robert Downey. Like Allen Funt's What Do You Say to a Naked Lady?, The Gong Show Movie was marketed as a treat for fans, too hot for network censors. Unfortunately, Barris had made a fatal mistake: Unlike The Gong Show, The Gong Show Movie took itself very, very seriously. It flopped hard, even with Gong Show fans like newspaper critic Joe Baltake, who described it as "cheerless, self-pitying, sentimental schtick."

The boos were everywhere, by then: at the movie's premiere, where viewers jeered when Barris's daughter, Della, appeared on-screen; at a Flyers game in Philly, where Barris got booed when his face flashed on the jumbotron. He couldn't shrug off the reviews anymore—they were getting under his skin. In March 1980, two months before The Gong Show Movie debuted, The Saturday Review published "The Hating Game," an evisceration of five Barris shows by Peter Andrews. In it, the critic damned Barris's shows for vapidity, but he also diagnosed something else: an "almost psychotic hatred of women." "No opportunity is ever missed to show a woman as some sort of Daffy Duck who doubles as the town moron and the community punchboard . . . that his victims skip to the executioner's block fairly squealing with delight at the prospect is no defense," wrote Andrews.

That spring, Chuck Barris Productions laid off most of the staff. Fuming at how he'd fallen, Barris holed up in the Wyndham hotel, where he began to hammer out an "unauthorized autobiography" called *Confessions of a Dangerous Mind*, a ragged, free-associative manifesto about his life, which took a very different tone from the sunny *You and Me, Babe*. In it, Barris told a story he'd never hinted at before.* He claimed that throughout his Hollywood career, he'd been working as an assassin for the CIA, killing targets while he was chaperoning *Dating Game* winners to the romantic capitals of the world.

Confessions of a Dangerous Mind, which was published in 1984, is studded with both absurd spy plots and lewd sex scenes (one hookup is simply described as "The Monumental Suck"). It's a fascinatingly wrathful document, punctuated by flashes of self-awareness: At one point, he describes reading "The Hating Game" on a flight, lingering over Andrews's accusations of misogyny, then running into the bathroom, sick with rage and fear. But the heart of the book is a tender lament for the Barris Productions of the late 1960s, which Barris described as "a beautiful, phantasmagoric subculture," a short-lived, delicate utopia that, from his account, went sour just after that 1969 *Life* profile came out. He describes that era as his own personal Camelot, lost to history: "a meteor flash, a falling star, a precious moment of chest X-rays and vaginal cream."

No one who worked with Barris believed the CIA assassin story. Unlike *You and Me, Babe*, *Confessions* didn't sell. After it came out, Barris would sometimes describe the CIA plot as a satire, an attack on the hypocrites who gave medals to soldiers but demonized game

---

* Although the idea does briefly come up in *You and Me, Babe*, in which the narrator tells some party guests that he works for the CIA and that he trusts them never to tell anyone.

shows. Once, in a 1984 interview on the *Today* show, he admitted that he'd never been in the CIA, although he said that he had applied and wondered about what could have been. Other times, he liked to hint that it was true. But in the 2010 book *Della,* Barris's poignant, self-lacerating final memoir, an account of his late daughter's life, Barris wrote that she, at least, had ultimately come to believe his story. The idea that her father was a globe-trotting assassin, emotionally scarred by the crimes he committed, was, in its way, a comfort: It helped to explain his long absences during her childhood.

After *Confessions,* Barris largely retreated, selling his shares in the company in 1987. He moved to the South of France, where he wrote memoirs and thrillers. In 2002, Sam Rockwell played Barris in *Confessions of a Dangerous Mind,* a movie that revived many people's affection for the producer. In the film's most memorable scene, Barris follows a temptress as she swims into the Playboy Mansion grotto, flirting, only to suddenly turn on him, calling him "the most insidious, despicable force in entertainment today." When Barris defends himself, she asks who he thinks he is, then cuts him off with a smile. "Oh, I forgot, you created *The Dating Game. Wow.* Right up there with the Sistine Chapel."

By the time Barris left town, the Reagan era was glimmering on the horizon. On Christmas Eve 1979, TV critic Michael Hill wrote a newspaper column that celebrated the schlock impresario's steep fall, and with it, the end of "gimmick programming." "Instant-gratification" television—the glittering protoreality game shows and tawdry confessionals that were Barris's specialty—had always been, and always would be, just a fad. Soon, Hollywood wouldn't have Chuck Barris to kick around anymore.

3

||||||

THE BETRAYAL
An American Family

STOP. HIT PAUSE (A BUTTON THAT DIDN'T EXIST FOR TV IN THE 1970s). Before we get to the Reagan era, we need to take a detour, back to 1973, when Chuck Barris was still riding high. That year, the biggest news story was the Senate Watergate hearings, which began airing in May—and the revelation, in July, that President Nixon had been secretly taping visitors to the Oval Office, using a set of voice-activated Sony TC-800B open-reel recorders. By the next year, the public was tearing through transcripts of the president's intimate conversations, which revealed that he'd known about the Watergate burglary all along. In August 1974, Nixon resigned.

Still, the White House was only the second glass house to shatter in 1973. Just four months before the Watergate hearings, TV viewers had been mesmerized by a *different* set of tapes, which were filmed in a ranch house in California for a series called *An American Family*. Like the Nixon tapes, this documentary footage shattered old notions of what was private and what was public. It also sent reality television down a new path. If *Candid Camera* had launched the prank show, and *Queen for a Day* the game show, *An American Family* would initiate the third, and maybe the most powerful, thread of reality programming: the real-life soap opera. Aired weekly from

January through March, the show would become the most divisive, explosive, endlessly debated pop-culture sensation of that complicated year—and then, it would disappear. Before it vanished, however, *An American Family* would do something astonishing, by creating the world's first reality stars, the Loud family of Santa Barbara, California.

An American Family had begun filming two years earlier, in 1971, during an era of pervasive unease. Violence soaked through the cultural landscape, from the morass of Vietnam to the Manson murders; drugs, sex, and radical politics were everywhere. At the sleepy New York public television station WNET, however, the programming reflected little of this mood: Its lineup comprised earnest, Peabody-winning, eat-your-spinach documentaries—virtuous downers. To jolt the network, which was in the midst of rebranding as Channel 13/PBS, the network's funders had deputized its new president, James Day, to produce a more modern program, a blockbuster "youthquake" series, with each episode focused on some hot topic like divorce or psychedelics.

Day was busy developing that show, which had the unpromising title *Priorities for Change,* when one of his producers, Craig Gilbert, showed up for a meeting—"a huge bear of a man, hulking, rumpled, and with a generous growth of beard," as Day described him in his autobiography. Stubbing out one cigarette after another, Gilbert pitched a more exciting idea: a documentary series that focused entirely on one family. If the station just kept the cameras rolling, Gilbert told Day, they would capture all of those youthquake themes, only they'd emerge organically, from the relationship between the parents and their children. The idea of filming a family wasn't totally unprecedented—it had echoes of *A Married Couple,* a 1970 documentary by the Canadian cinéma vérité pioneer Allan King—but it was a shocking proposition for WNET.

It was also a Hail Mary pitch for Gilbert, who was in the midst of a personal and professional breakdown. A Harvard-educated intellectual from a wealthy East Coast family, he was the son of a musical copyright lawyer for composers like Irving Berlin. He'd worked as an ambulance driver at the liberation of Bergen-Belsen; in the early

1950s, he'd edited the *March of Time* newsreels. Superficially, he seemed like a success story: He'd directed *Margaret Mead's New Guinea Journal*, a celebrated 1968 documentary in which the anthropologist revisited the villagers she'd studied forty years earlier, as well as the Emmy-nominated *The Triumph of Christy Brown*, in 1970, which would later inspire the Oscar-winning biopic *My Left Foot*.

Yet at forty-six, Gilbert was on the verge of quitting the business. He was depressed and had been drinking heavily. His sixteen-year marriage was unraveling, as were many other marriages in his social set; marriage itself, Gilbert had begun to feel, might be obsolete. And not just marriage—in the elite Manhattan intelligentsia that dominated production at WNET, there was a heavy mood of malaise, a sense that every social institution was broken, corrupt. Among those institutions was television, the greatest corrupter of them all.

Day gave Gilbert's project the green light right away. He also said yes to the project's massive budget. (A number that would rise, over seven months, to more than a million dollars.) The producer was so shocked, he got drunk for a week, he later told the *Los Angeles Times*. He also called up Alan and Susan Raymond, the young filmmakers with whom he'd collaborated on *The Triumph of Christy Brown*, to tell them about the new plan—and then, with the help of his associate producer Susan Lester, Gilbert set off across the country, seeking the ideal family.

Three months later, Gilbert met the Louds. In California, he had interviewed a few families referred by therapists, figuring they could cope better with being filmed, but none worked out. During this period, Gilbert had been reading Ross Macdonald's *The Underground Man*, a noir thriller about moral rot in Santa Barbara, California; intrigued, he went to the city to meet the novelist. Macdonald, in turn, arranged for him to go on a date with a local magazine editor, to whom Gilbert described the family he was looking for: rich, white, and good-looking, enviable from the outside, the sort of family that television glamorized. She knew just the people: Bill Loud, a local businessman, and his stylish wife, Pat, who had five kids and lived in a big house with several cars and a pool. The Loud children were a

bit younger than the college students that Gilbert had originally envisioned, but he liked that there were a lot of them: Lance, nineteen;
Kevin, eighteen; Grant, seventeen; Delilah, fifteen; and Michele,
thirteen.

That weekend, the Loud family met with Gilbert in their living
room. The producer explained that they would be one of several
families, to help viewers contrast the culture of the Midwest versus
California, and so on. It sounded like fun—an adventure. Bill Loud
had always enjoyed making home movies of his family. He worked at
a company that built equipment for strip mines, but his kids dreamed
of artistic careers: Lance, who had recently moved to Manhattan,
was a lifelong devotee of Andy Warhol; Grant and Kevin played in
bands; Delilah studied dance; and the shyest, youngest sister, Michele, liked to ride horses.

Grant knew that his parents fought a lot, but their troubles
weren't his priority. He was caught up in fantasies of becoming a
rock star, leaving home and getting a fresh start. Craig Gilbert struck
him as a welcome novelty, "a really fascinating, dark, mercurial kind
of a guy. He had these big bags under his eyes, so you could tell he
was carrying the weight of the world on his shoulders," he told me,
with an edge to his voice, when we spoke in 2020.

The innocence of that long-ago May afternoon was hard to re-
capture, he said. But the way Grant remembered it, saying yes to *An
American Family* had felt not risky, but high-minded. "When Craig
sold the idea to us—I know it sounds crazy and like the '60s, but he
said, 'This isn't going to be about you; when people watch this,
they're going to be thinking about *themselves*. The successes they
have, the troubles they have!'" Grant assumed the filming, which
started that weekend, with a student body election at the high school,
would take a few weeks.

His sister Delilah thought the same thing. For Delilah, the meeting seemed like just another casual conversation, part of their busy,
lively social life as a family. "Then Craig kind of . . . disappeared.
And all of a sudden, it was a go," she said.

FILMMAKERS ALAN RAYMOND, TWENTY-SEVEN, AND SUSAN RAY-
mond, twenty-five, had been married for five years. Early on, they'd
hit a few bumps—Susan found Alan stuck-up, with "New York
airs"—but they had quickly evolved into a tight team, united in love
and work. Growing up, Susan had revered the anthropologist Margaret Mead; Alan worshipped Robert Drew, the pioneer who helped
originate "direct cinema," a less contrived form of documentary. For
both of them, the cinéma vérité approach to filmmaking was not
merely a technique, but a deeper philosophy, almost a religion. If you
recorded with your camera and microphone for long enough, with
enough patience, eventually, the truth would emerge.

On Memorial Day weekend 1971, Gilbert called to let the Raymonds know that he'd found the right family. He told them to head
down to the Hotel Chelsea, where Lance Loud had been living for
two months. The couple grabbed their equipment (Alan did video,
Susan audio) and then, along with their colleague Tommy Goodwin,
who handled lighting, they went to 23rd Street. Like most New York-
ers, they were already familiar with the Chelsea, which was infamous
for its louche, outrageous social scene. Up in Lance's room, they
filmed some on-the-fly footage, capturing the handsome nineteen-
year-old as he changed his shirt and chatted brightly with his friend
Kristian, waiting for his mother to arrive for a weeklong visit.

The Raymonds then went across the street to wait. When Pat
Loud stepped out of her cab—in dark glasses and a white trench
coat, her luggage carried by a doorman—the Raymonds began to
trail her, in silence. They filmed Pat as she checked in, and then in the
elevator (where they introduced themselves), and kept filming as she
walked, disoriented, through the Chelsea's wide, dingy halls, the lens
capturing her alarm at the environment. When she arrived in Lance's
room, her son bubbled over with excitement, telling his mother
about the downtown artists on his wall, about "all the underground
stars" who performed at La MaMa. "All these wonderful people that
I've never even heard of," said Pat, deadpan. "Oh, I know!" Lance
shouted, swinging his silky shoulder-length hair like a veil. "But you
dreamed of them."

The next week of filming was a blissful experience, for the Raymonds. Once the footage was edited, a year later, it would establish Lance and Pat as the twin stars of *An American Family*: a gay man and his mother, each of them electric in their blend of vulnerability and glamour, each at a moment of metamorphosis, her in her marriage, him in both his artistic identity and his sexuality. For the filmmakers, that would always be the purest element of *An American Family,* a true collaboration between strangers. They captured Lance as he walked his mother to her room, greeting the trans actress Holly Woodlawn in the hall, then as he walked down more stairwells, through more halls, more shadows. The final sequence retained a lovely mark of self-consciousness: On the third floor, as Lance passed through a landing, he glanced back and held the door for the Raymonds, who walked through it, invisible to the viewer.

The Raymonds quickly recognized that they had found a miraculous partner in Lance, someone who understood and accepted what it meant to be on camera. With his hooded eyes, soft voice, and square jaw, his flowered shirt tied at the waist, the oldest Loud child was a font of Quentin Crisp–ish aphorisms, his behavior hovering, without any sense of contradiction, between authenticity and performance. There had never been anyone like him on television before. There had never been anything like the relationship they were documenting, either, the bond between a gay man and a mother who loved him deeply but also struggled to understand his choices.

Later that week, the Raymonds filmed the two Louds during a long, rambling walk through Central Park. It was a bravura sequence, winding through the trees and then down the stairs to Bethesda Fountain. Later on, in the press analysis of the series, this interaction would often be described as the "coming out" scene. But Lance was already out to his family as gay, insofar as such a label made any sense to the Louds at the time. He never spoke, in Central Park, about being attracted to men. Instead, Lance drew his mother—who was, during that week, shyer than her son, or maybe simply more wary of the camera—into a dialogue, as he spoke, in intimate, glancing ways, about what made him so unusual as a teenager, back when he'd struck up a correspondence with his hero, Andy Warhol, dyed his hair silver, and retreated into his room. "It was like being a little mouse trapped in a box or something. . . . There was so much you guys could have done with me, if you'd known about me."

Years later, Lance would say that when they filmed that day, he fantasized that he was a movie star, making a sequel to Warhol's *Chelsea Girls.* "Where does Jacqueline Onassis live?" Pat asked Lance as they walked through Central Park. "She lives under the water in a glass house," Lance told his mother, while the Raymonds filmed the water as it spilled down, split by the sunlight.

Susan told me that among cinéma vérité filmmakers, there's a theory that the best material comes early on. The filmmakers bond with their subjects while establishing the rules of the shoot: They won't speak to their subjects, or laugh at their jokes, or ask them any questions. Their subject slowly intuits that they shouldn't look directly into the camera. An intimacy builds, step by step. "You have to establish this choreography, like this *dance,* where I'm going to stand over here. You're going to pretend I'm not here," said Susan. It was an approach that didn't work with children, she added: "It's an adult game."

When Pat flew back to California, the Raymonds packed up and followed her to Santa Barbara. They stayed for seven months. Craig Gilbert hadn't given them much direction, they told me. "He just said, 'Film everything.' " As a home base, the couple rented a beachside cottage, while the crew (including Gilbert, when he was in town, as well as Susan Lester) spent most of their time at a 1930s-style hotel called the Miramar.

The process was loose and unstructured. Most mornings, the Raymonds would drive to the Louds' eight-room stucco ranch house, then ask everybody what their plans were. They'd follow along, documenting whatever story struck them as most promising, hoping something would happen, to someone. Most days, very little did. The house had been wired for sound, with a microphone placed inside the chandelier. To provide proper lighting for the cameras, each lightbulb had been replaced with a 500-watt quartz bulb.

Within weeks, the Loud children felt at ease with the cameras—and also with the Raymonds, who felt like hip, slightly older siblings, northeastern exotics with cool taste in music and art. The Raymonds filmed Grant and his friends as they horsed around by the pool. They tagged along when Delilah went to dance rehearsal. They filmed the kids spraying one another with shaving cream. They were self-centered teens, caught up in their own social lives, said Grant. "So, you know: *If you want to take pictures, go ahead!*"

At their rental cottage, the Raymonds began stacking Kodak film to the ceiling, around ten rolls per day, a hugely expensive amount of film. There were no digital shortcuts that they could take, no way to tell if there were errors, a "hair in the gate." They weren't able to watch daily rushes, since the film needed to be developed, printed, and transferred to 16 mm before it was possible for them to view it. Most days, Craig Gilbert wasn't around—and sometimes he was back in New York, wheedling for more funding and episodes (he wanted fifteen, while WNET wanted eight; they settled on twelve, as the budget ballooned from $600,000 to, by some accounts, $1.6 million). When he came west, he often spent evenings with Bill and Pat, but especially Pat.

Then, on September 3, three months in, something big did happen: Pat asked Bill for a divorce. The Raymonds were behind the camera when Pat—seething, chain-smoking, dressed all in white—handed Bill her lawyer's business card and asked him to move out. Maybe they shouldn't have been so surprised: For weeks, the Raymonds had been filming the couple's fights, their long silences, their heavy drinking. Yet the "divorce scene" came as a radical shock to them, and in time, the reverberations of that sequence would splinter the relationships of everyone involved in the production.

By then, Gilbert's blueprint seemed, to the Louds, to have shifted: Certainly, there was no plan to film any other families—nor had there ever been such a plan, according to the Raymonds.* It would not be a short shoot, either. Instead, the cameras would keep rolling for four more months, as Gilbert pushed for added footage, particularly of Bill, who was reveling in his new life as a single man. Legend-

---

* Pat's own account of the plan has varied over time: In an April 1973 interview with *Film Comment,* she described Gilbert telling her, in his first pitch, that the Louds would become one hour of a five-part series—and then, a few days later, flattering her by saying that the whole series should be about the Louds.

ary cinematographer Joan Churchill and sound recordist Peter Pilafian shot Bill at his hotel; John Terry and sound man Al Mecklenberg filmed Lance on a trip to Copenhagen. These outside crews didn't always follow strict cinéma vérité rules, which frustrated the Raymonds. By then, the couple saw the show as very much *their* creation, not Gilbert's.

In fact, even as Bill and Pat were splitting up, an uglier rupture had been taking place, between Gilbert and the Raymonds. Once the filming was completed, the three of them would argue about how the couple would be credited, as "filmmakers" or "directors." But on set, they fought about ethics. In the Raymonds' view, Gilbert had been "working" the family, manipulating his subjects, crossing boundaries. Whenever he was in town, Gilbert would spend the evening with Pat, the two of them socializing late at night, drinking and having long, intimate conversations, talking about art, life, and ideas. To Alan and Susan, comparative newlyweds, the situation was bewildering.

But many things had blindsided the Raymonds. Somehow, in three months of filming, they'd never suspected that Bill was cheating on Pat. They had no idea, even when Bill told them he had to go to the post office and then disappeared for three days. "We thought, 'Life is unfolding!' I was stunned that everyone knew but us," said Alan. One day, Lance, during a visit home, told the filmmakers, "I thought, this time, I'd *really* have to pull her together." Suddenly, in a flash, they understood: There was a marital history that had been invisible to them, one that had deep roots, going back years. Gazing through the camera, they hadn't seen it.

One day, several weeks before the divorce scene, after one of Bill's many mysterious trips out of town, Pat and Bill had gone to a local Mexican restaurant, El Paseo, which was hosting Santa Barbara's annual Fiesta, a Spanish history and heritage appreciation week. A mariachi band played, so loud that Susan could barely record the audio; Alan couldn't make out the conversation, either. But they knew the mood felt dark. Leaning sideways, Pat, her voice slurring, let loose at her husband, calling him "a goddamn asshole," describing him as "one of the most ludicrous, schizophrenic people," sneering, "If it weren't so sad, it would make me laugh." Uneasy, the Raymonds packed up and walked out of the restaurant. But Craig Gilbert—who was in town that day, observing the situation— followed them to insist that they keep on shooting.

In the parking lot, Alan argued with Gilbert, getting so fired up that he slammed the producer against a wall, nearly punching him. "Our position was that he was putting hot coals under the family," said Susan. Then Pat Loud came out the door, weaving and clearly drunk. Susan remembers worrying about Pat, thinking that one of them should stop her from driving. They didn't do that, though: Instead, they let her drive home, following her in their own car.

By September, Pat had begun dodging their cameras. The Raymonds didn't film her when she told the kids about the divorce; they didn't film her when she met with her lawyer. No one in the family ever asked the Raymonds to stop filming, but it had become a game of cat-and-mouse between them and the Louds. The situation finally came to a head the night Pat planned to talk to her brother and her sister-in-law about her decision to end her marriage. She intended to have that conversation, as well, in private.

Instead, when she showed up at her brother's house, Craig Gilbert was there, determined to convince her to let the Raymonds film the moment. For nearly three hours, Pat and Gilbert retreated, drinking heavily and debating. Pat needed to do this "scene" on camera, Craig insisted—otherwise, the story that they were telling in the show would make no sense to viewers. Why was she getting divorced? She had to help people understand. Finally, Pat agreed to be filmed— and Gilbert called the Raymonds, who set up their cameras. When Pat walked out onto the patio, she was clearly drunk. In the near-darkness, next to a loud rotisserie on which her sister-in-law was roasting a chicken, Pat sat down in a wire-frame chair and began to speak. By that point, Gilbert had gotten into his car and driven away.

That night, Pat spoke more openly than she ever had, in spiky, dark-humored spirals of revelation, telling her sister-in-law about Bill's cheating, his affairs with "big-bosomed, fat-assed blond businesswomen," describing her anxieties about her worth as a woman, her fears of the future. "I'm too old for women's lib but too young for *that*," she joked about staying in a sexless marriage. She talked about her children. Lance was "keen," she said, mournfully, but he "might have been keener if he thought his daddy really loved him, really cared about him." She listed her strengths and her weaknesses: "I'm not very intelligent! I'm perhaps a bit perceptive."

In response, her sister-in-law gave her old-school advice on how to save her marriage: Pat, she explained, had to learn to appreciate the stability her situation offered her. She needed to make Bill feel like a man. Alan felt uncomfortable behind the camera; he found himself hoping that the light would be too dim for the footage to be usable. "Also, there was the grinding of the rotisserie," he said. "They kept going until finally we didn't want to do it anymore."

The Raymonds are still of two minds about that footage. On one hand, they believe they may have crossed an ethical line. On the other hand, the result was a poignant sequence that had real social value, one that would affect the viewers who watched it, changing lives and helping people—both women and men, anyone struggling with the constraints of family life—feel less alone. Alan is a good talker with a confident ideology; he's been telling his side of this story for years. But on the value of that night, he stumbled. "It's kind of a difficult thing to really talk about," he said.

The truth was, the Raymonds had grown as close to their own subjects as Gilbert had. They simply believed that they were the Louds' friends, while they saw Gilbert as their enemy, the man who was exploiting their struggles. For many years, the Louds shared their interpretation.

"Of course, Grant, if you ever get to talk to him, will give you his sob story about when he went to pick Bill up at the airport," Alan warned me. He was referring to a key moment in the shoot, the night of the "divorce scene." That night, Grant had been hanging out with his girlfriend, in the dining room. Then his mother called out to him, to tell Grant to do something for her: He needed to pick his father up from the airport, from yet another business trip. And Grant needed to do something else: He had to tell his father to go to a hotel, instead of coming home. That way, no one would be filming Pat when she asked for a divorce.

Susan still marvels at the footage they captured that night. "And then, his *look*. I mean, it's something only vérité could capture. There's this look on this seventeen-year-old boy's face like, *Huh? Me? . . . Why me?* Because he knows what's about to happen." Had Bill decided to go stay at a hotel that night, the show's most famous confrontation might never have been filmed. "So he goes to the airport, we film him in the car. Yes, yes, we're with him, we're doggedly following him. He tries to suggest to Bill that it's kind of tense at home, but Bill doesn't get the suggestion. And Bill comes home. And that is the moment when Grant now cannot watch that series again. That scene—"

Alan breaks in: "That scene, that somehow or other, in the twisted machinations of his memory, we get blamed for."

AN AMERICAN FAMILY STOPPED FILMING ON NEW YEAR'S EVE, 1971. That night, Pat and Bill attended separate parties. Pat stayed home, wearing thick black glasses and a patchwork dress. Snuggling with her dog, she looked on, wistfully, as a crowd of teens—her kids, their friends—gyrated happily to "Boogie Woogie Bugle Boy." Meanwhile, Bill downed cocktails in a nightclub, surrounded by blondes in tight dresses. The next day, the crew that had filmed *An American Family* flew east, where the editors were waiting to get a look at their footage.

A year went by. For most of 1972, the Louds didn't worry, much, about the show they had starred in—they were distracted by Bill and Pat's divorce, with each of them figuring out their lives. The WNET series wouldn't be a big deal, they figured. It wasn't that crazy an assumption. *A Married Couple*, which debuted in 1970, had left few cultural ripples.* A similar American documentary experiment had

---

* In this "actuality drama," director Allan King spent ten weeks filming the fractured marriage of his friends Antoinette and Billy Edwards, and their three-year-old son, Bogart. In *The New York Times*, critic Vincent Canby praised the film's intimacy but also argued that it was tainted by self-awareness: "The unreality prompted by the camera's presence is acknowledged in the film, which then proceeds to pass off this conscious performance as some kind of meta-truth that is neither fact nor fiction."

also aired in November 1971, on CBS, a one-hour reported documentary by Charles Kuralt, which was titled, with hilarious gravitas, . . . *But What If the Dream Comes True?* Kuralt's film was a documentary deconstruction of the Greenawalts, a wealthy white family with three kids living in Birmingham, Michigan, with whom Kuralt's crew had embedded for eight weeks. It was an unrelentingly polemical project, whose critique of suburban privilege was imposed by Kuralt's know-it-all voiceover ("He has it all now, but when you listen to him, you detect the first faint shudder of discontent . . ."), full of disdain for the nascent feminism of local housewives. Although the Greenawalts got some flak from their neighbors, the program itself got good reviews, with *The New York Times* praising the family as "intelligent, sensitive, and disarmingly candid." Then it disappeared, like most TV.

In New York, meanwhile, Gilbert's editors had been wading through the footage from Santa Barbara—three hundred hours of the stuff, unsorted. From January until April, they watched the Louds for six hours a day, taking reams of notes, at once appalled and fascinated by what they saw, analyzing the family during smoke breaks. Gilbert believed that the editing had to be distinct from the filming, so he had deliberately hired editors who knew nothing about the Louds firsthand, in order to get a fresh eye.

The team shifted a few times. Charlotte Zwerin, the celebrated co-director and co-editor of *Gimme Shelter*, got fired, early, in a dispute over hiring. Ellie Hamerow was also fired, after she'd finished cutting the show's pilot. Hamerow, who thought the series should be cut down radically, clashed with Gilbert on a few points, including a concern about exposing Lance Loud to public judgment. In the end, the key editor was Gilbert's good friend David Hanser, who was midway through his own divorce. The editing team discussed a few possible structures for the series—dividing the episodes by theme or by character, for instance—but in the end, they decided to go chronologically, with one key exception: The first episode would be set on New Year's Eve, cutting between the two parties. That decision turned the show into a mystery: *What led to this divorce?* It had a pragmatic benefit, too: Since Gilbert was still negotiating about how many episodes would air, the show already had an ending.

The rest of the series would be a radical departure from anything WNET had ever aired, all those Peabody-winning documentaries with their earnest framing, expert voiceovers, and talking-head interviews. It also bore little resemblance to . . . *But What If the Dream Comes True?*, with its spoon-fed political thesis for CBS viewers. In contrast, most of *An American Family* had no narrator at all. The pace was slow and dreamy, even meditative, which left the viewer lots of space to contemplate the meaning of it all. A challengingly intimate aesthetic, it more closely resembled avant-garde independent movies than anything on TV. That raw, unmediated quality would make the show riveting—and, also, unnerving. Like *Candid Microphone,* it felt like eavesdropping.

The editors did include a few devices to guide the viewer, some of them violating the Raymonds' strict cinéma vérité precepts. For the first episode, Lance provided a wickedly funny voiceover, giving his siblings nicknames like "Tricia Nixon with spice." The fourth episode, in which Pat visited her mother, included home movies from her childhood. Gilbert originally planned to include more of this material—like a history of American immigration, used as a way of exploring the Loud family's roots—but none made it into the final cut, which focused on the family in isolation, interacting with one another.

The second episode was cut from the Raymonds' first week filming in Manhattan, starting at the Chelsea. That hour told a complete story of its own, full of tenderness and melancholy, streaked with remarkable footage of the downtown art scene: Pat and Lance at La MaMa, watching the drag-filled theatrical spectacular *Vain Victory;* dancing languorously in a disco; and visiting a Warhol exhibit. The final act focused on a painful conversation between mother and son, full of long silences, in which Pat gently encouraged her son to support himself financially. "You need some Murine or something in your eyes, your eyes are very red," she told him, worried. "Je suis fatigué," Lance murmured back.

Other episodes were less sharply structured. One was about Delilah's tap dancing classes; another focused on Bill's business. Grant crashed his car; the house nearly burned down. A few moments indicated that the Louds were aware that they were being filmed: In one scene, as Delilah and her boyfriend gazed into each other's eyes, Kevin walked by, then peeked back at the camera and announced, puckishly, "Brad and Delilah love scene, part two."

The first eight episodes were edited together from the first three months, leading up to the divorce scene. That sequence became the climax of the show, and it's brutal to watch, even decades later. In it, we view Pat from behind as she sits on the sofa, in loose white pants and a white blouse, her knees up, smoking. Even without seeing her face, it's clear she's seething. Bill saunters in, jaunty and clueless, but before his wife can say much, Delilah dances over to embrace her father. "Hello, big dude," Bill says to Delilah, warmly (it was his nickname for her), and the two of them joke about his tie, which he pulls off through his collar. "Did Grant say anything to you?" Pat asks Bill. "No, about what?" says Bill—and then, clearly realizing what is about to go down, Delilah pivots, then glides away, exiting the room.

Pat rises from the sofa and walks over to Bill. "I have spoken to a lawyer and this is his card. And I'd like to have you move out, just like that," she says. The Raymonds' lens zooms in on Bill's weathered features as he absorbs the news. "Well, that's a fair deal," Bill says, staring at the card. He pauses and adds, mildly, "I think it's short-sighted on your part, really—"

The two continue exchanging information, their voices calm, as the camera homes in on Bill's face, just as it had on Viva's on *Queen for a Day*, giving off glimmers of shock, amusement, and weariness, sparks struck from a stone monument. After another long pause, Bill remarks, wryly, "Well, then I don't have to unpack my bag, do I?" and begins putting his tie back through his collar. He packs some clothes; he makes a few phone calls; and finally, he leaves, never once glancing into the camera, even as it follows him to his car.

Just before Bill carries his bags out to the white Jaguar, the cameras, hovering by a bedroom door, catch a glimpse of Pat, alone on her bed. There is a sweet, strange shot of thirteen-year-old Michele, playfully making their cat "fight" with their dog. "God, how cruel! The cat can chew him up but he can't chew the cat up, right?" Delilah says to Michele. Then, a cut to black.

The rest of the episode is bleak. There are long, silent scenes of Pat sitting by the pool, hidden by sunglasses. There is a two-minute shot of Pat and Delilah dancing together to Artie Shaw, some opaque family banter, and a tense phone call between Pat and Bill.

And then, a final scene—a tender and beautiful sequence. In it, the kids and Pat watch Grant play the guitar, first a lively version of The Kinks' "Apeman," and then "Mother Nature's Son," by The Beatles. "This one's for Mom, guys," Grant says, and glances, with a sweet grin, into the camera. The last shot is a freeze-frame of Pat's face, uplifted by her children's presence.

Late in the process, Craig Gilbert added one final framing device to the show: a spoken introduction, four minutes long, which he delivered himself. Standing on a hillside in Santa Barbara, above the caption "Craig Gilbert, Producer," Gilbert, wearing an air of depressed authority, announces: "This series is about the William C. Loud family. . . . This was a cooperative venture in every sense of the word." The Louds were changed by the presence of the cameras, Gilbert explains to viewers; the crew had also been changed. The show's subjects should not be seen as an average or typical family, he adds. "*No* family is. . . . They are not the American family—they are simply *an* American family."

Gilbert's analytical manifesto, which contained grand historical pronouncements that appeared nowhere else in the series, made a preemptive case to the critics. It rejected the notion that the camera was merely an observer. It suggested, somewhat confusingly, that critics should not use the show to draw broad conclusions about American culture—but also, it implied that they definitely should do that. "What is the current American dream?" Gilbert asked the television audience. "Why has marriage become something less than a permanent arrangement? What is left of the parent-child relationship? Where are America's children going?"

After Gilbert's speech had concluded, the camera panned to the Edenic Santa Barbara hillside and the credits began to roll. There were shots of each of the Louds, set in squares, gliding into place, as if they were puzzle pieces: Delilah dancing, Bill wearing a hard hat. And then, the show's logo: First, the words "an American," in lowercase. Underneath, the word "FAMILY" unfolded—in solid, connected capital letters. Then "FAMILY" cracked, like glass.

AN AMERICAN FAMILY DEBUTED ON JANUARY 11, 1973. TEN MILLION viewers watched it, every Thursday night at 9 P.M. The Loud kids were among them, curled in their mom's bed, eating Pat's broccoli casseroles. After a year of denial, they understood they were in for it.

Before the show aired, Pat had screened a few episodes. She expressed no objections, although she did tell James Day and Craig Gilbert that she hated the credit sequence, with that cracked "FAMILY." Still, she wrote gracious letters to the staff and to Gilbert, thanking them for the thoughtfulness of their portrayal. Then someone slipped her the WNET press packet—and her perspective changed, overnight. As she saw it, their series was being marketed not as a sophisticated documentary but as a lurid soap opera—a spectacle for the world to mock.

Each packet included a show summary, a set of character descriptions, and an essay from *Image*, WNET/13's membership magazine, written by a Canadian writer named Fredelle Maynard. In her essay, Maynard regarded the family coldly, as a text to dissect: "These people touch without meeting, meet without touching," she wrote, describing the Louds as a vapid group, incapable of communication and suffering from "an American disease." In another section, Gilbert himself speculated on why the Louds had participated—they'd done it for the ego boost, he theorized, and, also, out of the hope that the camera might help them with their bad communication, that it might work like "the presence of a good friend." Maynard's essay was stapled to the *Image* cover that depicted one of the Louds' Christmas portraits, with black cracks added, splitting them apart.

The print ads were just as damaging. Before the second episode had aired, one ad blared, in all caps, "HE DYED HIS HAIR SILVER." Small print explained, of Lance, "He lives in the Chelsea

Hotel on Manhattan's lower West Side. And lives a lifestyle that might shock a lot of people back home in California." Dyeing his clothes purple was, the copy smirked, "a personal expression of . . . something . . . something he wasn't fully aware of at the time."

Early press for the show amplified these themes—and sometimes directly echoed their language. Joyce Wagner, in *The Kansas City Times,* wrote that the Louds "touch without meeting and meet without touching," cribbing the promotional line verbatim. This type of titillated press coverage kept on expanding, week after week, with each review feeding on what came before. WNET had hit its goal: They'd managed to produce a "youthquake," a blockbuster, a messily intimate, aesthetically provocative series that had triggered an energetic subindustry of op-eds, essays, and TV panels, arguing about what it all meant. The problem was, critics were reviewing not the show but the *family*.

Not all of the coverage was negative: In the *Los Angeles Times,* Cecil Smith celebrated the hour devoted to Pat and Lance at the Chelsea Hotel as "a most painful episode to watch in its depth of honesty and love." It was doubtful, Smith wrote, that *An American Family* was the kind of show that WNET's funders, who included President Nixon's telecommunications advisers, ever intended to create. "They seem to want public television to be bland and lifeless. That, 'An American Family' decidedly is not." In *The New York Times,* critic John J. O'Connor was similarly sympathetic, diagnosing the problem in the marketing, not the show. Most strikingly, anthropologist Margaret Mead, who had been the subject of Gilbert's earlier documentary, praised the series as the launch of a new genre, "as important for our time as were the invention of drama and the novel for earlier generations: a new way to help people understand themselves."

Still, the majority of the coverage was both hostile and personal—and to Pat, it felt like an emergency. Quickly, she held a family meeting: The Louds needed to reintroduce themselves to the world, on their own terms, she argued. In some ways, that tactic turned out to be an effective one, since it let the family make a noisy public case against Gilbert and WNET. But it also inflamed the problem of their own celebrity. To many observers, the Louds were now not merely a rich California family who had mysteriously allowed their personal lives to be televised to the nation, but a family who *kept* going on television—this time, to explain why they'd gone on television.

The media tour was all a bit amateur hour, in Delilah's amused recollection. Pat hired the kids' drama teacher from Santa Barbara High School to work as their press handler. Together and separately, the Louds began to show up on every possible platform, from *The Mike Douglas Show* to *Ladies' Home Journal*. "I feel like Joan of Arc on a jackass riding backwards," Pat Loud told the New York *Daily News* on February 20, slamming Craig Gilbert as an "instant anthropologist." The Louds needed to go on talk shows, she explained to the newspaper, so people could "see us as we are on a program that won't be edited or shaped to a concept."

The same night, the family appeared on *The Dick Cavett Show,* the classiest chat show around. Grant and Kevin played guitar for a national audience; Lance's band, then called Loud!, played as well. But despite Pat's hopes, a talk show had a shape, too. Much of their time was spent sparring with Cavett, whose mannerly disdain reflected an era in which even sophisticates treated homosexuality as a sideshow. "We don't say 'homo.' That's what the newspapers say," said Kevin, defending his brother. "I don't know, Dick, I don't sleep with my son, so I don't know what his preference is," said Pat, deadpan.

Lance, who wore a baggy blazer and pink socks, like some time traveler from the 1980s, undermined Cavett at every turn, slyly critiquing *An American Family* in the process, explaining that he only ever watched the last ten minutes. "No matter how draggy the entire hour seemed, they suddenly *pull themselves together* and really *throw on* that old drama at the end, and freeze out and play some good music or something. I really like that!" he said, grinning.

The same week, *The New York Times Magazine* published a major essay about the Louds, "An American Family: Things Are Keen but Could Be Keener," written by Anne Roiphe. It started out cruel and got crueler. "The patient viewer begins to absorb these people, their culture. Their level and kind of civilization is exposed as clearly as if it were under a microscope," Roiphe wrote. Roiphe, who was a novelist, had met Pat and Bill briefly at the Carnegie Deli, but she'd spent much more time with Craig Gilbert, who told her stories about the Louds' history that were not included in the show. Gilbert appeared to be "a soft and kind man, intellectual, artistic, an amateur anthropologist, a worrier, an introvert," Roiphe gushed. In her view, he was a genius who was saddled with clingy narcissists— and in his way, he was a novelist, just like her. Pat, on the other hand, struck her as a pathetic housewife with a crush on her producer.

The piece's worst sting, however, came from Roiphe's analysis of Lance, whom she described as "the evil flower of the Loud family." Even for 1973, the year that homosexuality was removed from the *Diagnostic and Statistical Manual of Mental Disorders,* Roiphe's essay is virulently homophobic. Long sections deride Lance's "flamboyant, leechlike homosexuality," his "camping and queening about like a pathetic court jester, a Goyaesque emotional dwarf." Roiphe theorized at length about what "caused" Lance, concluding that he'd been born damaged, "like swimming alongside an electric eel." She even theorized that Bill's cheating had somehow been Lance's fault. As a kicker, Roiphe managed to condemn the entire Loud clan for not talking more about politics during the show. "Delilah, like the rest of the Louds, never grieved for the migrant workers, the lettuce pickers, the war dead."

When she read the piece, Pat called Gilbert in the middle of the night, screaming with fury. Roiphe's essay also came up on *The Dick Cavett Show,* when the host asked Lance about the press. "Well, I don't know—some people might *like* swimming next to an electric eel," Lance said wryly. Roiphe's essay had been the only response that "truly hurt" him, he added, in a soft voice—and then, with impeccable timing, he dropped the punchline: ". . . but I took two aspirin and it was gone." The audience burst into laughter and supportive applause.*

---

* They weren't alone: Despite bad press, the Louds got tons of supportive fan mail, often from people sharing private struggles. One letter began, "Although you do not know us, I'm sure you don't mind me treating you as a friend. Pat, it's just unbelievable how many things we have in common." Another read, "To hell with the critics." Fans spilled out their deepest family secrets to the Louds, including a closeted gay man who wrote a moving account of his life to Lance, a letter which ended, "Highest regards to you and your very fine family. I regret that I cannot sign my name."

A month later, the Louds were pictured on the cover of *News-week,* with a banner reading "The Broken Family." In the aftermath of the show's debut, prominent journalist Shana Alexander had written two pieces about the Louds, describing the family as "afflu-ent zombies" and calling their show "a glimpse into the pit." Like seemingly every other East Coast cultural thinker, Alexander drew broad, borderline apocalyptic conclusions about the project's larger meaning for American culture: "The silence of the Louds is also a scream, a scream that people matter, that they matter and we matter. I think that it is a scream whose echoes will shake up all America."

The critics weren't alone in believing the show felt like the end of the world: Even as critics torched his work, Gilbert himself gave several bridge-burning interviews, in which he dished about his mar-ital troubles, speculated on the Louds' neuroses, defended himself against Pat's accusations, and theorized, at length, about American decay. The day before *An American Family* debuted, he told the *Los Angeles Times* that he should never have filmed the series, which he described as "a prolonged encounter group." In another Q and A, in February, Gilbert denounced television itself as a demeaning me-dium, which was ultimately corrosive both to those who made it and to those who watched it: "I think it is a mirror of everything that is wrong with the country." He also predicted that he'd be fired by WNET (which had now been rebranded as PBS) that March, because public television wasn't able to tolerate controversy.

After this burst of defensive fire, Gilbert retreated. He stopped giving interviews, and although he maintained relationships with friends like Susan Lester, he ultimately withdrew, living alone in downtown Manhattan. None of the projects he pitched—including, early on, an ambitious documentary about a dozen Midwesterners, through which he hoped to document the country's decline—got made. Once in a while, he would attend a panel about *An American Family,* then retreat again. In 1982, he published "Reflections on 'An American Family,'" a long essay in which he stated his case, relitigat-ing every detail. In it, he reprinted Pat Loud's letter, the one in which she thanked him for having "handled the film with as much kindness as is possible and still remain honest." He argued that *60 Minutes* had more manipulation than *An American Family.* He denounced the Raymonds for their claims that they were the true authors of his show. By retreating from the debate, Gilbert wrote, he had allowed the Raymonds—whom he described dismissively as "a man who had held a camera and a woman who had held a microphone"—to steal credit from him, and unfairly smear him as a "Svengali-like manipulator, a crass invader of privacy, and a brooding East Coast neurotic with a compelling need to foist my twisted vision of life on an unsuspecting public." None of that was fair, Gilbert wrote—and he, too, had suffered.

THE LOUDS' FAME DIDN'T END WHEN THE FINALE AIRED. THROUGH-out the 1970s, they remained household names, go-to laugh lines on *Saturday Night Live* and in *New Yorker* cartoons. They also continued to do press. Bill posed for *Esquire,* in bed, wearing a scarlet-and-black robe and a grin. Lance posed for *Screw*—full-frontal naked with dyed red hair—and gave out his telephone number in the interview, asking his fans to send "kisses and scarves." Pat wore a negligee for *Oui* magazine and got a makeover in *Ladies' Home Journal.* The press tour was not exactly torture, Delilah said—and at times, it was a fun, silly ride through 1970s pop media, like the time Delilah appeared as a bachelorette on *The Dating Game.* (She tried to plant Lance in the audience to signal which bachelor to choose, but an usher moved him. She wound up with "a dud" and won a trip to Pensacola, although she never went.)

Lance played at CBGB with his punk band, the Mumps. The least-known players in that club's legendary music scene, they played with Blondie and Talking Heads, but despite their witty, Kinks-inflected act, the Mumps never got signed—largely, according to Lance's lifelong friend and bandmate Kristian Hoffman, because of their unapologetic queerness. They were also hurt by Lance's fame: His notoriety attracted fans to the club but made the band look like a gimmick.

For many years, Pat was a household name. To her meanest critics, she was a fame-hungry joke—a much-mocked Real Housewife a decade before Bravo was a wink in NBC's eye. But other viewers, especially young gay men, embraced her as a feminist icon. To them, she was a glamorous truth teller who had bravely left a lousy marriage and loved her son for who he was, back when that was an act of courage. In 1974, she published *Pat Loud: A Woman's Story,* co-written with Nora Johnson, a dishy, direct book in which she went into detail about Bill's affairs, as well as the couple's failed attempts at an open marriage. She also described the effects of appearing on camera: Being filmed for so long, so intimately, felt like missing REM sleep, she wrote; the camera ("that eye of half-truth") had thrown her off-kilter, turning her into someone she no longer recognized. She'd done the book for the money—the Louds were in bad shape financially, due to Bill's overspending—but it was also another attempt to tell her story directly, without WNET or Dick Cavett in the way.

Pat's book was received respectfully, other than a scathing pan by Nora Ephron in *New York* magazine. Although Ephron hadn't watched *An American Family,* she'd found the publicity for the show repellent. "She has made a fool of herself on television, and now she is making a fool of herself in print," Ephron wrote, expressing revulsion at Pat's "letting-it-all-hang-out candor" and her confessions about finding out about Bill's cheating while she was pregnant.

At the time, Ephron, thirty-three, a clever essayist on the rise in Manhattan media, was still married to her first husband. Two years later, she would meet and marry Carl Bernstein. After he cheated on her while she was pregnant, Ephron would write *Heartburn,* a merry, score-settling bestseller full of delicious recipes. It was a case of instant karma: *Heartburn* would be attacked by critics for the same crime she'd dunned Pat for—spinning her public divorce into a personal brand.

That irony wasn't an exception when it came to the journalists who covered the Louds. Each of the family's chief media critics had a bizarrely similar biography. Fredelle Maynard, their tormentor in the WNET press packet, published a memoir about her childhood and marriage in 1972, which led to a divorce from her alcoholic husband—fallout that she wrote about in a *later* memoir. Her daughter, Joyce Maynard, wrote the bombshell essay "An 18-Year-Old Looks Back on Life," in *The New York Times Magazine*, also in 1972—and later, Joyce would go on to write about her abusive relationship with J. D. Salinger. Anne Roiphe and Shana Alexander would each wind up documenting their own marital crack-ups (in Roiphe's case, in a 1977 roman à clef in which she denounced her ex as a pervert; in Alexander's, in both a 1979 book about Patty Hearst and a 1996 family memoir). There was something in the water in their social circle: a deep urge to confess, rooted in feminist rage, in the 1970s insight that the personal could be political—and also, commercial. Yet if these journalists' life stories had parallels to Pat Loud's, it didn't seem to make them feel for her. If anything, it sharpened their knives.

One powerful defense of *An American Family* did emerge, a month after the finale aired. Written by Merle Miller and published in *Esquire,* the essay, titled "Dear Pat, Bill, Lance, Delilah, Grant, Kevin and Michele: I Loved You," is a witty, humane meditation on both *An American Family* and the vitriol that greeted it. Miller had had his own experience of the public confessional, having come out as gay in *The New York Times Magazine* two years earlier, as a defiant response to the open homophobia of the media world. He took delicious jabs at the hypocrisy of the chorus of critics of *An American Family,* all those writers in lousy relationships gleefully judging the Louds. "People I know for a fact haven't spoken to anybody in years, have simply talked at people, gave the Louds low marks for communicating," he wrote.

In a deeply divided country, Miller wrote, *An American Family* had united the population in feeling superior to its subjects. Miller himself had joined that "euphoric" mob at first, he confessed—and then, he had been won over by the Louds themselves, who struck him as tender, vulnerable, and, ultimately, decent people. Their show was funny; sometimes, it was boring. But it also made him scream at the screen, in a way that few TV shows ever had before: "Stop the cameras. Get those intruders the hell out. As Andy Warhol said in another context, you'll be famous for twenty-nine minutes, but you'll also be demeaned, vilified, and eventually, dismissed. A lot of people are going to recognize more of themselves in you than they are will-ing to admit, and they'll never forgive you for that."

Decades before reality programming became both an industry and a way of seeing the world, Miller argued for the potential of the new genre as a force for empathy, if people could just stop their finger-pointing. When Pat, on the night of the rotisserie, had opened up about her desperation at the idea of being single, the woman Miller was watching with had yelled out, "That's right. We're all basket cases when that happens." *An American Family* wasn't a shameful overshare, Miller wrote: It simply put a sharper lens on humanity than its audiences seemed capable of tolerating. "When the series is repeated, as surely it will be, we may even be able to set our personal discomfort aside and learn something from it."

IT NEVER HAPPENED. MAYBE THE STRANGEST ASPECT OF *AN American Family* was how quickly it disappeared. The episodes were unavailable in reruns, and then, as technology shifted, they were never released on VCR tapes, DVDs, or even streaming platforms. Shockingly, WNET had destroyed all of the outtakes from the show, as a cost-saving mechanism. The music rights were expensive. And the network, after its rebrand, seemed to view its former blockbuster as an embarrassment. There were a few screenings, one on New Year's Eve in 1990, a single airing of the New York episode in 2003, and another marathon airing in 2011. In 2023, the show's fiftieth an-niversary, no special devoted to the show was aired.

Even out of sight, however, *An American Family* left echoes—most often, reflected in satire. In 1976, Norman Lear produced a scathing experimental sitcom called *Mary Hartman, Mary Hart-man,* a satire of commercial television in which Louise Lasser played Mary Hartman, a housewife in a bad marriage, living inside a soap opera. In the first season's final episode, Mary appears as a guest on *The David Susskind Show,* representing "America's typical consumer housewife," just as Pat Loud had gone on *The Dick Cavett Show.* On TV, she is peppered with invasive questions by a panel of experts: How is her sex life? Does she feel "*fulfilled*"? Mary answers earnestly, only to realize that she's said too much, that she's told everyone about her chaotic family, her impotent husband. Her secrets now belong to the television-viewing public. Panicked, Mary stares into the camera, then holds up her hand, making a wiping motion and droning "Erase! Erase!" It's the primal scene of reality TV stardom, rendered as bleak comedy.

In 1979, the comedian Albert Brooks wrote and directed his first film, *Real Life*. Brooks, like many Angelenos, had been glued to *An American Family*, which had impressed him, he told me, as somehow simultaneously sleazy and revolutionary, an ethical mess that you couldn't look away from. At the time, Brooks was struggling to develop a high-budget movie about a cult leader, but then he stumbled on the Margaret Mead quote praising *An American Family* as a masterpiece. Inspired, he changed course, setting his sights on a new kind of satire, cheaper to film and more relevant, too.

Real Life opens with a deadpan description of the 1973 TV show *An American Family* along with Mead's quote, scrolling up the screen in a white font. In the film, Brooks plays "Albert Brooks," a smug documentarian who is like Craig Gilbert mixed together with Brooks's own self-lacerating comedic persona, a smug Hollywood climber. This Albert Brooks hopes to film a year in the lives of a couple from Phoenix, Arizona: veterinarian Warren Yeager (Charles Grodin, whom Brooks spotted on *Candid Camera*) and his wife, Jeanette (Frances Lee McCain). After convincing his subjects they are part of a high-minded social experiment, he sets up shop nearby and begins to film their silent family dinners. Brooks hovers over Warren as he performs surgery on a horse; he crashes Jeanette's gynecologist visit. After just two months of filming, the family begs the filmmaker to leave them alone. "Albert, the children are afraid to go to school," Jeanette says. "That's normal, trust me," says Brooks.

In the final scene, Brooks, holed up in his bathroom, explodes with frustration. "Why did I pick reality? Why did I pick *that*? Out of all the subjects? I don't know anything about it," he moans to the cameraman, who is still filming him. By then, the studio has pulled the plug; the Yeagers are across the street, finalizing their paperwork. Then suddenly, Brooks's eyes light up. "There's no law that says

'Start real, can't end fake,'" he announces. "What are they gonna do, put me in movie jail? It's a fake jail!" Inspired by the ending of *Gone with the Wind,* the deranged reality producer proceeds to torch the Yeagers' house, with the family in it—and as the flames rise higher, he screams, in delirium, "It's real! It's real! Their house is really burning!"

AFTER *AN AMERICAN FAMILY* ENDED, THE RAYMONDS FELT PROtective of the Louds, whose press tour they had supported. But they were also worried about their own reputation: As they saw it, they were the ones who had been robbed of credit for their biggest hit—and somehow, at the same time, smeared by their association with it.

Then a miracle happened: The Raymonds got a small grant from the New York State Council of the Arts, which they used to film *The Police Tapes,* a gritty, immersive film about a precinct in the South Bronx. *The Police Tapes,* which aired on television in 1977, won every prize available. It also forged the path toward two very different television shows: the NBC drama *Hill Street Blues* and the Fox reality show *Cops.* With their documentary career back in full swing, the Raymonds rarely ran into Gilbert, and the few times they did, at academic panels about *An American Family,* it only revived old grudges. They'd never bought Gilbert's hand-wringing. "This whole thing about how he was tortured is baloney," scoffed Susan.

The couple would go on to make multiple documentaries, most of them focusing on large institutions, including prisons, churches, and refugee camps. The Raymonds became more guarded, personally as well as professionally, building thicker emotional boundaries with their subjects. "We just changed, completely, so as not to go back to that living room," said Susan.

Still, every decade or so, they'd revisit their old friends, the Louds. In 1983, the Raymonds produced and directed *An American Family Revisited: The Louds Ten Years Later,* for the emergent cable network HBO, the first ever reality TV reunion show. The hour-long program was full of contradictions. In her interview, Pat described the WNET show as a humiliating experience; Bill, sitting behind a huge desk with a framed picture of Ronald Reagan, insisted, "I don't think it affected anybody," calling the series "a great, big, fun experience." At the height of the AIDS epidemic, Bill said of his son Lance, "I detest his way of life." Meanwhile, Lance breezily described his father as a "That's-life kind of guy, straight from the heart of Frank Sinatra." The other Loud kids gave brief interviews, visibly wary of the camera.

As the years passed, the family's stardom dimmed. Pat worked in publishing in New York, then moved, for a few years, to Bath, England. In the late 1990s, Grant took a steady gig as a producer at *Jeopardy!* Kevin went into business and technology, Michele into fashion, and Delilah rocketed up the Hollywood ladder, becoming a senior vice president at CBS and then a vice president at Sony Pictures. Bill remarried and divorced, then moved to Texas.

Lance stayed in New York, working as a journalist and writing several columns, including for Andy Warhol's magazine, *Interview*. He was still famous and an inspiring figure to gay men, but his life was full of shadows, among them a serious crystal meth addiction. At forty-nine, Lance, who had been diagnosed with HIV in the mid-1980s, became seriously ill with HIV and hepatitis C co-infection. He flew out to California, where he was cared for by his family, especially Michele and Pat.

In 2001, Lance wrote to the Raymonds. He was checking in to hospice, he explained to them—and he wanted them to fly west again and document his final days. Lance had a thesis in mind for this new film, one that would invert the original show's poisonous marketing campaign: He wanted the world to see that the Louds were ultimately a loving, united family. Alan was wary, but Susan argued that they had a moral obligation to Lance. Only after they flew to California did they understand that the family wasn't necessarily on board with his plan. "They were going, 'Oh God, you guys again, what are you *doing*? Okay, I'll have coffee, but please put down the camera,'" said Susan.

Lance reassured the Raymonds, even putting together a kind of manifesto, asking the other Louds to open their hearts to the project, for his sake. Delilah, who had helped Lance write to the Raymonds, sat for an interview, reluctantly. At first, Pat refused to talk on camera at all. But in what Alan described as "Susan Raymond's greatest moment," the filmmaker managed to talk her into it, bringing in "thirty years of friendship, all the water over the dam, knowing very well where the skeletons are buried." It was Lance's film, not Pat's, Susan argued—and Pat had to do the scene for her son.

The resulting film debuted on PBS in 2003. It was just a year after Lance's death on December 22, 2001, which was also the day of Grant's wedding, at which Lance was supposed to be Grant's best man. *Lance Loud! A Death in An American Family* begins with Lance declaiming, *Sunset Boulevard*–style, "I'm still big! It's the documentaries that got small." Unlike the awkward HBO reunion show, it's a poignant, powerful project, weaving together Lance's past and his present, illuminated by testimony from many of his friends. There are shots from his memorial service in the garden of Hollywood's Chateau Marmont, where Rufus Wainwright sang "Over the Rainbow." Pat and Bill sat in separate rows: The Raymonds struggled to capture them in a frame together. During his interview, Bill, now frail and elderly, spoke warmly about Lance, walking back his remarks in the '80s. Grant declined to participate, but Alan Raymond had tried to film him anyway, at a flea market where he was pushing Lance in a wheelchair, which led to another blowup between Alan and Grant, the most resistant Loud.

The way the Raymonds saw it, Lance was the true center of the Loud family, a rebel who changed the world. They heard the same story about him, wherever they went: "It's always the same, that someone was a small kid in Nowheresville, they were gay, they were hiding it, and then they saw Lance and realized they weren't alone," Susan told me. Lance recognized his celebrity as a vocation, which meant that he alone among the Louds accepted the Raymonds' role, too.

The couple did one final interview with Lance, a "highly edited" version of which appears on their website. It was too much, even for the Raymonds: Lance was saying "all these X-rated things," listing his regrets, they told me, even when they tried to talk him out of it. "He wanted to do—" said Susan. "Confess *everything*," said Alan.

"It was like something a priest should be listening to, not even a therapist, the priest. . . . Someone to give him absolution." Susan called it "the most extreme cinéma vérité moment ever. I can't find the words. It was sad. I mean, obviously, it was really sad—but then, you knew, he was talking to the camera."

Lance's final wish was one many children of divorce might understand: He wanted his parents back together. Miraculously, it came true. Bill was frail by then. He and Pat lived together, in Los Angeles. Susan Raymond went to visit the reunited Louds, twice. The first time, she said, Pat was still furious at Bill: "Like, for eternity." The second time, the couple were more at peace. That had always been the show's true irony, in Susan's eyes. "Craig didn't destroy the family. Craig destroyed himself, and the family's fine."

AFTER THAT EXPERIENCE, THE RAYMONDS THOUGHT THEY WERE done. Then, in 2008, they got an email from a producer named Gavin Polone, who was developing a scripted movie about *An American Family* for HBO, called *Cinema Verite*. Hoping to have a say in their own portrayal, the Raymonds signed on as consultants. That act severed their relationship with the Louds for good. "We were like, Nobody's gonna take a free ride on our name again," said Delilah.

Cinema Verite, which aired in 2011, starred James Gandolfini as Craig Gilbert, Tim Robbins as Bill Loud, and Diane Lane as Pat Loud. Both the Louds and the Raymonds agreed that Lane captured Pat's guarded elegance perfectly. The Raymonds, however, were frustrated with the outcome of the project. They had been hoping to see a stirring story about two young married filmmakers, a pair of artistic purists who had fought a valiant battle over ethics with an exploitative Svengali, a man who was "ruthless and crude." Gilbert had been "an insensitive boob," the Raymonds told me, repeatedly. He had mocked Lance, with a limp-wrist imitation, Alan said; he'd done the same with Christy Brown, imitating his cerebral palsy.

Gandolfini, however, had his own ideas about the role he was playing. After years as Tony Soprano, he wasn't interested in playing a cartoonish heavy—and he wanted a love story. Over dinner, Gandolfini had pressed Craig Gilbert about whether he'd slept with Pat Loud, which Gilbert denied "in twenty ways," he told *The New Yorker* in 2011. Alan Raymond also argued with Gandolfini, during a phone conversation: Gandolfini was playing the story's villain, Alan told him, a statement that was met with silence. In the end, HBO's most powerful star got his way, in an ambiguous scene in which Craig tells Pat that her husband is cheating on her, and then the two go up to his hotel room. The sequence irritated everyone. Still, the underlying problem was less that *Cinema Verite* was an inaccurate film but that compared to *An American Family,* it felt stagey, dead at heart, lacking the heat and spontaneity of the original. When the final credit sequence cut to footage of the Louds, there was no comparison.

The HBO movie *did* have one surprising side effect: It led to a détente between the Louds and Gilbert, to whom they hadn't spoken in thirty years. Paley Center curator Ron Simon, who had arranged that dinner between Gilbert and Gandolfini, described Gilbert as having a haunted affect, as if he were "carrying some heavy sin." Now he had a chance to expiate it. Although he sought no money for himself, Gilbert paid for the lawyer the Louds hired to negotiate with HBO. According to a document in Lance Loud's archives at Yale University, the family received $175,000 ($58,533 for Bill, $29,166 for Pat, Michele, Delilah, and Grant) and signed a nondisparagement agreement, which bound them not to slam HBO or the production. It wasn't a perfect resolution, but it was more money than the nothing at all they'd made from the series.

Since *Cinema Verite* aired, the Raymonds haven't had any contact with the Louds. After Lance's death, Grant became the Loud who made decisions for the family—and although the Raymonds know that he's angry, they don't understand why. If they made a mistake, Susan told me, she was certain that it was a simple one. "We did one too many films about them."

"IT'S STILL VERY EMOTIONAL TO ME," GRANT LOUD SAID WHEN I asked him about the scene the Raymonds had mentioned, the one in which Grant picked up his father at the airport, the moment the Raymonds said they "lost" him. "This is going to get very uncomfortable and awkward."

Grant had made clear to me, many times, that he is not the enemy of *An American Family*. He knew that the show had played an important role in television history. He was proud of how his family had handled their fame. The documentary series's creation was a Rashomon story, he said—and everyone, including the Raymonds, had a right to tell their side.

Still, some subjects caused him pain. Grant was particularly frustrated by the way that HBO's *Cinema Verite* portrayed the night Pat asked Bill for a divorce. In the scripted version of their story, Pat asked her son, discreetly, and more important off camera, if he could pick his dad up, in order to "save the family." That was false, Grant told me: The whole exchange had happened on camera. Still, the rest of that scene—the part where the Raymonds' cameras had gleamed in Grant's rearview mirror as he drove to the airport, full of dread— was all too accurate, a painful flashback to the night that changed his life.

During a newspaper interview, Kevin and Delilah had joked that that ride to the airport was the moment that Grant had "chickened out." He'd felt dumbstruck, when they put it that way: To him, that evening was not a joke, but a "primal wound." He'd been a moody, grandiose teenager, Grant told me, "not the brightest"—not his mother's favorite kid, like Lance, or his father's favorite, Delilah. When his mother asked him to pick up his father, to tell him to go to a hotel, Grant had crumbled, emotionally. It was too much pressure to put on a teenager, he said, particularly on camera. "Honestly? At that moment I just shut down." Grant's voice broke as we spoke and he began to cry; then he pulled himself together, a man in his mid-sixties again. "I didn't turn back on again for about fifteen years."

Grant hadn't gone to therapy, but he had been able to slowly process the experience, over the decades—getting married had helped, he said. So had becoming the family spokesman. Grant loved his brother Lance, but he also found him unsettling, a figure of chaos as well as charisma. "It was a bit like growing up with Loki as your older brother," he said. Grant and Lance had very different approaches to publicity: Grant wanted clear boundaries with the world.

At sixty-six, Grant also felt that he had gained some perspective on what had happened to his family. When he called the filming a Rashomon story, he meant something specific. Like most people, Grant had assumed that the phrase meant that everyone remembered a story their own way. Then he saw the movie *Rashomon* and realized that that wasn't the theme, after all: "It's about how everyone tells the story with himself as the hero."

GRANT HAD NEVER REWATCHED *AN AMERICAN FAMILY* WHEN WE spoke. Neither had Pat. When Michele sent me her personal DVD copies, she couldn't find episode eleven. "We are not very good custodians of our own legacy," she wrote to me. She never answered requests for interviews or for fact-checking.

Delilah still sometimes watches the Cavett clip on YouTube, marveling at Lance's wit and her mother's fierceness. She finds reality shows "humiliating." She has a few criticisms of *An American Family*, particularly the crude way the network had portrayed her father, who died in 2018: He'd never been granted his real-life vigor and humor, she said—all the reasons his children adored him. But she had no gripe with Craig Gilbert, whom she called an "equal intellectual," who shared true camaraderie with her mother. The Raymonds, she said, "never shied away from taking as much credit as possible." Delilah said that she had also gained something when she had watched the show, back in 1973, curled on her mother's bed. Seeing Pat's face, alone, in her bedroom, in that brief shot the Raymonds caught on the night Bill left, Delilah felt startled—suddenly, she could see the divorce through her mother's eyes, not her own.

The one Loud who had rewatched the whole series again is Kevin, who got a bootleg copy from a fan on Facebook. Kevin has a unique perspective on *An American Family*, maybe because he barely appears in it, having flown to Southeast Asia to work for a friend of his dad's, equipped with a video camera—footage that never got edited in. Kevin was a businessman, working in early-stage tech start-ups.

He lives in Arizona; he's the only Loud child who had children, with his ex-wife. A Republican in a family of liberals (he was enthusiastic about Trump when we first spoke, but later preferred RFK, Jr.), he also has an unusual opinion about the series that made his family into household names: He wishes it had had a second season.

The network screwed up when they squandered their biggest hit, he argued. They could have shown Kevin in college, at his frat; and Lance at CBGB—and his mother, a real-life Mary Tyler Moore, starting over in a new city. Kevin wished he'd been in Santa Barbara more during the filming—and also, that he had been the one his mother asked to drive his father home. He and Grant were eighteen months apart and they were very close, "but he is very sensitive and I am very insensitive." He believes something that no other Loud child believes: that without the presence of the cameras, his parents would have stayed married. Kevin was "the family negotiator": Had he been there, he told me, the divorce wouldn't have happened.

PAT LOUD DIED ON JANUARY 10, 2021, AT NINETY-FOUR YEARS old, surrounded by family. We'd spoken several months earlier, when she was holed up in her pied-à-terre in Los Angeles, with the pandemic raging. At the time, she was watching a lot of television, including *American Pickers,* a reality show about junk shop owners on the hunt for precious Americana. Her children came by to visit and help care for her, along with a circle of gay men, with whom she'd been intimate friends for years. Each night she held a cocktail hour, laying out her special hors d'oeuvres, gruyere and crackers. "Oh, it's a wonderful way to separate the day from the evening," she said.

Pat was fun to talk to and full of contradictions. She was proud of the show and full of regrets; she was bored by the subject ("everyone asks the same stupid questions") and knew that she was defined by it and, ultimately, didn't mind. She said that *An American Family* had led her to a bigger life than the one she had been leading—it helped her meet fascinating people, move to New York, and begin a career in publishing, with prized achievements like helping publish Andrew Holleran's novel of gay life, *Dancer from the Dance.*

Still, she regretted a lot. She told me, mournfully, that she had been "crazy," a "wreck," during those seven months of filming and that she regretted hurting her children. That night on the porch, with the rotisserie grinding, she was drunk and unstable—and instead of filming her, someone should have fed her Xanax or locked her up. Still, she said, the cameras weren't what wrecked her marriage. Five years before Gilbert arrived in Santa Barbara, Pat had confirmed that Bill was cheating, on what she called "the night of the files," when she'd rifled through his desk hunting for receipts. She had left Bill at the time, but then she came back. When she agreed to appear on television, her motive hadn't been fame. She wasn't trying to increase the store of human knowledge, either. What she wanted was simple: to rub her happy family in the face of Bill's mistresses. They were the one audience she had ever imagined.

After Lance's death, Pat compiled a beautiful book called *Lance Out Loud,* full of her son's photos and art. It was true that she had once had a deep emotional bond with the Raymonds: In her April 1973 interview with *Film Comment,* she had described the couple as "so close to us, they will be friends all of our lives." But as the years went by, she had come to see them the way Grant did, as predatory figures. Still, she expressed some sympathy for the couple. She and Bill might have been naïve when they signed the contract with WNET, but the Raymonds were the true innocents. "Alan and Susan had a good marriage." A young couple in love couldn't grasp how much could go wrong in a marriage, not from that "deep inside perspective."

Craig Gilbert died not long before Pat and I spoke, in April 2020, in his apartment in the West Village, at ninety-four. Pat described him to me as a wonderful man, worldly and brilliant. "He did *The Triumph of Christy Brown.* He did that thing with Margaret Mead. He was incredibly well-read and he had wonderful stories. He was beautifully educated. I just loved talking to him. I had no sexual interest in him whatsoever, nor he in me, but we were good buddies. He would come up about every six weeks or so and he'd bring a bottle of Laphroaig."

Her voice grew dreamy. "We'd demolish the bottle and talk all night. . . . And then, when this happened, I began to feel that he had never—that he had lied to me, that he had only contempt for us. And it was devastating." When Susan Lester, the associate producer for *An American Family,* called Pat to tell her the news of his death, she felt sad that he'd had such isolated final years. "I had always hoped that somehow or other, we could be friends again. I miss him."

Pat held on to certain grudges: She hated the way the media had portrayed Lance ("They got the gayness, without the grandeur."); she loathed Roiphe for having written that "vituperative" essay ("It was so nasty, and it was directed at a bunch of teenagers!"); and she despised the network, for selling them all out. But she was proud of her children, praising their accomplishments and their kindness. Grant's lasting marriage felt like its own special achievement, she told me. If she was still "bewildered" by the events of the past, there was no reason to dwell on them. Her life had been a blessing. "A lot of it was probably due to the fact that I was, for fifteen minutes, famous."

4

||||||||

THE CLIP

America's Funniest Home Videos and *Cops*

IN 1980, RONALD REAGAN WAS ELECTED PRESIDENT IN A LAND-slide, swept along on a wave of jingoistic nostalgia. Chuck Barris, still licking his wounds, would soon flee to the South of France. The Louds were moving on with their lives, their fame fading. And seemingly in a flash, television had started cleaning up its act. It got safe, it got wholesome, and for nearly a decade, it got boring. The prime-time lineup was full of formula: family sitcoms, legal procedurals, and slick soaps like *Dynasty*. The few shows that broke fresh ground—like *Roseanne, Moonlighting,* and *A Different World*—felt like outliers, exceptions in an industry that was ad-driven and mass, suburban and white. If the '70s had given off the funk of a stained shag carpet after a basement orgy, the '80s were more like a plastic slipcovered sofa in the living room, ready for company.

In place of *The Gong Show,* there was *Real People,* a sweetly cornball newsmagazine about ordinary Americans. The series, which debuted on NBC in 1979, was executive produced by George Schlatter, whom *The New York Times* once described as "the least cynical man in Hollywood." Best known for the variety show *Laugh-In*—he'd talked President Nixon into saying "Sock it to me!"—Schlatter had begun his show-biz career back in the audience participation era. (His wife, Jolene, had been a model on *Queen for a Day*.) *Real People* was proudly upbeat, conservative with a small "C," a patriotic approach for which Schlatter, a kind of anti-Barris, made no apologies: "I'm for the little guy, the underdog," he told *The New York Times*. It shot to #1.

Fred Willard—who would satirize his jut-jawed Midwestern persona in Christopher Guest's films—used that same vibe unironically as a host on *Real People*. The show profiled small-town eccentrics, like a man building a spaceship from used auto parts; celebrated military heroes, like the Navajo Code Talkers; and delved into quirky subcultures, like a society of bald men. No matter where *Real People* went, it found the upside: In a segment on punk cuisine (like a cake frosted with "Who Cares?"), the narrator gushed over footage of a mosh pit at Manhattan's Mudd Club, "These wacky, tacky street urchins come to wail away the wee hours at a typical funky punk party!"

Although *Real People* caught some flak for blurring the line between news and entertainment, it was largely scandal-free. Its success inspired a flood of network imitators: ABC's *That's Incredible!* (risky stunts, like juggling knives) and *Those Amazing Animals* (amazing animals), CBS's *That's My Line* (average people with unusual jobs), and NBC's *Games People Play* (weird sports competitions). These shows amounted to a safe, domesticated brand of reality programming, with fewer pranks or soapy twists—just the chance for regular people to enjoy the spotlight. (Or in the case of *That's Incredible!*, the *Jackass* of the bunch, risk human combustion.) It was a short-lived vogue, which faded away by 1984.

In 1985, reality television had a lesser-known breakthrough: NBC's *OceanQuest,* a five-episode spree of aquatic lunacy that might be seen as a precursor to *The Amazing Race,* if you cut a few corners and added a cameo by Fidel Castro. Created by underwater photographer Al Giddings, the series had an absurd yet ambitious premise: It documented the true-life adventures of Miss Universe winner Shawn Weatherly as she traveled the globe for a one-year "test of her spirit." Weatherly went deep-sea diving; she escaped from an underwater cage, surrounded by sharks; at one point, she met the Cuban dictator, a friend of Giddings.* It was hard to tell—perhaps deliberately—if the show was real or staged. In a *New York Times* review titled "'OceanQuest': Afloat in Suspended Disbelief," TV critic John Corry marveled at its slippery aesthetic. Were the sharks banging against Weatherly's cage real? How about the ropes breaking? Her terrified sobs? If this flashy show was hokum, he concluded, it was too watchable to dismiss. "Indeed, if anyone is faking in *OceanQuest,* we'd really rather not know," Corry wrote, establishing an audience standard that would, in time, define the reality genre.

The one other significant reality format of the period was *The People's Court,* which lacked sharks or Fidel Castro but was the first television show to feature binding arbitration. The brainchild of retired TV producer John Masterson, who had helped create *Queen for a Day,* the show, which was set in small-claims court, had echoes of early radio shows like *A. L. Alexander's Goodwill Court.* Filmed in a fake courtroom, *The People's Court* featured a real defendant, a real plaintiff, and a fake court reporter conducting real-ish interviews. The defendants ranged from bad plumbers to a Smurf performer sued for scaring children. Litigants could recover up to $1,500. Although *People* magazine described the show as "*The Gong Show* of U.S. jurisprudence," it wasn't especially wacky—and in fact, its creators had resisted NBC's original plan, which was to cast Pigmeat Markham, a comic known for his "Here Comes the Judge" routine on *Laugh-In.* Instead, they booked a retired Los Angeles County superior court judge named Joseph Wapner, a brilliantly counterintuitive choice that transformed the resolutely rational TV judge into a household name (and also, a running joke in the movie *Rain Man*).

Like electricity deprived of an outlet, the reality impulse welled up in the late '80s, forced to flow into any space that felt welcoming. It streamed into public access cable TV, where performers could be

---

* Giddings had met Castro during a period when the dictator was a scuba-diving enthusiast, a hobby that ended when someone made an attempt on his life by poisoning one of his diving suits.

filthy and flamboyant in a way that would never fly on network shows. It spilled into professional wrestling, a carnival of quasi-scripted violence that ruled cable in the mid-1980s, fueled by the concept of "kayfabe," the commitment that performers never acknowledge that they were faking it.

It surged, especially, into daytime talk shows, which had always acted as a truth serum for ordinary people. A half-century after John J. Anthony's misery hour, these shows had become a TV ritual, a place where eager civilians could tell their story. In the '80s, there was a brutal arms race between two superstar hosts: the twinkle-eyed Irish American male feminist Phil Donahue, an icon since the late '60s, and the breakout newcomer Oprah Winfrey, an empathetic Black news anchor from Chicago, who bonded with guests by describing her own early traumas, among them childhood sexual abuse and a stillbirth at fourteen. These two liberal powerhouses fought for the dishiest guests and the highest ratings—and over time, they faced a slate of competitors, among them the perky Sally Jessy Raphael (whose show had launched pre-Oprah), the peppy Ricki Lake, the suave Montel Williams, and the gruff Maury Povich. As the field tightened, these hosts began to fold in protoreality elements—gimmicks like DNA reveals or catfights—and by the early 1990s, a few of them had embraced shameless humbuggery, most notoriously on the visual tabloid *The Jerry Springer Show,* which minted fake news back when Fox News was still a twinkle in Rupert Murdoch's eye.

Critics saw daytime talk shows as tacky at best, tawdry at worst—but like the audience participation shows, they had a liberatory streak. At night, viewers watched tycoons cavort on shows like *Dallas, Dynasty,* and Robin Leach's *Lifestyles of the Rich and Famous.* In the afternoon, the rest of the world was invited to the party. Talk shows featured teen moms and drag queens, trailer trash and the ghetto fabulous—guests from every racial and sexual background, all the categories that mainstream culture viewed as marginal: the mentally ill, disabled people, fat people, transgender people, sex workers, and addicts (although in the '80s, people used different words). There was frank talk about rape, domestic abuse, and anorexia—the types of topics that the nightly news condescended to as "women's stories." Daytime talk shows were educational; they were exploitative; like Shimmer Floor Wax, they were both. A colorful personal story would get you seen and heard—and, also, jeered at, or at least interrogated by nosy strangers. That was the bargain TV had always struck, the price for being visible.

IN 1989, THE PLASTIC COVER SLIPPED OFF THE SOFA. THE THIRST for reality, diverted and repressed for a decade, reasserted itself in two hit prime-time formats: ABC's *America's Funniest Home Videos* and the Fox series *Cops.* Weird twins with extremely different personalities, *AFV* and *Cops* were both "clip shows," fueled by brief, outrageous bursts of action. Each of them freely blended slapstick and violence. Each relied on viewer faith that what they saw was real. And although one show was family-friendly fluff and the other a raw glimpse of urban poverty, together they became bellwethers of a new age of technology. They were the first draft of internet culture.

The catalyst for these protoreality shows was, as ever, a labor strike: Members of the Writers Guild of America—a powerful force since the mid-1950s, when five entertainment unions had merged—walked off the job in March 1988, with its members seeking greater creative input and higher residual pay from reruns (digital rights didn't exist yet). It was the longest strike in TV history, lasting twenty-two weeks. Production froze from March until August. The fall television season was pushed back into late October. To fill the vacuum, networks frantically pumped out whatever content was available—reruns, news broadcasts, sports events. NBC found a reprieve with the Summer Olympics in Seoul; the network also churned out endless episodes of *Unsolved Mysteries,* tabloid stories packaged like hard news. CBS leaned on *48 Hours* and *West 57th,* a slick newsmagazine that *The New York Times* derided as "a supermarket tabloid set to music."

In theory, this should have been a juicy climate for a reality TV resurgence, a creative eruption like the one that would blow up in 2000. The problem was, there *was* no "reality genre" yet. Even after four messy decades of experimentation, each format—from *Queen for a Day* to *Candid Camera, The Newlywed Game* to *An American*

Family—was still viewed as its own thing, a one-off fad, a gimmick that came and went. These shows had left no legacy—and, more crucially, no institutional structure. Network executives weren't trained to take unscripted pitches. There were no veteran reality producers, let alone a pool of casting directors, field producers, directors, camera operators, audio technicians, or editors.

Still, with the door propped open by the strike, two new shows managed to wriggle through. The shamelessly dopey *America's Funniest Home Videos* was, despite that flag-waving title, an adaptation of a hit Japanese series called *Fun TV with Kato-chan and Ken-chan*, which had featured a segment using viewer-made videos. In 1989, the U.S. producer Vin Di Bona spun the concept into a hit special for ABC, and then, in 1990, he built it into a weekly series. As his host he cast the comedian Bob Saget, who played the twinkle-eyed dad on the ABC family comedy *Full House*. Like *Candid Camera*, *America's Funniest Home Videos* had an unholy earworm of a theme song, whose lyrics held up a flattering mirror to its viewers: "You're the red, white, and blue! / The funny things you do / America, America—this is you."

America's Funniest Home Videos was an unusually easy show to produce, since it relied on videotapes sent in by viewers and filmed on camcorders, which were increasingly lightweight and affordable. It also cost ABC almost nothing: The network could air zany action footage without hiring any actors, directors, or stunt professionals, let alone building sets or paying for special effects. In each episode, Saget—and later on, John Fugelsang and Daisy Fuentes—would chat with the audience, introduce a dozen or so short videos, then tally the vote. The weekly winner got $10,000, based on votes from the studio audience; later in the season, the best tapes competed for grand prizes, including $100,000 and a Disney vacation. But for many people who dropped their videotapes into bubble-wrap envelopes, money wasn't the main point: The real prize was a shot at TV fame and the fun of meeting Bob Saget.

Each *AFV* episode ended with Saget shouting, "Keep those cameras safely rolling!" It was a warning not everyone listened to. Like ultraviolent Saturday morning cartoons, the show worked off a blend of sadism and sweetness, with a typical episode featuring a *yikes* (golfer thwacks himself in the groin) followed by a *whoa* (man water-skis through flooded streets), broken up by variations on an *awwww* (a man wearing a gorilla suit proposes to his girlfriend). The show's editors added dorky sound effects and dad-joke voiceovers, like a "1-2-3 LAWSUIT!," as teens tumbled through a broken trampoline. Saget mimicked Mel Blanc, the bard of *Looney Tunes,* for these voiceovers; the editors cut in Hanna-Barbera sound effects. While critics regarded the series as a genial time-waster, not a Barris-level war crime (one critic called it as "complicated as a bowl of noodles"), an occasional outlier called it out as a bad influence: In *The Washington Post,* Howard Rosenberg wrote a scathing column, arguing that the show encouraged child abuse.

Saget and I spoke in 2020, early in the pandemic. Secluded in his home in California, he had found himself looking back on that first season with both nostalgia and chagrin, remembering the innocence that had surrounded the show, including his own. "It took off like a wildflower," he said dreamily, recalling the day he got a call on his car phone—"with the curly wire on it!" he added—to deliver the news that the program had just hit #1 in the Nielsens. "When you're thirty years old and have two shows in the top ten, you're an idiot if you complain," said Saget. "And I was an idiot."

Hosting *America's Funniest Home Videos* was the world's easiest job, he told me—all he had to do was pick tapes and banter with the crowd. Over time, choosing the tapes got a little trickier. Instead of sending in short, clever clips, viewers began mailing in full two-hour videotapes—and increasingly, they took death-defying risks to get shocking material. One man propped a ladder up against a tree, and then as the camera rolled, yelled out, "Bob Saget, this is for you!"—and tried to jump into a pool, only to trip and hit the concrete, hard. When Saget saw the tape, he called the staff in alarm: "They were like, 'He's fine, he broke a rib.'"

Other viewers sent in porn. In one tape, a heavyset couple had sex in their shower stall, then broke the shower door and fell out of the camera's frame and onto the broken glass, giggling and grinding. It was hard for Saget to tell what was going on with that kind of footage—how much was an accident and how much a prank, trolling the producers. "They didn't know the line," Saget groaned, complaining about endless videos of dogs humping people's legs.

Saget had much fonder memories of "found comedy," the stuff that required no explanation at all, like a guy falling into a manhole and then climbing out. "It's a silent film!" said Saget, comparing the high points of *AFV* to Buster Keaton. He also praised the show's comparative diversity, the way it featured people of every race and class, with an international appeal. (Specific episodes were devoted to global clips.) Slapstick needed no translation, making the series "modular"—YouTube before the internet existed.

Unlike *Candid Camera*, there was no question of consent. In fact, the manipulation ran the opposite way: The producers were vulnerable to getting pranked by the contestants. At the time he aired it, Saget believed that the material was genuine, the sort of silly mistakes people captured organically when they filmed sports events, weddings, or backyard barbecues. But he could be naïve. In one of Saget's favorite clips, a little boy laid his jacket over a mud puddle so that a little girl could walk across it. Only years later did he realize the scene was obviously staged.

It wasn't long before Saget started sabotaging his own success. Early on, Saget had been a fun, filthy stand-up comic; now, he felt trapped as a wholesome TV host. He started breaking character, throwing rude remarks into the banter ("This is gonna be a blood-bath!"), and trying, semi-consciously and then on purpose, to break the terms of his contract—self-destructing, like Barris before him, by rattling the bars of his network cage. Still, Saget stuck around a long time—until 1997, when he finally left the show for good, resuming his comedy career and making movies. Back then, he was sure he'd sold out. Decades later, eighteen months before his tragic death at sixty-five, Saget felt much more comfortable about his legacy. One of TV's least-respected television shows now seemed, to Saget, like a lost idyll, worth revisiting—"that kinder, gentler, goofy time."

JOHN LANGLEY, THE CO-CREATOR OF *COPS,* INSISTED ON A HUG, not a handshake. Unlike most of the people I spoke to while researching this book, we met in person, the week before the country shut down in 2020. "I'm old, I'm going soon anyway," he said with a shrug when I worried about giving him Covid. We settled in at his office, on two dark leather sofas as big as boats. At seventy-six, Langley was a genial conversationalist with a habit of throwing in a "blah blah blah" now and then, a verbal hand wave for when the talk got sticky. He was proud of his peppery, eccentric résumé, which included early gigs like directing a Dolph Lundgren exercise video with Quentin Tarantino and Roger Avary as his PAs (he knew them from the local video store). But Langley understood that the first line of his obituary would be about *Cops,* the longest-lasting reality show ever—a show so successful it would outlast his death, a year later.

Born in 1943 in Oklahoma but raised in Manhattan Beach, California, Langley descended from what he once called "a long line of alkies and ne'er-do-wells," among them, an oil wildcatter grandfather. At eighteen, on the verge of being drafted, Langley joined the army, where he worked in military intelligence during the Cuban Missile Crisis. He went AWOL—more than once—and got court-martialed. After his service ended, he went to school, earning a BA and an MA in comparative literature, then nearly completing a doctorate in philosophy at the University of California, Irvine, studying what he described as "Longinus and philosophy of aesthetics as applied to literature, literary criticism, blah blah blah." In 1971, he quit, alienated by "white-tower politics." He still considered himself an educator, though: "It sounds corny, but I've always believed in a Horatian idea, to teach and delight."

By his thirties, Langley was married with three kids, working at a dull PR job at Northwest Airlines. After hours, he struggled to mount an independent film about a psychedelic anthropologist, a project that was "a little bit *Zelig,* a little bit *Mondo Cane.*" Langley, who had had a brief bout of cocaine use, was fascinated by drugs; he was also crazy about avant-garde filmmaking. In 1983, he made a movie combining those passions, *Cocaine Blues: The Myth & Reality of Cocaine,* co-produced with his creative partner Malcolm Barbour and financed with a $100,000 loan from a relative. As manic as any tweaker, *Cocaine Blues* had been stitched together from all kinds of footage: interviews with a DEA agent and a sulky, mustachioed drug dealer on a yacht; movie scenes from the 1930s; shots of monkeys twitching in withdrawal; sultry images of skinny junkies; and clips of needles, open-heart surgery, and brain scans, all of it scored to cha-cha and steel guitar. The movie warned about cocaine's risks—particularly to white professionals, shown snorting away their savings—but its tone was more *Mondo Cane* than PSA.

Langley's next anti-drug project, the 1985 music video "Stop the Madness"—which you must google immediately—was a for-hire project produced by actor Tim Reid, a member of the Entertainment Industries Council for a Drug-Free Society. "Stop the Madness" somehow managed to be *more* surreal than *Cocaine Blues*, as well as more racially layered. It opens with images repurposed from *Cocaine Blues*—the twitching monkey, the beating heart—scored to the howls of Herb Alpert's trumpet. Then, the camera reveals the person *watching* this anti-drug film: a sulky white teenager (Claudia Grace Wells, Marty McFly's girlfriend in *Back to the Future*), clearly unimpressed. Wells clicks the television off and walks to her bedroom, then opens her closet door—revealing a smirking drug dealer in a Panama hat, toting a casino tray of drugs.

As a celebrity chorus belts out "Stop the madness!" the video begins to cut between the story of this suburban white girl and another addict, a Black boy from the inner city (played by Boogaloo Shrimp, from the *Breakin'* franchise). Like the charity single "We Are the World," which debuted the same year, "Stop the Madness" attracted a truly bananas array of celebrity participants, including a twenty-two-year-old Whitney Houston, singing "Everyone's a loser in this deadly game," along with Casey Kasem, Stacy Keach, La Toya Jackson, Toni Basil, Kim Fields, David Hasselhoff, and Kareem Abdul-Jabbar. First Lady Nancy Reagan showed up in the White House, harmonizing with a multiracial chorus. At the video's climax, our heroes dump their drugs into a garbage truck—which is driven by a grinning Arnold Schwarzenegger—and then they high-five in ecstatic sobriety, as a joyful crowd boogies in the street, combining breakdance moves with balletic leaps (and also, because it's 1985, the robot). The Goodyear Blimp floats overhead, blinking the words STOP THE MADNESS.

Both *Cocaine Blues* and "Stop the Madness" were a perfect reflection of the dizzy, contradictory "Just Say No" era, which is to say, they were best watched while stoned. But they also led Langley to his eureka moment, when, during the production of *Cocaine Blues,* he went on a drive-along and got the chance to watch cops make street arrests. Every interaction he saw felt electric, full of spontaneity and real-life drama. Langley was convinced that there was a TV show in the subject—but he wanted to make it in a new, stripped-down style. There would be no more twitching monkeys, no Herb Alpert and no educational narration. Instead, this show would be cinéma vérité, "with no filters, as direct as possible."

Around 1985, Langley began shopping *Cops* to every network. They all turned him down. Filming live arrests seemed like too big of a legal risk to cautious network executives, but Langley's concept also struck the C-suite decisionmakers as flat-out weird—it was chaotic and uncontrolled in a way that scripted police dramas were not. The few executives who *did* express interest encouraged Langley to make a more straightforward documentary, with an authoritative narrator and maybe some scripted reenactments to help guide viewers. Langley stuck to his guns: He was convinced that *Cops* had to be filmed using a raw, unmediated, fly-on-the-wall aesthetic.

One opportunity *did* emerge from these pitches, however: the chance to work with Geraldo Rivera, a former ABC investigative reporter who was infamous for his flamboyant personality and over-the-top television specials. Langley was initially wary of Rivera, who had just hosted *The Mystery of Al Capone's Vaults,* a syndicated special that became a national joke when the vault turned out to be empty. Still, Langley pitched something big, when they met: He told the investigative reporter that he could film drug busts, live, and then added that "this time, there will be something in the vault." It was a bluff—he had no idea if he could pull off that kind of stunt.

The result was a bombastic 1986 special called *American Vice: The Doping of a Nation,* which combined live elements with pretaped ones. In *American Vice,* Rivera and the studio audience were drug tested (12 percent tested positive for pot, 10 percent for co-caine). The anchor held "crack babies" up to the camera; he con-fronted mothers in drug houses ("Who *are* you?" one irritated woman asked); and he berated "drug whores," asking one, "Don't you have any self-respect?" There was a moodily xenophobic seg-ment about "illegals" at the Mexican border and another in which Rivera posed as a buyer. Throughout, Geraldo warned viewers that drugs were drifting from "the ghetto" to suburbia, hurting "typical American families."

The show's climax was Langley's contribution, the one he'd promised during their first meeting: three live drug busts, which were filmed in San Jose, Houston, and Fort Lauderdale. In 1986, pulling off these busts was a technological marvel, requiring the use of a helicopter; a satellite-equipped van, which Langley used to bounce images using microwave dishes; and a live director in New York, who coordinated with Langley over the phone.

There were a few bumps. When the Fort Lauderdale raid started, the director tried to cut to a commercial. The audio guy panicked, so Langley grabbed the boom mic himself and raced into the house. Inside, to his amazement, they discovered that their target—a drug-trafficking Bahamian police officer—was in the living room, watch-ing the same show that they were filming. The crew scrambled to turn the television set off. "It was so postmodern, it freaked me out. Dimensions within dimensions," Langley told me, laughing.

The people that Langley filmed weren't required to sign a release, since a "live drug bust" was categorized as news programming, not documentary. Still, judging from his narration, Rivera was aware that they were in dicey territory. When the Florida raid began, he explained to viewers that the cameras weren't allowed to show the suspects' faces—only to have a lens suddenly swerve to the left, re-vealing the distressed face of a woman holding a baby. Startled, Ri-vera stuttered, "Obviously, that woman is not involved in the bust. . . . It's live television, we have no control over it, it's *risky business*!"

The Florida bust nabbed a dealer named Nelson Scott, who served time in prison. But in Houston, they had a problem. While

Geraldo breathlessly described an upcoming raid on a pimp and some prostitutes dealing coke, the cops smashed in the door with a battering ram, revealing only a confused-looking woman, Terry Rouse. As the woman muttered, "What did I do?," struggling to hide her face from the cameras, the sheriff shoved her into a wall and handcuffed her. Later on, Rouse would explain that she was staying at the house to paint it; she sued Rivera, reaching a private settlement. The San Jose raid had a similar problem: The show broadcast the arrest of a man named Manuel Chavez, but he was released after police decided that he was just a visitor in the house. Even the Nelson Scott case went sour, exposing Broward County's corruption.

The ratings were sky-high. From Langley's perspective, the project had been a success, any legal blunders notwithstanding. "It was interesting, revealing, informative, exciting—all the things you want in television," he said.

Critics disagreed. In the *Los Angeles Times,* Howard Rosenberg described *American Vice* as "live TV at its most revolting, with cops kicking down doors and bagging alleged pushers in front of TV cameras that beamed coast-to-coast pictures of suspects along with apparently innocent bystanders." Having your arrest televised was basically a trial with no jury, Rosenberg pointed out. "But what if the man was not guilty? There was no taking back the pictures."

THROUGHOUT THE LATE 1980S, JOHN LANGLEY WORKED WITH Geraldo on more *American Vice* specials, some of which made him proud (runaways, the mafia), others less so (devil worship). If Geraldo was more of a showman than a journalist, that distinction didn't bother Langley.

Their collaboration also scored him a crucial meeting, with Fox development executive Stephen Chao. Chao—who would later become the president of Fox TV, for an extremely short time, which we'll get into later—was a protégé of Rupert Murdoch, the Australian magnate who owned the upstart "fourth network," Fox. Launched in 1986, Fox had a simple mission: to throw tomatoes at the uptight networks and make money. Its lineup was more blue collar, more diverse, and much ruder than the Big Three, with signature hits that would include *Married . . . with Children* and *The Simpsons.* Fox hired Joan Rivers and Arsenio Hall, the first female and first African American late-night hosts. The network already had one major reality hit about criminal justice on its lineup, the notorious *America's Most Wanted,* which had been Steve Chao's invention: It was a "manhunt" show, featuring crime reenactments with wanted fugitives, who then got tracked down by Fox viewers.

Langley's first meeting with Chao went poorly, when Chao—"a Harvard puke," in Langley's eyes—rejected every pitch, including something Langley called *Funny Home Videos.* Still, Langley scored a second meeting, and eventually, Chao put him in the room with Fox CEO Barry Diller. To Langley's frustration, Diller had familiar notes: He wanted the show to use a narrator, reenactments, and also a bit of mood music. Langley said no. Finally, his stubbornness paid off. There was a Hollywood writers' strike going on by then. "They were desperate for programming," said Langley with a smile, thirty years later.

Cops would have a catalytic effect on television. Together with *America's Funniest Home Videos,* it jump-started the reality genre, which had been static for nearly a decade. It changed the way the police were portrayed and perceived. But for all of *Cops's* shaky-cam, unpolished aesthetic, which reflected a new era of surveillance cameras, it was also a continuation of an earlier tradition, a direct descendant of one of television's oldest hits, the 1951 police procedural *Dragnet.*

While *Dragnet* wasn't a reality show, it played one on TV, down to its iconic opening: "Ladies and gentlemen, the story you are about to see is true."

Dragnet's creator, Jack Webb—who also played the show's hero, the laconic Joe Friday ("Just the facts, ma'am")—was a radio actor who had grown up in Los Angeles, fatherless, living in what he once described as "poverty and slime." In the late 1940s, he'd had a conversion experience much like Langley's: While filming *He Walked by Night,* a 1948 movie about a cop killer, Webb went on exciting ride-alongs with a Hollywood police consultant, who griped about how badly Hollywood treated his profession. At the time, the police were generally portrayed as the bad guys, on the radio and in movies—they were corrupt thugs in noir dramas or incompetent idiots in comedies, like the Keystone Kops. Inspired by his experience, Webb set out to turn them into heroes: middle-class pros, rational to the core, holding back a tide of misery in the dirty streets of Los Angeles. He would do this by working hand in hand with the cops, using actual LAPD cop cars, hiring cops as extras, and basing his stories on real cases.

The authoritarian LAPD police chief William H. Parker, who was a notorious racist and also a genius at PR, quickly grasped the TV show's potential. He formalized the department's relationship with Webb, requiring that scripts be okayed twice—for accuracy and for permission. The department and *Dragnet* (and Webb and Parker, whom Webb saw as a father figure), swiftly became mutually reinforcing institutions. In the press, *Dragnet* was widely praised for its authenticity, with *Time* magazine describing it as "a sort of peephole into a grim new world." In 1954, when the magazine published a biting (and, also, remarkably racist) profile of Webb,* the writer admitted that the producer had pulled off a seemingly impossible feat: He had cleaned up the LAPD's terrible reputation, even in the wake of bad press like the 1951 "Bloody Christmas" scandal, a racist police attack on Mexican Americans.

Dragnet was both a top-notch TV show and what modern critics would come to describe as "copaganda." Even decades later, when police dramas deepened, becoming more ambitious and also more critical of the institution they portrayed, on shows like *Hill Street Blues* and *The Wire*, they continued to walk the path cut by *Dragnet*. The police procedural's calling card was gritty authenticity, with the cop as an existential hero, seeking truth in a world of slippery lies.

Cops had two other key forerunners: the 1969 Frederick Wiseman

---

* According to *Time,* Webb was a friendless workaholic, a Hollywood climber who had "gone up, up, up, limber as an Indian brave," who reacted to threats to his creative control "with the ferocity of a Boer trekker defending his oxen against the howling blacks," and hated working for NBC "as the captive Grecian maiden hates the mustachioed Turk."

documentary *Law and Order,* which Langley didn't see until he was already producing *Cops,* and the 1977 TV movie *The Police Tapes,* which was filmed by Alan and Susan Raymond in the wake of *An American Family.* Made with a $43,000 grant, *The Police Tapes,* the first TV program to show real police ride-alongs, was a technical marvel, filmed with lightweight cameras and, for lighting, Newvicon tubes, which allowed the Raymonds to capture night scenes without floodlights. Like Wiseman, who'd filmed the Kansas City police department, the Raymonds worked directly with the police, embedding for weeks in the South Bronx. They filmed the cops as they described the account of a rape victim, and then as they arrested the accused man (who smirked, unconcerned). They filmed street arrests and a hostage negotiation. All of the officers in *The Police Tapes* were white; nearly everyone they arrested was Black. With no narration, the film's singular moral guidance came through a remarkable monologue delivered by Bronx police chief Anthony Bouza, in which he explained how idealistic rookies became violent cynics. "We are manufacturing criminals, we are manufacturing brutality," argued Bouza—and he suggested that maybe, by keeping his precinct "cool," he kept America from confronting inequality: "Maybe I should do my job less well."

Cops would share some DNA with both the scripted *Dragnet* and the unscripted *Police Tapes.* Like Jack Webb, Langley intended to tell true stories. Like the Raymonds, he would embed with police departments, going on ride-alongs and filming street arrests as they happened. But the *Cops* approach to realism—its dark verve, its spikes of voyeuristic comedy, and its utter shamelessness as both copaganda and entertainment—would cut a wild new path.

LANGLEY'S FIRST CUT OF THE *COPS* PILOT WAS DELIBERATELY crude. Filmed in Broward County, Florida, it included what Langley described as a "gay homicide," blood splashed on a wall and a bloated corpse in a river. The aesthetic was raw, using handheld cameras with no tripods, along with organic audio. Langley wanted to make a strong impression—and also to give his bosses at Fox something to cut. According to a story Langley enjoys telling but which you probably shouldn't bank on for accuracy, at the initial screening, Barry Diller, who found the show engaging but excessively graphic, started to argue with a marketing guy, who worried that *Cops* would alienate sponsors. Just then, an unprepossessing figure wandered in, whom Langley initially took for an accountant. It was Rupert Murdoch. "Order four of 'em," Murdoch barked, ending the debate.

The first season of *Cops* centered on a group of colorful characters, among them Cuban-born anti-drug crusader Sheriff Nick Navarro; rookie cop Jerry Wurms and his officer girlfriend, a Farrah-haired bombshell named Linda Canada; and Ron "Chicken" Cacciatore, the head of the organized crime division. For all his bravado about rejecting network notes, Langley did compromise, early on: He included music and, more clumsily, scenes of the cops' home lives, including a stilted argument between Cacciatore and his wife. Wurms also proposed to Canada, as she said, laughing, "I can't believe you just did this on TV!" Decades later, these stagey exchanges feel oddly familiar: They're less like *Cops* and more like the arch, uncanny fake dialogue of shows like *The Real Housewives*. A few episodes in, Langley cut them out of the show.

What was left was the formula that would fuel *Cops* for decades: three seven-minute vignettes of street policing per episode, swinging crazily in tone from comedy to action, pathos to horror. Cut from hundreds of hours of footage, these clips included drug busts, kicked-in doors, overdoses, marital fights, street fights, bar fights, and undercover work, all of it set in the type of slums that rarely showed up on television, particularly in 1989. Some scenes were quick and brutal, others slow and philosophical. But like *Candid Camera*, *Cops* was at its heart a prank show—an ambush show— with the cops as Allen Funt. In the credits, Langley used a funky, knowing theme song, "Bad Boys," sung by the Kingston-based reggae band Inner Circle: "Bad boys, bad boys, what you gonna do? / What you gonna do when they come for you?"

"Vice Is Nice but Cops Is Tops," raved one article in *The Boston Globe*, comparing the show favorably to the scripted *Miami Vice*. But there was also criticism of the show's ethics, of those domestic scenes, and, most damningly, of the racial dynamics. In *The New York Times*, critic John J. O'Connor denounced *Cops* as "tabloid sensationalism," in which the racism was "so casual, so taken for granted, that the only response might well be despair." The show's primal image was "hammered home again and again: the overwhelmingly white troops of police are the good guys; the bad guys are overwhelmingly black. Little is said about the ultimate sources of the drugs, and nothing is mentioned about Florida's periodic scandals in which the police themselves are found to be trafficking in drugs." The show's production method was existentially corrupt, O'Connor argued. "The court of law is the video camera, which is kept running even when the trapped suspect protests its presence."

Langley preferred to describe the arrangement with a euphemistic phrase: *Cops* was an "invitational show." Wiseman and the Raymonds *also* had agreements with the police departments they filmed, Langley pointed out—how else could they go on those ride-alongs?

The way he saw it, the real difference was about class status. Wiseman's *Law and Order* included scenes of jaw-dropping violence, like a white cop doing a chokehold on a Black prostitute. *The Police Tapes* featured a searing glimpse of a Black man's corpse lying in the street, as a woman wailed in grief by his side.* Yet because those filmmakers were liberals who made black-and-white films for public TV, they won Peabodys and Emmys! Still, Langley acknowledged the key problem: The police could censor any scene they wanted to on *Cops,* although he claimed they'd rarely done so. This was likely because they didn't have to: As Paul Stojanovich, one of Langley's producers, once put it, the show was called *Cops,* not *Crooks.*

That first season of *Cops* was marked by another, less visible power dynamic: Langley had a longstanding relationship with Deputy Wurms, one of the stars of season 1. The thirty-two-year-old

---

* Susan Raymond also described a scene that didn't appear in the film, in which a pregnant woman wept uncontrollably upon hearing that her husband had died—a reaction that led Susan to freeze in horror and fail to record it. It was their job to make clear-eyed moral distinctions about what appeared on film, both Raymonds told me, which distinguished *The Police Tapes* from pure voyeurism, the insidious quality they saw in *Cops.*

rookie cop cut an odd figure on the air, compulsively narrating his own heroism from behind dark sunglasses. "We're here just to look for some drugs and clean up the bad people off the street," Wurms announced, in a typical scene. "It's a game out there, a cat and mouse game!" Among fans of the show, Wurms became famous (and to some, notorious) for chasing an unarmed kid, yelling, "Stop—or I'll shoot you in the back!" When I asked about it, Langley said the show didn't glamorize the incident: Wurms's supervisor was shown later on, dressing down his reckless employee.

If Wurms came across less as a rookie cop than a rookie actor on a cop show, that made sense. He'd gotten into show business early, as the assistant to his high school friend John Travolta. Wurms was an assistant director on Langley's 1987 Dolph Lundgren exercise video, and in 1986, he'd been a producer on *American Vice,* helping televise the live bust in Florida performed by Sheriff Navarro's department. When that job ended, Wurms trained as a cop—and then, he took a job working for Navarro, who knew Wurms's father, a DEA agent.

Langley never hid Wurms's Hollywood résumé, but most of the media coverage treated Wurms as if he were just another beat cop. "If it helps people see that we have a tough job out there and we're on their side, it's worth it," he told the *Miami Herald* about his sudden fame. Canada, Wurms's fiancée, would become the season's breakout celebrity, bantering with David Letterman in a black leather jacket and praised by *People* magazine as "the most compelling character to fill a serge suit since Angie Dickinson."

Canada showed up in many of the first season's most affecting scenes, including one in which she comforted a little girl terrified that her mother's boyfriend might return home from jail. "About four nights?" the girl said, tearfully, holding up her fingers, asking how long the boyfriend would stay away. "About ten nights?" It was heart-rending material. But the gulf between Canada—an adult who knew she was being filmed—and the child, in her frilly white dress and braids, exposing her fears to an audience she didn't understand was watching her, lay at the dark heart of *Cops.* The show's most illuminating moments lay side by side with its most exploitative ones—and there was no way to thread them apart.

III

OVER TIME, LANGLEY HONED THE *COPS* FORMULA TO WHAT HE described as "an existential variety show." His ideal episode had a three-part story arc. The first segment was an action piece, meant to grab the viewer's attention. The second was "what I, in a highfalutin way, called a lyrical piece or emotional piece, a slower piece," such as "a domestic"—a family dispute, like the one with Canada and the little girl—or sometimes a comic dialogue. The final segment was ideally a "thought piece." As an example, Langley described a conversation between a cop and a Rastafarian about the spiritual use of pot.

Still, Langley worked with what he got. He had no regrets about anything he aired. If viewers felt disturbed by what they saw, the truth was sometimes disturbing, he told me. If some of the scenes on *Cops* played as slapstick—like the one in which a beefy, wild-eyed strongman refused to leave a bar, then got pepper-sprayed and did kung fu moves—well, ugly events could be funny, too. People who were honest about the world accepted these realities, Langley said: "This is what happened." It was up to the viewer—it was their responsibility—to interpret what they saw.

Watching *Cops* could feel like absorbing a series of short stories that starred characters we'd never see again. "I can't tell my momma nothing," said a young woman with a weary shrug, explaining that her mother had been attending medical school and also dealing crack. A sad-eyed prostitute, her legs coated in scabs, confided in Officer Canada about the abuse and rapes that had made getting high feel like a necessity, a way to numb herself. In the sixth episode of *Cops,* a female cop brought a toddler to Child Protective Services, then sobbed in her car about how ill-equipped the system was. Buried inside the show were grim revelations about criminal justice: A Black man knelt in a police station and told a white cop, "I studied law for a year and a half at Rutgers University," as the officer and a room of suspects, all of them Black men, burst into mocking laughter, joking at the very idea that he could ever represent them.

Langley trained his camera operators to follow the action, to avoid getting hurt—and to get a release, immediately. (Unlike Geraldo's *American Vice* special, *Cops* didn't qualify as news.) In his memoir, *Shoot to Thrill*, *Cops* cameraman Sean Michael Davis described learning this skill, crucial if he didn't want to get canned. Since crew members on *Cops* had nothing to offer arrestees—they couldn't give them money or lower their charges; they had to wait until anyone drunk had sobered up—Davis, who had arrived on the job acting cocky, identifying with the cops, learned how to "chill out" and show empathy, in order to collect the signatures he needed. "The releases started coming in, and my shows started to air."

For some crew members, the job was a joyride. One of Langley's early hires was Bertram van Munster, a Dutch filmmaker who had also worked on *Candid Camera* and who would go on to create *The Amazing Race.* Van Munster, who filmed *Cops* for eight years, adored the looseness of Langley's all-handheld, no-tripods school of street cinema, which let him leap straight into action. In an interview with the Television Academy, he scoffed at the idea that *Cops* was exploitative or excessively violent. "Violent? *Cops* is not a violent show. *Cops* is a comedy," he said.

Occasionally, a critic would praise the show in Langley's terms: In 1992, Alan Bunce, in the *Los Angeles Times,* described it as the only true cinéma vérité TV series, "innocent of reenactments, free of fancy production effects, and doggedly faithful to its format," a "stickler for authenticity" that was a rebuke to other reality productions. Most press was bad, though—at best, dismissive. Although Langley bristled at his critics, he did agree on one issue with the first season: Showing an endless stream of Black "perps" was a mistake. To even the numbers out, he began to film what Fox producer Stephen Chao described, on the podcast *Running from Cops*, as "white criminals, white hotheads, white trash, white something, you know."

The second season of *Cops* was set in Portland, Oregon. Over its original run of thirty-two seasons, the production would film in forty-one states, as well as the USSR and Hong Kong. It became a solid Fox hit, getting more than eight million viewers per episode. Unsurprisingly, cops themselves were some of its biggest fans.

Police departments also quickly learned the value of cooperating with the hit Fox series, especially after a scandal, just as *Dragnet* had helped the LAPD after the Bloody Christmas attack. Early on, LAPD commander Daryl Gates had said no to *Cops* filming in his city. Then, in 1991, George Holliday recorded the beating of Rodney King, graphic evidence of police brutality that led to a mass uprising a year later, after the jury delivered a not-guilty verdict. In 1994, the new LAPD police chief, Willie Williams, agreed to let *Cops* film his officers. "At this juncture, it makes certain sense for the department to receive some positive coverage," said Gary Greenebaum, the president of the police commission, in the *Los Angeles Times.*

Not every official agreed. David Gascon, a local commander, dismissed *Cops* as a "highlights reel," a distorted, overly violent version of the life of a street cop. Former police chief Gates, who had resigned in 1992, also continued to raise objections: "If someone broke into my house, and I called for help, and the police showed up with TV cameras, I would resent the hell out of that." Signing a release was meaningless, he argued: "The pressure is there for those people to consent, because the police have allowed them to be there."

Frank Berry, then the head of the NAACP, also objected to the show, but from a different angle. The way he saw it, the problem with *Cops* wasn't that it worked with the police—it was that cops behaved *better* on camera than they did in real life, concealing their racism. Commander Gascon disagreed: Surely, after what happened with Rodney King, every cop would now be aware that there were cameras watching them, at all times.

OVER THE DECADES, *COPS* CONTINUED TO REFLECT CHANGES IN law enforcement, as drug laws grew harsher in the 1990s, as departments militarized and the carceral state expanded—and, eventually, as prisons privatized, giving control to corporations whose goal was pure profit.

In 2013, the advocacy group Color of Change, which had emerged in the wake of Trayvon Martin's death, campaigned to get *Cops* taken off the air. Whether or not that effort had any impact (Langley claimed it didn't), Fox *did* cancel *Cops,* in 2013, after it had run for twenty-four years. The show was promptly picked up by Paramount Network, then called Spike TV—a channel aimed at young men. On Spike, *Cops* bounced back, reaching a new audience.

In 2019, Dan Taberski, a documentarian who had worked in reality TV, began the investigatory podcast *Running from Cops,* about Langley's series. For eighteen months, his team watched nearly 850 episodes of *Cops,* looking for patterns. He concluded that Langley was right about the numbers: Black suspects weren't overrepresented. Still, Taberski found many other problems, among them the fact that Black crime was frontloaded, dominating the opening "action" sequences. The show also exaggerated the sheer level of drug-related crime in cities, he argued—and he also believed that it fudged evidence. Taberski interviewed suspects who had filed lawsuits, some of whom said they were too high to consent, were intimidated by the cameras, or believed that signing would get them a fairer shake in court. These ethical problems were ultimately insurmountable, Taberski concluded. The issue was significantly worse on a similar show, *Live PD,* which was like the bastard offspring of *American Vice,* airing a series of streaming drug busts, broadcast live.

By 2020, when Langley and I first spoke in his office, Fox's cameras were also no longer the only ones documenting the police. There were cameras at every bodega, on street corners, at subway turnstiles, in doorbells. The police wore body cameras, too. What's more, anyone who got arrested or was harassed—or had any interaction at all with a cop—likely had a camera-phone in their hand, or tucked into their back pocket (and if they didn't have a phone, a bystander did). It was a new model of citizen journalism that reached a horrible climax that May, with the death of George Floyd, a crime recorded by a teenage girl on her phone, in a brutal ten-minute-and-nine-second clip that ignited mass protests. That kind of clip would never have aired on Fox.

A month later, *Cops* was re-canceled, this time by Paramount. Langley and I spoke again that fall. During our first interview, Langley had expanded on his legacy with amused confidence. He had described himself as a child of the 1960s, a hippie at heart—the kind of person who might, early on, have made a show called *Pigs*. (It had become his go-to line.) After years working with law enforcement, he'd changed his mind on some issues. He now viewed the drug war as a failure, along with the expansion of the carceral state. He was strongly opposed to private prisons. In 2007, he and his son Morgan made a reality show called *Jail,* which ran for five seasons but got little traction. He had plans to make a show that would follow an accused person from their arrest through their trial, as well as another project called *Lady Justice,* which was focused on women's approaches to law enforcement. "They deescalate, they don't inflate the problem. I've seen it happen," he said, enthusiastically.

Still, Langley defended *Cops.* "I didn't create the content and I didn't create the laws. And I'm not necessarily *endorsing* those laws," he told me. Viewers, he insisted, could interpret the show in multiple ways—they could see it as a powerful case against the police system and, really, against capitalism itself. "They should think, 'Well, why is all this happening in *this* area? Hmm. Why are so many people doing drugs? Hmm. Why do people sell drugs? Hmm.'" He argued that *Running from Cops* had warped the data, that *Cops* was a target because it was so entertaining. "I guess my achievement was putting it into a form that worked for network TV."

If anything, the true mystery of *Cops* is that—for all of its influence and financial success—it had no descendants on television. No other show did quite what *Cops* did, by filming a primal human crisis—a surgery or a car crash, say—over and over, cinéma vérité–style, then mining it for humor and bleakness. *Cops* had lasted longer than any other reality show, and yet, its format was sui generis. Like *America's Funniest Home Videos,* its legacy was online.

Langley had become a wealthy man. He owned a home in Ojai, a vineyard in Argentina, and several restaurants; he was on the cover of *Cigar Aficionado* magazine, puffing a stogie. When we spoke in March 2021, the spring after the Black Lives Matter uprisings and two months after the January 6 insurrection, I wondered if he would feel humbled or, perhaps, self-questioning. Instead, he seemed energized. He spoke with amused contempt about Viacom, the multinational corporation that had canceled *Cops* through one corporate arm—and then picked it up on a new streaming service with the other. It was all hypocrisy, he said, all done for profit, not principle. He doubted the head of Viacom had ever watched *Cops*.

He had no intention of stopping production. In fact, now that he was no longer under the thumb of the network, Langley planned to pitch *more* shows, including some "that I have yet to sell because frankly, I'm waiting for the climate to settle down a bit." He loathed the phrase "defund the police," which he found naïve and harmful. He bridled when I used the phrase "systemic racism." Yet he insisted that he agreed with the principles of the Black Lives Matter movement, including their objections to the criminal justice system. When I asked Langley if he'd ever filmed police abuse, he said, "No. Because to be honest with you, they don't do abusive things," then added, "They do things *I* think are abusive, to be honest, in their treatment of suspects." If his critics saw *Cops* as evidence of a corrupt system, biased against poor people, in which police were trained to "overreact," Langley agreed. He just thought they were blaming the messenger.

A few months later, in June 2021, Langley died of a heart attack in Mexico, while competing in the Ensenada to San Felipe 250 coast-to-coast off-road race. In his final months, he had felt encouraged by what he saw. Filming during the pandemic, he had been struck by how many addicts were being sent to treatment instead of jail. Cops were deescalating, he said with excitement; they were talking more to suspects. "And it's because of Covid, it's because of changed rules, it's because of George Floyd. It's for a lot of reasons, right?"

Langley's dreamy tone felt delusional to me the day we spoke, so soon after January 6. But he insisted that he felt a "sea change" in the culture—and he fantasized about creating a new kind of show, in which suspects could speak about the roots of their unhappiness, their lost jobs, their addictions, their depression. "As a kid of the '60s, sometimes it takes extreme reactions to injustice in order to change everything," he said. As for reality television, he warned me not to blame him. "Some people say that I was the godfather of reality and all that stuff, which I think is nonsense. But if it were true, I'm not responsible for the bastards that followed."

THE
REV UP

||||||||||||||||||||||||||||||||||||||||||||||||||||||||||||

1990–2000

5

|||||||

THE HOUSE
The Real World

A FEW WEEKS INTO THE FILMING OF THE FIRST SEASON OF MTV'S *The Real World,* Eric Nies, a twenty-year-old model from New Jersey, walked into a swanky SoHo loft apartment on Broadway just below Prince Street. Two of his housemates, Heather B. Gardner and Julie Oliver, were in the kitchen, flipping through a coffee-table book and giggling. "Did you leave this out for us?" Julie asked. She held up the book to show him one of the photos: a black-and-white shot of Eric, full-frontal naked, as he took a cautious step through a forest, like some hunky innocent in Eden.

One floor down, in the show's control room, surrounded by monitors, Jon Murray and Mary-Ellis Bunim, the show's co-creators, looked on in excitement. They had planted that book—the fashion photographer Bruce Weber's glossy photo collection *Bear Pond,* which had been Eric's big break as a model—in the loft, hoping the nude photo would spark some drama among the housemates, a production method that Bunim, a seasoned soap opera producer, called "throwing pebbles in the pond." The gamble looked like it was about to pay off, igniting a flirtation or maybe a fight—either one was fine with them.

Nearby, associate producer Danielle Faraldo was staring at the screen in distress. She had begged her bosses not to plant *Bear Pond*, not to interfere with the house at all, convinced that any manipulation would taint the reality format's purity and break the cast's trust. Now she was fuming. Her worst fears were playing out, as Heather wondered out loud where the book came from and then Eric looked straight into the cameras and yelled, "What the *hell*?"

Three decades later, in 2020, Jon Murray smiled as he described the crisis—a small, dry smile. We were seated in his office in Santa Monica, in the beautiful home *The Real World* had built, a peaceful place where he'd raised his son, Dyllan, with his long-term partner, Harvey. All around were memorabilia tracing his years in Hollywood, including a shelf with framed vacation photos and Emmys for Outstanding Unstructured Reality Program and Outstanding Nonfiction Special. It all felt like ancient history, that heated battle over authenticity—a Gen X obsession, as obsolete as the Shakers. The first series that felt fully recognizable as modern reality TV, *The Real World* had forged the tools that would define the genre: the shared house, the deliberately diverse ensemble cast, and the "confessional." Yet the experiment had nearly ended, right as it started.

On that strange day in SoHo in 1992, the cast seemed to be on the verge of walking out of their own Eden. "We threw pebbles in the pond. And they threw back a boulder," said Murray.

THE REAL WORLD STARTED FILMING IN FEBRUARY 1992, JUST AS Bill Clinton was beginning his campaign to win the Democratic primary. The AIDS epidemic was raging; in Simi Valley, the trial against the cops who had beaten up Rodney King had just begun. Meanwhile, MTV—a hip cable network that aired marathons of Madonna and Michael Jackson music videos—had agreed to stage a peculiar experiment, putting seven young artists in a loft apartment, then filming their lives. Decades before TikTok, *The Real World* would give viewers a taste of a future in which everyone would grow up in public.

The roots of *The Real World* went back to two documentaries that Jon Murray had seen when he was growing up: Michael Apted's

Up series, which, beginning in 1964, traced the lives of British children, revisiting its subjects every seven years; and *An American Family*, which Murray watched with his parents at seventeen. *An American Family* had blown Murray's mind, in part for what it *wasn't*—it was not a scripted drama or an earnest, educational narrated film "with a booming voice, back when they all had the booming voices." Instead, the strange, dreamy documentary felt like eavesdropping, overflowing with the voices of teenagers—artsy, attractive kids, right around his age. Best of all, there was Lance Loud, with his sleepy eyes and loose hips, deep in a dance of love and disappointment with his mother. "It made an impact," said Murray.

Murray's father was a Veterans Affairs psychologist. His mother was a British war bride, a fiery figure who kept moving their family from city to city, hunting for the best education for her children. As a result, Murray spent his early childhood in Gulfport, Mississippi, then had two stints in upstate New York, with one alienated year in between in England, in 1962, when he was seven, the same age as the kids in the first installment of the Up series, *Seven Up*. A guarded, watchful child, Murray grew accustomed to life as a fish out of water: He was a liberal Unitarian in the Baptist South, then a Southern-accented child in the Northeast, then an American student at "a dodgy East Oxford public school." These experiences helped turn him into a natural observer, a quality that was intensified by his private awareness that he was gay, sensitive to the idea that a stranger might sense something hidden in him. His escape was television. Murray collected *TV Guide*s as if they were comic books. When he was ten years old, he even wrote to the editors of *TV Guide,* asking for copies of the Nielsen ratings—which, amazingly, they sent him.

The same year that *An American Family* aired, Murray's family went through a life-warping tragedy: His older brother, who had fled to Toronto to avoid the Vietnam draft, died after he fell out of a window, high on LSD. The loss devastated his parents; Murray was determined to spare them any further trouble. Laser-focused on his career, he transferred to the Missouri School of Journalism, where he showed an early streak of showmanship: Once, for a class project, he did a segment about a college prank, in which ping-pong balls had been poured from an airplane. During the editing process, he added in an anchor's voice, announcing, "The bombs are dropping over London!" The stunt impressed his professor—until he realized that the narration had been cut in after the fact, at which point he lectured Murray about media ethics.

For a decade, Murray thrived as a TV news producer, jumping from city to city, climbing the ladder; eventually, he landed a plush corporate gig, helping stations buy and schedule their syndicated programming. In his thirties, Murray was living in a Manhattan coach house with a steady boyfriend—a solid, stable life in the industry he loved. But like Chuck Barris, he felt stuck in the executive suites, eager to switch to the creative side of the business. In his off hours, Murray had been developing pitches—a set of unusual new formats, all of them attempts to merge documentary with drama. There was *Doctor, Doctor,* a real-life *Marcus Welby, M.D.;* there was *Crime Diaries,* about fictional detectives who solved real crimes. With his connections, Murray was confident he could sell one.

Instead, he hit wall after wall. Finally, his young agent, Mark Itkin, made a suggestion: Murray should team up with another TV veteran, the soap opera producer Mary-Ellis Bunim. Their chemistry was instant. Bunim was a sharp-elbowed, stylish Hollywood player who was unafraid of confrontation—an ideal match for the more mild-mannered Murray, who adored her fiery charisma. In 1987, the pair founded Bunim/Murray Productions in a small office in Beverly Hills, and for twelve years, they worked together like Dorothy Parker and Robert Benchley, on either side of a shared table. "We would bat around ideas, type them up on our IBM Selectric, then go off to have lunch with the secretaries in Beverly Hills and come back hoping that our message light would be blinking," said Murray.

It rarely was. Money was tight. From 1987 to 1991, they failed to sell any of their ideas, among them a competitive format called *Great American Road Race,* a decade before *The Amazing Race.* Frustrated, Bunim took a short-term money gig, working as a producer for the daytime soap opera *Loving,* but in her off hours, she kept collaborating with Murray. Their pet project was an update of one of Murray's favorite shows—the documentary that had blown his mind as a teenager in 1973. In an amazing coincidence, in 1988, Murray attended NATPE, the TV industry's yearly convention, only to find himself seated next to Delilah Loud, who was then working as a vice president at a company called Qintex. Starstruck, Murray peppered Delilah with questions for hours, curious about every aspect of *An American Family.*

When he left dinner that night, he was determined to create a modern version of his favorite show. For the next two years, Bunim and Murray poured the majority of their energy into *American Families,* ultimately filming six episodes, among them a pilot about an adopted daughter looking for her biological mother. The episode aired on Fox in 1991, but the ratings weren't quite high enough for a full-season pickup. It was a crushing disappointment.

Even while she worked to get *American Families* off the ground, the multitasking Bunim had taken yet another side gig, a work-for-hire job for a show called *St. Mark's Place,* to be produced by MTV. The idea had come from an MTV producer named Lauren Corrao, who had set out to make a scripted soap opera about young people living in the East Village, which would run five nights a week—hip, edgy counterprogramming to the bland teen shows on the networks. But even as Bunim developed the pilot script, she kept grumbling to Itkin that the project was almost certainly a dead end. There was no way that MTV—a small, low-budget, nonunion cable network, used to airing music videos for free—would agree to green-light a show that cost $500,000 per episode.

Sure enough, MTV passed on *St. Mark's Place.* Bunim and Murray flew to New York to have breakfast with Corrao. The producer, at twenty-seven, already had several triumphs under her belt at MTV, including the cool indie comedy *The Ben Stiller Show* and the game show *Remote Control.* Bunim and Murray initially struck Corrao as a bit stuffy, or maybe just more grown-up than her peers at MTV, but over scrambled eggs at the Mayflower Hotel, they pitched an idea that startled her. They wanted to make a soap opera, only one that was made without a script. The cast would be made up of real people, six young artists living in a cool loft. The plot would emerge from their conflicts, Murray explained: They'd make mistakes, then they'd work them out, and in the process, the group would bond, and slowly, the characters—their hopes, their dreams, their identities— would change. MTV would have a hot drama about young people, only it would be low-budget and nonunion.

Corrao clicked with the idea immediately, having lived in just that kind of a hothouse apartment after graduating from Brown University, where she'd majored in semiotics. Bunim and Murray gave her the *American Families* pilot, as proof that they could cut documentary footage that felt like TV drama. By lunchtime, Corrao had gotten the go-ahead from her boss, Doug Herzog, to film a pilot. She still needed "proof of concept," however, before MTV would take the show to series. No one was sure how regular people would act, surrounded by cameras. Would they shut down? Act phony? Would they break down under the pressure?

That night, when Corrao described the idea to her husband, MTV director Jim Jones, the couple cracked up—and both of them immediately thought of one of their favorite movies. A generation younger than Murray, they hadn't seen *An American Family,* but they were big fans of Albert Brooks's *Real Life.* That movie was the ultimate producer's nightmare, they agreed: filming people so boring, the only way to get drama was to burn down the house.

OVER MEMORIAL DAY WEEKEND IN 1991, JIM JONES, ALAN COHN, and Rob Klug co-directed the pilot for *The Real World,* Bunim and Murray's attempt to get MTV their "proof of concept." To cast their housemates, MTV had taped flyers up at laundromats, seeking people "willing to be themselves." They found Adam Wacht, a long-haired rocker; Dizzy, a pork-pie-wearing rapper; Eamee, a "free spirit"; and Peter Reisfeld, a bartender at the divey Raccoon Lodge. Two cast members were selected from inside MTV: Janel Scarborough, a *Club MTV* dancer, and Tracy Grandstaff, a twenty-two-year-old MTV employee who had seen a flyer in the break room, then applied as a lark. Scarborough, who was Black, was the last one to be cast—they'd sought her out for diversity's sake, she assumed.

That weekend, the six OG cast members moved into a fancy loft-style apartment. At first, Tracy found the process unsettling: Every two hours, a sound guy would tap her on the shoulder, then take her into the bathroom, lift her shirt, and change her mic's battery pack, a process that felt a bit skeevy. She worried about hidden cameras. But mainly, she was confused: She'd imagined the show would be more like MTV's *Spring Break* specials, which were full of music and celebrity cameos. Instead, they just wanted to film her hanging out.

Some mild drama did bubble up during the three days of filming. All weekend, Tracy and Peter hung out, riding his motorcycle across the Brooklyn Bridge, then lingering at the Raccoon Lodge. In the pilot, this wound up looking like a flirtation, which was an illusion—Tracy knew that Peter had a girlfriend. Still, the two of them could see that they were creating a story, and during their ride across the bridge, they joked about the scene being scored to the cheesy heavy metal band Winger. "It was U2, so we won that round," said Tracy.

On a different night, Mary-Ellis Bunim set Tracy up on a blind date. While the couple was walking home, co-director Alan Cohn gave Tracy and her date an ultimatum: He wasn't going to leave until they kissed. Tracy wasn't especially into the idea, but they did it, kissing under a streetlight. Jim Jones described the moment to me, jokingly, as "the original sin of reality television."

Murray, who had flown in to supervise the shoot from Los Angeles, where he was still working on *American Families,* screened the footage. He was thrilled by what he saw. The cast moved in loose, surprising ways—they sat on the window ledges, instead of chairs—and their language felt fresh, full of subtext and irony, with none of the arch obviousness of scripted dialogue. He was particularly bewitched by the shots of Tracy and Peter cruising across the bridge, both wearing leather jackets—an image of youthful romance, simple, sexy, and iconic.

That Monday night, Bunim lifted a glass to toast Cohn, who'd agreed to edit the pilot: "Alan, it's all up to you now!" Cohn lifted his glass, but internally, he was freaking out. It wasn't that he lacked relevant experience—he'd worked as an assistant to documentary legend Frederick Wiseman, then jumped to the corporate world, filming "industrials" for Drexel Burnham. Still, *The Real World* struck him as a big deal: It was a chance to translate cinéma vérité for Gen X, to convert kids who had been raised on MTV editing. Persnickety by nature, Cohn kept putting off the edit, until Bunim got concerned. To be fair, she was on to something: Although Cohn had told her that he knew how to do linear time-code editing—the grueling analog method editors used at the time—he'd lied. He studied the manual whenever she left. He had 125 hours of footage and just one note from MTV: Add music.

Slowly, laboriously, Cohn produced a short clip, around eighteen seconds long, which focused on Peter's disorientation the day he entered the loft. In it, Peter walked through the beat-up lobby, then into the elevator, dangling his motorcycle helmet. Upstairs, he shook Dizzy's hand—and then Cohn cut in a voiceover: "I was standing next to Dizzy." Then another cut, back to Peter, who was suddenly seated, rather mysteriously, in another room, with the noir-like shadow of a ceiling fan swirling above as he said, in voiceover, "I saw Tracy and Eamee, drinking orange juice." To illustrate *that* thought, Cohn stumbled upon an accidental shot in which the camera abruptly swooped down, then focused on a sandwich and some orange juice. It was a goofy pop of color that captured the vibe Cohn wanted: playful, ironic, romantic, spontaneous.

Once that was completed, Cohn felt liberated to edit the episodes. The camera operators had filmed the housemates using both regular cameras and Hi8s, which were canted to 45 degrees, producing a trippy "Dutch angle"—a slanted look inspired in part by the 1949 noir thriller *The Third Man*, but which was mostly an attempt to look cool. Using music as glue, Cohn cut montages, using snap zooms (aggressive sudden close-ups), with a focus on bright colors and visual jokes, like the Deee-Lite song "Groove Is in the Heart" cut over a shot of someone smoking, with the exhale synced to the song. Among his inspirations were Oliver Stone's *JFK* and Scorsese's *GoodFellas*—hot, ironized modern cinema. Even with only three days' worth of footage, he had plenty of fun stories to illustrate: Tracy and Peter's flirtation, the cast dancing at a club, hosting a party, and having several heated arguments about selling out.

After the pilot was completed, nine long, nerve-racking months went by. MTV kept putting off their decision. Janel and Tracy both heard rumors that the focus groups were positive, but by the time MTV finally committed to filming a full season, any notion of reusing the cast was gone. By then, Tracy had become Lauren Corrao's assistant, which meant that she was embedded inside the experiment that she'd helped launch.

Tracy would go on to have a big career at MTV, landing a *second* role on an iconic series: She became the deadpan voice of Daria, the ultimate Gen X cynic, on the eponymous animated show. Eventually, she found a high-up job at NBC, producing advertising. But when the first season of *The Real World* was filmed, she was busy working the phones, as the cast vented to her. She had no regrets about losing the chance to do the show. "I saw what it did to that cast. It sticks with you. . . . I don't think any of them signed up for the emotional side of it."

TO STAFF THE FIRST SEASON, CORRAO HIRED A YOUNG CREW with hip musical taste and a passion for indie documentary. To these MTV stalwarts, Jon Murray, who was thirty-seven, and Mary-Ellis Bunim, forty-six, felt like outsiders: squares and boomers, not "the Nirvana generation," as producer George Verschoor, right in the middle at thirty-two, summed up the younger crowd's perspective. Still, one person stood out: Danielle Faraldo, Bunim's twenty-six-year-old former production coordinator, a Gen X idealist who was deeply invested in the show's success.

Julie Oliver, a cast member from the first season, described Faraldo as "a tiny scrap of a person with blond hair, like teeny, teeny, tiny." From the accounts of everyone involved, Faraldo was almost helplessly emotional and passionate about the social experiment she'd helped create. She'd worked on the project from the beginning, helping to coordinate the pilot—and from her account, she had helped spark the show's creation, when she worked for Bunim at *Loving*. According to Faraldo, her boss was griping about the problems she was having developing *St. Mark's Place* when Faraldo made a suggestion: Bunim should put a few young artists together in a loft, then film them. They talked about the dramas of Faraldo's friend-ship circle, the emotional material that might feed the show—and according to Faraldo, she suggested Bunim call the show *The Reel World*. (Murray had never heard this story, although it was one that Faraldo told several cast members of *The Real World*. Verschoor also hadn't heard the story; he told me that he considered the show's origin story to be the night that Jon Murray met Delilah Loud.)

Bunim hired Faraldo to work on the pilot of the show, paying her $300 a week to scout for a loft in New York and interview potential housemates. She scribbled notes in composition books, building a "show bible," a description of how the format might work. A year later, when MTV picked up the series, Faraldo's job description shifted, although she was still an associate producer. Bunim/Murray had hired Verschoor, an experienced TV producer who worked at Qintex with Delilah Loud, as the showrunner. Although Faraldo did multi-ple tasks, her central role was as the go-between for the cast and the crew, a crucial job, since the two sides were meant to stay separate.

Bunim and Murray cast the show to mimic the pilot, looking for a rocker, a rapper, a free spirit, etc. Their Tracy Grandstaff analogue was Memphis State University freshman Julie Oliver, a white South-ern dance student with a droll wit and a conservative family, who'd heard a radio ad when she was driving home for Christmas break, then filmed an audition tape in which she clog-danced and also mocked Northerners for stereotyping people like her as hicks. Her dad was nicknamed "The Colonel"; she'd been to New York just once, for a school trip. When Murray met Julie, in December 1991, he recognized her immediately as be the perfect star for the show: an Alabama virgin in the big city, the ideal fish out of water.

At the time, Murray had been boning up on screenwriting guru Robert McKee's rules of story structure, hoping to raise his narrative game—to hold his own with the skilled Bunim, who had spent years spinning out soap opera plots. He began to "produce" Julie right away, calling a local minister and encouraging him to give a sermon about young people leaving home, so they could film it. When Julie's flight landed in New York, Murray hired a cabbie, then instructed him to drive her to SoHo via Harlem—a route that made no geographic sense—so that he could record her reaction. He even timed her arrival to make sure that Julie would be the last person to enter the loft. On the plane, Murray captured a shot of Julie as she gazed out the plane window, knowing that once the show was in editing, that could become a moment to insert a "memory," a flashback to her home.

The rest of the cast was made up of more established young artists. Heather B. Gardner, twenty-one, was a rapper from Jersey City and a member of the pioneering Boogie Down Productions. Andre Comeau, twenty, from Detroit, was the lead singer of the rock band Reigndance. Kevin Powell, twenty-five, was a spoken word poet and a freelance journalist, part of the staff at Quincy Jones's new magazine, *Vibe,* and taught a class at NYU for high school kids. Becky Blasband, twenty-four, was a singer-songwriter who worked as a waitress at Club Tatou, and Eric Nies, twenty, was a model. Few of them knew much about the show, just that it was a documentary about young artists, created by MTV—good exposure.

Late in the process, the production added a seventh character: Norman Korpi, a twenty-four-year-old artist from Michigan who was part of the Warhol Factory scene, which was bubbling downtown decades after Lance Loud's time at the Chelsea Hotel. Faraldo, who met Norm back when she scouted his Park Slope loft for the pilot, had spent a day getting high with him and talking about art. She told me she convinced Murray to cast him instead of a different gay person, who struck her as potentially "harmful to the gay cause." (Murray doesn't remember this.)

ON FEBRUARY 16, 1992, THE SEVEN STRANGERS MOVED INTO THE loft at 565 Broadway. The glamorous downtown space had originally been a 4,000-square-foot duplex, but for the show, the producers converted it into two lofts, then equipped it with fourteen microphones, which were embedded in the ceiling and the night tables. There was a massive living room, with a spiral staircase connecting the floors, and four bedrooms. The decor was bright and bold, with Keith Haring prints, a pool table, leopard-print throw pillows, and a massive fish tank—a metaphor that no one could miss.

The film technology was rudimentary: Most of the time, there were just two cameras (occasionally three), each with a massive battery pack and thick cords draping the floor like snakes. The producers showed up on Prince Street every morning, then picked someone to follow. Some days, they'd film Julie going to dance classes; on others, they filmed Heather as she recorded her rap album *The System Sucks,* or Eric at a modeling shoot, or Becky singing at a club. Despite the way it appeared in the edited episodes, the cast wasn't living in the loft full time, with the exception of Julie. Many of her housemates couldn't afford to break their leases for three months, so they came and went—Heather stayed over the least, she said.

Murray wanted a fly-on-the-wall effect, so at first, the camera operators weren't even allowed to say hello to the cast. Everyone objected to this setup, so Murray dropped it—and right away, the two sides began to bond. Like the Raymonds and the Loud kids, the crew members were not much older than the people they were filming. They, too, were struggling artists, working on a social experiment, for relatively low rates. After hours, at Gonzalez y Gonzalez, a local restaurant where the crew blew off steam over margaritas, some cast members would tag along. Late at night in the loft, director Bill Richmond would turn his camera off, to let the housemates vent.

Two days a week, Murray would film interviews with the cast members. He'd take each housemate into a back hallway, to the staircase, or up to the roof, then ask them detailed questions about everything that was happening in their lives—at one point, he even interviewed Norm while he was in the bathtub. To make sure that these interviews would work as voiceovers, Murray trained the cast to look straight into the camera and tell their stories in present tense: "I'm walking into the loft." He never used scripts and they didn't refilm scenes: If they happened to miss a good moment, he figured, they'd live with it.

Then they waited, hoping for drama to emerge. Nothing happened—and then nothing kept happening. A few weeks in,

Bunim and Murray were worried. No one was fighting—and, worse, no one was flirting, let alone hooking up. Sitting in the control room, watching the monitors, they began to brainstorm. Maybe they could send Becky, the singer, out on a fake date, the same way they'd done with Tracy back when they were filming the pilot? Maybe they could plant a copy of *Bear Pond,* to spark some drama with Eric?

These ideas weren't pure cinéma vérité. But they weren't scripted drama, either—they were somewhere in between, a form of puppeteering, of social engineering. *The Real World* was already an artificial setting, designed to provoke reactions: The housemates were living in a fancy loft they couldn't afford, with people they might never have met otherwise. Now the producers wanted to add a little more provocation, to stir a dash of *Candid Camera* into *An American Family.* During a meeting with the cast, they warned the group that MTV had found an early cut of the footage boring—and they told everyone that they should expect some games, some surprises, to spark more drama.

Instead, they had a new problem to deal with: Their Gen X crew hated all of their ideas, convinced that these stunts would taint the project. "[Co-director] Rob Fox and I got really mad about that, frustrated: You know, *You're fucking with reality,*" said Bill Richmond. Richmond was especially upset when Bunim got a guy at a club where Becky performed to ask her out on a date. What if Becky fell in love and then found out that the guy was a plant? he argued. Faraldo told Bunim that she needed to "trust the process"—that if she didn't, the cast would turn on them.

The executive producers swatted away these concerns. "She was very young at the time," said Verschoor of Faraldo. "And she was considered, to me, kind of *turned* by the cast." His own perspective landed somewhere in between, while he struggled to sort out his principles. "At that time, it was very binary: It's either a documentary series or it's not. Like, 'If it's a game show, tell them!'—and that was blasphemy, to say that to Jon and Mary-Ellis."

Then Bunim and Murray planted a copy of *Bear Pond* in the house—and just as Faraldo had feared, the cast rebelled. When Eric blew up and demanded to know where the photo book had come from, Faraldo glared at her bosses. She understood that it was her job to talk to the cast, but before she approached them, she tried to make a bargain, to get Bunim and Murray to agree not to air the footage. Bunim refused; Murray backed Bunim up. "And I was like, 'How can you *do* that?' I'm like, 'You see how upset they are. Eric's crying!'" Bunim told Faraldo to do her job: She needed to get Eric back on board with the filming.

When Faraldo walked into Eric's bedroom, she knew the mics were on; she didn't want to say anything that would antagonize her bosses further. Instead, she stared into Eric's eyes, trying to communicate with him nonverbally, to let him know how upset she was, too. Eric can't recall the events clearly, but he remembers Faraldo helping calm him down.

After that clash, production stopped. Although memories are fuzzy, the producers seem to have held a series of meetings, at the loft and at Gonzalez y Gonzalez. At one of these meetings—which was attended by the cast, Bunim, Faraldo, and Verschoor (Murray was in Los Angeles)—the debate flared up. According to several people who were present, the conversation turned into a shouting match, as cast members, particularly Eric, Heather, Becky, and Norm, insisted that they needed to understand the rules of the show. The way Verschoor read the mood, they were threatening to walk—and Bunim's response only inflamed matters. Yes, she told the housemates, the producers would be planting provocations, but instead of resisting it, they should embrace that idea as a fun game, a way to help the show succeed. As an experienced soap opera producer, she knew a lot about "packaging people," she told them—it was a term she'd used when talking to crew members, as well.

"The cast was looking at her, saying, 'What? I'm a human. I'm not an actor that you can package,'" said Verschoor. Murray, who wasn't present that day, said he had a tape of the event but he wouldn't share it: He denied that there was any shouting and said that the way he understood it, Bunim was explaining that the show was pivoting away from these methods, telling everyone that there would be no more "pebbles in the pond."

In the end, the decision was MTV executive Lauren Corrao's to make—and she wound up siding with the cast. She "put down the hammer," Corrao said, decreeing that there would be no more interference from the producers. Verschoor remembers being impressed and also surprised. Many executives would simply have fired everyone involved in the rebellion.

Production started up again, but the crisis had triggered a period of deep disillusionment for Faraldo. Bunim was angry at her former assistant, whom she no longer trusted. The cast, however, was deeply bonded to her. To Julie, Faraldo seemed to have "no walls," transparent in all her emotions. "She reminded me of an RA," said Heather, who described the associate producer as "the eighth cast member." With no poker face, Faraldo tended to leak information, in both directions: She would talk to the producers about the cast, but she also told the cast what she'd heard from the crew—or sometimes, she simply showed it on her face. "I'd look green and they'd ask me what was going on, and I'd say, 'Don't ask.'"

For Verschoor, the situation was a difficult one to maneuver. He felt bad for Faraldo, but he also believed that she was "unraveling," losing perspective. She played an irreplaceable role for the production, though. "They really liked her and they would open up to her. I didn't want to betray that trust, because she was getting information we needed."

THE SHOW WENT ON, WITH THE CAST DOING THE KINDS OF THINGS artsy kids did in New York in 1992. The housemates cooked spaghetti; they had fun at a roller disco. A few of them road-tripped to a pro-choice rally in Washington and also worked as volunteers for Jerry Brown's presidential campaign. Julie befriended a homeless woman, then spent the night with her in the West Side Boat Basin. Becky recorded music with her close friend Adam Schlesinger, a brilliant musician who would later form Fountains of Wayne with Chris Collingwood (who also hung around during the shoot, but refused to sign the MTV release, so he doesn't appear in the show). Julie and Heather visited the class Kevin was teaching at NYU. There were a few contrived events, like a photo shoot that was booked by Bunim/

Murray Productions, but mostly, the housemates did as they pleased. The hunt for authenticity had its absurd side: When Andre's band tidied up their crash pad before the camera operators showed up, the MTV crew spilled the Cheerios back on the floor, to maintain proper grittiness. (Verschoor doesn't think this happened.)

Murray had dreamed that the show would spark deep friendships, spanning social divides—and one of these did emerge, between Julie, the white dancer from Alabama, and Heather, the Black hip-hop artist from New Jersey. According to Heather, their closeness emerged, ironically enough, off camera—when both cameras were out of the house, the two women would hang out in Julie's room alone, having intense personal conversations the show didn't record.

For other cast members, however, the loft could feel alienating. Like Janel Scarborough, the one Black cast member on the pilot (and arguably, the first regular Black cast member on any reality show), Kevin Powell had been "scouted" to appear on the show, approached by MTV at Ellen's Stardust Diner. Right away, he felt intrigued, viewing the show, with unusual prescience, as a "branding" opportunity, in a way most people didn't think in those days. A heavy TV buff, Kevin had a deeper sense of the show's roots than his housemates, since he saw it as a part of a larger history—he thought about *Gilligan's Island, Candid Camera,* and *Real People.* During the audition process, he didn't talk about politics; instead, he shyly answered the questions Bunim and Murray asked about sex. He also talked about the house music he loved.

The show's timing changed everything. Filming began on February 16, the Rodney King trial presented its opening arguments on March 6, the jury acquitted the police officers who had beaten King on April 29, and by May, Los Angeles was in flames, as the streets filled with protesters, looters, and police. There was an incendiary national debate going on about race and power—one that Kevin, who had studied Black history and worked in the anti-apartheid movement, was deeply engaged in, but which his roommates knew very little about.

The Los Angeles uprising became the subtext of the season, setting off a series of clashes between Kevin and his housemates. Kevin and Becky had long, tangled debates about race and gender, one of which broke down when he called her a bitch. He wrote Eric a letter explaining structural racism, which baffled Eric. He clashed with Andre and Norm, too. In the edited version of the season, the same scenario kept repeating: Kevin as a finger-pointing polemicist, arguing with a white roommate. "I didn't understand the difference between proactive and reactionary anger. I didn't understand that there were other ways to have conversations with people about hard subject matter other than yelling and screaming," Kevin told me. When he had signed up, he'd hoped to repair the stereotypical images of Black men on television, from *Amos 'n' Andy* to J.J. on *Good Times*, only to land in a different trap.

One clash got uglier. It began with a truly 1992 technological glitch, when Kevin, who was making a work call on the loft's only landline, was interrupted by Julie, who picked up the other receiver. According to Julie, Kevin came downstairs and "lost his shit," screaming and smashing the phone against the wall behind her head, then lifting up a candlestick. Frightened, Julie called the production office, only to have Kevin grab the phone and throw it—which meant that the crew heard him yelling at her, said Julie. (Jon Murray doesn't remember this.)

In the episode that aired, this conflict was laid out as a "he said/she said" mystery, which Julie told me wasn't accurate. The way she understood it, MTV likely didn't want to portray Kevin as a stereotype, "an angry Black man"; while she understood that impulse, she also wondered why, if that was the case, they needed to use *any* of the footage. "They were thrilled to have real emotion and real action, something current to what was going on in Los Angeles. But in retrospect, none of it was really honest or helpful," she said.

Kevin, who has never rewatched the season, remembered the fight but has no recollection of the details, although he was certain he didn't throw anything. "I was just at my wit's end," said Kevin. "And anything was triggering to me, at that point, because I just wanted it to be over."

The argument hadn't happened on camera. But soon after, Kevin and Julie had another argument, one that began in the loft, then spilled outside onto Broadway, as Verschoor frantically flung camera cords out the window, determined not to miss a key moment. It was a stressful day for everyone: With violence in the streets of Los Angeles, New York was on alert. By the time the cameras got hooked up, a crowd had gathered around Julie and Kevin, baffled about what they were witnessing: Was this a movie shoot or was it real? It was precisely the kind of conflict that Murray had dreamed of documenting—a fiery, layered conversation full of mutual misunderstandings, requiring no pebbles in the pond at all.

"I have a lot of misdirected anger but I have a lot of anger that's justifiable, too," Kevin told Julie, stepping closer to her. Julie, visibly frustrated, asked Kevin to step back and give her some space. Kevin told Julie that Black people were emotional, that she should see his behavior as cultural. "Get off the Black-white thing," yelled Julie. "I'm sick of it!" "Look at Los Angeles!" he shouted back. "What are you gonna do, hit me?" she snapped. "Why do you assume because I'm a Black man, I'm going to hit you?" he shot back. In the final edit, the viewer's perspective depended very much on one's sympathies, on whether you believed Kevin was being threatening or Julie was being hyperbolic. But it was powerful TV.

After that clash, production hired a security guard. In the decades since, Julie and Kevin have made amends; like the rest of the cast, they became part of a group text chain. Back in 1992, after the argument in the house, Kevin felt angry, he said, but mostly, he felt endangered, "profoundly victimized," by the accusation that he'd thrown something. "At that moment, I felt like Bigger Thomas in *Native Son*, like I'm just doomed to the gallows."[*]

Heather, who was Julie's best friend and also the one other Black person in the house, had felt little sympathy for Kevin's behavior in 1992. "I was just like, 'Yo, why are you so serious about everything? This is not the place and the platform.'" Decades later, she thought

---

[*] A few months after these interviews, the cast filmed a reunion special for Paramount+. That filming sparked its own racial clash, only this time, the polarities were reversed: When Kevin called Becky out for white privilege, Becky walked out of the filming, complaining that she felt entrapped. This time, everyone else was on Kevin's side.

her reaction had missed the mark. "He was a twenty-five-year-old professor and he was dealing with so much more stuff than I knew about. And he was frustrated, the same way that people are frustrated now. I didn't understand it and I didn't *want* to understand it, because I was in party mode." Kevin was angry, she said, "and sometimes, you don't know where to put that anger. But he was not wrong for feeling that way."

IN ICY MID-MARCH, BUNIM AND MURRAY CAME UP WITH A NEW plan: While Faraldo stayed in New York with the guys, Verschoor flew the three women down to Jamaica, to the Hedonism II resort. The producers hoped to spark some kind of vacation hookup—or, at the very least, to film bikinis instead of down jackets. Instead, they wound up capturing a *different* kind of drama, one involving Becky, the cast's stylish Suzanne Vega–esque singer-songwriter. Viewers were alerted to the scandal through a witty edit, in which a plane was shown lifting off, heading back to New York—and then freezing in midair, to a voiceover from Becky explaining, sheepishly, "Well, one thing *did* happen." Then there was a cut to a paparazzi-like shot of Becky and Bill Richmond canoodling on a sailboat, along with a scribbled arrow and the words, "Bill, Ex-*Real World* Director."

For viewers watching MTV, the fling between a cast member and a crew member seemed to come out of nowhere. In reality, there was a dramatic backstory: A few days into the trip, Verschoor arranged for the cast to go to a local reggae festival, driving everyone to a nearby town, at night, in a small pickup truck. At first, the cast members had fun, dancing and eating jerk chicken. Soon, however, they began to draw hostile stares. Several strapping local band managers strode over, clearly unhappy that MTV had been filming their concert for free. They demanded that Verschoor give them $20,000.

When Verschoor said he didn't have the money, the situation got tense, fast. The crew yelled for the girls to jump into the truck and lie down flat—and they all screeched away, pursued by the band managers, who (depending on who is telling the story) may or may not have had guns. "They chased us all the way back into the resort and

threatened our lives—they scared the hell out of all of us," said Verschoor. Becky was pissed, convinced that Verschoor had caused the
problem. "George hoisted that camera and turned on the sun-gun
and *blam,* me and Julie and Heather were just spotlighted." She remembered Heather yelling for them to lower their heads as Verschoor
tossed cash from the truck, while she and Julie laughed hysterically,
still holding chicken bones. In retrospect, Heather told me that she
found the whole drama a bit ridiculous: "I mean, of course the pro-
moters wanted to be paid. . . . Just *pay* them."

Back at Hedonism, Becky felt shaken up and worried that the
band managers would come after them—there wasn't much security,
just a fence out front. Verschoor was in the lobby, speaking with the
cops. Becky didn't want to be alone, so rather than go back to her
own room, she went to Bill Richmond's room. Richmond heard a
knock—and when he opened the door, neither he nor Becky spoke.
Instead, they went to bed together, in total silence. When he woke
up, Richmond stared up at the ceiling, where there was a mirror that
reflected their bodies. His first thought was *I just wrote the next episode.* His second thought was that he'd lost his job.

The affair didn't stay secret for long. When Verschoor went to the
bar with his director of photography, they found his cast member
and his director kissing. Both men froze, uncertain how to react.
"Then we both said, 'Go get the camera,'" said Verschoor. Becky
and Bill's flirtation wasn't entirely new—it had started back in New
York, during those hangouts at Gonzalez y Gonzalez. It also wasn't
the only workplace romance on *The Real World*: Richmond had
dated other MTV employees, among them Tracy Grandstaff, the
"Julie" from the pilot, who joked that he was "a serial dater." Housemate Andre—who described himself as being in a "very noncommit-
tal" phase during the show—hooked up with crew members, too.

Becky was the only one whose fling became a plot point. The way
she viewed the situation, she was being slut-shamed by MTV puri-
tans, who had cast her as the whore to Julie's virgin. She didn't blame
Bill—and although she spoke up in his defense, he got fired. Instead,
she put the blame on Bunim and Murray, who Faraldo had once told

her had compared her to Annette Bening's character in *The Grifters,* a manipulative seducer. When they got back to New York, Becky found herself acting out, intoxicated by screw-you defiance. "I thought, maybe Middle America needs a dose of sexuality. Either you're a little squeaky-clean Jennifer Aniston or you're the deep-throat girl. You can't get a natural girl who's okay with her body."

Murray was proud that he managed, amid this chaos, to produce the perfect voiceover from Becky—her sheepish, amused quip: "I literally sucked Bill through the fourth wall." In retrospect, leaving aside any questions about workplace sexual dynamics, the story does raise one obvious issue: Why on earth did a show that was desperate for drama not include the story about a gun-toting car chase in Jamaica? Murray told me they didn't include it because there was no footage and the story was more about the band managers than the cast. Julie brought up a more cynical theory: Maybe MTV didn't want Hedonism to look bad, since they'd gotten the trip for free.

WHEN NORM KORPI SIGNED UP FOR *THE REAL WORLD*, HE WAS excited, imagining the show as a fun, even somewhat avant-garde experiment, like an MTV twist on Biosphere 2, the 1991 project in which a bunch of people were confined in an Arizona research facility. He hadn't told his Italian Catholic parents that he dated men yet, and after he joined the cast, he wavered about how "out" to be. On the one hand, Norm wanted to show queer viewers that "your life isn't going to be some miserable, nasty thing." On the other, he worried about exposing his younger sister to bullying. A designer and video artist, Norm knew Lance Loud, who was part of the downtown Warhol arts scene, and when he imagined being "out," it was in the same way Lance had been out, way back in 1973: implicitly queer, perceived primarily through his talent and taste, with his charisma his calling card.

The show's creators struggled to respond to Norm's uncertainty about just how "out" he wanted to be—and from Norm's perspective, the fact that Jon Murray himself was gay didn't help. Although

Murray would go on to raise a child with his long-term partner, Harvey, and become a philanthropist for gay causes, at the time the show was filming, the producer—like most other gay men in his industry, including his own agent—was discreet about his sexuality. Murray lived with Harvey; he brought him to parties. But although Bunim dropped hints to Norm ("You know Jon, he's like you"), the way the cast members remember the situation, it all felt coded, rather than explicit. Or as Julie put it, "I didn't know that he *wasn't* gay."

The result was a clash of perspective: Although Norm had warm relationships with his housemates, he was an impossible interview, a "dyslexic monster," in his own words, who gave long, rambling answers, evading Murray's questions. He refused to "come out" in a sentence. He refused to invite his parents to the loft. If Murray had imagined anything like a 1990s reboot of Pat Loud's visit to Lance at the Chelsea (he says he didn't), Norm wasn't going to deliver it.

Ultimately, however, Norm *did* come out to his family—or at least he spoke with them on the phone about the fact that he would be "out" on TV, an experience that Faraldo remembers as a low point of her job. The call got recorded but never aired. Norm *did* end up dating a man on *The Real World* (the future talk show host Charles Perez) and they kissed, on the air—a major TV breakthrough, especially given that *Melrose Place*, one of the rare network shows with a gay character, would lose advertisers two years later when they planned to air a scene with two men kissing.

Still, when the season aired, Norm was labeled as bisexual, a choice that satisfied no one. Julie remembers Murray approaching her for a clarifying voiceover. "The game was that you had to answer everything back in a complete sentence. And the question was 'What are your thoughts about Norman's bisexuality?'"Julie said. She had hesitated—and the way she remembered it, Murray told her that this was her chance to put the topic in perspective. Worried that if she didn't offer up a positive spin, Norm might get a negative one, she delivered. Murray told me that Julie misremembered the interaction: He said Mary-Ellis Bunim was the one who did that interview with Julie, which he knew because he'd rewatched the tapes in preparation for the for the 2021 series *Reunion: Homecoming.* He also added that because Norm was "open about being gay/bisexual," it wasn't an inappropriate question to ask.

Decades later, Norm looked back on the experience with frustration. In the early 1990s, gay men often viewed male bisexuality as a cop-out—a fake identity on the road to Gaysville. Gay journalists like Michael Musto, who had initially embraced him, gave him the cold shoulder when the show came out; he wound up feeling less like a pioneer than a footnote. Two seasons later, when Bunim/Murray cast Pedro Zamora, a young gay Cuban American who had HIV, Pedro would often be described as the first gay man to appear on reality television.

ALAN COHN EDITED SEVEN EPISODES OF *THE REAL WORLD* AND supervised the other six. Following the model he'd innovated for the pilot, he filled it with quick cuts, Dutch angles, and bold, ironic, and occasionally wacky music cues. Among his co-editors was the Ukrainian-born Oskar Dektyar, who had edited the Russian version of *Cops*. Dektyar was a true romantic about art, but he wasn't a cinéma vérité purist. Assigned to deliver a romance between Julie and Eric, he hunted through seventy hours of film, foraging for chemistry. One day, he found the ideal sequence: Eric slurping spaghetti off Julie's plate, scored to "I'm Too Sexy," by Right Said Fred. As if he were constructing fan fiction, he built a playful montage of the two falling for each other, with shots of Eric making cow eyes at Julie, then cuddling a kitten. After he completed the sequence, he walked out to the parking lot, dancing with exhilaration.

From the beginning, the editors understood who their star was: Julie Oliver, making friends from diverse backgrounds. In the first episode, Julie flew to New York, gazing out the window, and then viewers saw a flashback: Julie fighting with her old-fashioned father. When Cohn edited in the preacher's sermon, he added the melodic throb of "Personal Jesus" by Depeche Mode. When Julie's cab drove through Harlem, he used the Guns N' Roses song "Welcome to the Jungle." In the next scene, when Julie showed up last at the loft, Heather's beeper went off. Julie asked her new housemate, playfully,

"Do you sell drugs? Why do you have a beeper?" The editors added a musical sting—and then a freeze-frame, providing an instant cliff-hanger. The implicit question: Was Julie a *racist*?

Julie and Eric's flirtation—which didn't exist, according to everyone involved, including Julie and Eric—became the central plot of the season. But everyone got their moment, in small, satisfying stories about Norm going roller-skating or Heather recording a rap song about date rape. The truth is, even three decades later, the first season of *The Real World* remains absurdly charming to rewatch, driven as it is by the naïveté of its attractive cast, who lounge around their SoHo loft wearing clown hats and cowrie beads, obsessively analyzing their own level of "realness." Heather mocks Eric as a phony, fascinated by his own image; Andre speaks earnestly about wanting his band to be authentic. In a late episode, the group plays a prank on Kevin by swapping personalities, only to have Kevin take them seriously, worried that Julie—who purrs "sex sells" at him in crimson lipstick—had been corrupted by MTV. It's a time capsule of a lost generation, consumed by the ultimate horror: selling out.

During the final episode, the housemates break into the control room, seize the cameras, and point them at the crew—it was a meta-episode that doubled as a celebration of the production. Each talking-head interview emphasized the purity of the project. "There was nothing set up. We were all very much real about everything! We didn't think about the cameras after, probably, like, the first week," said Becky, looking festive in pink lipstick and a gray power blazer. In the background, her housemates horsed around, pretending to have a threesome, the kind of outrageous hookup their producers had hoped for all along.

Shortly after filming ended, on May 18, the cast of *The Real World* gathered with MTV executives and the crew to watch the first episode on a small monitor at the loft. They were flabbergasted. "We were really hung up on—it sounds stupid now—but how *inaccurate* it was. 'That's not what Day Two was!'" said Julie. Norm fumed as he absorbed the show's goofy visual jokes—a schlock aesthetic, he thought. Andre felt sick watching himself speak earnestly about his music. Becky was less upset than she was "philosophically angered," she told me: She could see that the show was "fluff."

Eric, who was about to begin a career as an MTV dance host, was less upset. And Heather found the pilot episode downright funny and cool. "I know how storyline works," she said. Meanwhile, Verschoor was over the moon. "Watching them watch themselves was just another groundbreaking moment for all of us, too . . . seeing them witness how their lives were compressed into a three-act structure—and how they were elevated to TV stars, really."

That screening would become a Bunim/Murray tradition: Whenever filming ended, the cast always watched the first episode—a cathartic moment, but also, a moment that let them purge their emotions, everything that pissed them off, before it aired. Murray compared the process to bringing astronauts back from space. The *Real World* casts always had the same gripes, he said. "They'd say, 'We had that really good discussion of homelessness!' We knew that if people wanted to watch that, they'll watch CNN."

THE REAL WORLD DEBUTED ON MTV ON MAY 21. IT OPENED WITH a gorgeous credit sequence put together by an indie film producer named Lauren Zalaznick, a sequence designed to establish the premise of the show as efficiently as did the theme song from *Gilligan's Island*. In it, colorful images of the seven housemates alternated with moody black-and-white images of New York City, a jittery montage of iconic spots from CBGB to the World Trade Center. As each housemate's face appeared on screen, their voice said a phrase, building a sentence: "This is the true story (True story!) of seven strangers picked to live in a loft (*guitar pluck*) and have their lives taped (*snare drum*) to find out what happens (What?) when people stop being polite (Could you get the phone?) and start getting real." Then, "*The Real World.*"

Critical response was mixed. In *The New York Times*, John J. O'Connor joked about the dizzy editing, but praised the show as both emotionally affecting and more authentic than a soap opera.

"There are no writers here who can manipulate incidents with a flip of a word processor." On the other extreme was *The Washington Post*'s Tom Shales, who condemned the *Real World* cast as a bunch of slackers: "Ah to be young, cute and stupid, and to have too much free time," he wrote, sneering that the cast should "get a real job."

Luckily, the show's target audience wasn't cranky boomers. It quickly became a hit—and at $107,000 per episode, with a soundtrack that MTV got for free, it was a bargain. The first night it aired, *The Real World* tripled MTV's audience in the prime-time 10 P.M. slot. *Entertainment Weekly* and the *New York Times* Arts section featured the show in splashy spreads. That summer, MTV aired weekend marathons of the whole season, a scheduling innovation that sent the ratings soaring. Like the Louds, two decades earlier, *The Real World* housemates were suddenly globally, destabilizingly, mind-bendingly famous.

The Video Music Awards, that September, were a revelatory night for every member of the cast. They knew their show was popular, but they were also aware of something else: Plenty of people at MTV saw the network's hottest hit as extremely uncool—and worse, as a threat, a tacky fill-in that was sure to displace MTV's music programming. Norm had made angry calls to network brass on the group's behalf, pushing for star treatment. When they walked down the red carpet, it felt like a vindication. "They screamed like we were The Beatles," said Kevin, who was handed Hershey's Kisses to toss to the crowd full of celebrities and fans. Even weirder, the stars recognized *them*. Magic Johnson ambled over to Heather, saying, "Oh, I know y'all!"

Norm felt exhilarated. Then, at the after-party, he had a brief interaction that soured the glamour: A drunk advertising executive confided in him that having a gay man in the cast made it harder to sell ads. Norm spun out, emotionally—and he wasn't alone. With the possible exception of Eric—whom MTV had hired to be the MC of a dance show called *Hangin' w/MTV*—each housemate was having a hard time adjusting to their new circumstances. Part of the problem was emotional, part financial. It was the reality paradox that would, in later years, became endemic: They were superstars, but without the paycheck or social protection that usually accompanied mind-blowing celebrity. Each cast member had earned $2,600, with the first half paid out weekly to cover expenses. They understood so little about marketing and product integration, someone had to explain that they should wear their free Levis—the company was a sponsor.

For a while, Julie took a day job at Viacom, the same company that had turned her into a household name, where she sneakily dug up the cast's fan mail, which had been kept from them. (Julie had always had a spy's impulses: In the loft, she dug through the trash near the control room, looking for hints about the producers' plans.) When she tried going to dance auditions, she was dismissed as "Julie from *The Real World*." After a brief spell out west, where she roomed with Norm—who had a big home in Los Angeles, where cast members often crashed—she went back to Alabama to care for her parents. She got married; she had kids. She didn't feel ripped off, exactly: Even at nineteen, Julie had known that the MTV contract (which she passed to a family friend, a lawyer) was a bad deal. She had signed it, anyway. She had to, if she wanted the adventure.

Two years after the debut of *The Real World*, the movie *Reality Bites* was released. The first film directed by Ben Stiller, *Reality Bites* was a Gen X romantic comedy, which satirized *The Real World*, just as Albert Brooks's *Real Life* had once roasted *An American Family*. The movie's heroine was Lelaina (Winona Ryder), a recent college grad who films a cinéma vérité documentary about her friends, only to have it co-opted by In Your Face, an MTVish cable network. In the end, Lelaina chooses the guy who knows the meaning of the word "irony" over a sweet cable executive—and, implicitly, artistic purity over compromised success. A meditation on the horrors of selling out, the movie was also a bit of an inside job for the MTV community, since it was directed by an MTV comedy star and studded with other MTV talent. *Real World: Los Angeles* cast members played extras in the scene when Lelaina storms out of her own screening, horrified that her film has Dutch angles. Lauren Corrao's husband, Jim Jones, who had directed the *Real World* pilot, produced the movie; Lelaina's best friend was played by Janeane Garofalo, a cast member from *The Ben Stiller Show.* More than one MTV employee—among them Danielle Faraldo, although she never saw *Reality Bites*—wondered if Lelaina was based on them.

In reality, Lelaina was a stand-in for Helen Childress, an earnest, twenty-three-year-old Noam Chomsky devotee who had written the screenplay in college, inspired not by MTV or *The Real World* but by OK Soda, a cola brand that had been cynically marketed to Gen X. Making *Reality Bites* was a learning experience for Childress, one that involved its own set of compromises, all of which led Childress to a Lelainaish breakdown—a meta moment that she looked back on, decades later, with amused chagrin.* The rest of Generation X had a similarly polemical reaction to the movie: During one preview screening, the audience booed as soon as they saw the United Artists logo.

Real World cast member Andre Comeau attended a screening of *Reality Bites,* but walked out partway through, recoiling "as if burned." Andre, who was as much of a Gen X purist as Faraldo, had had one of the strongest negative reactions to the show's debut. He cut his hair, broke up with his girlfriend, and dropped out of his heavy metal band. He changed genres, to folk music. Years later, Andre was doing fine: He was a married music executive with a child, and didn't want to sound whiny—he'd long ago come to terms with the show's legacy. But he did find it irresponsible that MTV hadn't offered the cast any counseling. Part of the problem with reality fame was having trusted the producers in the first place, absorbing their praise, he pointed out: If you hated your portrayal, you had to confront the fact that maybe your "puppet masters" hadn't cared about you, after all.

Not everyone had regrets. For Heather, *The Real World* had been

---

* Childress sold the screenplay, then collaborated with Stiller, improvising dialogue as they changed his character from an ad executive to an MTV-ish bigwig. By the time the movie debuted, however, she was as disenchanted as Danielle Faraldo: Her pet project felt less like a scathing attack on capitalism and more like "gentle teasing"—and what's more, it was being marketed by MTV. Childress was "a real downer" during the press tour, she said, laughing. "It seems very jejune now, Lelaina's anger. Honestly, the way I reacted to the actual movie is the way she reacted to the show. I thought, 'I'll take a stand. Write a novel. Say, This is all bullshit!' You had to be twenty-three to feel that way. . . . It's almost endearing to think of what we were worried about."

nothing but a sweet, youthful adventure—in part, she said, because the hip-hop community didn't reject her the way the rock world did Andre, her close friend. Hip-hop was more comfortable with self-promotion, she thought. Her one regret echoed Kevin Loud's, from *An American Family:* She had wanted there to be a second season, starring the whole cast. MTV had considered the idea of putting Julie, Eric, and Heather together in a Winnebago, a plan that fell apart. "It should have been all of us," she said.

THE FIRST SEASON OF *THE REAL WORLD* WAS A UNIQUELY INNO-cent experience, for both its cast and crew. From then on, the young people who signed up to appear on MTV might get hurt, but they understood what the show was. That was the catch-22 of the reality genre: The savvier its subjects became, the more self-aware about their roles, the less authentic the footage was—but, arguably, the more ethical.

Bunim/Murray became more professional, too. The company moved into fancy new digs, which were paid for by MTV; they hired a story-editing department and bought modern Avid editing consoles; they went on a hiring spree, training a new generation of reality crew workers. By season 2, much of the original creative team had left the show. After the season 1 wrap party, Faraldo had one last argument with Murray about Norm's portrayal, then never came back. Alan Cohn filmed two episodes of *The Real World: Los Angeles,* then never watched the show again. ("Maybe half an episode," he said.) The final straw was the day he pointed his camera at a cast member holding a copy of *Spin* magazine that featured a cover story about *The Real World*—it was all getting way too meta for him.*

---

* That *Spin* article included dismissive quotes from legendary documentarian Albert Maysles. After he read it, Cohn called his filmmaking hero up. "I had stolen a book about the movie *Salesman* from my college library, so I *knew* some stuff," Cohn said, jokingly. "I said to Maysles, 'I'm taking your stuff and sugarcoating it for an audience today, who you may think is dumber, but the truth is, they're taking in a hundred times more information per second than you were dishing out.' Which has pluses and minuses, obviously." Maysles hadn't even watched *The Real World,* as it turned out. He said that he'd call Cohn back—and forty-five minutes later, he did, saying, "Hey, you know what? I see what you're doing here."

Lauren Corrao left after the second season, too, put off by the fame-hungry new cast. Verschoor acted as showrunner for three more seasons, which were set in Los Angeles, San Francisco, and London. Along the way, he helped pioneer crucial elements of the format, particularly the confessional: a closet that was equipped with a sofa and a video camera, so cast members could retreat, then talk directly into the camera, without having to interact with any camera operators. It was a public space that everyone pretended was a private space, a better metaphor than that fish tank in SoHo.

Verschoor also managed to oversee the rare season of reality television to get near-universal acclaim: *The Real World: San Francisco*. By then, the *Real World* casting process had evolved, as had the people who applied for the show. Many of the people who sent in videotapes—in particular, the season's hero, the warmhearted Cuban American AIDS activist Pedro Zamora, and its villain, the crusty street punk David "Puck" Rainey—had a strong sense of what they were getting into. It was the first reality show to succeed not due to the cast's naïveté but because of their sophistication, their eagerness to collaborate with the people who were filming them.

At twenty-one, Pedro had already gone through multiple traumas: When he was eight, he'd escaped to Miami on the Mariel boatlift, and his mother died when he was thirteen. At fourteen, Pedro came out as gay to his Catholic family, and then, at seventeen, he found out after donating blood that he was HIV positive—he'd never gotten any safe-sex education. When a fellow AIDS activist encouraged him to apply to *The Real World,* Pedro quickly grasped the show's potential, hoping to harness his warmth and charisma to personalize the disease for MTV's young viewers. By the time he died, the day after the finale aired, this tragic calculation had paid off. His death inspired national grieving, with President Clinton delivering a video eulogy at his service, calling him "a member of all of our families." For many viewers, Pedro Zamora would become the first gay man, and the first person with AIDS, that they'd known intimately.

Still, the season likely wouldn't have worked without Pedro's nemesis, the tattooed street courier Puck, whom the cast initially assumed was the member with HIV (he'd arrived fresh from jail, his face coated in scabs). From the start, the cast befriended one another: Cory, a sweet white UCSD student from Fresno; Rachel, a flirty Mexican American Republican Catholic; Judd, a warm, nerdy Jewish cartoonist from New York (cast over the writer Dave Eggers, who was eliminated because the crew worried that he would punk them); Pam, a Chinese American med student with a red skunk-stripe in her hair; and Mohammed, a Black local musician with a Cheshire cat grin. All of them were open, liberal-minded, and eager to learn about one another—except for Puck.

In one of the purer metaphors for societal dysfunction ever to air on television, Puck blew snot rockets and made fun of Pedro, even as Pedro's T cells dropped. He undermined every diplomatic gesture the roommates made, burning down every bridge they built. A few weeks into filming, there was a showdown. It was a perfect payoff for Murray's original vision of the show: While season 1 had been rocked when the cast united against the producers, in San Francisco, they clashed with *one another,* creating a three-act drama that felt as rich and layered as any fictional script.

Unsurprisingly, the housemates chose Pedro over Puck. Even after Puck was expelled from the house, however, the MTV cameras continued to follow him, making him the first reality TV character to lean into the "villain edit." His bratty antics were contrasted with the season's more heartwarming plots, among them, a love story—and marriage—between Pedro and his boyfriend, Sean Sasser, as well as Judd's sweet crush on Pam, who had a boyfriend. Not everyone was okay with MTV's final edit: Judd, for one, felt frustrated that Puck came off, on the air, as a charming rascal, not the man he knew, whom he describes as a bigoted creep who wore a swastika T-shirt.* Judd and Pam, who got married in 2001, became the keep-

---

* MTV VJ Kennedy, for one, agrees: In her memoir, she describes Puck ruining her family's Christmas by wearing lederhosen to their Greek Orthodox church, throwing a shoe at her broken arm, and ultimately breaking down when her family imitated scenes from *The Real World.* "I blame him for everything. Ever. Even the Kardashians are his fault," she wrote.

ers of Pedro's legacy. In 2000, Judd wrote a lovely graphic novel called *Pedro and Me*, an homage to their friend's life. They still live in San Francisco, raising two children who aren't allowed to use social media.

After Verschoor left *The Real World*, he kept in touch with many former cast members, as well as with Bunim and Murray, for whom he felt intense gratitude, as mentors who had helped him launch a career in a brand-new TV genre. Julie, Heather, and Norm went to Verschoor's wedding; he considered them family, he said. He knew there were housemates who felt burned by their experience, either exploited or misrepresented. (Becky had once yelled that he was "a used-car salesman.") But Verschoor's memories were mainly fond ones, of the show's sweetness, back when they had heatedly debated ethics at Gonzalez y Gonzalez. "It was the early days of rock and roll, right? Where is the music going to take us? What's more important, selling records or being true to your musical roots? Yeah, it was fun."

IN THE YEARS THAT FOLLOWED, BUNIM/MURRAY WOULD BECOME a powerhouse institution, producing influential experiments like *Making the Band*; early "celebreality" shows like *The Simple Life*; and the Brentwood game-changer *Keeping Up with the Kardashians*. Their agent Mark Itkin—who had brokered a smart deal for them, which let them control their own franchises—would become one of reality TV's top power brokers. Over the years, Bunim enjoyed mentoring new employees, bringing them into the business, although she sometimes had a certain brutality of method when it came to layoffs. "She even looked at firing someone as a story," Murray told me, fondly.

In 1995, the company launched a travel-oriented spin-off of *The Real World: Road Rules*, which replaced the house with a traveling RV. In 1998, they debuted *Real World/Road Rules Challenge*, a crossover competition show that starred old cast members from both shows. In 2010, *that* show became *The Challenge*. Year by year, the Bunim/Murray project had evolved, in Darwinian stages, into a hard-core extreme-sports competition—a kind of soap opera Thunder-dome, bigger, wilder, and far more aggressive than anything that had come before. The show that was rebranded *The Challenge* bore little resemblance to that earnest miked-up loft back in SoHo. But by then, a different type of personality dominated the franchise: preening, hot-bodied stars whose explicit ambition was to market themselves as brands, with space for ads on their T-shirts and biceps. The Gen X fetish for authenticity had shriveled away, as defunct as the desire for Zima.

Although Bunim's work had helped usher in an era of personal revelation, she kept her own life private. In 2004, when Bunim died of breast cancer at fifty-seven, few people knew she was ill. Murray knew, of course: When they met with Paris Hilton, Bunim hid her oxygen tanks under the table, and the partners had a signal in case Bunim needed to stop. Her memorial service, on a beautiful hilltop, was attended by cast members from many seasons of *The Real World*. After the ceremony, Millee Taggart-Ratcliffe, who knew Bunim from their days working in soap operas, praised her to me as an honest person in an industry that had always been devoted to superficiality and surfaces. "She wasn't nicer than she was, and she didn't have a phony bone in her body. She didn't apologize for it. And she was always about the story, about the journey. She was always about making it better."

As proud as Jon Murray was of his legacy, his voice took on an edge when he spoke about the years of condescension from his Hollywood peers, the people who had looked down on the genre he'd helped build from scratch. He knew that some people would always see reality production as "a dirty thing." But although he had a few regrets—like the night vision cameras he'd put in the *Real World* bedrooms in Chicago, the ones that had captured graphic footage of a character having sex, footage he'd later cut out of the reruns—he made no apologies. He'd saved more cast members from making fools of themselves than he'd hurt, he said. The way he saw it, his biggest accomplishment wasn't helping to invent a new kind of television, it was creating a new type of viewer. For the generation who had grown up with *The Real World,* reality TV wasn't a compromise, some crummy stopgap when scripted TV wasn't available.

Reality was what they preferred.

Thinking back on his relationship with the new generation, Murray described sitting at a conference table, years earlier, surrounded by Annie Leibovitz–style shots of the Denver season's cast. Set in massive frames, the images looked like movie stars, although nobody knew who these people were, not yet. As producers brainstormed about potential stories, Murray would gesture up to the pictures. "I would say, 'You know, their eyes are watching us.'"

6

||||||

THE CON

The Nihilistic Fox '90s

MIKE DARNELL GOT HIS JOB AT THE FOX NETWORK THE OLD-fashioned way: He stalked Barry Diller, then sent him a self-destructing briefcase.

The day we met in early 2020, Darnell wore his trademark uniform: a mop of wild curls, shredded jeans, a denim jacket, and dangling silver necklaces, plus boots with stacked heels. A former child actor, he radiated a Tigger-like enthusiasm. Seated on couches all around us was his loyal work posse, including his wife, Carolyn, whom he'd met in middle school, when the two had split the role of Puck in a school production of *A Midsummer Night's Dream*. The office suite, on the Warner lot, felt more like a rec room, with an *American Idol* popcorn machine, a foosball table, and a pillow that read "Remember, as Far as Anyone Knows We Are a Nice Normal Family."

Darnell had first arrived in Hollywood as a kid, booking roles in 1970s sitcoms and ads, mostly mouthy ethnics, from Puerto Ricans to "tough Jews." The son of a cop who had retired when he got shot, Darnell grew up in Philadelphia. At ten, he won a singing contest, belting out "The Candy Man" at a police benefit. That gig got him a manager, and two years later, Darnell's family headed west, where

Darnell made a decent living, biking to Universal studios to do guest shots on *Kojak,* eating in the commissary with his "hotsy-totsy" mom. He was only an okay actor, but he had one significant advantage over his peers: He reached his full height at 5'2", which let him book gigs long after the other kids aged out.

At twenty, Darnell quit acting, knowing the odds were against him. His true passion wasn't performing, anyway: It was television itself—the stars, the money, the ratings, even the scheduling. Like Jon Murray, Darnell collected *TV Guide*s as if they were baseball cards. He memorized Top 10 lists; he studied the Nielsens as if they were sports statistics, betting on the winners. He was an omnivorous viewer, watching everything on the networks, including competition shows like *Star Search*, the kind of show that launched amateurs into fame, among them his high school classmate Brad Garrett.

Darnell studied business at California State University, Northridge, then angled for an internship at CBS's *Entertainment Tonight,* only to discover that it was scut work (his boss also mocked him for being unable to reach high-up shelves). In 1986, he jumped to the Los Angeles news station KTTV, which had recently been bought by Fox. He wound up in an offbeat job, working as the station librarian, a powerless role that consisted mostly of organizing tapes, but he felt certain that with enough hustle, he could make his way to the C-suites, which he was confident could use his help.

Instead, Darnell got stuck. For seven years, he ground his gears at KTTV, surrounded by hard-news anchors who condescended to him as a tacky chatterbox, lacking the chops to do real journalism. Darnell had always had his own idea of good television, his values having been shaped by his adolescence, which took place just as the line between news and entertainment was eroding like the California coastline. In 1980, the hottest local news show was *Eye on L.A.*, known to fans as "Thigh on L.A.," a show that churned out crass, outrageous stunts and contests, along with tabloid segments like "Inside Liberace's Closet" (a tour of his dry cleaning). Critics panned the format as sexist sleaze, but *Eye on L.A.* trounced the competition—at one point crushing a rival show's sweeps week documentary about the Philippines and forcing them to air their own bikini special. Darnell had similar ideas about what made good entertainment—and he remembers being fascinated by Geraldo Rivera's 1986 special *The Mystery of Al Capone's Vaults,* in which Rivera scored bonkers ratings while discovering nothing at all.

Crazy with frustration, Darnell had started slacking off at his job, dumping tapes into the trash instead of filing them, as he focused on a side hustle, a project called *Life After Reruns.* Somehow, he talked Burt Ward, the actor who played Robin on the TV version of *Batman,* into doing an interview. Siphoning off KTTV resources—an editor here, a cameraman there—Darnell created a clip, which he showed to everyone he ran into, from his bosses to the janitor. And then, finally, Darnell had a stroke of good luck: In 1989, Tim Burton's *Batman* movie came out—and the station needed material to cover it. With admirable chutzpah, Darnell agreed to let his bosses air *Life After Reruns,* but only if they kept his voice in the narration. The miracle arrived just in time: He'd just had another screaming fight with a higher-up when he heard that he'd been promoted. Fox president Barry Diller had liked his *Batman* piece.

In his new role as a news producer, Darnell designed segments that only a truly TV-scrambled mind would invent, like a piece accusing *Beverly Hills, 90210* of stealing the concept of sideburns from *The Beverly Hillbillies.* He used his camera like a paparazzo, recording snatches of celebrity conversations at movie screenings for a segment called "Overheard." Still, his main goal was to get Diller to notice him again—and eventually, at an *L.A. Story* premiere, he pulled it off by jumping out from behind an escalator, getting Diller and his girlfriend Diane von Fürstenberg to laugh and praise his guts.

This small interaction was enough to encourage Darnell to follow through with a truly cockamamie scheme. On a Panasonic tape recorder, Darnell recorded a message: First, the *Mission: Impossible* music, then Darnell's own voice, intoning the words, "Good evening, Mr. Diller." Darnell explained that he wanted to work at Fox. The message ended with "This tape or my career will self-destruct in five seconds." He taped an arrow to the play button, hid the recorder in

a briefcase, and bribed a parking attendant to pass it to Diller. After
an anxious weekend, his phone rang. It was the Fox president, asking
Darnell what kind of job he wanted.

IN 1994, DARNELL BECAME FOX'S "HEAD OF SPECIALS," WORKING
under vice president of specials Bob Bain. He oversaw glitzy spec-
taculars, like a rock 'n' roll skating special featuring Olympic skaters
Nancy Kerrigan and Oksana Baiul. He was also assigned to oversee
Encounters: The Hidden Truth, a magazine show that featured segments about crop circles, ghosts, and Bigfoot. By the mid-1990s,
paranormal series had become a core programming focus for Fox, a
creative cycle that had begun back in 1992 with the success of the
quasi-documentary series *Sightings,* a show that, in turn, had inspired the scripted series *The X-Files* in 1993, with its pair of FBI
investigators, the open-minded Mulder and the skeptical Scully. *Encounters,* like *Sightings,* presented itself as a form of investigative
journalism, but it hovered on the line between real and fake, which
had always been Darnell's sweet spot.

It was also an entertainment model with deep roots, one that
went back to the spiritualism craze of the nineteenth century, when
scammers had hosted séances for wealthy women and hucksters sold
"spirit photography." In the 1840s, crowds had swarmed to P. T. Barnum's American Museum to see his big breakthrough, the Fiji Mermaid, a hideous half-fish/half-monkey that he marketed to visitors
as a beautiful sea maiden. Now Darnell—Barnum's clearest spiritual
descendant—needed a Fiji Mermaid of his own.

One day, Robert Kiviat, the coordinating producer of *Encounters,* showed up in Bain's office. Kiviat was an old hand at tabloid TV,
having produced segments for Geraldo Rivera's splashy 1991 investigative news show *Now It Can Be Told.* He had also helped to inspire
David Duchovny's conspiracy-obsessed character, Fox Mulder, having grown up with *X-Files* producer Howard Gordan. Kiviat had an
astonishing find, he announced—a videotape of an alien autopsy
from 1947. He'd gotten the tape, which contained seventeen minutes
of black-and-white footage, from a British music producer named

Ray Santilli, who had, in turn, apparently stumbled across this shocking material at a rock 'n' roll archive in Cleveland, Ohio.

Bain wasn't impressed by this strange story, but Darnell's eyes lit up. After pitching multiple networks with the tape, Kiviat had gotten only one bite, at UPN, which insisted on a full investigation. Darnell wasn't so picky: Once Kiviat showed him a letter from Kodak, which verified that the film was from either 1947 or 1967, he was on board. His Fox colleagues were initially wary—CBS had just been embarrassed by a hoax show about Noah's Ark—but at the marketing meeting, Darnell laid out his strategy, which was pure Barnum: If they didn't say the footage was real, nobody could call it a lie. Bain agreed to go forward, although he told the room, "I want everybody to know this is all Mike's. I got nothing to do with it."

In 1995, *Alien Autopsy: Fact or Fiction?* became Darnell's first hit for Fox. Aesthetically speaking, the show was an artisanal blend of solemnity and hokum, broken up by moody shots of Roswell, New Mexico. Scientific experts inspected Kiviat's footage and then weighed in, with theatrical levels of ambiguity, on the question of whether the autopsy footage—in which a long gray creature was dismantled, section by section, like some paranormal salami—was a hoax. Prominent pathologist Cyril Wecht, who had reviewed JFK's autopsy, confirmed that whoever made the film certainly knew how to do an autopsy. Stan Winston, a major special effects specialist, marveled, with an open mind, "My hats are off to the people who created it *or* the poor alien who is dead on the table."

Fox Standards and Practices had laid down a few rules, forbidding Darnell to show the alien's head being cut up. Hilariously, they also insisted that he digitize the alien's genitals, despite the fact that the alien *had* no genitals. The editing only made the footage look dirtier, in the tradition of "censored censored censored" on *Candid Microphone.*

To read the narration for the show, Fox hired actor Jonathan Frakes, who had played the studly Commander Riker on *Star Trek: The Next Generation.* Frakes knew he wasn't their first choice, he told me. "Patrick [Stewart] turns all this shit down. . . ." he joked. "Because I'm such a whore, I took this, and the producer hired me for another couple of jobs." *Alien Autopsy* wound up steering Frakes into a fresh revenue stream as a narrator for paranormal shows, and in time, a starring role playing himself on the WB drama *Roswell*. With medium pride, he described *Alien Autopsy* as "if not the first of its kind, the first of its niche."

One thing about *Alien Autopsy* was undeniably authentic: the ratings. The show became the highest-rated Fox special in the history of the network, with a 25 share—the percentage of viewers watching TV that night who watched that show. Fox reran the special again and again, and by the second airing, nobody objected to Darnell showing the head cut open. It got the kind of reviews one might expect. "Tonight marks the third time Fox is televising its *Alien Autopsy* special, each time luring viewers with the promise of updates and unseen footage," wrote David Bianculli in the *Fort Worth Star-Telegram*. "By the time it's repeated for the 13th time, all the producers will be able to do that's new is to admit the first 12 showings were a hoax."

Bianculli might have been joking, but he'd pinpointed Darnell's business model. After the regular *Alien Autopsy* had worn out its welcome, Darnell simply repackaged the fraud as an exposé of the fraud, in the 1998 special *World's Greatest Hoaxes: Secrets Finally Revealed*, which was also directed, written, and produced by Robert Kiviat. Meanwhile, the original special had become a campy pop-culture reference on shows like *Seinfeld* and *The Simpsons*. It even inspired three separate episodes of *The X-Files*, among them the meta episode "Jose Chung's from Outer Space," which was about a made-up show called *Dead Alien! Truth or Humbug?*

It took a few years before the tangled backstory of *Alien Autopsy* emerged, or at least, became slightly detangled. In 2006, Ray Santilli admitted that he'd faked the autopsy—although he continued to claim he'd merely "reconstructed" the material, in order to replace *actual* footage of an alien autopsy, which was real but had deteriorated. This supposed "reconstruction" was performed by a British artist named John Humphreys, who'd worked on shows like *Doctor Who* and *Max Headroom*. Working in total secrecy, Humphreys had based the plaster cast for the alien model on his six-year-old son, then filled the cast with sheep brains set in jam, chicken entrails, and knuckle joints. Although he had no experience doing autopsies, he played the chief examiner in the video; a homeless man had played the cameraman.

These details were likely not a revelation to Fox, although good luck getting anyone's stories to match up, three decades later. In conversation, each participant made their own involvement sound innocent: Humphreys told me the art project was a favor he did for a friend, kept secret for a decade. Kiviat told me multiple contradictory things, at length, in circles, loudly, but mainly he emphasized that he was an investigative journalist who had always known that the footage might be a hoax, but also, that he believed it might have been real—and he hinted, during our last conversation, that sources from the Department of Defense had added to that impression.

The show's field director, John Jopson, was more straightforward. A music video director who also worked in theater, Jopson spent the mid-1990s working on paranormal shows as a side job, a "grubby" gig that had some enjoyable aspects, like filming crop circles. When he first saw the alien autopsy footage, he was genuinely impressed—until he flew to England and met Santilli, who struck him as obviously shady. Suspicious, Jopson sought out a private eye to investigate the story, only to have his boss, Kiviat, tell him to cut the Perry Mason act and finish the show. (Kiviat was furious when I asked him about Jopson's claims, calling Jopson a liar who was "working above his pay grade.")

Ironically, the next year, while filming a preview for the 1996 UPN show *The Paranormal Borderline*, Jopson *himself* wound up producing a paranormal hoax when he created convincing footage of a "Yeti" in a Himalayan snowstorm (actually, a man in a gorilla suit in Northern California). Looking back, Jopson was ambivalent about his years in "the hoax machine." He knew these shows were sold as entertainment; he understood that many viewers didn't care if they were real or not. Still, he felt guilty duping scientists. *The Paranormal Borderline* had had two teams of producers, he said: a "black team," which created the fakes, and another team that "investigated" them. In 1998, when the special *World's Greatest Hoaxes: Secrets*

Finally Revealed debuted, Jopson decided that he wanted to speak out, writing a letter detailing his attempts to warn Fox about *Alien Autopsy*. One sentence was in bold font: "It was then made clear to me that if the footage was exposed as a hoax, the ratings would suffer."

Alien Autopsy was less a reality show than a fake documentary that mimicked legitimate journalism, like the TV analogue to the *Weekly World News*. But it would wind up becoming the first draft of Fox's cable news model, with its emphasis on entertainment over reporting. The show's tone (high camp, low tabloid) and its subject matter (the spirit world, conspiracy theories) let its creators merge the serious and the silly in a way that made it hard to criticize. If the show you were watching was a joke, who cared if it was also a fake? Marketed correctly, these productions managed to be simultaneously authentic and phony, news and anti-news, without that feeling like any kind of contradiction.

More than a century earlier, P. T. Barnum, during his testimony at the trial of the spiritualist photographer William H. Mumler, had drawn just this kind of distinction. On the stand, Barnum didn't merely denounce Mumler, a scammer who sold fake photos of ghosts. He also argued that his work shouldn't be compared to Mumler's "spirit photos," which qualified as actual frauds, marketed by people who knew they were selling fakes. Barnum might not be certain that his exhibits were real, but he'd been told they were real—and maybe, he argued, he had even convinced himself.

Fox television trained its audience to adopt a similar attitude. Like Mulder, they should want to believe; like Scully, they could revel in their skepticism. That cynical credulity (or credulous cynicism) would become the defining quality of American culture, in the reality genre, on the news, and in politics. Shortly after the turn of the twenty-first century, a Manhattan hotel owner turned reality star would bank on it.

AFTER THE SUCCESS OF *ALIEN AUTOPSY*, DARNELL FELT LIBER-ated at Fox, gleefully panning for ratings gold in the rapids of outrage. His signature innovation was a variation on the "clip show" model, with titles like *When Animals Attack!*, *The World's Deadliest Swarms*, *When Good Pets Go Bad*, and *When Stunts Go Bad*. (He did a few cuddlier ones, too, like *The World's Most Incredible Animal Rescues*.) These specials were patched together from preexisting footage of piranha attacks and trucks blowing up, a secretary xeroxing her boobs or a chef licking his food, like a cruder, more graphic version of *America's Funniest Home Videos*—or, sometimes, like *Cops*, only cut together from the outtakes. Many of these specials were narrated with comic gravitas by an old colleague of Darnell's named Mark Thompson, a former weatherman from KTTV. Fox devotees found these compilations jaw-dropping and hilarious; their critics saw them as evidence of the collapse of Western civilization. The bad press, as ever, only goosed the ratings higher.

Reality TV production had always relied on low budgets, and strategically speaking, Darnell's approach had something in common with that of baseball impresario Billy Beane, who built winning teams using cheap, mediocre players. Instead of paying for expensive stunts, Darnell used footage filmed by news crews or surveillance cameras—the type of undervalued materials he'd thrown in the trash as a librarian at KTTV. The way he saw it, these shows were just like the tabloid news show *Dateline*, except that they cut the boring parts out. Titles were key, the bigger the better—although Darnell knew when to pivot, for pragmatic reasons. When he was warned that the title *World's Scariest Car Chases* might alienate automobile sponsors, Darnell changed it to *World's Scariest Police Chases*, transforming it from a show that car companies hated into one that cops loved.

In 1996, Darnell got a new boss, Peter Roth, who embraced his methods, as long as ratings were high. Only one show caught real flak—and, ironically, it was not an especially disgusting one, unless you were a David Blaine superfan. *Breaking the Magician's Code: Magic's Biggest Secrets Finally Revealed*, from 1997, was inspired by a night Darnell had spent at the private club the Magic Castle, where a magician refused to explain a trick, citing his "code." "That's not *my* code," Darnell thought—and he set out to make a series to "show that magic tricks are dumb." Magicians were outraged—and also, litigious. (Although every one of those lawsuits failed, Darnell emphasized.) His parents, who had always been his biggest boosters ("According to my mom, I should've gotten an Emmy for 'World's Scariest Police Chases 3,' okay?"), nearly had a brawl with a magician at a canasta night. Star illusionist (and *Seinfeld* star) Jason Alexander snubbed Darnell, who got banned from the Magic Castle.

Darnell also aired extreme-sports shows, including live motorcycle jumps by Robbie Knievel, the son of Evel Knievel, using a line of razzle-dazzle that any magician might envy. When a Grand Canyon shoot was canceled due to a freak snowstorm, Darnell insisted Knievel say nothing, as, on live TV, Mark Thompson vamped for an hour, delivering anxious weather reports and upbeat weather reports, and also repeated airings of a lurid cartoon animation of what might happen *if* the motorcycle crashed. Finally, Knievel canceled.

Darnell got angry letters, but he pointed his bosses to the ratings: The non-jump had gotten a 15 share, winning the night. When three weeks later, Knievel *did* jump the canyon successfully, he got the same rating. From Darnell's perspective, this was TV's primal creative act: scoring crazy ratings numbers and huge outrage, just like Geraldo at Capone's vault. He had his limits, but only a few: He wouldn't air a live execution. His epitaph, he once told a journalist, should be "However he died, he hopes someone caught it on video."

BY THE LATE 1990S, DARNELL WAS PRODUCING FIFTY TO SEVENTY specials per year. Like the man behind the Fiji Mermaid, he understood that part of the job was charming journalists. In 1999, Rick Kushman from *The Sacramento Bee*, who'd once denounced the Fox executive as the scourge of Western civilization, wrote a glowing profile, marveling at Darnell's childlike enthusiasm. "It's like pizza," Darnell told Kushman of his style of TV. "It doesn't matter what your SAT scores are or how much money you make, most people still like pizza." In 1998, Tom Vanderbilt became the rare critic to celebrate Darnell's magpie artistry, with a piece in *The New York Times* that drew a line between Darnell's clip shows and "the lengthier, character-driven vignettes of 'Cops,'" which had, in a decade, gone from young punk to respectable grandpa. Darnell had taken "the highlight sports reel, the all-climax porn compilation" and turned it into modern pop art, wrote Vanderbilt. "No matter what the footage, it is processed uniformly: a quick setup (location, players, motive), followed by a period of escalating tension (a hostage situation, a chase or foot pursuit, an approaching tornado or shark), finished off with a 'money shot' (a crash, an attack, or a rescue). And then, if possible, a lesson." Vanderbilt quoted Paul Stojanovich, a producer on both *Cops* and *World's Scariest Police Chases*, on the production's philosophy: "It's a quantity show."

There were setbacks along the way. In 1998, Fox pulled Darnell's *Prisoners Out of Control*, about violent prison rioting, off the air; *The World's Most Embarrassing Throw-up Moments* never aired, not because it was gross, but because too many clips were reenactments. Like Barris, Darnell had a few dream projects he never got off the ground, sometimes literally, as with *Space Jump*, a plan to take a man up in a weather balloon, then parachute him into a free fall.

He was also making enemies—among them his new boss at Fox, Sandy Grushow, who became chairman of Fox Entertainment in 1999. At competing networks, top executives regularly laid into Darnell, swearing they'd never copy his trashy hits—until they did. In 1996, NBC West Coast president Don Ohlmeyer called Darnell's clip shows "one step short of a snuff film." In 1997, he called them "the equivalent of auto-accident programming." In 1999, just before Scott Sassa replaced Ohlmeyer as president, Ohlmeyer bought *World's Most Amazing Videos* from Bruce Nash, the Fox producer who had worked as one of Darnell's steady partners.

In the first episode of that show, a man stuck his head up an elephant's ass, a clip that Darnell told me he'd never been able to get Fox to air. (NBC did, however, remove the *squish* sound effect.) By then, Darnell's influence felt inescapable, with echoes even on uptight PBS, which produced a show called *Escape! Because Accidents Happen*. Like *Eye on L.A.*, Darnell had shoved the Overton window wide open, forcing his competitors to program leather bikinis.

III

WITH THE TURN OF THE MILLENNIUM ON THE HORIZON, DARNELL had become the new Barry Diller, a powerful network mentor who could make your career, if you could just grab his attention. Sure enough, a TV-loving striver was angling for his sight line. The way Mike Fleiss tells the story, he met Darnell when, while helping his boss Bruce Nash pitch a format for *Breaking the Magician's Code*, he went rogue, impressing Darnell with the nastiness of his spiel. (Nash has denied this, saying the pitch was always designed to be nasty.) The two Mikes synced instantly, Fleiss told me, sounding like a giddy contestant on *The Bachelor,* the franchise he'd go on to create. "It was one of those moments where you realize you're not alone. There's another guy like you! It was wonderful. I saw him there at Fox, this little tiny man with a big office, and I fucking *loved* him. I would have done anything for him."

A chubby stoner who had grown up in Fullerton, California, Fleiss was the son of a nurse and a father whose career had been sidelined by epilepsy (and yes, Fleiss is also related to Hollywood madam Heidi Fleiss: He's her cousin). Like Darnell, he was a TV buff, a huge enough fan of TV producer Aaron Spelling—the creator of "jiggle TV" like *Charlie's Angels*—that he named his first son after him. In his twenties, Fleiss was a newspaper sportswriter, but a few years in, he got fired: He had been slacking off, blazing up and binging *The Simpsons* and *Married . . . with Children*. TV struck him as a much wilder, freer landscape than journalism—and when he stumbled on Howard Stern's short-lived cable show, which had sketches like "Guess Who's the Jew" and "The Lesbian Dating Game," it felt like a tractor beam, pulling him toward his home planet.

For a year, Fleiss was unemployed. Finally, in 1990, he landed an entry-level gig at Fox's *Totally Hidden Video*, a *Candid Camera* rip-off.*

---

* This was the same shoddy show that Allen Funt fumed about in his memoir—early on, the producers had faked stunts using paid actors.

The pay was $450 a week, to the disappointment of Fleiss's pregnant wife. But even in "the TV dregs," Fleiss was in heaven. He never got writer's block; asked to deliver five hidden-camera gags, he'd write thirty. What other people saw as exploitative, he found exhilarating. "There's nothing more fun than smoking some weed and spending $20,000 to play a practical joke, being young and high and tricking some unsuspecting Americans," said Fleiss.

One day, he got a call from the man who would become his other mentor: Steve Chao, the president of Fox TV. Chao—the same "Harvard puke" who had bought *Cops* from John Langley—was a fellow oddball in the C-suites. The son of elite Chinese government officials, Chao had been raised in Ann Arbor, Michigan, and, after studying classics at Harvard, he'd written for the *National Enquirer,* and then, after business school, become a Rupert Murdoch protégé. Even in an industry full of extreme personalities, Chao stood out: Reality TV agent Mark Itkin remembers once walking in on Chao screening "snuff films," for either fun or research, Itkin couldn't tell. Chao also had a strong track record in reality formats. Along with having helped to produce *Cops,* Chao had created *America's Most Wanted,* a show that was originally conceived of as "electronic lynching."

Chao wouldn't last long in the top job. In 1992, just eight weeks after Murdoch had promoted him to president of Fox Television, he was fired, after an incident at a corporate retreat in Colorado. Midway through a presentation titled "The Threat to Democratic Capitalism Posed by Modern Culture," Chao used a male stripper to illustrate a point he was making onstage, mortally offending Rupert Murdoch's wife, Anna. (Forgive the parenthetical, but the details feel important: In his presentation, Chao had been trying to demonstrate that American audiences were excessively outraged by sex and not enough by violence, in contrast to the Netherlands. Chao's plan had been to set off some explosives, fake-shoot the male stripper, and then announce, "Would you rather see a healthy naked body or a bloody corpse?" Unfortunately, then–secretary of defense Dick Cheney and his wife were seated in the audience, so his security wouldn't let Chao use a gun or explosives. Instead, Chao pointed to the male stripper, using his fingers as a gun—and somehow found himself looking directly at Anna Murdoch and telling her, "Anna, can I please have your undivided attention?"

Anna might have let that faux pas go, but Chao already had a history with her, having been thrown out of her parties three separate times. In the most striking of these incidents, he had grabbed Mrs. Murdoch's newly adopted puppy—which she was bragging had webbed feet—and tossed it into her swimming pool, to see whether it could swim. The puppy sank to the bottom of the pool. Chao then jumped in, fully clothed, to save the dog, but it left a bad impression.)

Anyway! During his brief, chaotic reign, "Crazy President Chao" (as Fleiss called him, with affection) inspired Fleiss with his vision for modern television. "He just kept on saying, 'We have *got* to be able to do shows without writers.'" He encouraged Fleiss to pitch his own reality formats, a plan that made sense to Fleiss, who was increasingly spooked by the finances of TV writing, convinced that the only way to make real money was to own his own show.

Fleiss took a job at Nash Entertainment, and in the mid-'90s, he sold his first series, *Before They Were Stars*—the mirror image of Darnell's *Life After Reruns*. The pay was subpar. As low-level "scrubs," he and Bruce Nash were perpetually partnered with do-nothing executive producers, men who siphoned off $30,000 an episode while Fleiss, who had been diligently faxing out requests for Farrah Fawcett's yearbook picture, made $1,500. "I was so mad! But my agent at the time said, 'This is how it works. You get ripped off the first time. Next time you get ripped off a little less. And finally, you stop getting ripped off, and then it's your turn to rip somebody off'— which is just straight out of *The Sopranos*. Christopher has to pay for lobster and Cristal for Silvio, because he's the new kid on the block."

Fleiss wasn't any happier working for Nash, who was "a typical Hollywood shyster," in Fleiss's estimation, so eventually, he quit, launching Next Entertainment in 1997, with a boost from Darnell. The two men's first project as a team was called *The World's Mean-*

est People Caught on Tape, a format that was spawned from a clip that Darnell passed to Fleiss, in which a bartender stirred a customer's martini with his penis. Fleiss, a quick hand at research, set out to find more "gotcha" surveillance footage, only to hit a wall. Eventually, he told me, he asked for Darnell's source, a detective named Fred, who was from Calgary. Fred from Calgary offered him more material. Then Fleiss noticed something odd: Some of the new clips had multiple takes. "I called Tom Sheets, Darnell's right-hand man, and said, 'I think some of this is bullshit, man. I think some of this stuff is fake.' And Tom said, 'Don't worry about it.'"

Fleiss's naïveté dissolved in a flash. It was *all* fake, he realized. "All that busted-on-the-job shit, all that shocking behavior stuff—there weren't cameras set up everywhere around town! There were guys making these fake videos and selling them to producers, who then turned around and made them into shows for the Fox Broadcasting Company." It was like Saget's realization about the video of a little boy putting his coat on a mud puddle, but much seedier.

The revelation didn't turn Fleiss off, exactly. Mainly, it just opened his eyes to the business he had chosen. "I had such reverence for television in general, and for Mike, also, I couldn't fathom that something was falsified or a fraud, and of course it was," Fleiss said with a dark laugh. "Fake news! Fake news." (Darnell denies this entire story, adding that he's never heard of Fred from Calgary. Somewhat confusingly, Darnell also claims at the time the show aired, Fleiss knew the clip was fake—but neither Darnell nor Sheets was aware of anything sketchy about it.)

The show, retitled *Shocking Behavior Caught on Tape,* earned a 19 share, a strong rating. After Nash jumped networks and went to work for NBC, Darnell and Fleiss—now mutual competitors with Nash—grew closer. Darnell would throw out goofy ideas—like *World's Dumbest Drivers*—and then Fleiss would bring them to life. Some of these concepts, like the provisionally titled *World's Biggest Bitches,* never made it on the air. As Fleiss described it to me, that show's introduction featured a "cat scratch" sound, just like *Bitch Hunter,* the parody later featured on *30 Rock.* There were few shows nearly as outrageous anywhere on the cable dial, with rare exceptions, like the hidden-camera series *Taxicab Confessions,* which debuted in 1995 on HBO. Still, *Taxicab Confessions,* which featured plenty of graphic sexual and violent stories, ultimately took a subtle, empathetic view of human nature. That wasn't the Darnell way.

Fleiss worked hard, absorbing lessons from his beloved Fox guru. Their key philosophical precept: The more divisive a show was, the more it infuriated critics, the higher the ratings. The ideal Fox show was one that smashed every button, managing to piss off both conservatives and feminists. "We didn't like an idea unless it had a little bit of 'You can't put that on television.'"

WITH THE NEW MILLENNIUM LOOMING, FLEISS WAS CRAVING THE big get, the kind of wild idea that could push him to the next level: a network hit, in prime time, with his name all over it—a show for which he would get all the credit. In 1999, his moment finally arrived.

That year, the entire TV industry was obsessed with an ABC quiz show called *Who Wants to Be a Millionaire,* a tense, glamorous British import with high ratings. One weekend, Mike Darnell flew to Parsippany, New Jersey, to attend a wedding. Plane phones were new at the time, so he made a call—and when he heard *Millionaire's* numbers were rising, he grew fixated on the problem. "All I could think about is, 'Who? Who?? *Who Wants to Be a Millionaire?* What *else* do the people want?'" Darnell stared at the wedding; he thought about that quiz show jackpot. Then, like the genius who combined peanut butter and chocolate, he merged the two things: *Who Wants to Marry a Millionaire?*

Once Darnell had a title, he called Fleiss, looking for concepts. It wouldn't be the first time that a couple got married, live, on the air: There had been similar stunts pulled, on a radio program called *Two Strangers and a Wedding* in 1998 in Australia and again the following year in England. In 1988, a provocative British show called *Network 7* had staged a gay secular wedding, to protest anti-gay policies. Way back in the 1950s, during the heyday of the American audience participation era, *Bride and Groom* had aired live ceremonies, including one with a rabbi. But Darnell was looking for something wilder and stranger: not merely a wedding, but the sort of glittery, dystopian spectacle that no one could look away from. Fleiss had an idea: They should stage a parody of the Miss America pageant, taking the piss out of one of TV's corniest brands. Darnell loved it—and added a twist, one-upping ABC by making their groom a *multimillionaire.*

The idea was a natural match for the Fox brand, which was devoted to twisted, satirical takes on the shows that aired on ABC, CBS, and NBC. *Breaking the Magician's Code* had been a raspberry in the face of CBS's self-serious *The Magic of David Copperfield* specials; his clip shows were twisted variants on Saget's cute home videos. Now *Who Wants to Marry a Multi-Millionaire?* would be a jab in the guts of frothy televised weddings, all those syrupy displays of hypocrisy—most notably, the royal wedding of Charles and Diana in 1981. Mutually exhilarated by the outrageousness of their concept, Fleiss and Darnell went into production overdrive. They had just ten weeks to pull off their plan if they wanted to catch February sweeps.

They quickly found fifty single women willing to participate in the competition; as hosts, they hired Jay Thomas and former Miss America Leanza Cornett. The groom turned out to be more of a problem, though. The few rich men they scraped up got cold feet; others seemed like closeted gay men, said Fleiss (Darnell denied this). Finally, they settled on Rick Rockwell, a forty-two-year-old real estate developer from San Diego. Rockwell struck Fleiss as telegenic, but also dorky. He looked rich, if you made a few adjustments. "He owned a condo in Vancouver, which was probably worth like $65,000; he had a house—although it was max leveraged and in Encinitas. He had a net worth of about $1.3 million. I said, 'Does that really count as a multimillionaire?' And Mikey said, 'Well, 0.3 is a multiple . . .' So we rolled the dice."

Darva Conger, a thirty-four-year-old ER nurse in Los Angeles, was three months into her new job when she heard about the show from a TV producer, who was married to a doctor she worked with. Conger, the daughter of Susan Harrison—an actress who'd starred in *Sweet Smell of Success,* then fallen off the map of Hollywood—

had had a rough childhood, bohemian and broke, drifting around California. At twenty-one, seeking stability, she joined the military, where she trained as a medic and worked in the reserves on a base in Illinois, as well as on active duty in Korea and Utah. She'd had a hard year in 1999: Her estranged father, with whom she'd recently reconciled, had died. Her mother and brother were both sick. Conger figured she could use an all-expenses-paid trip to Las Vegas.

When she showed up in Sin City, however, things weren't so glamorous. She worked all day filming B-roll and learning moves, which were supposed to be part of an elaborate opening number. The other women were mostly aspiring actresses; like Conger, they weren't there to find husbands. In fact, she thought the show was probably rigged—and she even believed she knew who the "ringer" was, until the moment she was chosen.

That Saturday was one of the best days of Fleiss's life. During rehearsals, Darnell had cut the campy musical number that Fleiss wanted, because Darnell always preferred, in Fleiss's estimation, a tone of "stress and dread and consequences." But once the cameras began rolling, Fleiss was on top of the world. Word had spread about the extravagant event, so the auditorium was packed. He could feel the energy rise, as the women posed in little black dresses and answered questions, then modeled bathing suits—and finally, wedding dresses. The groom, who was shown only in silhouette, winnowed the contestants down from fifty women to ten, then to five.

At the show's climax, when Rockwell picked Conger from the line of finalists wearing white gowns and lacy veils, the audience surged toward the stage, hysterical with excitement. Rockwell, his face finally revealed to the world, got down on one knee to propose. Conger said, "Yes." Backstage, Fleiss dropped to his own knees, overcome by pure joy. His writing and producing partner Chris Briggs was standing next to him. "He goes, 'Dude, what are you doing?' I said, 'Dude, we're going to be rich and famous.'"

For Conger, the show was a blur—although she did remember some lines that she read off a teleprompter, offering to be "your friend, your lover, and your partner throughout whatever life has to offer us." She was in shock, she said—and on autopilot, figuring that she could fix things later. As the moment was described in the *Pittsburgh Post-Gazette,* "When chosen, the platinum-blond bride looked stunned, her face frozen in a smile bordering on terror. She began shaking visibly. Rockwell led her to center stage, enfolded her in his arms and initiated a long, passionate kiss, during which her shoulders appeared as stiff as a coat-hanger's. He fixed his gaze on his bride-to-be, drinking her in and grinning in triumph. His lips could be seen forming the words, 'You are so beautiful,' and 'I'm so happy.'" Nevada judge Diane Steele married them. As the credits rolled, they did a slow dance to the Savage Garden lyrics "I knew I loved you before I met you / I think I dreamed you into life!"

If Conger viewed the night as a surreal charade, Rockwell quite clearly did not. That night, Fox paid for a honeymoon suite with two bedrooms. From her account, as she sat on her bed, Rockwell walked in freshly showered, with a towel around his waist, then offered her a massage. She said she wasn't in the mood and, trying to be polite, talked him down, then locked the door. It wasn't a major trauma, compared to a few other experiences she'd had. She'd nearly been raped in high school and had several other "Me Too" moments while she was in the military. But she was unnerved. "He kept saying that I'd met his family. I was like, I just met you!"

Within the next few days, she told the producers she didn't want to be left alone with Rockwell. She'd go on their scheduled cruise to Barbados only if she had a separate room—and a female chaperone. On board, she posed for publicity photos, but otherwise avoided Rockwell—instead, she had fun with her chaperone, with whom, by coincidence, she'd gone to grade school.

Meanwhile, Fleiss was busy editing the show. Rockwell kept on calling him from the cruise, begging him to mediate, so during breaks in the editing, Fleiss stood outside the building, trying to wheedle Conger into giving her husband a chance. Fleiss's sympathy was entirely with Rockwell, who might be dorky, but was mainly, in his view, "a nice guy who just wanted a pretty wife." Conger, he barely knew. He had more trouble understanding her motives, but he knew that she was disrupting his pet project.

The two-hour special aired on Tuesday, February 15, the day after

Valentine's Day. Ten million people tuned in, and then that number began to rise, spiking at twenty-three million during the last half-hour, a record number for Fox, trouncing *Who Wants to Be a Millionaire*. For Darnell and Fleiss, it was a spectacular success, on every level—a schmaltzy, sexist carnival that doubled, for viewers, as a swoony stunt, the Evel Knievel canyon leap of matrimony.

Fleiss was floating on air. *Rolling Stone* wanted to write a profile about him; top agents were calling. Fox ordered up three more specials, along with a follow-up interview with the bride and groom, set to air after a rerun. There were delicious condemnations from both the National Organization for Women and the conservative Media Research Center. The *San Francisco Examiner* called the show "a real-life demonstration of how to cheapen marriage through unapologetic cynicism, gold-digger avarice, and meat-market notions of true romance." Darnell ate the hostility like fuel, feeling special satisfaction when he made the front page of *The New York Times*.

Days later, the bomb landed. On February 20, Conger and Rockwell, back from the cruise, were smuggled into separate hotel rooms near the Santa Barbara airport, where they were supposed to film the after-special interview. Mark Thompson spoke to the two of them, trying to present the situation in a soft glow: Yes, the couple were taking things slow, but they were giving it a shot. Conger said she made it clear that the marriage hadn't worked out.

Whatever she said, the footage would never air. As Fleiss left in a limo with Rockwell and Thompson, the phone rang. All week, there had been revelations in the press, questioning the groom's credentials. Rockwell, whose original name was Richard S. Balkey, was less a real estate mogul and more a failed stand-up comic, whose credits included a role in a straight-to-video sequel to *Attack of the Killer Tomatoes*. He owned a cheap house with two broken toilets in the backyard. He had once given someone a $25 gift certificate as a wedding present. Fleiss wasn't thrilled, but it wasn't a disaster: Fox knew about most of this stuff.

On the phone was Mike Darnell, who was hyperventilating. Chairman of Fox Entertainment Sandy Grushow had just told him about an article that was set to appear on The Smoking Gun, an online investigative website. Nine years earlier, Rick Rockwell had had a restraining order filed against him by an ex-fiancée, who accused him of hitting her and letting the air out of her tires. Fleiss was certain this couldn't be right—he had done a background check on Rockwell, using an online service called 007. But when he turned to Rockwell and asked him about the story, Rockwell, who was holding a drink, said casually, "Oh, yeah, yeah, yeah. But it was no big deal!" (Later, Rockwell would deny all of his ex-girlfriend's allegations.)

Fleiss got dizzy all over again; he popped a Xanax, which was slipped to him by Mark Thompson. He could hear Darnell panicking on the line. "He said, 'They're out for blood. Sandy is going to come out and say, in an interview with [*New York Times* journalist] Bill Carter, that he's not going to allow any more reality TV ever on his network.' He was going to say that I was a scourge—it was just unbelievable." (Darnell remembered the call differently and pointed out that the Bill Carter interview didn't come out until a few days later, so he couldn't have mentioned it.)

There's something touchingly innocent, looking back, in the depth of personal betrayal that Fleiss and Darnell—the nihilistic maestros behind *World's Scariest Police Shootouts*—felt about the Rick Rockwell revelations, given the types of reality TV scandals that would follow in the show's wake. But that day in February 2000, their careers looked like they were dead. Fox not only canceled the rerun of *Who Wants to Marry a Multi-Millionaire?*, they shoved the special down the memory hole, just as WNET had disappeared any trace of *An American Family*.

The disaster became a big story on *NBC Nightly News,* with Tom Brokaw solemnly announcing, "Scandal rocks Hollywood," and in the next few weeks, every paper took a bite. Even bystanders got dinged. The guy who booked the production at the Hilton in Vegas was fired. Like so many reality experiments before it, *Multi-Millionaire* had become a flaming symbol of the decline of civilization.

At an all-company meeting, Sandy Grushow dictated a new Fox policy: There would be no more reality shows, from that day forward. "And everybody applauded. A hundred people," said Darnell, bitterly, still seething at the memory, decades later. Grushow had told the press, "I would rather fail with quality than succeed with garbage," and when Grushow resigned four years later, Darnell liked to joke that his nemesis had done just that.

Things were worse for Fleiss, who had lost his job. There was an internal investigation at Fox; there were lawsuits to settle. The year that followed, spent brooding in the shadows, bonded him deeply with Darnell (although, as is probably apparent from these parentheticals, which emerged during fact-checking, that bond seems to have weakened since our original interviews). According to Fleiss (Darnell denies this, too), Darnell helped Fleiss get back on his feet by passing him sub-rosa jobs, without putting his name in the credits—until eventually, Fleiss found a way to stage a comeback.

The crisis inaugurated the reign of The Smoking Gun, until then just a fledgling e-zine that was co-founded by an investigative journalist from *The Village Voice*. The week they uploaded the Rockwell restraining order, the site's traffic grew twentyfold, reaching two million hits a day. It was the first tremor of a larger media earthquake, as gossip sites began to proliferate online, informational kudzu that wound itself around ordinary news organizations, sometimes obscuring the original institution. These sites would play a significant role in the reality genre—as a scourge, but also a source of valuable publicity.

Meanwhile, the stars of *Who Wants to Marry a Multi-Millionaire?* had fallen deep into the reality-fame paradox. Paparazzi trailed them, but they couldn't pay for security. News outlets, desperate for tidbits, were slipping cash to their exes for gossip. To make matters even juicier, their stories kept clashing: Conger called Rockwell creepy and said she'd done the show as a lark; Rockwell called Conger frigid and said that he was heartbroken. Who you sympathized with came down to which kind of behavior you found more unstable: the notion of marrying a stranger to get a free week in Vegas or the idea of seeking your soulmate on a Fox game show.

Conger's early strategy was to do one classy interview, with Diane Sawyer, then retreat. But after she lost her nursing job, she changed her mind. When offers poured in, she decided to take advantage of them—she was already being smeared as a gold-digger, so she might as well get some kind of jackpot. "I made a stupid mistake. It doesn't mean that I am a stupid woman," she told Reuters. She sold some of her prizes at auction, then donated her ring and Isuzu Trooper to a cerebral palsy foundation. She posed for *Playboy*, wearing a wedding dress on the cover—a choice that "saved my bacon, honestly," she told me. (She turned down an offer from *Penthouse*.) A few years later, she also showed up on Darnell's show *Celebrity Boxing*, an appearance that helped to finance her own lavish wedding and honeymoon in New Zealand.

Meanwhile, Rockwell went on *Dateline*, doing an interview in which he acknowledged that he'd threatened to kill his ex-fiancée, but denied that he'd slapped her and called the restraining order "somewhat of a nonevent." Asked what he'd learned, he joked, "Don't screw up on a slow news day." In April, the couple was granted an annulment on the basis of fraud. Rockwell wrote a memoir called *What Was I Thinking?*, then went on a comedy tour titled "The Annulment Tour." In 2001, the pair made a stiff mutual appearance on *Larry King Live*, in which Conger apologized to Rockwell, saying that she'd gone on the show, foolishly, to get the attention of an ex. Rockwell was clearly still angry. Both of them were publicizing projects—his book, her website—that didn't pan out. By 2003, their fame had faded into tabloid history.

Two decades later, Conger was mostly amused, looking back. "People are mean and it was probably a dumb idea, but it's not even on the scale of the bad things people experience," she said. At the height of her reality celebrity, she had tried to launch a lifestyle brand called Darva's House, which was focused on gardening, fitness, and cooking, the sort of brand-building that would become par for the course for reality stars twenty years later. Back in 2000—before Instagram or, for most people, Wi-Fi—it had no chance to succeed.

Instead, Conger retrained and became a nurse anesthesiologist. She got married to a paramedic. She had a child, then divorced. When I reached her, during the pandemic, she was working long shifts at the OR. Her Instagram showed her hiking and doing woodworking projects. There were loving memorials to her mother and selfies with her beloved autistic son, but there was no sign of her own fame, other than the words "accidental celebrity." When I looked at the app a year later, even that had disappeared.

IN THE AFTERMATH OF *WHO WANTS TO MARRY A MULTI-Millionaire?*, the press gleefully celebrated the death of reality TV, a sick, sad fad that was finally gone for good. In the San Angelo *Standard-Times*, TV critic Tim Goodman wrote a column comparing reality shows to hard drugs, arguing that with *Who Wants to Marry a Multi-Millionaire?*, TV had finally hit rock bottom and was getting sober. *World's Biggest Bitches*, *World's Nastiest Neighbors*, and *Plastic Surgery Nightmares* were dropped from the Fox schedule. To the casual observer, it looked like the genre was flat-lining, at last.

Behind the scenes, however, Darnell had been getting calls: from ABC, from NBC, from top executives. The *Multi-Millionaire* numbers were too big to ignore. In his own view, he hadn't done anything wrong, and soon he was back in the game. Still, those frightening months had changed the producer. Colleagues who had given negative quotes to the media were now his enemies, forever; the few who stood by him were permanent allies. "Stick with me or don't, right?"

Meanwhile, a revolution was brewing, just across the horizon—and just south of the equator. Even as the cover of *People* magazine asked "Has TV gone too far?," CBS producers were setting up camp in Borneo, preparing to film a new series, one that would revive the scandalous, resilient tradition of reality programming for good. Just twenty-three days after the disastrous airing of *Who Wants to Marry a Multi-Millionaire?*, *Survivor* started production. And after *Survivor*, the deluge.

7

|||||||

THE GAME

The Invention of *Survivor* (and Mark Burnett)

SURVIVOR WAS THE FIRST SERIES TO TAKE THE REALITY GENRE mainstream in the United States, turning the fringe, faddish phenomenon of "dirty documentary" into a legitimate institution. If *The Real World* had modernized the genre, *Survivor* supersized it. Like a summer blockbuster, it was full of bright, brutal images, with flaming torches, aerial shots, and gorgeous underwater cinematography. The main characters became iconic figures—Richard Hatch, stark naked, spearing fish in the Pacific; the grizzled Rudy Boesch, his hand held up against a totem pole; Sue Hawk, ranting about snakes and rats. Other reality shows might have been gimmicks. *Survivor* was an *event*.

What really made *Survivor* stand out, however, was its ingenious format, which managed to unite three key traditions: Allen Funt's prank show model; the Chuck Barris-esque game show; and the real-life soap opera, which was launched by *An American Family*. This singular, powerful structure would ultimately influence nearly everything that followed it—and when *Survivor* broke out as a prime-time hit for CBS in 2000, it struck many viewers as a distinctly American program, big, brash, and Hollywood, as if manifest destiny had been crossbred with the Super Bowl.

But in fact, *Survivor* wasn't American at all.

Instead, the show was the spear tip of a *different* reality boom, a parallel creative expansion that had been taking place across the Atlantic, particularly in the UK and the Netherlands. The European reality phenomenon has its own complicated history, involving a separate set of pioneers, many of them easily as shameless and piratical as any Hollywood hustler. One of the most significant of these men is, of course, Mark Burnett, a white-toothed pitchman wearing an Indiana Jones–esque Akubra hat. A British immigrant, Burnett would become one of the key innovators behind modern American reality TV—and then, through the transitive property, a kingmaker in U.S. politics.

Burnett didn't create the *Survivor* format, though. Instead, the idea began with a *different* British television creator, Charlie Parsons. Born in 1958, Parsons, a dreamy boy from a posh family, had attended Tonbridge, a centuries-old, all-male boarding school he once described as "an isolated world where you had to fight for yourself." He escaped by watching 1960s TV, as well as his favorite show, a 1975 American TV adaptation of the children's novel *The Swiss Family Robinson,* the story of a shipwreck survivor raising his kids on a volcanic island.

In 1987, Parsons, who had studied at Oxford, found a job at a broadcast tabloid called *Network 7.* It was an absolute eye-opener for the young journalist—an education in what was possible. Parsons's new boss was a wildcat TV producer named Janet Street-Porter, a self-described "illiterate cockney with big teeth" who was at once adored and feared at her network, Channel 4. A veteran of the punk and fashion scenes of the 1970s, Street-Porter had been married three times and spoke candidly about topics like her illegal abortion. If Darnell was the shortest producer at Fox, Street-Porter was one of the tallest at Channel 4, at six feet. In a 1988 interview, she described television as her ideal medium, "as exciting now as rock was in the '60s." She abhorred old-school BBC, a style she dismissed as "radiovision—deadwood TV."

Network 7, which Street-Porter co-created with Jane Hewland, was her attempt to create an alternative media landscape, with the slogan "News is entertainment. Entertainment is news." The newsmagazine—which aired live for two hours each Sunday morning, broadcast from inside a bohemian caravan city in a Docklands banana warehouse—was kinetic, rude, and densely visual, full of Claymation and graphical infobars, filmed with handheld cameras and focused on "citizen journalism." There were mini news segments called "blipverts," as well as video diaries from amateurs, titled "This Is Me." Experts were banned. Viewers were encouraged to dip in and out—if one segment didn't click, the next might. Though it lasted for only two seasons, *Network 7,* which was designed to resemble a "channel within a channel"—as if Channel 4 had been hacked by pirates—was hugely influential, a po-mo middle finger to the tradition-bound British networks, just as Fox and MTV had been to ABC, CBS, and NBC.

Like MTV, *Network 7* relied on a set of charming presenters, among them Charlie Parsons. During the second season, when Parsons was twenty-nine, he became a showrunner, helping produce the show's gonzo stunts, many of which used regular people. He aired a live gay wedding, at the height of the debate over the Thatcher government's Section 28, a law that outlawed the "promotion" of homosexuality (six years before Pedro Zamora got married on *The Real World*). He aired a live interview with a death-row prisoner, then asked viewers to vote on his fate. One day, their mischievous production team bugged the Channel 4 boardroom, then broadcast what the executives had said about their show.

In 1988, *Network 7* aired a segment called "Castaway," set on a desert island. The stunt, which had been pitched by a new hire, Murray Boland, was based on a segment aired by Boland's former employer, the Irish radio program *The Gay Byrne Show.* A year earlier, that show's producer, Philip Kampf, had decided to send some strangers into the wilderness of rural Connemara, armed only with a popular book called the *SAS Survival Guide.* After a few days of boring daily check-ins, there was a shocking development: One member of the group, Gerry Ryan, announced live, on the air, that they'd beaten a lamb to death, in order to have something to eat. "He said he put a rock in a sock, looked this lamb in the eye, and said, 'I'm sorry, but it's me or you,' and bludgeoned the defenseless creature," as Kampf remembered the moment in 2013.

The show was catnip for listeners—and then it became a national scandal. Under fire for airing an account of animal cruelty, the producers conducted a full investigation, even digging up the remains of the lamb, like some Irish *CSI*. In the end, it transpired that Ryan—who would go on to become a famous TV host—had lied: A farmer had actually killed the lamb for the group, but Ryan didn't want it to look as if they'd cheated.

Charlie Parsons immediately saw the concept's potential, but he decided to set his version on a desert island, just like the one in his favorite book. "Castaway" comprised three ten-minute segments, which were filmed in Sri Lanka, featuring four strangers who were "marooned" together: soap opera star Simon O'Brien; tennis champion Annabel Croft; a London stockbroker, whose name no one seems to remember; and Pete Gillett, a former Parkhurst Prison inmate (and gangster Reggie Kray's self-promoting adopted son). Each got to pick one item to take with them, like a machete or a live chicken.

"Castaway" featured no games or competitions; it was more like *The Real World* on a beach, with C-list stars, minor food deprivation, and a breezy holiday vibe. In 2017, Annabel Croft* praised the experience as "delightful." "We were given a machete, a roll of loo paper, a tinderbox, and a chicken. No food or water and we had to build our own shelter," she effused. "But I had the most amazing time. I wasn't stressed about winning tennis matches. Instead, I was talking to a man about how he ended up in jail. . . . We had to live without light, credit cards, or money—it was literally survival. We ate coconuts until someone eventually killed the chicken. I couldn't eat it—not after it had been one of the gang."

After "Castaway" aired, Parsons was convinced that there was a brilliant TV show in the concept: Like Jon Murray marveling at the

---

* Croft ultimately quit tennis and became a serial reality TV star, appearing on shows including *Treasure Hunt, Celebrity Wrestling,* and the BBC's *Famous, Rich and Homeless,* which is just what it sounds like: stars playing homeless to teach viewers about poverty.

way the *Real World* cast sat on ledges instead of chairs, he had been struck by the unusual intimacy of seeing strangers bond under pressure. Even this rudimentary version suggested all sorts of stories: Which sort of personality would thrive in these extreme conditions—and which would crack? It was a blend of *The Swiss Family Robinson*, the rigors of Tonbridge, and one of Parsons's favorite novels, *Lord of the Flies*. He just had to figure out how to build a sturdy TV format that could run for years.

PARSONS'S BRAINSTORM WASN'T, AS IT HAPPENS, THE FIRST TIME a British television producer had marooned a group of strangers in the wilderness. Back in 1977, at the height of the hippie era, John Percival—a documentarian-provocateur trained in archaeology and anthropology—had produced *Living in the Past* for BBC Two, a series designed to re-create life during the Iron Age. For the project, Percival cast six couples, including the Ainsworths, who had three children. Each person was paid one thousand pounds. Percival stranded the cast in a remote corner of Wiltshire, where they were deputized to build a new society, together, from scratch.

The project was significantly more serious-minded than the shows that would follow in its wake, with experts tutoring the cast members in welding, leatherwork, and Iron Age architecture. Then, they were left alone for a year. Camera operators stopped by just two times a week. If "Castaway" had been a curaçao-flavored 1980s lark, *Living in the Past* was more like homebrewed mead, a charmingly earnest product, reflecting the era's vogue for DIY homesteading. In a departure from Iron Age authenticity, the show's participants—who included a nurse, a construction worker, and a teacher—operated as a hippie commune, working by consensus. Despite bad weather, they got by, erecting thatched buildings, milling corn, and slaughtering pigs. They even held pagan festivals, lighting up a fifteen-foot wicker man and chanting "Burn him! Burn him!" Percival made a few modern allowances, for birth control and tampons, but by and large, it was a genuine attempt to live like Britons in 500 BC.

When conflict *did* bubble up, the producers kept it under wraps, even after the family with children left the show. In a 2008 "Where Are They Now?" reunion show, one participant spilled the tea: The childless couples weren't thrilled by the presence of kids. In his 1980 book *Living in the Past,* Percival described battles between a neatnik and a vegetarian. In the edited version, however, there was no Real Housewives of the Iron Age drama—instead, the emphasis was on the struggle for peaceful co-existence. In Percival's book, he gripes that too many hot single people applied for the show. "I had an alarming and slightly prurient vision of a dozen young people who had hardly met each other before, settling down to live in close proximity for twelve months. It would take them all of their time to sort out their sex lives, let alone build an Iron Age village." It was a dystopian vision that would take decades to emerge on the 2001 Fox series *Temptation Island.*

There was a high level of nudity. As cast member Helen Elphick explained sheepishly in the reunion show, it was an unusually hot summer in Wiltshire, and in a classic reality-TV bonding ritual, the Iron Age cast got so friendly with the filmmakers they forgot they were being filmed naked in a swamp, let alone that the footage would be shown to a national audience.

Despite its low-conflict approach, *Living in the Past* drew eighteen million viewers a week. In fact, given its popularity, one might have expected that the series would mount a second season, maybe set in the Stone Age. Instead, Percival burned the settlement to the ground, to keep it from attracting tourists. Sadly, his own experience had been complicated by tragedy: In 1972, Percival; his wife, Jacky Gillott, a pioneering journalist; and their two small children had themselves moved off the grid, to live on a farm in Somerset, an experience that Gillott turned into a book and radio show. Then Gillott killed herself in 1980. In the aftermath of these sad experiences, Percival went back to making documentaries, along with a beloved series about gardening.

The *Living in the Past* ensemble, too, returned to their lives. They continued to meet up a few times a year, without any cameras, and some of them kept up their blacksmithing skills.

III

IN 1992, CHARLIE PARSONS LEFT *NETWORK 7* AND CO-FOUNDED A
production company called Planet 24 with two high-profile partners:
the Irish rock star Bob Geldof and Parsons's long-term boyfriend,
Baron Waheed Alli, an Indo-Caribbean immigrant who became the
first openly gay and Muslim peer in the House of Lords. The gay
power couple and the rock star were determined to create a slate of
fun, noisy TV hits, lucrative and controversial. Their slate included
the popular morning show *The Big Breakfast,* the frothy *Gaytime
TV,* and the late-night music program *The Word.*

The Word, which debuted in 1990, was more debauched than
anything on British TV. At once innovative and indefensible, it was
stuffed with Darnellian stunts that drew young male viewers, eager
for edgy, nasty humor. The production could be just as unsettling
behind the scenes, according to Duncan Gray, who worked on the
show. One day, he was overseeing auditions for new presenters with
his manager, Paul Ross, whom Gray considered "a very clever man,
but a real sociopath." To test applicants, the managers would often
fake malfunctions, like broken earphones, in order to determine
their capacity to improvise on the air. Once, Ross upped the ante: He
told Gray to tell the applicants to bark like dogs. They were to walk
on all fours, he commanded them, while barking, "I want this job! I
want this job!"

"I'm a pretty nice person," said Gray. "But back then, you know,
it was a pretty fascist organization. It was unpleasant." He followed
orders—and so did the applicants. The experience inspired a shocking new segment on *The Word,* "The Hopefuls," which was devoted
entirely to people who would do anything to get on television, from
eating a toenail sandwich to a young man tongue-kissing a toothless
"granny," a stunt that sent shockwaves across Great Britain.

Parsons knew *The Word* crossed ethical lines, but the show's success, along with the ratings for *The Big Breakfast,* had him feeling
cocky, proud of his ability to smash taboos and attract press. He
hoped for something bigger, though—a game show format, the kind
of format that would be more than a one-time sensation, that could

sell across the globe. The "Castaway" concept was the magical idea, he believed—he just needed to find a network that agreed.

For nearly a decade, Parsons pitched *Survivor,* which was then titled *Survive!* He got rejected by every British network, then by all the American ones. In the mid-1990s, Parsons found a booster in a British expat in Los Angeles: Michael Davies, a former writer for *Let's Make a Deal* who was a fan of *Network 7.* At the time, Davies was a producer at Disney's Buena Vista studios, funding oddball, unscripted projects, among them an American version of *The Big Breakfast.* Parsons flew to L.A. for that project, and when it sank, Davies agreed to help him develop *Survive!,* which was, at the time, a one-page pitch: A group of strangers are stranded together on a desert island, where they play games and get kicked off, one by one.

Davies helped Parsons build a significantly more detailed pitch, then set up a meeting with Stu Bloomberg at ABC, who rejected it. CBS and NBC also said no. In 1995, one executive *was* intrigued by the concept: *Real World* producer Lauren Corrao, who had, at that point, jumped to Fox. But although Corrao liked the premise for the show, she insisted that Parsons needed to team up with a more experienced producer, someone who was able to handle the complexities of a nature shoot. Before she could finalize a contract, that deal got scuttled by bigger forces: Disney bought ABC, then insisted that Davies bring *Survive!* back into the ABC fold, leaving them all at square one.

This might feel like a long, tangled corporate story, but it's important to understand just how many people were determined *not* to make the show that transformed reality television. Around 1993, Buena Vista gave Parsons $130,000 for added development, which allowed him to construct a model of the island and run some tests. The team took yet *another* meeting, this time with ABC Entertainment president Jamie Tarses, who was just three weeks into the job. Parsons explained that he needed $13 million to produce *Survive!,* and although Tarses showed some interest, she, too, ultimately passed. Parsons's Hollywood dreams were fading—and to make things worse, he felt certain that he had finally "cracked the nut" of the desert-island format with the help of a dream team of clever game-show minds, recruited from both sides of the Atlantic.

This team included Duncan Gray from *The Word; Real World* producer George Verschoor; British producer Dan Cutforth, who would later go on to produce *Project Runway;* a former *Candid Camera* segment producer named Lincoln Hiatt; and Channel 4 producer Frankie Glass, who was in charge of logistics. Their assignment was to sort out the precise *Survive!* gameplay, down to the tiniest details. During the summer of 1996, they began meeting in a conference room on West Olive Avenue, in an obscure building far from the Buena Vista lot, "almost as if Michael [Davies] were running a rogue set of agents," Gray joked. Davies helped brainstorm ideas, as did Charlie Parsons, who came and went.

For the first three weeks of these brainstorms, Gray remembers feeling baffled by the task at hand, stubbornly objecting to the entire premise of the show: *Why* were these people stuck on an island in the first place? Why would they ignore the cameras? Also, if the contestants were for-real starving, why would they play a bunch of silly games? Then one day, someone—he can't remember who, maybe Cutforth, maybe Verschoor—shouted out an answer: "They want immunity." The players just wanted to be safe, to be protected from death, symbolically speaking. "Suddenly, everything fell into place," Gray said. "We understood what we were making: the Game of Life as a game show, right? That became the log line."

After that key breakthrough, the development process sped up, as they giddily dreamed up the two imaginary tribes, the games, the rewards, the crucial psychology of how the plot would play out. The group had finally begun to understand that they weren't making a game show: *Survive!* was a drama with three acts.

The *Survive!* format began with a simple setup: Sixteen castaways would get ferried to an island, then split into two tribes. Those teams, half men and half women, would compete in a set of challenges, which, in the original draft, had titles like Coconut Slingshot, Bury Caesar, and Fountain of Tantalus. Some competitions were "reward" challenges, to win food and other comforts; others were "immunity" challenges, which protected players from expulsion. Every three days, one of the castaways would be voted out.

Early on, Parsons had imagined that the show might feature a charismatic host—a mysterious billionaire on a luxury yacht, floating just off the island, who would expel the players. At some point, that idea was dropped, replaced by a better approach: During a weekly Island Council, the teammates would vote *one another* off. In the seventh episode, the two teams would merge, scrambling the power dynamics. The way Parsons imagined the island, the landscape would bear some relationship to the bohemian warehouse where he'd filmed *Network 7*—an exciting, artificial space where the producers would have control, changing the rules as they wished.

That summer, Duncan Gray and Dan Cutforth wrote a detailed pitch book, which touted *Survive!* as not merely a fun TV game show but a culture-rattling phenomenon, one that would spark global debate. They invoked grand comparisons to Odysseus and Robinson Crusoe, *The Tempest* and *Lord of the Flies*, arguing that this new format would create a "heroic, almost mythical situation," taking the eternal themes of fiction and adding "a brilliant, contemporary twist." At the climax of each episode, the castaways, "summoned by the sound of a blast on a conch shell," would meet with an empathetic host, who would ask them probing questions, and then, dramatically, reveal the results of a secret vote.

This imaginary season would move through three acts, they wrote: first, six playful episodes, to introduce the characters; then six more, in which relationships intensified, beginning with the episode 7 merge, which the text compared to "Christmas Day in World War I," when soldiers met between opposing bunkers. The climax would be the finale, at which point the show would have honed four finalists down to two, using a pair of contests: a "How well do you know your teammates?" quiz and a balance competition. The finalists would then make their case to a jury of players who had been kicked out—and finally, one winner would get a million dollars.

In addition to the details of gameplay, the pitch book emphasized the look of *Survive!*, which it described as more sophisticated than *The Real World*: "Grown-up—this is not MTV." Scenes of daily life would resemble a gritty TV drama, exploring the contestants' relationships and daily crises ("How hungry do you have to be to eat insect stew?"). The Island Council, in contrast, would be glamorous, filmed on a set, using a Steadicam and crane shots.

Gary Carter, a South African–born former actor who was the business manager for Planet 24, showed up in Los Angeles halfway through the summer. When he read the first draft of the proposal, he pushed Gray and Cutforth to rewrite it, to make the language more consistent—they were creating intellectual property, he warned them, not writing a short story. By the end, it was an unusually fully formed prospectus, particularly for a genre that barely existed. With remarkable confidence, the text predicted a hit that "the whole nation will talk about," with diverse contestants who would rocket to fame. Parsons even had the group mock up a *Newsweek* cover, using a fake cast portrait, in order to dramatize the media mayhem.

By the time ABC and Buena Vista turned down his pitch again, in 1996, the mojo of Parsons's glory days had faded. A self-deprecating Brit, he knew he was a dud at pitching in American boardrooms. For years, he had resisted taking notes from executives who proposed reimagining *Survive!* by turning it into a two-hour special or maybe dropping the games.* When Corrao had suggested that he pair up with a different producer, a British military veteran named Mark Burnett, he had resisted that, too. "I was quite naïve and quite arrogant, and I didn't want to share my winnings, if you like."

He couldn't seem to get past the key problem for executives: *Survive!* didn't fit into any programming category. It was part soap opera, part game show, part sports, part nature film, a gamble for any ad-driven network. It seemed too strange—too dangerous and, maybe, too embarrassing—to work. The format couldn't even be tested out as a pilot, since Parsons insisted on a full season commitment. Like John Langley with *Cops,* he wouldn't bend. But eventually, he had to.

III

* Two British networks eventually made shows along those lines: Channel 4's *Shipwrecked,* from 1999, and BBC One's *Castaway 2000,* set in rural Scotland. (A few years later, they added games.)

IN LATE 1996, PLANET 24 FINALLY CUT A DEAL WITH ANNA Bråkenhielm, a producer for SVT, the Swedish analogue to the BBC. By then, Gary Carter had already sold a yearlong option on *Survive!* to a Dutch company, Endemol Entertainment, which never produced it. From Carter's perspective, the newly liberalized airwaves of Stockholm, unlike Los Angeles, were primed for a risk. Sure enough, Bråkenhielm—who hoped to shake up her stodgy public network—said yes one minute into his pitch.

Renamed *Expedition: Robinson,* the series was filmed in Malaysia. Even before it began to air, Swedish pundits were skeptical, with some warning that the project took a "fascist approach" to entertainment. During filming, however, the *Survive!* blueprint played out beautifully. The castaways bonded and clashed, there were idyllic nature shots, there were sweaty physical challenges (the teams swung over a mud pool) and philosophical debates—among them an argument about killing a goat, an issue that seemed to emerge organically in every version of the show. Aesthetically, *Expedition: Robinson* looked cheaper than the grand, immersive series that Parsons had envisioned—the Council was shot in the daytime, around a campfire—but it was exciting TV, down to the sequence when the players wrote their votes on pieces of parchment, then held them up to explain their choice. SVT got ready for a wave of exciting media debate and top ratings.

Instead, there was a tragedy. One month after filming, Sinisa Savija, a Bosnian/Serbian immigrant who was the first person voted off the island, killed himself by walking in front of a commuter train. It was nine weeks before *Expedition: Robinson* was scheduled to premiere. In the footage of that first Council, Sinisa, who had immigrated to Sweden five years earlier, got a round of gentle handshakes, then departed with a quiet smile. He'd lasted four days. In 2002, in a poignant essay about the tragedy, *Guardian* writer Esther Addley wrote, "It is a dignified reaction—one would hope to appear so composed having been told, with several cameras in your face, that you were a loser, a reject, the least popular person in the group."

In the Swedish newspaper *Aftonbladet,* Sinisa's widow claimed that he had been "a glad and stable person" before those four days.

"When he came back he told me, 'They are going to cut away the good things I did and make me look like a fool, to show that I was the worst and that I was the one that had to go.' " She didn't sue the network, but she did ask that the series be discontinued.

Carter had two responses simultaneously. "I was horrified that someone would die on a show I was associated with—and also horrified that someone would die just before it would air." SVT denied responsibility for Sinisa's death, arguing that he was already unstable; a Swedish TV board upheld that claim. Cast members signed a letter defending the program. Whatever the truth, it was clear that Sinisa was innately vulnerable, as an outsider in Sweden. He also wasn't the only cast member with a painful history: One man had been raped as a child, while another spent time in prison. The way Sinisa's widow saw matters, the fact that the series required psychological testing at all demonstrated that it was unsavory, intrinsically dangerous to mental health.

The producers quickly edited the footage to deemphasize Sinisa's role by combining two Councils for the show's debut episode, on September 13, 1997.* But by the time the series aired another episode, three weeks later, the shock had begun wearing off—and the cultural mood shifted. The ratings were good, after all. By its second season, *Expedition: Robinson* had become a bona fide hit. It continued to run, under the simpler title *Robinson*.

At first, the suicide tainted the project's reputation in the global TV market, but then that shadow faded, too. For some, the tragedy even became part of the show's allure. In a documentary about Sinisa's death, *Survivor* host Jeff Probst, who was filmed on the *Survivor* set in Borneo, described the suicide as the first thing he'd read about in his research. It had made him think, "Okay, this show is for real. This really is a show about saying, 'We don't want you around anymore. We don't *like* you.' " Probst paused. "Yeah, hearing about the

---

* In a documentary about the show, a cameraman described an especially awkward factor: Amid the chaos of the early shoot, they had captured no footage of Sinisa leaving the group, so they had to reconstruct the scene and make him leave twice.

suicide made me"—and then he smirked, with a naughty-boy knowingness—"*much* more interested than I was initially."

The next year, the rules of *Expedition: Robinson* shifted. Now the contestants would be voted *in* by their mates, not kicked out. Over the years, the format would continue to adjust, as an expulsion that had once seemed cruel become just another part of the game.

IN THE EARLY 1990S, JUST AS CHARLIE PARSONS'S CAREER WAS entering a nosedive, fellow British immigrant Mark Burnett had been shinnying, rung by rung, up the Hollywood ladder. Unlike Parsons, Burnett had grown up working-class in the dingy East London suburb of Dagenham, the only child of doting Scottish parents who worked at a Ford auto plant. As a boy, he was obsessed with war stories and tales of derring-do, watching American TV shows like the Western *Rawhide* and the cop show *CHiPs*—anything with adventure, anything with heroes. Burnett did share one taste with Parsons: He, too, was fascinated by *Lord of the Flies*.

At seventeen, Burnett volunteered for the British Army's Parachute Regiment, serving as a section commander in Northern Ireland and the Falkland Islands, where members of his unit nicknamed him "the Male Model." In the Falklands, he saw action, including a battle in which twenty-four men of the three hundred in his regiment died, an experience he once described as "horrific, but on the other hand, in a sick way, exciting." Then, at twenty-two, he took another leap of faith. At the time, he'd left the service and was considering a job as "a weapons and tactics adviser" in Central America. During a stopover in Los Angeles, he decided to stay, swayed in part by his mother's plea for him to give up the "gun stuff." (He had lied to her and said he was taking a security job in L.A.) It was October 18, 1982. Burnett had $200 and no green card. He was an illegal immigrant who knew one person in town, a friend whose sofa he could sleep on.

By the next day, Burnett had a job: His friend, a chauffeur, had introduced him to one of his clients, a Beverly Hills businessman who was seeking a nanny for his son. That unusual gig began a de-

cade of cheerful entrepreneurial zeal, as Burnett leapt nimbly from
job to job, a charismatic striver with a gift for networking. His third
nannying boss became his mentor, getting Burnett a job selling insurance. His first wife, Kym Gold, with whom he sold T-shirts on
Venice Beach, got him a green card. Kym's rich stepfather, in turn,
hired Burnett as a vice president at *Face International,* a magazine
that sold promotional pages to Hollywood hopefuls. A few years
into his new life, Burnett started his own business, a telemarketing
firm that sold credit cards to Latino immigrants. It wasn't a glamorous situation, but Burnett had become an American success story: a
businessman living in a big house in Tarzana, with his second wife,
Dianne, who had been one of his employees at *Face International.*

Burnett was infatuated by America, which struck him as a utopia
of social mobility. In Los Angeles, he was no longer judged by his
working-class accent—and in fact, as a white immigrant from the
UK, he was granted a dose of extra class privilege, since strangers
frequently assumed that he'd gone to Oxford or met the queen. It felt
like a relief to him after the "Tall Poppy Syndrome" of his native
Dagenham, he once told former Fox TV president Stephen Chao in
an interview, characterizing Americans as a "giving and trusting"
people. Determined to make the most of his good fortune, he started
attending Tony Robbins seminars, hoping to Unleash the Power
Within.

One Sunday morning in August 1990, when Burnett was lying in
bed with Dianne, reading the *Los Angeles Times,* he stumbled on an
account of a French adventure-sports competition called "Raid
Gauloises." Launched the year before, the exotic sport was not
merely an athletic event but a confrontation with "the rules of the
jungle; a race for survival," with events like bushwhacking up a volcano, camel riding, and skydiving. No American team had ever raced
it before—and the race's creator, a haughty French sports journalist
named Gérard Fusil, openly pooh-poohed the notion that any American team ever could. America was a nation of weaklings, Fusil told
journalists, made soft by air-conditioning.

Burnett was riveted: Here, at last, was the perfect challenge for a
newly minted American citizen—and even better, a fantastic busi-

ness concept. He was determined to launch a U.S. version of the Raid Gauloises, although first, he would compete in it. In 1992, Burnett put together "Team American Pride," recruiting a ragtag group through his gym in West L.A., including an actor from New Zealand, a stockbroker, a "workout instructor to the stars," and a TV producer, Susan Hemond, since they were required to have one female member.

It was an expensive plan. With a valuable blend of naïveté and gumption, Burnett built a marketing package from scratch, cold-calling sponsors and journalists. He struck a deal with a sports equipment company; he talked Prime Ticket, a regional sports network owned by Fox television, into airing a segment on the race. He even managed to get coverage in *Runner's World* by first convincing the editor in chief to run a story about him written by Martin Dugard, then calling Dugard and telling him the piece had already been presold to the magazine.

Burnett had always been an aggressive salesman; in Dianne Burnett's memoir, she describes her ex-husband upselling a client at *Face* so hard that the man had a seizure. Now he was flexing in a new realm, building skills that he would use in TV for decades. Unfortunately, his marketing savvy wasn't enough to help Team American Pride win the Raid Gauloises. When they landed in the Sultanate of Oman, the group imploded. Burnett, the team navigator, kept getting lost. One member was rescued by helicopter. The personal trainer broke his ankle. The actor quit in a huff, kayaking off in a stormy sea. In the *Los Angeles Times,* in a piece titled, "Endurance Race Started Badly, Ended Worse," Susan Hemond described their time in Oman as "the Outward Bound trip from hell," while the personal trainer, Michael Carson, denounced her as "a very hard woman." Burnett was more upbeat. "The race is a lot like life," he told the *Times*. He would do better next time.

He did, in 1993, with a reconstructed Team American Pride made up of himself, Hemond—and, this time, three Navy SEALs. The team came in ninth, despite 120-degree temperatures and (judging from Dugard's amused account in a book about the race, *Surviving the Toughest Race on Earth*) French teams who loathed Burnett for his chipper braggadocio. Group dynamics remained fractious. Toward the end, "a tight-lipped Hemond and a shivering, chattering Burnett" called each other "awful, anatomically explicit names," and Hemond nearly died from internal bleeding. But Burnett—who wore laminated photos of his new son and of his mother, who had died shortly before he left to compete—framed the experience as a triumph, once again. "When things seem impossible and all seems lost—it never really is if you work together," Burnett told the *Los Angeles Times*. "That's what the Raid teaches you."

The truth was that whatever his team endured, finishing was a triumph—and for Burnett, a mark of credibility. Before he even competed, he had bought the North American rights from Fusil, and now he began to hustle, with his partner, a former investment banker named Brian Terkelsen, to launch the sport in the States, creating a company with a less Gallic title: Eco-Challenge Lifestyles, a green-tinted brand meant to attract outdoor apparel companies as sponsors. Fifty teams paid $10,000 each to participate—and MTV agreed to air the event.

Then, Burnett made a rare mistake: He decided that he needed to run the Raid Gauloises one final time, in 1995, in Borneo—confident, as always, that he'd win. It was a miscalculation. Once again, he drove the French teams nuts by bragging that he'd come in first and also flacking the Eco-Challenge. This time, however, it was Burnett who wound up desperate to quit the game. "Unshaven, exhausted, with jungle filth covering their clothing and hands, the five looked thoroughly ashamed," wrote Dugard, calling the collapse "the saddest, most humbling sight I have ever witnessed at the Raid." By then, Burnett and Gérard Fusil were alienated; the two men turned to lawyers after Burnett's failed attempt to purchase the world rights to the race.

Burnett would fold these low points into his memoirs, converting them into a series of Tony Robbins–like life lessons. It was important to trust your gut, it was crucial to choose good teammates—and, ideally, you should not sign up for a third French endurance race in Borneo when you were preoccupied with launching an American one on MTV.

BURNETT'S OFFICES AT MTV WERE RIGHT DOWN THE HALL FROM Bunim/Murray, so, just as Jon Murray had once studied *Cops* for hints about how to make his show, Burnett visited *The Real World*. In the mid-1990s, he produced several iterations of *Eco-Challenge*, first at MTV, then at ESPN, and finally at the Discovery Channel, where he struggled to get the production to match his ideal.

The 1995 version of *Eco-Challenge* was a forty-five-minute special on MTV, made with handheld cameras. The ESPN *Eco-Challenge* was a subset of the channel's X Games. And although the 1996 Discovery series, which Burnett filmed in British Columbia, was closer to his vision—it featured emotional stories about teams clashing, over five episodes, filmed with fourteen camera crews—by 1997, Burnett was at odds with the network. He wanted characters, while they wanted pure nature footage, like the original Raid Gauloises, which had featured images of tiny figures struggling within a grand landscape. Eventually, he licensed the rights to the Eco-Challenge brand to the network for three years, in exchange for a steep raise.

By the late '90s, Burnett was becoming nearly as frustrated as Charlie Parsons—he couldn't seem to launch the sort of flamboyantly theatrical sporting event that he envisioned, something more cinematic than Gérard Fusil's Raid, more emotionally intense than the Ironman competition in Hawaii, "more epic, more dramatic, more bombastic," as he wrote in his memoir, *Jump In!*

Unlike Charlie Parsons, however, Burnett was a master deal-maker, at ease in the ad-driven landscape of Hollywood. Beginning with Team American Pride, he had shrewdly negotiated a thick cut of the profits—at ESPN, he'd managed to double his money by arranging to own 30 percent of ESPN's ad minutes, which he then sold to his own sponsors, with whom he'd *already* cut deals. At Discovery, Burnett spearheaded a radical new density of product integration, putting logos on *Eco-Challenge* bags, players' jackets, and anywhere else they'd fit. In the edit bay, Burnett pushed for his producer Mike Sears to add shots of Land Rovers—and when Sears cut some footage into the sequence, Burnett told him he wanted more. "I said, 'What exactly did you sell them?'" Sears told me, laughing at the memory. Burnett sheepishly admitted that he'd promised the sponsor twenty minutes of car footage.

That was the underlying paradox of Mark Burnett's success: Unlike early reality auteurs, writers like Allen Funt and Chuck Barris, or producers and directors like Craig Gilbert, Jon Murray, Mary-Ellis Bunim, and John Langley, Burnett's Hollywood career had basically emerged in reverse order. At heart, he was a shrewd, passionate marketer with a product to sell: adventure racing. The best way to fund that product was to find sponsors. The best way to get sponsors was to give them a media platform. And television—which Burnett once described as "a necessary evil"—was the sturdiest media platform available, capable of reaching a global audience of consumers.

Along the way, Burnett made some enemies, judging from a *New York Times* article in which Don Mann, whose own adventure competition was squashed by *Eco-Challenge,* compared Burnett to a rattlesnake. "If you're close enough long enough, you're going to get bit." If you admired Burnett, however, you might see that as a compliment. "He could sell a ketchup Popsicle to a woman in white gloves," his former executive assistant (and then his reality show coordinator) Kristen Parks told me, fondly.

Even as he was producing *Eco-Challenge,* however, Burnett had his eye on another project. He'd first heard about the *Survive!* format in 1995, when he met Lauren Corrao at Fox. After Burnett pitched her on *Eco-Challenge,* Corrao had described a similar idea, a bit more like a game show—Parsons's strange vision of a showdown on a desert island, a Darwinian battle that could result in only one winner. "Yeah, I was the person who put Mark together with *Survivor,*" Corrao said, sounding more amused than livid, as she had been back in the 1990s, when she lost the golden opportunity to be not just the TV executive who had greenlighted *The Real World* but also the one who launched *Survivor*—only to hear, five years later, that Burnett was producing the reality show formerly known as *Survive!* without her, for CBS.

After his meeting with Corrao, Burnett went straight to his fellow Brit Michael Davies, then pushed him to introduce Burnett to Parsons, whom he met at a Christmas party. The two men hit it off—and Burnett offered, right away, to buy *Survive!* Parsons said no, as ever. But Burnett never let up: "He hustled me, if you like, for ages," said Parsons. Even after *Expedition: Robinson* was produced in Sweden, Burnett was "very, very keen" on the rights, which Parsons had wisely retained after the sale of Planet 24.

At the time, Parsons had just endured the worst professional experience of his life, developing a show with Keenen Ivory Wayans. He missed England; his father had died. Melancholic and adrift, he got yet another note from Mark Burnett, in 1998, asking to buy the format. Finally, he agreed to sell it. And in two years, Burnett managed to close the deal, at last.

HOW DID BURNETT PULL IT OFF? CBS, AKA THE "TIFFANY NETwork," was the squarest of the three major networks, the sort of stodgy place that MTV and Fox took shots at. Les Moonves, the network's president, was establishing a mass-market mandate, seeking glossy, formulaic hits—cop shows and loud sitcoms, aimed at an aging audience. In fact, if it hadn't been for Ghen Maynard, a junior executive with a passion for 1980s soap operas and social psychology, *Survivor* might never have made it to Borneo.

Maynard was the youngest executive at the Tiffany Network, and also one of the few nonwhite ones, the son of an American military veteran and a Japanese-born mother and raised in Pasadena. He was almost certainly the only CBS executive who was crazy about both *The Real World* and *Dynasty*. At Harvard, where Maynard had studied social psychology, he butted heads with a few professors, who were baffled by their student's interest in the socially positive effects of *Dallas*. As a student, Maynard took a job publishing the *Let's Go* guides, but he left to pursue his passion: TV, specifically network shows—the kind of populist hits that he was confident were the best way to shape the culture.

As the manager of drama development at CBS, however, Maynard wasn't shaping much of anything. Instead, he was stuck in a cubicle by the bathroom near Doug Prochilo, the assistant to the pioneering Black TV director Anita Addison, who was Maynard's mentor. One day, Prochilo gave him a lead: a pitch from Conrad Riggs, Mark Burnett's manager. Everyone in town had turned the pitch down, starting with Discovery, Burnett's old partner. NBC, Fox, and MTV had passed; UPN couldn't afford the show. At ABC, Michael Davies and his mentee Andrea Wong had expressed interest, until internal politics (and then, Davies's quitting his job to produce *Who Wants to Be a Millionaire*) sidelined the project.

Nobody at CBS wanted *Survivor*, either (the name had been changed after Burnett's partner Conrad Riggs noticed a Discovery show called *Survive*), but Maynard fell in love with it, right away. He was drawn to the new format's emotional darkness—and he was fascinated by its radical approach to TV demographics. If they produced *Survivor*, CBS would be able to cast a contestant to represent every type of person—rural, urban, Black, white, rich, poor, young, old—pulling in youthful viewers without alienating the AARP crowd. After a senior executive passed on the idea, Maynard simply ignored him, and then, for a year, he worked strategically, behind the scenes.

Maynard never screened the *Expedition: Robinson* footage for anyone, because he thought it "looked like garbage"; he never mentioned the suicide, either. When he finally finagled a meeting with Moonves, his boss chuckled, then gave him the verbal equivalent of a shrug—which Maynard took as a green light. After he was promoted to vice president, he worked with scheduling head Kelly Kahl and the ad sales team, who were able to pull in sponsors at low rates. For the show to be a success, it also had to be a bargain.

In late 1999, Maynard finally got the meeting he had been angling for, between Les Moonves and Mark Burnett, a day he still remembers as magical. As Bill Carter described the sizzling pitch in his book *Desperate Networks,* Burnett spooled out *Survivor* as a hypnotic campfire story. "Imagine what would happen if a plane went down," said Burnett, describing a diverse group of shipwreck survivors, trapped on an island, as their behavior descended into chaos, à la *Lord of the Flies.* Step by step, Burnett described the tribes, the challenges, the votes—the whole season, down to a vivid scene of the castaways walking "barefoot in the sand at the water's edge." Clearly pulling from the 1996 pitch book, he wowed Moonves with two mocked-up magazine covers—*Newsweek* and *Time*—that celebrated the show's success as a global blockbuster.

Then Burnett highlighted something that hadn't been in Parsons's original prospectus: He explained that the series would be catnip to advertisers. Imagine, Burnett argued, how valuable a pizza slice—or an ice-cold beer or a cellphone—might seem, when they were offered to people who were starving on a desert island?

If Moonves was still dubious, the numbers were unbeatable: *Survivor* not only wouldn't cost $13 million, anymore, it had become a risk-free proposition. Burnett could guarantee CBS the full price in advance, prepurchased by sponsors: $800,000 to offset the loss of CBS reruns, plus $750,000 for the budget. That rock-bottom budget was what won him the green light—and Moonves quickly scheduled the show as a summer tryout. Burnett would be paid just $35,000 an episode.

The two men sealed the deal over a fishing trip, and soon after, Burnett created a company called The Survivor Company, which was split between CBS and Burnett. The network would come to regret this deal—because, at least the way that Burnett understood the scheme, he would keep half of the ad money, just as he had done when he cut that canny deal with ESPN. The legal wrangling would go on for years.

For reality fans, none of that would matter. After decades of experimentation, *Survivor* would release the genre's potential at last.

8

||||||

THE ISLAND
Survivor: Borneo

IN DECEMBER 1999, *SURVIVOR* CASTING DIRECTOR LYNNE SPILL-man began slapping headshots up on Mark Burnett's refrigerator. Spillman herself wasn't especially outdoorsy—her last job had been stalking nightclubs, casting hot guys for the MTV dating show *Singled Out*—but she understood her mission. She needed to find sixteen "castaways," two from each of eight network affiliate regions, so that viewers could root for them like home teams. A few of those contestants had to be over sixty years old, to match the CBS demographic. All of them had to be resilient, to handle the wilderness. This time, there would be no suicides.

Spillman was impressed, right away, by her boss's media-savvy methods: He turned every media hit into a recruitment ad and a chance to build buzz for the show. An early radio promo, "Can You Survive?," had pulled in too many survivalists, so producer Mike Sears, who had worked with Burnett on *Eco-Challenge,* came up with a clever new slogan to attract applicants, brainstorming with line editor Beth Holmes. That slogan—"Outwit, Outplay, Outlast"—would attract a broader, livelier crowd of players, around two thousand in all. It would come to define *Survivor,* long after Sears had left the show, which happened before filming had started.

Each wannabe survivor had to answer the same question: "Which character would you be on *Gilligan's Island*?" They sent in two-minute videotapes, in which they dodged plastic bugs in the shower (Sean Kenniff, a doctor from Long Island) or shot at firewood (Dirk Been, a dairy farmer from Wisconsin) or wore a goofy wig (Brown University anthropology graduate Greg Buis) or parodied the then-popular movie *The Blair Witch Project* (both Gretchen Cordy, a former Air Force survival instructor, and Ramona Gray, a Howard-educated chemist from New Jersey) or dressed up like Mary Ann from *Gilligan's Island* (Colleen Haskell, an advertising student from Miami, and Sue Hawk, a truck driver from Wisconsin, who dressed up as *all* the characters, minus the Howells). Navy SEAL Rudy Boesch's video was thirty seconds long, just a shot of the septuagenarian growling, "I've led a lot of missions and I can lead one more!"

Fifty-eight potential castaways were flown to Los Angeles, to a DoubleTree hotel, under strict orders not to interact with anyone (a rule not everyone honored: Gervase Peterson, a basketball coach from Philadelphia, brought some female friends up to his hotel room, only to have management assume they were prostitutes). Over several days, the contestants were subjected to an intense, and at times bizarre, casting process, an experience that Scott Messick, the show's director, remembered with fondness, decades later, calling it "some of the deepest, most unlicensed psychology that ever existed." Like any hazing ritual, the process bonded the people who performed it as much as the ones who went through it.

Each candidate got a medical checkup. They took in-depth personality quizzes with two psychologists, the surf-loving Dr. Richard Levak and Dr. Gene Ondrusek, whom Burnett had met during the taping of an NPR show about thrill-seeking behavior. Then, to test the candidates' mettle, the producers set out to probe their castaways for weaknesses. They interrogated them, alone or in groups, sometimes waking contestants up in the middle of the night, to see if they'd crack. Kelly Wiglesworth, a river rafting guide from California, got woken by cameras and lights at 2 A.M., then peppered with bizarre questions—If someone stole a pineapple, would she eat it?—as if she were being interrogated by the police. Sean Kenniff walked into a room where he was told to answer three simple questions. Then he was left alone with the camera. Eager to stand out from the crowd, he did Jim Carrey impersonations.

There was a point to these aggressive techniques, Ghen Maynard told me—they needed a resilient cast, made up of people who could improvise under pressure. Still, the gonzo experience was an undeniable thrill for the producers, who felt liberated to delve into the minds of their subjects in a way that you couldn't do with professional actors. One day, Burnett's co-producer Craig Piligian, an "unfiltered" ex-Marine, glared at a religious contestant whom he'd mistaken for a Seventh-day Adventist, then screamed, "What the fuck is *with* you anyway? You go and knock on people's doors?"

Some questions left contestants wondering just what kind of show they were trying out for. A repeated one: "If you were lying in a tent and on one side there was a man and on the other side a woman, and they both came on to you sexually, what would you do?"

After ten days, Spillman and Burnett lugged carts of VHS tapes into the conference room to screen them for Les Moonves. The meeting went poorly: The CBS president declared every participant "abrasive," from Kansas real estate tycoon B. B. Andersen to Los Angeles corporate lawyer Stacey Stillman. There was a single exception: Sonja Christopher, a sweet, ukulele-playing sixty-three-year-old breast cancer survivor from California. Still, over four hours, the CBS brass managed to winnow the group down to sixteen finalists. These sixteen got a final interview, with dozens of CBS executives, who were seated around a massive U-shaped table.

Spillman coached her prospects before they went in. In the hallway, she grabbed the hand of one of her favorites, Jenna Lewis, a "sarcastic and kind of badass" single mom from New Hampshire, telling her, "Funnel the *nicest* side of yourself. You are the sweetest girl on the lane. Seriously. Don't curse." It worked: Jenna charmed the skeptical Moonves. Colleen Haskell got a similar neg: "Don't be that stuck-up country club girl that everyone thinks you are. Be yourself!"

Many of the applicants understood that they were playing a role. Joel Klug, a twenty-seven-year-old gym marketer, could see that he would be the show's "abrasive womanizer, like, the guy who dumped you in high school," so he deliberately insulted a female CBS executive. Sue Hawk told a brassy story about warehouse rats. But mostly, they winged it, hoping to strike a chord with their corporate judges. Ramona Gray, a bisexual African American chemist, took questions from the all-white group of executives for over an hour. "Would you prefer to sleep with a Black woman versus a white man?" ("Duh," she said.) And "Have you experienced racism?" (Another "duh"— and when they asked her how she'd respond to a racist castaway, she joked that she had a black belt.)

This elaborate process, like an E-ZPass to strangers' psyches, got Moonves, who was himself a former actor, excited about the summer series that he'd green-lighted largely because it was free. The producers, too, felt liberated by the novelty of talking to *real people,* who felt unpredictable, loose, and strange.

Still, there were a few divisive choices. Richard Hatch, a corporate consultant from Rhode Island, struck everyone as arrogant and often downright hostile. When he was left alone in a room with a camera, as Sean had been, he mooned the lens. He also scrawled the words "the winner" on the Polaroid portrait they'd hung on the wall. During Richard's final interview, he told the executives, "Listen, you know that you're going to pick me, but what you *don't* know is I'm going to win. And next year, I'll host the show!"

Spillman thought of Richard as "funny, cocky, a little arrogant— and his story was so unique." He was a gay man with an adopted ten-year-old son. He'd studied, briefly, at West Point. Everyone was excited by the prospect of a clash between Richard and Navy SEAL Rudy Boesch, who was openly homophobic. When Moonves polled the room about who they thought would win the final prize, no one picked Richard.

SURVIVOR BEGAN FILMING ON MARCH 13, 2000. THE SIXTEEN castaways, who knew very little about the format, based their expectations on previous reality shows. Gretchen, a former Survival Evasion Resistance and Escape trainer for the Air Force, imagined a gritty adventure-sports series, like Burnett's *Eco-Challenge.* College student Colleen thought of *The Real World*. Several players—Sean, Jenna, Joel, Gervase, and even evangelical Dirk—had Hollywood dreams; they all wanted the prize money. But a significant proportion had applied primarily as an existential adventure, like skydiving or a silent Buddhist retreat—a test of their strength, of who they were and what they were capable of. They wanted to do well but also, to be good. It was a moral dimension that would be key to the first season of *Survivor*, then never quite the same again.

The cast flew to Borneo, still forbidden to speak to one another. For two days, they stayed at the Magellan hotel in Kota Kinabalu, eating heartily, getting schooled on survival skills, and learning the rules (no hitting, no splitting the money). Each of them was cleared for one "luxury" item, like tweezers (Sue) or the Bible (Dirk). Finally, they boarded a long schooner ride to the island, Pulau Tiga. During that four-hour ride, the rules against fraternization were finally lifted. Gervase gave Ramona, the only other Black contestant, a nod. Sue struck up a rapport with Gretchen, her fellow practical tomboy, about how they might use the equipment on the ship. Gretchen also walked over to Richard, hoping to share first impressions. He told her that he was gay and asked if she had a problem with that—and when she said that she didn't, that her father was gay, he cut her off to tell her that she was wasting her time and should probably just quit, since the game would have one winner: him.

When the island was glimmering in the distance, Mark Burnett stepped forward, then divided the group into two tribes, Pagong and Tagi, which were named after the two beaches. Jeff Probst announced that they had sixty seconds to grab any tools or equipment. And then, as the cameras swung around, soaking up the anarchy, the castaways raced wildly around the ship, grabbing anything that seemed useful—tarps, machetes—then jumped into the water and scrambled aboard two rafts, rowing desperately toward Pulau Tiga, against the current. It was a brutal marathon to shore, which was more than two hours away.*

---

* A bold moment, but one that could have been *more* dramatic: supervising producer Brady Connell had lobbied Burnett for the show to *sink* the boat, for real, a plan that fizzled when he couldn't nail the specs.

When they arrived, field producer John Russell Feist was waiting on the beach, with a camera operator and a "soundie." The castaways were vomiting and panicking, struggling to figure out where to sleep. Feist felt over the moon with excitement. A middle-class kid from Texas, he was a daredevil photojournalist who had covered heavy political stories, like a KKK march, as well as tabloid TV, "whatever I had to do to live." He'd fought to get this peculiar job in Borneo, smelling a hit—and now, the scene on the beach confirmed his impulses. It was all real and uncontrived, with raw emotions that couldn't be faked.

Unfortunately, there was a catch. When his team was done filming, Feist radioed headquarters to let them know that they were ready to sleep. They told him to go ahead. "And I go, 'Where do they sleep?' They go, 'In the tents.' And I go, 'What tents?'" Headquarters put him on hold.

As it turned out, there *was* no plan for the crew's sleeping arrangements—and they were too far from camp to walk back in the dark. Feist wound up sleeping on the beach for three days, with cameras that cost $125,000. Sliding over his body were white sea snakes with tiny jaws, too small to bite, unless they snagged the webs between your fingers. Rats scampered in the sand, running from the snakes.

These conditions would get much worse for both the cast and the crew over the next thirty-eight days. That was the paradox of the first season of *Survivor*: CBS had launched a wildly ambitious, masterfully structured television show, one that would elevate the scrappy, low-fi reality genre into something more like a slick, hypnotic blockbuster movie. They were inventing new production techniques on the fly—ways to gamify personal relationships, to turn real life into plot points, to make suffering beautiful. But the *Survivor* production was simultaneously understaffed and underbudgeted, full of people who were literally starving in both the cast and the crew. It was a brutal work environment that left those who endured it even prouder of what they had accomplished, given the conditions.

Not everyone was okay with this bargain. Right away, one member of the Pagong tribe, sixty-four-year-old business tycoon B. B. Andersen, wanted out. He cornered Feist, demanding to speak to Burnett and to hire a helicopter off the island. Feist told him that was impossible: If B. B. wanted to leave, he had to be voted off. Eventually, B. B. agreed to participate. After a risky night journey—with both cast and crew hiking through the pitch-black jungle and the shoreline, as the camera operators walked backward over slippery rocks—B. B. became the second person to be voted out by his tribe.

The first one had been Sonja, Moonves's favorite cast member, the Californian breast cancer survivor. During the first challenge, she had stumbled in her ill-fitting Reebok sandals, slipping under the water. It was just six days into the season, and already two out of three of the older cast members had been voted out. The CBS demo would have to root for someone else.

PRODUCTION WAS DIVIDED INTO THREE SECTIONS: "CHALLENGes," which designed, tested, and oversaw competitions; "Reality," which traced the personal interactions of the castaways; and "Tribal Council," which staged the dramatic ejection ceremony on an elaborate set on the other side of the island. (Brady Connell had suggested Burnett rename the ceremony, originally titled the Island Council, so it would work for future seasons.) At the top of this hierarchical ladder were Mark Burnett and then Craig Piligian, two swaggering, Type-A former military men; below them were supervising producer Brady Connell, who'd worked on everything from Japanese game shows to *Rescue 911* and was in charge of the gameplay, and director Scott Messick, an advertising and sports-TV veteran whose trademark was an edgy, blow-'em-up style and who was in charge of the filmic aesthetic of the show. John Kirhoffer ran the Challenges team; Kelly Van Patter was the production designer. Jeff Probst, the show's host, was hired at the last minute—so late, the rest of the crew was deep in preproduction when he arrived.

The inner circle also contained four field producers—John Feist, the photojournalist; a travel producer named Maria Baltazzi; and two more *Eco-Challenge* veterans, Tom Shelly and Jay Bienstock—

the only four people who were officially allowed to speak to the castaways. These field producers, in turn, oversaw teams of camera operators and audio technicians, around eighty people total, all of them nonunion. There were a few dozen Malaysian locals, as well: a group working as Sherpas and two high-level "fixers," with logistics overseen by the experienced operations manager for the island, Terence Lim.* Psychologist Dr. Ondrusek was there as well. Early on, two film editors cut footage in an editing suite behind the Tribal Council set.

Basic functioning was a struggle from the beginning. The producers had provided each tribe with mosquito netting, canned food, and one sack of rice (initially, they were told that the rice was unlimited—a rule that shifted nine days in). To eat, they had to fish or forage in the jungle. Water was a mile away. Both tribes tried to light a fire, which was crucial for their survival—in Pagong's case, they used magnifying eyeglasses that B. B. had snuck in as his "personal item." Rats crawled over them while they slept in leaky, makeshift shelters—eventually, they would wind up eating those rats. Every two days, the players would compete in a challenge; every three days, one person got voted out. But after a few weeks of near-starvation, the only prize the castaways wanted was food.

Meanwhile, on the other side of the island, the crew was nearly as hungry as the cast, unhappy with the "tish," a local fish stew, which almost everybody hated and nobody seemed to have enough of. They slept in tents or hammocks in brutal heat. There were no lunch breaks, just energy bars scarfed down in the jungle. Intensifying the situation was the danger of Pulau Tiga itself, which was no Hollywood illusion. "Everything on that island wanted to kill you," Dr. Ondrusek told me, remembering "six-foot monitor lizards roaming outside your tent looking for leftovers." Monkeys threw nuts on the tin roofs, infuriating field producer Tom Shelly so much he fantasized about using a slingshot to kill one. Snake Island, where the show staged challenges, was notorious for its banded sea kraits and

---

* Lim, now working for the NGO Stop Fish Bombing USA, expressed special respect for Eric Thein, the show's lead fixer, "the godfather of reality TV fixers."

venomous vipers. The island was also a handoff point for pirates, which meant that it was patrolled by Australian special forces, who carried guns. "I love the outdoors. Used to. *Survivor* beat that out of me," joked Shelly.

Things went wrong, regularly. During preproduction, the beaches were coated in debris—Barbie dolls, plastic bottles, and disposable cameras, swirling in from passing ships—so Malaysian helpers bagged it up. A delivery of ironwood, which everyone had assumed would float, sank—the art department had to put on scuba gear to retrieve it. At the Tribal Council area, gasoline-filled tiki torches leaked all over the wooden floor, with no fire extinguishers nearby, until Peter "Babylon" Owens, the prop master, raised the alarm. Amid this chaos, key details were improvised. "We didn't even realize we needed an island life department," Messick told me. "How do they get water? Medevacs? What happens at four in the morning—how do we get messages to them?" (Associate producer Jude Weng pioneered one solution: "tree-mail," boxes that let the crew send notes to the cast.)

Meanwhile, the castaways were struggling to figure out the game. On Tagi, river guide Kelly Wiglesworth had decided to focus on impressing her teammates, shucking coconuts, trying to make fire in humidity so extreme she felt like she could sip the air with a straw. At first, she butted heads with the geriatric military veteran Rudy, who felt like dead weight to her, unable to build a fire or tie a knot. "And I was like, 'You are the most useless military man ever.' And he was like, 'Well, I was a Navy SEAL. We weren't supposed to build fires. . . . We weren't supposed to be *seen*. I just came in and killed people!' And I was like, 'Okay, point taken.'"

Neither tribe was ever truly alone. Camera operators and sound technicians hovered around them, dangling boom mics; tiny, lipstick-sized cameras were tucked into the roofs of the shelters. Burnett and Piligian showed up on the beach regularly, chatting with the cast and assuring them that their show would be a hit. Still, the people with the greatest power were the field producers, who scribbled in their yellow Rite in the Rain notepads, observing what was going on. They had studied the cast's psychological assessments; they knew what was happening in the other tribe; they knew what the next task would be. Everything they said carried weight, as a guidepost to what was solid and what was an illusion.

Still, some things felt undeniably real. For Joel Klug, the turning point arrived a few days in, when they were handed a bowl of live, squirming grubs in dirt, then told that if they didn't eat one, their tribe would lose the competition. "I thought, no way they'd have us eat a live thing on television, but sure enough—holy shit, it was *terrible*. . . . That's when I thought, this is not going to be some little thing. This is going to be crazy, people have never seen anything like this before."

ASSOCIATE PRODUCER JUDE WENG WAS PART OF THE FOUR-person team that helped develop that challenge, using butods: white grubs, with hard black heads, which Malaysian crew members scooped up from a banyan tree on the mainland. In Los Angeles, her team members had spent months designing and rehearsing competitions, from "attrition" games, which let both genders compete; to goofy creative competitions, like making an SOS sign; to athletic challenges. There were stunts based on military exercises, like a "rescue mission" in which the tribes saved a kidnapped contestant from a tree; there was a race along planks set in the ocean. On the island, the producers talked with the two native fixers, one of them a shaman, looking for ways to incorporate local traditions—and a few elements were also thrown together on the fly, like a *Blair Witch Project* quiz.

The child of Taiwanese immigrants, Weng was a former "preditor" for the Travel Channel, a job she had taken out of pragmatism after graduating from a women's film directing program, at which point she learned how few women got hired as directors. Like Feist, she'd fought hard to get the gig, which let her do a bit of everything, from testing challenges to collating notes from the producers (summaries called "the downloads") to writing questions for Probst for the Tribal Council.

No task was too extreme. The tasks team had sent the butods to an entomologist to make sure that they were safe to eat, but they didn't wait for the results, in Weng's recollection. "We were a bunch of ding-dongs," she said. "We're like, 'Well, shit, if the locals eat them, we'll eat them, too.'" It wasn't easy: The pincers were so powerful that if you swallowed the live grubs whole, they'd damage your throat. Instead, you had to bite the head off and spit it out, then throw the wriggling body back into your mouth and chew.*

To critics of the show, eating live grubs would become a symbol of *Survivor,* a sign of how debased and humiliating the show was. To Weng, who was the daughter of a chef, that missed the point—they were a local delicacy, a source of protein. "Once you got past the movement on your tongue, it tasted like a cross between raw shrimp and bacon."

The entire crew tested the show's challenges together, multiple times—including Burnett and Piligian, who had an intense, competitive vibe. Weng was cautious when it came to Burnett. "I just had an instinctive feeling that he was not your friend, even though he was so charming." Burnett struck her challenges team member Fernando Mills as both jocular and ultracompetitive: The producer threatened to fire him once, if he couldn't finish a race: "I think he was joking!"

Piligian had his own brand of prickly, foul-mouthed macho. In a story that Weng would dine out on for years, the two once shared a boat with eight U.S. Army soldiers, who had flown in to oversee the obstacle course challenge. Piligian, a proud Marine, kept muttering insults about the army until suddenly, he turned to Weng, alarmed, and whispered five words: "My balls are on fire." In yet another production snafu, kerosene for the tiki torches had spilled, leaking into Piligian's shorts. Weng found herself pouring bottled water into her boss's hand as he tugged his waistband out, so he could clean his testicles. It was that kind of workplace—there was no point complaining. The way Weng viewed it, the real problem was not the

---

* Weng's colleague Fernando Mills had sought out that entomologist and secured the doctor's go-ahead the night before the challenge ran. Then he got a follow-up call the next night, after they'd already filmed the sequence—the grubs might have had a deadly parasite, after all. Mills spent the day freaking out, worried that a castaway was about to drop dead.

boundary-crossing request, it was that Piligian never thanked her. "He acted like it never happened."

CAMERA OPERATOR RANDALL EINHORN, WHO HAD WORKED ON *Eco-Challenge,* had years of experience with the outdoors—he was an experienced white water kayaker who'd contracted dengue fever in New Guinea—but he laughed when he first heard about the format for *Survivor.* "We were like, 'Nobody's going to watch that! They're going to be aware that the camera's there, it's not going to feel like they're "surviving"—what are you going to do, let them die?'" Still, he applied, assuring Burnett that he could do more than hold a camera: He knew how to tell a story.

Privately, Einhorn wasn't as sure of himself. He'd filmed emotional meltdowns on *Eco-Challenge,* but in Borneo, the rules were stricter. He wore sunglasses and rarely spoke, except to ask brief questions during interviews. Not everyone that he worked with followed the rules, he knew—a few colleagues were much chattier— but, like the Raymonds on *An American Family,* Einhorn was a cinéma vérité purist. "You let it happen. You don't let it affect the experiment."

Einhorn worked thirteen- to eighteen-hour days, in every section of the show, filming the Reality, the Challenges, and the Tribal Council. On a team with a story producer, another cameraman, and two soundies, he'd hike miles in the rain, carrying heavy digital Betacams in a backpack draped in a garbage bag. An Indigenous crew accompanied them, shoeless, having learned basic English to communicate: "sticks" for tripods, "bricks" for batteries.

As Einhorn worked, he experimented with methods to capture stolen moments. Sometimes, he'd let the contestants wander far away, so they'd forget the cameras were there. He'd put a castaway in the corner of the frame, to emphasize the looming jungle. He took special pride in his water shots. One morning, he approached Rudy, who was standing alone in the ocean, to ask how he felt about his tribe. Rudy, usually taciturn, reeled off a few deadpan sound bites, with the camera an inch above the water, bouncing with the waves.

The moment felt loose, intimate, and funny; Burnett loved it, urging others to imitate it, to interview contestants "on the fly," away from other contestants. Einhorn relished that kind of film-craft; he loved the unspoken dance between him and the soundies, who held fifteen-foot booms, intuitively adjusting to maintain the "line," the 180-degree relationship between two people interacting, to make the scene comprehensible to the viewer. (The audio department, some of whom came from *The Real World,* had initially tried using portable microphones, then ditched them when it was clear that they made recording impossible.)

This work was more difficult than filming a scripted show. None of it could be planned in advance. During the shoot's most satisfying moments, Einhorn felt as if they were building a new vocabulary of cinema, in profound but unspoken collaboration with their subjects.

Not every aspect of the show was strict documentary. Messick, the show's director, had made his bones in TV sports and advertising, building flashy, fun visuals for the Olympics and MTV and creating high-octane sneaker ads. He found the Swedish version of *Expedition: Robinson* visually dull—a brilliant format, without much glory. Messick made sure that the camera operators collected a wide variety of footage: close-ups and long shots, lush B-roll from nature and soaring aerial footage. He filmed the castaways even when they were rehearsing their challenges, to get enough options to use multiple angles. After one swimming challenge, Messick even tried a new approach: He had Malaysian crew members dress up like the castaways, then swim the same course again, imitating the players as they were filmed from a helicopter—a glorious, Olympian view, without cameras visible on the side.

Messick's favorite moment was the Wicker Man event, which had been inspired by the time he and the head of challenges, John Kirhoffer, had spent at Burning Man. It exemplified his vision of the show's aesthetic, using dizzying aerial footage of the castaways. The sequence was shot from a helicopter as the teams trudged across the sand, holding torches, then touched the flames to a massive straw statue of a man. That was the kind of glory he wanted: as if they were playing roles in a primal ritual at the beginning of the world.

Every three days, the production filmed another Tribal Council, the ritual gathering in which a player was voted off the island. The cast and crew were always exhausted that night, after a grueling, hours-long hike in the dark, then across a rickety rope bridge. Unlike the Reality scenes on the beach, the Council scenes took place in an artificial location, a one-piece set that was shipped, at enormous expense, to Pulau Tiga. The set had columns, a gong, wooden benches, a bonfire, and a line of tiki torches, one to symbolize each castaway. There was also a pirate's chest overflowing with fake cash, on Burnett's insistence; production designer Van Patter, who kept trying to add locally sourced authentic touches, to make it "less Flintstones," less like a game show, loathed the cheesy thing, but Burnett wouldn't give in. Castaway Jenna Lewis's first impression of the set was "something out of *The Jungle Book*."

The inner circle, which included Probst, Messick, and Connell, as well as Burnett and Piligian, had met with their Malaysian advisers, then cobbled together a fake mythology for the island, an ersatz ritual that Probst performed with theatrical solemnity. In later years, this ritual would sometimes be criticized by media-studies scholars, who viewed it as part of the show's aura of imperialist schlock. Terence Lim, the Malaysian logistics director, saw it differently. He'd always taken care to safeguard the island's spiritual health, he told me: Two weeks before preproduction, a shaman had performed a ritual on the beach, sacrificing a goat with one clean cut, burying the goat's head in the sand, and then roasting and eating the body. Pulau Tiga was the home for a set of spirits, who needed to be treated with respect. (You weren't supposed to shout out people's names in the jungle, for instance.) But the made-up voting ritual didn't bother him: "If they were to prepare an exact local version, like a head-hunter's house or a longhouse, that would really upset the spirit. In a way, because it's not exactly the same, it's not disrespectful," he said.

Jeff Probst had lobbied hard for the hosting job, which he recognized might be his big breakthrough. He'd sent in a goofy audition video, in which he strutted like John Travolta; then, he'd had a disastrous interview. When Burnett doubted the dimpled game show host's wilderness abilities, he told the Television Academy, he'd ripped up his headshot, shouting, "That's not me. I'm not a studio guy, I'm a writer, I've been in therapy, I *get* the show. *I'm the guy!*" (Burnett said he didn't remember this.) Ultimately, Probst turned to a gimmick not unlike Mike Darnell's *Mission: Impossible* tape: He sent a "letter in a bottle" to Burnett and Ghen Maynard, which he stuffed with mocked-up newspaper articles, each one praising *Survivor* and chalking up the show's success to "the very likeable but unknown Jeff Probst."

Still, if Probst had been a late pick, he caught up quickly, with what Connell described as a near-photographic memory. Like Freud in a safari hat, he passed the conch shell during Tribal Council, probing the castaways' feelings. Then he tallied the votes and dramatically snuffed out the loser's torch, which symbolized a person's life on the island. Early on, when Probst first tossed out the show's signature line, "The tribe has spoken"—a Burnett coinage, according to Probst—it sounded silly. But the castaways were hungry and tired; the shadowy setting, both tacky and majestic, was seductive. The minute you dropped your guard, it all felt real.

Lighting was crucial to this effect. During preproduction, the lighting director had made the set dazzlingly bright, like a game show. After some internal debates, Burnett insisted they turn it down, using firelight and flickering torches instead—and when the lighting manager resisted that note, Piligian pulled his bad-cop producer act, screaming, "Throw that fucking light into the jungle!," then stormed off, throwing a wink at camera operator Scott Sandman. The Malaysian crew stood by, fascinated by what Terence Lim described as "the show within the show." ("We always knew whatever happened, we would be the ones to end up fixing it," he added.)

In an interview with the Television Academy, Burnett described his philosophy for the Tribal Council: The flames were meant to make the castaways feel as if they were literal sacrifices, part of some ancient tradition. Darkness lowered people's defenses; it made them more malleable—every cult leader knew that. Burnett would often speak about *Survivor* in these terms, as a Joseph Campbell–esque cycle of rebirth, with the players moving from the amber light of life into the blue light of death, then back. In Dianne Burnett's memoir, she described watching the first Tribal Council. When Burnett had asked her if it was hokey, she told him that it was—but it worked.

Messick oversaw the filming of this ritual like a conductor. He'd added a key dramatic element during preproduction: a ramp that the ejected castaway walked across, straight into a confessional, a private/public place like the one on *The Real World*, letting them speak directly into the camera. It was a bit like a deathbed confession, their last chance to tell the viewers what it all meant.

OVER THIRTY-NINE DAYS, A PLOT EMERGED FROM THIS PROCESS, full of neck-snapping twists, bold character arcs, and snappy dialogue. The story went like this: In Pagong, the younger tribe, the castaways goofed around as if they were on vacation, taking treks through the jungle and splashing around in a mud volcano, trying and failing to catch fish. They nicknamed their shelter the "MTV Beach House"; they played a joke version of *The Newlywed Game*. Greg and Colleen, who kept sneaking off into the jungle, were the designated Julie and Eric. Gretchen, whom everyone regarded as a warm, practical "mom," was the tribe's leader.

Meanwhile, in Tagi, four players conspired, building a secret alliance. Instead of clashing, the way the producers thought they might, Richard, the gay corporate consultant, had formed a tight bond with Rudy, the homophobic Navy SEAL. The two men then joined forces with truck driver Sue and river rafting guide Kelly, who was just twenty-two. The Tagi tribe members worked hard and built a comfortable shelter, even as the secret alliance geared up, then began to exert their power. Once Sonja and Stacey had been voted out, the alliance knocked off Dirk, then Sean. When the two tribes merged, the alliance targeted the Pagong members, starting with Gretchen, Pagong's beloved captain, a shocking twist.

By the final week, the alliance members were the only ones left. During a totem-pole attrition challenge called "Hands on a Hard Idol" (inspired by the documentary *Hands on a Hardbody*), there was a new twist—Richard deliberately took his hand off the totem pole first, gambling that whoever won the challenge would decide to keep him in the game, since he was so widely disliked that a jury of his former teammates would never vote for him. The gambit paid off. With only three people left, Kelly voted to keep Richard. She'd made the same calculation in an even more dramatic way, during an earlier challenge: During a tie-breaker vote, she'd chosen to eliminate her friend Sue.

Sue took her vengeance: At the final Tribal Council, she delivered a fiery monologue, condemning Kelly. When the jury's votes were cast and tallied, Richard Hatch—the arrogant castaway Burnett had thought would be the first out—had won one million dollars.

No one wrote or directed this drama. Instead, it emerged, organically, from the game format itself, just as Charlie Parsons had hoped it would. It was a breakthrough for the reality genre, and more specifically a win for the approach that *Survivor* co-creator Duncan Gray described to me as "situationalism": building an artificial setting so self-contained, a story was forced to blossom inside it, like a bonsai tree. For several decades, reality productions had experimented with ways to nudge real people, maneuvering them to produce conflict. Allen Funt used pranks to knock strangers off-kilter. Craig Gilbert talked Pat Loud into venting about her marriage while drunk. Chuck Barris set spouse against spouse, while Mary-Ellis Bunim and Jon Murray threw a few pebbles into the pond, then used editing to heighten tensions among the housemates.

On *Survivor,* the inner circle had architected an elaborate-enough false reality—a combination of the isolated rigors of the island, the pressured competitions, and the absurd Jedi mind trick of that firelit Tribal Council—that a captivating drama had emerged, authentically, from those circumstances, complete with villains, heroes, and comical dupes. It was a thrilling development. Just as the pitch book for *Survive!* had predicted it would, *Survivor* rippled with grand literary themes, among them, questions about just what kind of personality ultimately triumphed in a varied human community—and what, exactly, counted as fair play, on TV and off.

Richard Hatch was the one person who seemed to understand the show's premise from the start. *Survivor* wasn't an athletic contest, it was a game of manipulation. Richard didn't invent alliances: *Expedition: Robinson* season 2 had featured a "girl alliance." In Borneo, corporate lawyer Stacey Stillman also had to build an all-female team early on, while gym coach Gervase had an unspoken agreement with Ramona and Joel, his fellow "alphas." But Richard's strategy was more sophisticated: He explicitly sought out players that he could control—and also, players that he could defeat.

Not only had Richard pulled this off, he'd gloated about his schemes during on-camera interviews, while lying to his allies. Like Lance Loud on *An American Family,* he viewed himself as a kind of co-director of the series he was in. One day, he walked by producer Tom Shelly and whispered, "You're going to want to film this," before making his next move.

It can be affecting—and oddly funny—to rewatch the first season of *Survivor,* which is centrally consumed with the question of whether it is ethical to compete in the first season of *Survivor.* Although everyone in the cast came to this conclusion from a different place—from Dirk's evangelical faith to Greg's antiauthoritarianism; from Gretchen's earnest military code to Sonja's Californian empathy—as an ensemble, the castaways nearly universally clung to the notion that the show must be a meritocracy, designed to produce a worthy winner. If you voted to expel another castaway, that person should "deserve" it: They were the weakest player, the most unpleasant player, or maybe the most immoral player.

When you looked at the game through this idealistic lens, forming an alliance was *itself* a corrupt act—one that meant that you should be voted out. "We were like, people are forming *teams*? That's not fair!" said Colleen. Sonja laughed, remembering her response to Sue's early suggestion that they vote Rudy off. "I said, should we even be *talking* like this?"

Despite their isolation, the castaways were all aware that their behavior would be televised—and also, judged. During one Tribal Council, when Gervase denied making a sexist remark, Gretchen shot back, "You know what, Gervase? Right now is when they're going to play you *saying* those words." Joel fretted that if he lied to his teammates on camera, his business clients might blackball him; Sonja worried that her retirement community might disapprove.

The most skeptical of the castaways was twenty-four-year-old Greg—who, much like rock musician Andre on *The Real World* a decade earlier, was a Generation X purist. From early on, Greg was worried that he'd stumbled into something corrupt . . . and also, kind of cheesy. The Brown University graduate was heavily into environmental self-sufficiency (Colleen joked to me that instead of making out, she spent most of her time in the jungle absorbing Greg's lectures on how to collect rainwater off leaves). But although Greg loved the island, he hated the game. Even once it became clear that a secret alliance was decimating his teammates, he dismissed any participation in the process as "sleaziness, duplicity."

"I didn't want to be a bad person, or not a nice person, on TV, for the money," Greg told me, ruefully. Decades later, he looked back on that attitude as a "binary, adolescent" mindset, a way of opting out of the tricky ethical challenge of *Survivor,* maybe by forming his own alliance, to protect his friends. "I should have helped everybody, as much as I can," he said.

Sean, the doctor from Long Island who hoped to become a TV medical expert, suffered from overlapping types of self-consciousness. He wanted to *be* a good guy, he wanted to *seem* like a good guy, and he wanted to impress future employers. His unique approach to this dilemma was to vote the other castaways off in alphabetical order, while talking openly about his method. This strategy wasn't quite as goofy as it looked on the series, Sean told me: Everyone on the Pagong tribe had a first name that came early in the alphabet, so voting alphabetically let him look neutral—even to his own producer, Jay Bienstock, who he worried might reveal his plans.

It took the entire game for everyone to fully absorb the fact that there *was* no "clean" way to win. As river guide Kelly put it, wearily, during one of her confessional interviews on the show: "How do you, you know, stay true to yourself and maintain integrity and still play the game? And you know what . . . you can't."

As clever as Richard Hatch was, he did get a few breaks, like winning fishing equipment a week or two in—a tool that made him invaluable to the team, as a Rhode Islander with solid seafaring skills. The day Richard won that equipment, Burnett bawled the production team out, Weng said. The crew could easily tilt the gameplay if they gave away prizes that weren't equally useful to every player. It was important not to swing the game, even unintentionally.

Field producer Feist, for his part, felt fascinated by Richard, a contestant who initially struck him as too chubby and middle-aged to win a brutal survival competition. The corporate consultant was clearly smart; he could be dryly funny. On Richard's birthday, which he planned to spend naked, Feist had teased him, joking that if he, too, were "hung like a snail," he wouldn't show it off on television. That same day, he filmed Richard when he was underwater fishing, using a spear. Suddenly, Feist saw Richard in an entirely new way—he was a confident predator, spearing a shark, easily outpacing his more physically fit producer. Even Richard's nudity began to seem to Feist like a strategy, a way to look vulnerable and appear less threatening to the people around him.

Later on, when Feist was back in L.A. to focus on editing, he found some unused footage from a camera hidden near the cistern. In it, Richard walked up to the buried water supply, unscrewed the top, and drank his fill of the clean water. Then he squatted on top of the cistern. He washed his genitals and his backside in the water—and he let the water drip back in. Finally, he bottled the water and returned to camp, to give it to his teammates. The moment confirmed for Feist exactly what he had sensed about Richard: that for all his charm, his focus was on control. He was intent on showing dominance over the group, even when he thought he was alone. (Richard denied this incident ever occurred.)

Richard, for his part, said he was blindsided by the idea that anyone might view him as a villain. "I thought I'd be the MVP of the baseball game: 'Look how well he played!' " The way Richard viewed the situation, any hatred directed at him was ultimately about homophobia. He'd gotten naked because it was hot out—and if the nudity was a ploy, it was more that he was trying to repel straight camera operators, winning him moments of privacy.

Whatever the truth, for many observers, Richard's behavior on the air added up to the impression that he was not merely a gay man, but a twisted one: cold, rude, exhibitionistic. Like Lance Loud before him, Richard would become the sort of representational pioneer who divided viewers, repulsive to some and inspiring to others. With his big belly and urge to exert power, he bore some resemblance to the other inescapable antihero of that year, the charismatic mobster holding court on HBO's *The Sopranos*.

Richard's sexuality might have played differently on screen had it been clearer to viewers that he was not the only gay castaway. There were three: Richard; Ramona, whose bisexuality never came up during the show; and the ukulele-playing Sonja, the first contestant to be voted out. Sonja, who had come out in her forties, had had a painful history: Her father had told her homosexuality was a sickness, and she'd had a traumatic early marriage to a man. Her female partner had also cheated on her during her breast cancer treatment. For Sonja, applying to *Survivor* had been a joyful midlife adventure, inspired by a trip that she had taken with other cancer survivors, reviving her lost athleticism. When producer Tom Shelly asked her if she planned to come out as a gay woman to the rest of the Tagi tribe, she told him she wasn't sure.

Three days in, the subject had already come up, twice. On the beach, just before the first Tribal Council began, Richard theorized, out loud, that he must have "a counterpart" in the cast—another gay castaway. Sonja piped up, "You're sitting next to her, Rich!" Then, during that night's Council, Probst brought the subject up with Rudy, who said that he liked Richard and Sonja just fine, since they "didn't look like the queers [he'd] met in the Navy." Sonja remembers telling Rudy off, arguing that attitudes like his kept his gay shipmates stuck in the closet.

Neither exchange made it into the show, a decision that came from the top. Shortly before the episode aired, months later, Burnett called Sonja to reassure her that she wouldn't be outed. She hadn't requested the edit, but Sonja, who felt humiliated at being the first cast member to be voted out, felt grateful. She was fearful of public backlash—and she was afraid of getting pigeonholed as the lesbian castaway, reduced to her identity. When the queer magazine *The Advocate* called her for an interview, she turned them down.

SONJA WASN'T THE ONLY CASTAWAY WHO WAS WORRIED ABOUT being stereotyped, in a cast that was dominated by white, straight contestants. During one challenge, Gervase, one of the two Black castaways, refused to pick up a spear, irritating Gretchen until he explained the problem: Holding that weapon on camera would make him look like "a spear chucker from Africa" to the CBS audience. While he never felt racism from his fellow cast members, it was also true that they didn't see the problem until he explained it.

The producers were the cast's only sounding board. Their opinions held sway for everyone, particularly during interviews, which felt like therapy sessions, but therapy with godlike figures. Shelly always told cast members that they were speaking to him in confidence; he tried to be vigilant about not ramping up drama, letting things develop on their own. Even so, small remarks steered everyone's thinking. When a producer kept asking Greg what he thought about Colleen, Greg thought about Colleen. When Gervase's producer wondered if other people viewed him as sexist, Gervase assumed someone viewed him as sexist. The most leading question: "What would you do if the other team were planning an alliance?"

Burnett and Piligian, during their occasional visits to the tribes, had their own ability to pull strings. Greg remembered sitting in a boat with Joel when Mark Burnett showed up, then leaned over Joel in order to speak to Greg, congratulating Greg on a sexy beach photo shoot Pagong had done for *TV Guide*—maybe to bait Joel by ignoring him in favor of his competition, maybe to get Greg more excited about the show.

These cast-crew dynamics ran in both directions. Gervase snuck glances at the crew's laminated cards, which had biographical info printed on them, while Joel chatted up camera operators, looking for gossip about voting patterns. He knew what they thought of the show. "The crew would talk constantly about what garbage TV this was. They all wanted to be little Scorseses," said Joel.

Occasionally, however, true intimacy emerged between the two sides. About three and a half weeks in, the Pagong tribe roasted one of their chickens. That night, they begged field producer Feist to join them for dinner, worried that he'd lost weight. Figuring it might help with interviews, Feist turned off the cameras. Over coconuts full of chicken and rice, the group had a lovely, easy conversation, a rare break from the stress of production. That night, Colleen told Feist that she was sure nobody would remember their show, that it would disappear. He told her that she was wrong—he'd seen the footage of the first episode, and in just a month or two, she would be famous.

There were also some clashes, mainly between the producers and the young Pagongers, who kept breaking the rules. When they found tiny microphones concealed in the roof of their hut, Greg macheted them out. Knowing brand names were forbidden, Gervase would shout out, "I could really go for Doritos and a Coke!"—or praise Reebok, hoping to score a sponsorship. (A realistic goal: Early on, two cast members, Stacey and B. B., nailed deals to appear in Reebok ads that parodied *Survivor.*)

The rebellious environmentalist Greg Buis became the group's Bugs Bunny, a prankster who kept slipping away, running off to sleep in the woods. He went barefoot, refusing to wear the Reeboks they were contractually bound to put on, even when he stepped on a snake. When the crew filmed a sequence with a time-lapse camera, Greg stepped in front of it, naked, every hour or so, to spoil the shoot. Like Norm on *The Real World*, he refused to give the producers straight answers, taking pretend phone calls from a *Gilligan's Island*–esque "coconut phone." Eventually, Feist warned Greg that with one bad edit, he would get trimmed from the show.

Greg told me he was just trying to be playful, but the crew saw his jokes as threats—particularly his persistent trolling of Probst's sacred island ritual, which infuriated both Probst and Burnett. At the Pagong tribe's first Tribal Council, Greg responded to B. B.'s departure in a pirate accent, "Arrrr, you were a fitting sea captain!" When Probst tried to explore Greg's feelings, he talked about his shorts instead. The producers had to restart the cameras, while the castaways got rowdy, shouting, "We're voting you off, Jeff!" (Probst read about three votes for himself before the production stepped in.) When Greg was finally voted off, he got hustled to a boat, with producers on every side, rather than getting to stay overnight in a hut. There had been rumors that he was planning to mess with the electricity and maybe refuse to leave the island at all.

Gretchen—the Pagong tribe's de facto leader and a much more earnest person—felt grateful for Greg's clowning. Unlike him, she was agonized by the emotions of the show, especially by voting people off, which still gave her pangs of guilt years later. Just before the tribes merged, Gretchen thought about quitting, but she didn't want to be selfish, knowing that the money could change her kids' lives. After the merge, she turned down the offer to enter a "girls' alliance" with Kelly and Sue. Then she got voted out. Afterward, the production did what they always did with ousted castaways, taking her to a cabin behind the Tribal Council and leaving her alone. "That was when I could have used some psychological support," she said, dryly.

Gretchen's mind was racing, ruminating over everything that had happened. Unable to sleep, she went out for a walk on the beach, where she ran into an Australian commando with his gun. Then, on the way back to the cabin, she glimpsed something odd, glimmering in the sunrise—a big mass, something that looked like Styrofoam. With a jolt, she recognized what it was: the back of the Tribal Council set. It was Gretchen's *Truman Show* moment, when it finally hit her that she had been living inside a game show. "I can't tell you how stupid I felt about the whole thing."

BY THE SHOW'S FINAL DAYS, THE CAST STANK, THEY WERE LOW on sleep, and a few were getting seriously sick, including Colleen, who had fleas that had laid eggs under her skin. Their sex drives had evaporated, so any early flirtations were beside the point. But mainly, they were starving. Two crises broke out, both of them involving food. The first was a minor blowup, about a sponsored prize: a single Bud Light, the one Burnett had been confident the castaways would fight for. In Borneo, no one wanted a beer. After some negotiations,

Burnett agreed to offer the winner a spaghetti dinner as well, along with the chance to see five minutes of the debut episode.

That was enough motivation for them to play—although Kelly, who won the competition, loathed Bud Light so much that when Probst handed her the bottle, she waved it away, as Probst muttered, "Wiglesworth, drink the damn beer. The Budweiser people are here." (The sponsors, who were visiting the island, were in the jungle, watching them film the scene.) Kelly drank it, and then she was ferried away blindfolded to a fake "local bar," which was full of Malaysian extras, all of them drinking Bud Light. The spaghetti tasted more like noodles with ketchup, but it was something.

The second food fight nearly sank the show. Shortly after Colleen was voted off, when the cast was down to five players, Richard made a serious accusation. He claimed that Kelly had cheated by taking a Clif Bar from one of the camera operators, Scott Sandman. At first, he complained to Jeff Probst, who, according to Richard, made sympathetic sounds but did nothing. Two days later, he told his main producer, Maria Baltazzi, that he was going to walk out.

Rumors began to spread wildly among the crew: Over his earphones, Lim heard they needed a boat—and at first, he thought either a cast or crew member had been seriously injured. Everyone left the beach. Then, Burnett and Piligian met privately with Richard. From Richard's account, the discussion swung wildly in tone, with the producers alternating between promises and threats, charm and pressure. At times, Burnett told him they were family. "You and I are together for life! This is an *adventure*." Burnett also warned Richard that he was ruining his life's work—and he called Richard bitter for not having figured out how to get extra food. "I'm like, 'Whoa, this dude is corrupt,'" said Richard. He recalls that Piligian played bad cop, yelling, "I *am* Standards and Practices."

Nobody but the people present know what actually happened—and Richard, who is a skilled manipulator by everyone's account including his own, is hardly a reliable witness, particularly since his claims became part of a later legal struggle, when he was convicted of tax evasion, then spent fifty-one months in prison. But Richard insisted that that afternoon, the show's executive producers assured him he'd ultimately get *more* than a million dollars, because, among other things, the taxes on his winnings would be paid.*

Kelly has a different version of the story. In her telling, Richard and she were both standing in the same area when Scott Sandman announced that he was taking a nap, then let a Clif Bar slip out of his pocket, whether intentionally or by accident. She and Richard discussed the find, then buried it in the sand to hide it—and then, later on, offered it to the other cast members, who split it, with only Rudy turning it down.

She agreed with Richard that some extra food had made its way to the cast by the end of the show: The Pagong women were slipped treats from the crew, like Werther's caramels and cigarettes. But a full investigation proved she'd done nothing wrong, Kelly said. She had no secret stash of food, as Richard claimed; no one was trading sexual favors, his other accusation. The crew had simply pitied the starving cast, she told me—and there was no rule that they couldn't take a Clif Bar that had seemingly fallen from the sky. (Sue Hawk, for her part, didn't judge the women for taking food. "Can I get down on you for being smart enough to let your boobies get you some extra food? No. What the hell? Why not?" Sue told me that Kelly gave her part of a candy bar, and that, although she felt guilty, she ate it. She viewed Richard as "a whining motherfucker.")

Scott Sandman's version is close to Kelly's, although not identical. From his account, he was napping on a bench, his knee propped up, wearing his usual multipocketed cargo pants, when a Clif Bar accidentally fell out. Later on, he saw Kelly holding it. He reassured her that he wouldn't demand it back and hugged her—and when Richard, nearby, pretending to sleep, saw them, he reported it. Kelly, for her part, says there was never any hug between her and Sandman.

Like the "pebbles in the pond" shutdown on *The Real World,* the crisis shook the production, but only briefly. Sandman got fired, even

---

* Sean, who visited Richard in Rhode Island on the day he cashed his $1 million check, says Richard never mentioned this promise until years later, when he was in legal trouble. Sean also told me that he was continually audited for his own winnings and knew he had to pay taxes.

after he begged to be reassigned (although he continued to work for Burnett, later, on *Eco-Challenge*). Then the cameras started rolling again, a juggernaut heading toward the finale.

THE FINAL TRIBAL COUNCIL TOOK PLACE ON APRIL 20, THEIR thirty-ninth day on the island. The jury comprised the last seven castaways who had been voted out, all of whom had been staying together in a hotel in Kota Kinabalu, on the main island: Rudy, Sue, Sean, Colleen, Gervase, Jenna, and Greg. Ramona wasn't one of the jury members, but she'd stayed on in the region anyway, touring Thailand and Malaysia with her fellow early evictees Joel and Stacey. As a result, Ramona wound up witnessing these events in a way that no other castaway was able to—as just another viewer, standing with the crew and reveling in the fireworks.

She watched as Kelly and Richard, the two finalists, each explained to the jury why they should win; she watched them take questions. And then, as each jury member voted, offering up a few brief words of explanation, Sue Hawk stood up. Her eyes were burning. Seething, Sue laid out her case against Kelly, her former friend. Kelly and Richard were like a rat and a snake, Sue raged. They were like the animals who had dominated the island—and Sue encouraged the jury to vote for Richard, an openly malicious predator, a venomous snake, over Kelly, whom she viewed as an underhanded rat.

Sue ended her speech with a florid, indelible vow of vengeance. "If I were ever to pass you along in life again and you were laying there dying of thirst, I would not give you a drink of water. I would let the vultures take you and do whatever they want with ya. With no ill regrets." The crew members who were gathered around Ramona all made silent, exhilarated eye contact with one another, overwhelmed by the sheer drama of the moment.

Later on, Ramona would hear speculation that Sue couldn't have composed that speech herself, something that was easy for her to believe, given the power that field producers held. Maybe she was right: Feist told me that as Sue vented to him, hashing out her feelings about Kelly and Richard, Feist asked her, "Don't you think this whole game is like this island, where it's inhabited by just rats and snakes?" Sue's eyes lit up; she got the idea immediately, then went and wrote it into her speech.

Sue doesn't remember Feist saying that—and Sean told me that he watched Sue write the speech herself, scribbling furiously for an hour on computer paper, in a fugue state. A self-proclaimed "redneck tomboy" from Wisconsin, Sue was a truck driver, working twelve hours a day. She had imagined that her trip to Borneo would be a vacation from the grind of her daily life, the opportunity of a lifetime. That day, however, she was full of bile, having been sure that Kelly would choose her over Richard, that they would both get to "screw Rich royally and blow his mind." After writing a few drafts, she winged it as they filmed, delivering the best bits from memory. "I couldn't hit nobody, you know what I mean? So I was like, fuck it, I'll just slice you open with my tongue," she told me.

Several jurors were alienated by the sheer intensity of Sue's bitterness, especially Gervase, who changed his vote in order to support Kelly. But Sue had no regrets. Years later, she had the draft of the speech laminated, to hang on her wall.

Watching this all go down, Ramona wasn't thinking about any of those details. Instead, she was watching as a fan. "And then the guy that everybody hates, he *wins*? It was an epic, epic moment. If we had thought bubbles, you could have seen, 'Oh shit! No way! This is great.' Or—maybe it would be money signs in their eyes. 'This is gonna be ratings gold. Like, a finale with this speech? We did it! Whoever had anything to do with this, you need a raise.'"

EDITING BEGAN ON PULAU TIGA, IN A DIGITAL SUITE TUCKED BE-hind the Tribal Council set. Early cuts fell flat: When the crew screened some footage, Van Patter, the art director, remembers griping to a producer, "We're killing ourselves for that piece of crap?" It felt like a game show, with gimmicky effects, zooms that resembled peepholes. Soon, though, the editing team found their groove. They began to build in clear, dramatic act breaks; they let the viewers see the action instead of just hearing about it. Two editors left, while the other two, Sean Foley and Brian Barefoot, moved back to Los Angeles. There, working with Ivan Ladizinsky and Jonathon Braun, they rolled out stories right up until they aired. It was a surreal blur of deadlines, making decisions on the fly. "Why did I use so many dissolves?" Barefoot once moaned in *CineMontage*.

Even so, everyone involved was confident that they had a hit on their hands. Together, the producers and editors had mapped out each episode's six acts on the wall, with A, B, and C plots, cleverly intertwined, the way they would be in a scripted drama. The aim, in every episode, was to offer viewers a powerful sense of cause and effect, making the final ejection feel at once surprising and inevitable. To inject a sense of grandeur, they wove in intoxicating B-roll, with underwater shots and images of scuttling lizards, embedding viewers in the world's riskiest tropical getaway.

An "old-school guy" with a film background, Ladizinsky worked intuitively, scribbling notes on yellow pads to pinpoint funny moments. From his perspective, there was a cultural split between the producers, who were obsessed with the plotline, and the editors, who were all about images, emotions, and music. In his ideal episode, interviews would be used sparingly, even if that risked confusing the audience. He was resolutely opposed to any trickery, like creating dialogue from scraps of audio, the sort of shoddy shortcut that might happen on Fox. "If they didn't say it, I'm not going to *make* them say it."

Still, there were many opportunities for creativity, for flair that went beyond the ordinary. In the episode where the tribes merged, Ladizinsky got to break format. When the Tagi tribe rafted away from the beach, he used an aerial shot to turn their boat into a speck in the ocean—and then he added a clever shot which had been taken through two abandoned crates, in imitation of a scene from *Jaws*, putting the viewer inside the mouth of the monster. It was a witty visual joke that had a deeper emotional undercurrent, the ideal edit.

Ladizinsky took just as much pride in pacing each episode correctly, so it would be hard for viewers to predict that week's loser.

The week Gretchen was expelled, his wife screamed out loud. "The audience loves a good left hook to the jaw," he told me, with pride.

SURVIVOR DEBUTED ON MAY 31, 2000, SIX WEEKS AFTER FILMING had wrapped. It promptly smashed every ratings record around. One day, Mark Burnett walked into the editing suite and slapped the viewership sheet up on the wall: They'd beaten *Friends*. Glowing coverage saturated the media—as did outraged commentary, by observers horrified by the bug-eating and Richard's amoral behavior. "We were cutting the show in these little offices in Santa Monica, near the 10, and we would walk to the deli for lunch and all of the magazines, every one of them, had pictures of *Survivor*, headlines on *Survivor*," said Shelly. When the castaways appeared on Bryant Gumbel's *Early Show* after each week's Tribal Council was aired, they boosted his ratings, too.

In late August, the "Final Four" appeared on the cover of *Newsweek*, just as Parsons's early prospectus had predicted. Inside, the magazine described the show's success as having blotted out any criticism of the reality genre: "Before 'Survivor' debuted 13 weeks ago, the pundits whined that 'reality' shows were the beginning of the end of television—or worse. They'd kill the sitcom, because they don't require writers and are cheaper to produce. They'd obliterate what's left of Americans' sense of privacy and dignity, too. Nobody's complaining now. . . ."* Ghen Maynard—the executive who had shepherded *Survivor* into the world, back when nobody saw it as a winner—felt utterly vindicated. And Tom Shelly, who had adored *An American Family* in film school, made a cold call to one of his heroes, Craig Gilbert, to thank him for having "put that type of storytelling into my DNA."

Miraculously, CBS managed to keep the winner of the show secret until the finale aired. At one point, a rumor spread online that Gervase had won—followed by a second rumor that CBS had spread the first rumor. Every bit of gossip, however superficial, stirred up

---

* There were a few exceptions: PETA picketed CBS on behalf of the beleaguered island rats, with signs reading, "Rats have rights! Survive on veggies!"

press. Not every story was insignificant, however. The most alarming one concerned Richard Hatch, who had been arrested for child abuse, having physically disciplined his son while they were out jogging. The charges were eventually dropped, but the story was covered heavily on a growing set of *Survivor* gossip sites, particularly The Stingray, a website launched by an investigative journalist named Peter Lance, who had a personal gripe against Richard Hatch, with whom he'd once planned to co-write a biography. When their book contract fell apart, Lance became a full-time muckraker, digging up dirt on *Survivor* and other reality shows. The vehemence of the online reactions was new to Maynard, who watched, in alarm, as viewers streamed into the AOL chat rooms to rip his cast to shreds. Ultimately, however, any press was good press—and the production even created a website for its haters, survivorsucks.com.

On August 23, 57.3 million fans of *Survivor* gathered, all around the world, to watch the finale—almost half of the people who were watching television that night. Partygoers dressed up as their favorite castaways and sipped Mai Tais. Charlie Parsons, sitting at a bar in London, caught a glimpse of these celebrations on the BBC. He took a sip of his own drink, feeling melancholy. He owned a cut of the profits, but the world was celebrating *Survivor* as an American show, a brilliant and original new format, invented by Mark Burnett.

WHEN LES MOONVES ORDERED UP A LIVE REUNION SPECIAL TO follow the finale, Stacey Stillman, the third person voted off, saw an opening. The reunion hadn't been covered in their original contract, so Stacey, a lawyer, encouraged her fellow castaways to unite to demand higher pay. CBS was selling thirty-second ad slots for $600K; Stacey figured they each deserved $100K. Instead, another castaway ratted her out and new contracts were FedExed to all of them, for $10K, to be signed in two days. The truth is, Stacey's plan was probably doomed from the start. Many of the contestants needed that $10K—and they had no desire to alienate CBS, which controlled their job opportunities. Stacey herself wasn't a popular figure among her castmates, some of whom found her obnoxious.

Before the reunion special, which was hosted by Bryant Gumbel, the cast watched the *Survivor* finale together in the greenroom—Gretchen held Kelly's hand during Sue's speech—and then they all walked out onstage. There were boos when Sue walked in. The audience booed Richard, too. They cheered the loudest for Colleen, "America's Sweetheart." The reunion special is an odd document of the cultural moment: Among other things, Rudy's homophobia is treated as a lovable quirk and everyone, including Richard, laughs at Sean's jokes about creating a brand for him called "Fat Naked Fag." The special's focus is almost entirely on the ethics of *Survivor,* with the audience polled on questions like "Did the right person win?" (65 percent said no). At one point, Richard gave a speech defending CBS's editing against complaints of deception, which led Gumbel to joke, "You already won, Richard."

By the time they filmed that special, the cast was vibrating with stress, coping with the fame hangover that afflicted nearly all reality stars, intensified by what they'd been through physically. Gervase felt unstable for a month and a half, flooded with PTSD symptoms and unable to sleep. He was unimpressed by CBS's aftercare. Dr. Ondrusek had been a casual presence at best, he said, with bad boundaries—he had partied with the cast at the Magellan bar, rather than actually treating anyone. A reflexively upbeat person, Gervase told me that he was extremely grateful for the head start the show had given him in Hollywood, and overall, he was fine with his edit. (He did have clarifications: The remark he had made comparing women to cows was a logical offshoot of a discussion about how willing people were to humiliate themselves for love, he argued.)

But the racial politics of the show bugged him, and would continue to do so, even decades later. "It sucks. It's terrible," he said of being one of the few people of color in a show made by white people. "It starts off as an uneven playing field, number one. And it's a weight you have to carry around. Everyone else has to represent themself and their family, their city. But as the Black guy, I'm representing the whole Black race."

Ramona had similar feelings: She had been mortified to be shown napping—portrayed, like Gervase, as lazy, when in reality, she was just recovering from rowing out to the island, which made her intensely seasick. Decades later, the two castaways would become part of a group of Black castaways who lobbied CBS for change, and in 2020, they won an agreement to have 50 percent of the cast and 40 percent of the crew come from diverse backgrounds.

WITH *SURVIVOR* A TRIUMPH, THE PRODUCTION WAS VULNERABLE to anyone who challenged its mystique. Shortly after the season finale aired, that threat arrived, in the form of a lawsuit from Stacey Stillman. Although Stacey had been voted off early and was barely a presence in the series, her accusation struck at the heart of the *Survivor* premise: that it wasn't a fair fight.

The crisis started in September, just after the Emmys. At that time, Joel was dating Stacey, and during a red carpet event, she joined him and Dirk Been in a limo. Stacey was teary-eyed that day, shaken up by a bad interaction she'd had with Burnett. As the two men comforted her, Dirk apologized to Stacey for having voted her out. It wasn't the first time he'd apologized: Six months earlier, at the Magellan hotel, he had told her, during a brief exchange, that he regretted his vote, which he said was the result of "some bad advice."

Now Dirk explained who had given him that advice: Mark Burnett. The show's executive producer had encouraged Dirk to vote Stacey out and keep Rudy in, Dirk confessed—and he'd given Sean the same advice. Startled, Joel chimed in with his own story: Early in the game, Burnett had urged him to talk B. B. out of quitting, something he'd thought nothing of at the time. Stacey was furious. The way she saw it, she'd been cheated. Burnett had favored Rudy over her—or maybe he just didn't want the three oldest contestants, the CBS demographic, to be voted off first.*

---

* In 2018, Probst, while answering a question about how much sway *Survivor* producers held over who won which challenge—and whether it was ever tempting to push for a specific player—said the top brass rarely even thought about that idea anymore. That was not as true during the early seasons, he added: "Nobody wanted Richard Hatch to win. . . . We thought it was the end of the show: The big naked evil villain wins!" Instead, they had hoped the winner would be Rudy, "this Navy SEAL vet," he told Jeff Garner in 2023 on the podcast *The Producer's Guide.* Another potential bias in Rudy's favor had emerged in Stacey's lawsuit: Rudy had worked on logistics for *Eco-Challenge,* back in 1996. Mark Burnett testified that he didn't know that fact until after the show was filming.

At first, Stacey didn't go public. Instead, she asked CBS for money—and then, she asked them to cast her on an upcoming *Amazing Race*–like series that the network had been developing. (She wanted Joel to be her partner, but he declined.) In early 2001, Stillman sued CBS and Burnett for fraud, breach of contract, and unlawful business practices, seeking $75,000 plus lost prize money. CBS countersued for $5 million, for breach of contract and defamation. Eventually, CBS settled, for an undisclosed amount. Stacey didn't respond to my requests for an interview; Dirk Been politely declined. It's likely that they'd signed NDAs.

Why did CBS settle? It's impossible to say for certain, but it might have been due to the six-hour, 603-page deposition given by Dirk Been, who spoke to legal authorities as an "independent third party," not linked to either side of the dispute. Originally sealed, the documents were released by Peter Lance, the muckraking journalist who ran The Stingray. Only selected portions of his testimony made the news at the time, but decades later, Dirk's deposition is a heartbreaking, sometimes darkly funny read, a near-biblical fable about the power of reality producers, as well as a touching account of disillusionment, right at the genesis of the genre.

Under oath, Dirk described the events of his ninth day in Borneo. After his team lost a challenge, when Dirk was standing on the beach, waiting for the boat to arrive, Burnett walked over, friendly as ever. At the time, Dirk was planning to vote Rudy off, since their oldest team member hadn't been winning challenges and his main skill, cooking rice, seemed like something that anyone could do. Burnett made a suggestion: Rudy had skills that might come in handy during later challenges. Maybe Stacey was a better target?

It was a brief interaction, just five minutes, and then Burnett left and walked over to Sean, who was standing nearby. Later on, when Dirk and Sean went off together to get water, they had a conversation about voting Stacey off, agreeing to speak to Richard about it. That night, in a rainstorm so heavy that it blew out Stacey's torch before it could be snuffed, she was voted out, 5 to 2.

After the vote, Dirk started to worry. As a result of the downpour, the Tagi tribe had stayed overnight near the Council set, giving him time to think. "I was not feeling good about myself in—in—in—in what I had just done," he testified. The conversation on the beach made him uneasy. Why had Burnett spoken to him? He'd assumed the producer was trying to be helpful—and he trusted Burnett, a person who understood everything about the show, including what the upcoming challenges were. Still, it felt wrong. Over the next few days, he grew more guarded with the producers. Two councils later, he was voted off.

Just before he left, Dirk had another encounter, in which a crew member, who seemed to be drunk, began dishing to him, spilling out surprising details about the production process, like the fact that the producers had at one point considered helping his starving tribe out by filling some empty fishing traps with fish. The tapioca that Dirk harvested had been planted by the crew, too, because it wasn't indigenous to the island.* To Dirk, these small bits of stagecraft felt profound. "I just remember feeling like, 'Man, I just had this huge, awesome, wonderful experience that was such—more than just a physical thing, such a spiritual journey for me where I learned so much, grew so much as a person.'" Now it looked different to him, contrived and artificial, not a challenge but a cheat.

Whenever a castaway got voted out, Burnett asked them to write him a letter. Gretchen had written one of these notes, which she assumed was an honorable request for feedback on the production— although in retrospect, she wondered if Burnett was trying to unearth any complaints. In Dirk Been's letter, he effusively thanked Burnett for casting him. Then he laid out his concerns. The fact that Burnett had swung those early votes had "tainted the entire experience," Dirk wrote; the fakery made him feel "cheap and used." Somehow, he still viewed Burnett as a friend, perceiving the two as "partners in a project"—and he explained that he hoped that his candor could help Burnett to improve the show and change his ways.

---

* This was true, according to Lim: The two fixers were often deputized to do similar small tasks, like planting tapioca and quietly refilling the water reservoir.

For a month, Dirk heard nothing. Then, in late June, Burnett left a few phone messages for him, just as he was about to embark on his media tour, the one each castaway took after their final Tribal Council aired. When the two men spoke, Dirk brought up their beachside conversation about Stacey, only to have Burnett deny that it had ever happened. Dirk was flabbergasted. In his deposition, he described himself as distraught, shocked that a man he admired was "telling me something I know that happened didn't happen. And one of us was a liar."

Then Burnett changed his tone. Maybe Dirk had a point, he said; he would consider his concerns. He also added that if Dirk wanted endorsement deals, he needed to be upbeat. *Stacey* had been upbeat! That's the way she'd booked that Reebok ad. Dirk interpreted Burnett's statement as a coded warning: If he spoke out about the behind-the-scenes manipulation, he'd be off the CBS gravy train, for good. Even worse, Burnett appeared to be revealing something more insidious, which was that he had never respected Dirk's Christian faith, that he thought he was the kind of man who could be bought. "And then he said, 'Well, you need to be positive—' That was the end of the conversation."

Burnett denied Dirk's story, under oath. In court, he testified, "At no point during the production of *Survivor* did I or any other producer, staff member, or crew member ever direct any of the participants to vote for or against a particular participant, or attempt to manipulate, coerce, induce, intimidate, or influence the participants' voting." He testified that he hadn't known that Rudy had worked on *Eco-Challenge* until the show was filming. Sean testified, as well, confirming that Burnett had spoken to him, but only to encourage him to "vote his conscience." Four other castaways also testified on CBS's behalf, including Joel.

To cynical observers, it's probably easy to shrug off Stacey's complaint as a shakedown, ginned up by a lawyer with a grudge who was voted out early and came across, on the air, as a high-handed diva. Dirk, however, had no real motive to lie. If anything, he was testifying *against* his own interests, since he was one of the least marketable members of the cast. To complicate matters further, in his deposition, Dirk came across as so determined to take responsibility for his own vote that he refused to say that Burnett "manipulated" him, even when he was describing explicitly manipulative behavior. Dirk's deposition tells a messy, ragged story, which makes it believable. Everyone I spoke to—from the cast to the crew to CBS executives—described Dirk as "the real thing." He was a true believer.

During one of our interviews, Joel asked to see Dirk's deposition, which he'd never read. The two men had stayed friends after the show ended; they'd acted together in a Christian thriller, *Gone*. Still, Joel was startled to read Dirk's words, which reminded him of an account by a kid molested by a priest. Dirk had been trusting and vulnerable, he said. Joel was not, maybe because he viewed Burnett mainly as a businessman, protecting his investment. The Tribal Council was never real to Joel. He knew that it was a TV set all along.

LIKE THE LOUDS AND THE CAST OF *THE REAL WORLD,* THE BORneo cast were, for a while, blindingly famous. A few of them retreated, including Greg Buis, who dropped off the grid—reemerging, briefly, to take an ill-fated gig with Donald Trump's modeling agency. Colleen scored the most high-profile opportunity, booking a role in a Rob Schneider movie. But most of the cast, whether they were interested in a Hollywood career or not, began to jump from gig to gig—charity events and paid speeches, cameos on *Baywatch* (Joel), *JAG* (Rudy), *Diagnosis: Murder* (Sonja), and *The Hughleys* (Gervase). It was fun and lucrative; by the turn of the millennium, the reality economy had finally begun to take shape. Sue Hawk interviewed presidential candidate George W. Bush on Regis Philbin's talk show. Sean booked a gig as a doctor on a soap opera and a medical expert on CNBC. Gervase did hundreds of gigs over the years, acting as a de facto agent for the group, passing along opportunities to other castaways. Colleen and Jenna both turned down

Playboy, while Sue declined to play a lesbian in *Dude, Where's My Car?*

For the first year, each of these opportunities had to be okayed by CBS, which barred the castaways from working for their competitors—nixing Richard's chance to host NBC's *Saturday Night Live,* to his lasting fury. (Six of them thumbed their noses at CBS by appearing on NBC's *Weakest Link* the minute the year ended.) But reality fame finally offered some potential for real employment, including the chance to reappear on *Survivor* itself, beginning with an "All-Stars" season in 2003. Many of the players took CBS up on these opportunities, including Kelly Wiglesworth, who returned to play in a "Second Chance" season in 2015.

Kelly, the runner-up to Richard Hatch, had suffered some of the show's most severe repercussions. "I went full *Lord of the Flies,*" said Kelly, describing her return to civilian life. While *Survivor* was airing on CBS, she ran river trips nonstop, trying to tough it out. Her feet bled, she had crushing fatigue, and, although she refused to admit it, she was getting sicker, both physically and mentally. Finally, Gretchen—one of the few cast members Kelly still spoke to—insisted that CBS step in. In Los Angeles, specialists found parasites and fungus in her intestines and her liver. Kelly's adrenal system was shot and she needed heavy medication.

Although the symptoms still linger for her, years later, she never considered suing: "I signed up for it," she said bluntly. She'd had a happy life, raising a child, and, for a time, hosting a show on the E! channel. Kelly also stayed close to the crew, although not the cast. Some of them had apologized for their votes against her—including Sue, who sent her letters and jewelry, which Kelly ignored. (Sue said that she sent her beads as a "good energy gift.")

Decades later, the one thing that truly bugged Kelly was a symbol of the show, at once literally and figuratively: the *Survivor* logo, a silhouette of a woman holding a torch—a picture of Kelly for which she'd never been compensated. "That's the thing, they try to nickel and dime you for everything. And you're like, 'Man, like at this point, twenty years in, you guys have made billions off of me.'" After the show, she'd gotten a gift basket from the production: a box of rice, some fruit, and a candle that smelled like rain.

"WHAT A DIFFERENCE A HIT MAKES," WROTE WILLIAM KECK IN the *Los Angeles Times* in 2001, predicting a deluge of new reality TV experiments. Although much of the *Survivor* crew stuck around, a few took jobs with these new shows. The most prominent refugee was Scott Messick, who had a falling out with Burnett, despite, or possibly because of, his contribution to the show's gritty, rock star visual aesthetic, as well as concepts like the fire symbolizing life. When he wasn't offered a pay bump, Messick got snapped up by Mike Darnell at Fox, who deputized him to film another reality show, *Boot Camp*. Burnett brutally sued that show off the air, on the basis of "trade dress"—the idea that viewers were being tricked into thinking the show was *Survivor.* It was one of the first of the aggressive lawsuits that would distinguish the era.

Having *Survivor* on your résumé could be a mixed blessing for the people who created it. When assistant producer Jude Weng's future mother-in-law introduced her to a powerful female TV executive, the woman grabbed Weng's hands and asked what she'd worked on—and when Weng said *Survivor,* the executive dropped her hands and snapped, "Those shows are garbage, they're ruining the culture," then marched away. Weng was mortified and resentful. She'd helped create a blockbuster, only to have it marginalize her further. Although Weng spent a few years working on reality shows, she became determined to break into scripted TV, even if it meant a pay cut. It took a lot of effort, but in time, she became a popular director on smart network comedies, including *Black-ish* and *Crazy Ex-Girlfriend,* and twenty years after *Survivor* aired, she finally got to direct her first film for Netflix, the *Goonies*-like *Finding 'Ohana.*

Camera operator Randall Einhorn took a similar path. He worked on *Survivor* for six seasons—"five too many," he said. He grew to hate the new cast members, always yammering about their Hollywood agents. To him, the whole show felt compromised: Production included more "do-overs," reshoots to get the right angle; the crew took shortcuts, collecting "sweet-and-lows," snippets of dialogue designed to be used as voiceovers for specific scenes. A few seasons in, the producers also incorporated "The Dream Team," a group of official stand-ins, who, like the Malaysian crew, dressed up like the castaways and helped pose for aerial shots and close-ups.

These techniques weren't cheating, depending on how you thought about it, just attempts to streamline the look of the show. But Einhorn, a purist who bridled at sweeteners, preferred footage that was "gleaned, not produced." Once, he took a gig as the director of photography on *American Idol,* a stable show with better hours and benefits, only to quit after five days. Ultimately, Einhorn found a miraculous off-ramp when, while he was filming a snowboarding series, an NBC executive introduced him to Greg Daniels, a writer who was working on an NBC sitcom called *The Office.* The show was an American adaptation of Ricky Gervais's scathing British mockumentary, a dark satire of reality TV, in which a cruel boss is made worse by the presence of the cameras. During his interview with Daniels, Einhorn told him that he hoped to use his reality skills to make something more wholesome, comparing his aesthetic goal to a tofu hot dog: "good food wrapped like bad food."

On *The Office,* Einhorn repurposed the tools he'd honed in Borneo, capturing stolen moments between Jim and Pam, just as he'd once filmed Greg and Colleen. He let the camera go in and out of focus, putting key interactions just out of frame. He also encouraged his camera operators to imagine themselves as characters, giving them notes, just like the actors, to help them show their motivations through their camera work. "You don't know this, but you suspect this. You *think* she's looking at Dwight, but you're not sure."

The American version of *The Office,* which took a less jaundiced perspective on reality TV than the original, inspired a wave of mockumentary sitcoms, among them *Parks and Recreation* and *Modern Family.* These shows used the aesthetics of reality TV—its liquid, spylike camera work; its "gotcha" flashbacks, which could expose snatches of hypocrisy or hidden backstories; its touching confessionals—as fuel for new types of comedy, cannibalizing the genre that was, in the eyes of many sitcom writers, an economic threat to their existence.

In the forty-five seasons that followed Borneo, *Survivor* kept changing, evolving in response to new conditions, new technology, new psychology. The challenges grew more baroque, the castaways more athletic. Spillman began casting for a fresh demographic: pretty Hollywood manipulators with thick skin and, ideally, sales experience. There were modern stars like Boston Rob and Amber, a showmance that became a marriage, as well as proud villains like Jonny Fairplay. There were castaways who did multiple seasons or jumped to other shows.

The editing changed, too, speeding up, as the producers incorporated drones and GoPros, and eventually switched to HD. Jeff Probst became an executive producer and, in time, replaced Burnett as the show's guiding visionary. But the primary change in the show had to do with strategy. After that first season, everyone knew enough to build an alliance—and the game became a meta-game, full of in-jokes about old seasons, like "Pagonging," slang for voting off the other tribe, one by one. Nobody starved on *Survivor* anymore, including the cast. Starving, in the end, wasn't good television.

The Stacey Stillman suit had faded into the Reddit threads of fanatics, many years ago. If Mark Burnett had put his thumb on the scale that day on the beach, did it really matter? *Survivor* wasn't a show about fairness, in the end. It was about something else: the thrill that swept over Ramona when she got the chance to watch the *Survivor* finale like any ordinary viewer, reveling in the sight of ordinary people under pressure, a drama more explosive than any fiction. After Borneo, TV executives knew what was possible.

9
‖‖‖‖‖

THE FEED
Big Brother

TIMING WAS EVERYTHING.

While *Survivor* lit the fuse in America, another show set off the reality explosion in Europe—*Big Brother*, which debuted in Holland almost simultaneously. Structurally, the two formats shared some DNA: A diverse group of strangers were trapped together, then nominated one another for expulsion. But in a technological sense, the two shows were centuries apart. As daring as *Survivor* was, it was produced like most TV: It was filmed, then edited, and then broadcast a few months later. *Big Brother*, in contrast, was a live fishbowl full of cameras, streaming immediately over the internet. With its Orwellian name, it hinted at a future in which everyone would live under surveillance, 24/7. It also took the risk of being boring, in a way that *Survivor* never had—and nearly paid the price for it.

Big Brother was created by John de Mol, Jr., the son of a crooner known as the Dutch Sinatra. A swashbuckling, chain-smoking media entrepreneur who had been a tabloid star since his teens, de Mol was more like the Dutch Chuck Barris, best known for a protoreality genre he called "emotainment." Among his early hits was *Love Letters,* in which couples competed for the most outlandish marriage proposal—a "marry me?" during a parachute jump, say—as hidden cameras recorded their partner's reaction. The Dutch TV market was tiny, but Endemol Entertainment (the company name after a merger with Joop van den Ende) punched above its weight, cannily flacking formats to other European countries. De Mol was confident that the lucrative United States market, the biggest jackpot of all, would be next, and in 1994, in *Television Business International,* he predicted he'd hit that goal within two years.

He didn't. Instead, by 1997, de Mol was getting itchy, eager to launch something more radical, attention-grabbing, and extreme. New technologies were changing the way people interacted; producers were raring to monetize these new tools. In 1996, he'd bought two six-month options for the *Survive!* format from Gary Carter, only to let them lapse.* Then, one rainy afternoon in September 1997, the same month that *Expedition: Robinson* debuted in Sweden, de Mol gathered key staff members—Patrick Scholtze and brothers Bart and Paul Römer—around his desk, for one of their regular brainstorms. Their goal was to come up with something truly original, richer than mere emotainment, a format to shock the world.

As de Mol chain-smoked, stubbing each cigarette out halfway through, his team talked in circles about various social phenomena, among them the trend of workers taking long sabbaticals and the omnipresence of surveillance cameras. Paul Römer brought up Jennicam, a website on which an American college student was documenting her life, stripping down in front of a webcam, but also letting people watch quotidian daily behavior, which visitors found mesmerizing. Then, just as the meeting was winding down, Bart Römer brought up an article that he'd read about Biosphere 2, the scientific project in which eight people were cut off from society.

Suddenly, these ideas seemed to combine, like Pop Rocks and Coca-Cola. The way Paul Römer remembered it, it was a collective eureka. Excited, de Mol put forth a provocative plan, which he called

---

* Instead, Endemol would soon hire Gary Carter himself, who moved to Amsterdam—in part, he told me, because it was a better place to live as a gay man in an interracial relationship, with an adopted autistic child.

"Project X": Endemol would find a group of unrelated strangers, then stick them inside a confined space for a full year, with no contact with the world, surrounded by cameras. The team discussed the concept for hours, giddy at the notion of this voyeuristic peek into human nature. Then de Mol swore everyone to secrecy.

Paul Römer oversaw the development of the format, which took a year and a half. In its earliest iteration, Project X was titled *The Golden Cage*. A group of contestants would live in a luxury mansion, then get chased out, one by one, by a "ghost," a manipulative voice determined to drive them all crazy. Römer tried a few dry runs, with his colleagues playing the contestants; to his delight, less than three hours in, someone had a teary meltdown. As part of their research, they consulted psychologists and interviewed people who'd spent long periods in submarines and spaceships. But it was soon apparent that the last-man-out format was a bust: "You could drive people crazy in a week."

Römer tried a new approach: Instead of competing, the contestants would work together. Their lodgings would be basic—and they'd earn their luxuries by performing challenges. On the advice of Gary Carter—who now worked for de Mol—the timeline shrank to a more doable three months. Then de Mol, who loved games, added a crucial element: The housemates would be evicted not by one another but by the show's audience, which would vote over the phone. Every few days, the housemates would nominate two people for eviction—and then the fans would pick one of them to walk out the door.

In early 1999, Endemol ran another test, setting up a house full of cameras and using six volunteers. Once again, things became emotional quickly, when, after a few drinks, a cast member began to open up about his sibling's suicide. "If a real person tells a real story with real emotions, not produced, and you have watched that guy for twenty-four hours, you start to connect . . . it's raw, it's unfiltered, it goes right from your brain to your heart," said Römer.

Project X was finally ready to go public.

Although the emotional footage he'd collected for the show— now called *Big Brother*—delighted Römer, it also nearly tanked the project when a network head, whose daughter had killed herself, got a look at it. The executive felt disturbed by the show's unsettling intimacy—and worried about bad PR, too, after the suicide linked to *Expedition: Robinson,* two years earlier. Indeed, critics had begun attacking the show long before it aired, warning that it was both unethical and dangerous. Martijn Raadgever, a recent college graduate who had taken a job working as an editor on the show, avoided mentioning it to his friends at parties. Even the Dutch parliament denounced the show. Paul Römer began doing regular television spots, prepublicity in which he urged viewers to see *Big Brother* as a profound experiment and a fun soap opera, not a threat, let alone the spear tip of fascism.

For the show's ensemble, the producers tried to cast a metaphorical family—specifically, a group who resembled the Ewings from the 1980s American prime-time drama *Dallas,* whose photo was pinned up at the casting office. The final group included Karin, a middle-aged mother recovering from breast cancer; Ruud, the "crazy uncle," a "funny regional person," as Raadgever described him to me; and assorted symbolic siblings, among them Bart, a hot, blond former soldier, and Sabine, a small-town fashion stylist on the rebound from a breakup.

Römer felt confident that *Big Brother* wasn't a psychologically risky project, as long as they cast "well-balanced, good-thinking" contestants. He wasn't worried about the show's ethics, either. The only time he felt any qualms was when they added some farm animals to the garden, during planning. "I thought to myself, 'Wait, can you have a *cow* there?'"

BIG BROTHER DEBUTED ON SEPTEMBER 16, 1999. THE HOUSE, which was located just outside Amsterdam, had been embedded with twenty-four cameras and fifty-nine microphones. Running through its center was a cross-shaped office, with wide passageways that enabled four cameras, rolled by camera operators, to peek into every room from behind two-way mirrors. Twelve directors worked in shifts. The technology had improved enough since *Expedition:*

Robinson that they were able to handle a deluge of footage. De Mol insisted that the audio quality had to be crystalline: The video was less important, he argued, since viewers were used to the glitchiness of surveillance footage. Still, in an era before digital editing, each tape still needed to be logged by hand, a grueling process that required a staff of more than a hundred people. The edited episodes would run on broadcast TV in prime time, five nights per week.

The online feed, on the other hand, would run all day and all night. Despite all of their early talk about Jennicam, the notion of live streaming all of the footage from the *Big Brother* house didn't emerge until relatively late in the show's development—and Römer himself was initially skeptical. It was an expensive experiment, not to mention tricky to pull off, on the then-rudimentary internet. The live feed also raised other concerns: Because Web viewers would know what happened, when it happened, Endemol would have less leeway to shape the story in edited episodes. In the end, all of those fears were unfounded. Far from spoiling the show, the live stream wound up whipping the audience into a frenzy—and it heightened media coverage, too, by giving journalists fresh tidbits to react to, on top of the nightly episode. As it turned out, nobody minded watching a juicy conflict twice.

That first season was pure cinéma vérité, Römer told me—and Sabine, the small-town girl in the cast, agreed. "There was no manipulation of the group. There was no staging. . . . It was really almost raw footage," she said. The producers did make a few allowances for danger, like chaining down an axe that was included for woodcutting, lest anyone impulsively decide to chop up their housemates. The group played goofy games, in order to win food. But the broader rules were largely improvised. When Ruud slept in the nude, the producers kept the cameras rolling. Housemates could smoke pot to relax.

That first night, 20 percent of the Netherlands tuned in. Then, the ratings dropped. For two weeks, the *Big Brother* feed was dominated by slow, *Godot*-ish dialogue, as the roommates napped and made corny jokes about how frequently they cooked beans for dinner. On the tenth day, one housemate quit, announcing that she was bored and found the program "false and hypocritical." Raadgever remembers a director joking that if things became too dull, de Mol would order the contestants to start killing chickens.

Then, a miracle happened. A significant plot had finally emerged: a love triangle involving Bart, the ex-soldier, and Martin, a thirty-two-year-old businessman, both of whom had developed crushes on Sabine. When Martin falsely accused Bart of being gay, Martin was nominated by his housemates for expulsion, then voted out by the audience. In the aftermath, in a sweet romance that entranced the nation, Bart and Sabine fell in love, in small glances, displaying delicious, authentic physical chemistry—at least, they fell into what Sabine described to me as a "holiday romance."

The ratings for *Big Brother* spiked; the advertisers poured in—and suddenly, the risky experiment was a hit. A competing television station became so desperate to get in on the action, they parachuted one of their presenters into the house, over the walls.

The other housemates—who felt left out of the steamy love affair—promptly nominated Bart and Sabine for expulsion, putting them in competition with each other. It was a dynamite twist and, from Römer's account, a storyline that would recur, organically, in nearly 70 percent of the early *Big Brother* seasons in multiple countries. The house always turned against the newly infatuated couple; the vote always pulled in viewers, eager to take sides—Team Sabine versus Team Bart.

Römer's voice grew dreamy as he narrated the events that followed, sounding triumphant, even decades later. "Of course, they were angry toward the group. They felt *betrayed* by the group," he said of Bart and Sabine. Feeling guilty, the other housemates offered the couple a private bedroom. Then, the day before the eviction, infrared cameras captured images of the couple's bodies as they shifted and moved beneath the blankets. One of that night's image still felt tattooed in Römer's head, he said: Sabine, reclining in bed, smoking a cigarette. It was a breakthrough visual: a filmic sex cliché made more powerful because it was really happening.

A certain self-consciousness was dawning inside the house by then. Soon after Sabine was voted out, Bart, as he was walking through the halls alone, glanced into one of the hidden cameras and said, "Now, you won't vote me out, will you?" Like Richard Hatch, he recognized that he might win—and that the people who were watching could help him. "And I thought, 'Ah, now you've got it.' It was like watching the birth of a theatrical aside," said Gary Carter.

One snowy day in mid-December, the cast, which was down to four people, gathered in the hot tub in the garden. While they soaked together, Karin began to speak, for the first time, about her breast cancer, sharing vulnerable details about her life. Suddenly, the finalists heard a sound—a roar. One of them jumped up, naked, and ran up to the roof to see where the noise was coming from. For the first time, he caught a glimpse of the show's audience: There were thousands of people, gathered around the perimeter fence of the house, cheering.

To Gary Carter, the naïveté of that cast had been something precious and unique. They were pure in a way that no *Big Brother* contestant would ever be again: "astronauts in an age of innocence," as he once put it in a keynote speech. For Paul Römer, the experience of making the show was a high that he'd keep on chasing for years.

For Sabine and Bart, however, the outcome was significantly bleaker. Five weeks in, when Sabine got evicted, she discovered that her country was united in its hatred of her. The "cigarette scene" had made her infamous, as if it were a leaked sex tape. To make matters worse, she had confided to another housemate that she wasn't really in love with Bart, that their relationship was "good for the time being." For this perfidy (the world's first televised "showmance," as the phenomenon of such temporary relationships would be known), Sabine became an early reality TV villain. The blond, buff Bart—who cried, seemed heartbroken, and, crucially, was a man—was widely adored.

On the penultimate day of the twentieth century, Bart, too, stepped out of the *Big Brother* house. He'd won 250,000 Dutch guilders, approximately 113,729 U.S. dollars. He was also blazingly, irredeemably, impossibly famous. Just three days into his new life as a reality TV celebrity, he had his first nervous breakdown. For the following two years, Bart lived his life in a state that he described, in 2008, in *The Times* UK, as "oblivion," behaving as if he were a rock star, doing "soft drugs," sleeping with fans, and taking full advantage of lucrative media gigs, all the while saturated with self-loathing. "I was a false saint," he told *The Times*.

Although Sabine and Bart remain friendly, there was a gulf in their perspectives—unlike Bart, Sabine retained many warm memories of her time in the house, which had felt like a sweet vacation from the pressures of the world outside. She's had therapy to deal with the aftermath; she wrote a self-published memoir, as well, hoping to speak to a younger generation of women. Decades later, however, she remains haunted by that cigarette scene. She didn't understand that there were infrared cameras recording, she said. She'd felt safe at night. The images were also deceptive, she added—she and Bart didn't have intercourse, they just made out. In 2020, she was still asking Endemol to take the scene down. "It sounds intense, but it was kind of like an assault," she said.

Like Bart, she had come to believe that the reality genre was intrinsically unethical. "It's not honest TV. It's not what you think it is. Producers can make a person out of you."

BEFORE THE DUTCH SEASON HAD EVEN ENDED, ENDEMOL WAS rolling out franchises around the globe. Each *Big Brother* franchise went through the same virtuous cycle: first, media outrage, then a tsunami of audience curiosity, and finally, always, those sweet, record-breaking ratings, as the European nations united, one by one, in their embrace of Endemol's shocking new television format as dishy, divisive must-watch. In Italy, a cardinal warned that the 24/7 *Big Brother* cameras would steal people's souls, while left-wing polemicists protested it with poetry readings. In Spain, the professional clown-activist Leo Bassi stood outside and read Orwell's *1984* through a megaphone. In Denmark, the cast went on strike. When the Norwegian minister of culture told Gary Carter that he had destroyed Norwegian culture, Carter snapped back at him: "I said,

'You are the minister of culture. *You* take responsibility for your culture!' All I did was put a frame around it and get Norwegians to perform being Norwegian."

Back at Planet 24, Charlie Parsons was fuming: The way he saw it, *Big Brother* was nothing but a rip-off of *Survivor*. He wound up filing an intellectual property lawsuit against de Mol, but the courts ultimately ruled in de Mol's favor—the two formats, the judge decided, weren't really all that similar. You couldn't trademark the broad idea of a group of people voting one another off a metaphorical island.

Meanwhile, de Mol's dreams of world media domination appeared to be coming true, culminating in a massive bidding war for the U.S. rights to *Big Brother*. When CBS won the prize, the franchise came with one condition attached: The Dutch producers would produce the U.S. show, following the exact blueprint that they had perfected, down to the design of the house. Paul Römer flew out to Los Angeles for preproduction. He remembers feeling not merely confident but downright cocky, ready to conquer "the Olympics of television." He understood that the schedule was tight, with just six months for prep—he'd be working with Evolution Media, a reality production company best known for *Bug Juice,* a Disney show about summer camp—but he was certain that he could pull it off. After all, it had worked in every other country.

Instead, Römer wound up overseeing one of the most notorious flops in reality TV history. The Dutch producer was frank about his own mistakes, when we spoke: He chose his battles poorly from the beginning, he said, sparring with Les Moonves over tiny decisions (Could they show a bare butt silhouetted behind a shower door?). He had also crossed swords with Ghen Maynard, who, in the wake of *Survivor,* had been promoted to vice president of the newly created alternative programs division. Standards and Practices hated him, too. But whatever his inability to work with the top brass at CBS, Römer also felt as if the new version of *Big Brother* was simply cursed, from the start.

One serious problem was timing. Since the American *Big Brother* began airing one month after Mark Burnett's blockbuster debut, it was widely perceived as a copycat show, bafflingly set in an ugly house in Studio City instead of a sexy jungle in Borneo. It aired five or six nights a week, with a cumbersome online-streaming component that felt designed for nerds. (Myself being one of them: I logged in every day.) There had been a few similar internet experiments that year—most notoriously, dot-com millionaire Josh Harris's *We Live in Public,* in which he streamed his relationship to an audience of chat-room voyeurs, but also, Dennis Rodman's RodmanTV.com, which gave fans a paid glimpse of his party pad in Newport Beach, California. Those projects were comparatively interesting, though: outré, oddball experiments. The CBS version of *Big Brother* just seemed dorky.

The casting went poorly, too. Römer felt unnerved by the placid Midwesterners who applied for the show, a part of American culture he didn't even realize existed. Still, he dutifully picked his fake family, which included Eddie McGee, twenty-one, a one-legged Irish American wheelchair athlete from New York; Curtis Kin, twenty-eight, a gentle, Stanford-educated Asian American lawyer from New York City; Josh Souza, twenty-three, a jock from California; Brittany Petros, twenty-five, a vivacious pink-haired punk virgin from Minnesota; then-current Miss Washington Jamie Kern, twenty-two; and Jean Jordan, a twenty-six-year-old bisexual stripper from Minneapolis. For the show's "mom and dad," he cast Karen Fowler, a forty-three-year-old Indiana woman in a bad marriage, and George Boswell, a forty-one-year-old hot-tar roofer from Illinois. Other than Curtis, they were all white, so to add diversity—or what he described as CBS's demand for "1.8 Black people"—he cast William "Will Mega" Collins, twenty-seven, a youth counselor and political activist from Philadelphia, and Cassandra Waldon, thirty-seven, an elegant U.N. employee from New York. He didn't have a choice about the host: Moonves had insisted they hire a low-level CBS news anchor named Julie Chen.

On July 5, 2000, *Big Brother* debuted on CBS. The first episode was produced live, as a special event designed to introduce the format to U.S. viewers. The special opened with a shot of the contestants milling around the parking lot of the "house," an elaborate set that had been built on a CBS Studio Center lot. As the cast members' friends and families cheered them on, Chen—reading from her vacuous script with a chipper brio—ushered the contestants through the front door. Once they were inside the house where they'd agreed to live for the next three months, the cast began to wander around aimlessly. They stared into the two-way mirrors; they inspected the chicken coop and the IKEA-style furniture. They made polite chitchat in the kitchen. When the credits rolled, Moonves turned to the Dutch producer, stone-faced, and told him, "I want you to know that was the worst hour of television that I've ever been associated with for my entire career."

Römer wasn't worried: *Big Brother* was always boring early on. He cued up some food competitions, like dominoes and jumping rope. He watched as inside jokes bubbled up, like Will Mega giving the hot-tar roofer the nickname "Chicken George," a hat tip to the slavery miniseries *Roots*, because George had decided to oversee the care of the chickens in the yard. Then Römer waited for the love triangle to emerge.

Instead, something strange happened: American viewers, who voted by calling in to CBS's "America's Choice" lines, began to eject the show's liveliest characters. The first to go was Will Mega Collins. A mischievous figure, like Greg Buis on *Survivor*, Mega had spotted a crack in the system right away: Every day, the cast members would walk into the "Red Room," the confessional space where they stared into a camera lens and spoke with the producers, through an overhead speaker. When they left, they'd tell everyone else what had happened, including anything the producers had told them.

Mega decided that he would lie to his housemates, instead. While no one was looking, he turned some furniture upside down; then, he told his housemates that the messed-up room was a puzzle, one that *Big Brother* wanted them to solve. Nothing in the rules specifically forbade these tactics, but, to Mega's frustration, the producers promptly told the housemates that he'd made the whole thing up— and then added a voiceover in the edited episode, explaining that Will had tried to break the housemates' trust in *Big Brother*. Years later, he still fumed at the injustice. Whatever conflicts Mega had with his housemates—who Cassandra had warned him perceived him as "a certain kind of brother," a "Mac Daddy" type—the top brass for the show had turned him into a target. They'd changed the rules midway through, the way society always did when Black men succeeded, he told me.

Will Mega also had a problem *outside* the house—one that he wasn't aware of. Nine days into the filming, the New York *Daily News* had printed a photo of him holding a gun at a 1998 rally in Texas, where he was protesting the dragging death of James Byrd, a Black man murdered by white supremacists. Unbeknownst to CBS, Mega was a former national field marshal for the New Black Panther Party for Self Defense, under the name Hiram Ashantee—a background that he'd never mentioned in interviews (the producers didn't ask, he said). Mega had set out to try to repair the weak image of Black men on television with a "confident, intelligent, and uncompromising" model of masculinity, but instead, like Kevin on *The Real World,* he spent a lot of his time debating racism with white strangers, for whom Mega didn't bother to hide his contempt. A handful of strategic gestures, like sharing cigarettes, fell flat; when he threw a competition, thinking that he might starve someone out, it just annoyed them. Then the producers gave everyone the food anyway. He felt as if he were trapped inside *The Brady Bunch.*

There was one bright spot: Mega's conversations with the other Black housemate, Cassandra, who encouraged him to try a different approach, to be more open to listening and bonding with the other people in the house. Unfortunately, as nuanced as their debates about racial identity and interpersonal strategy were, they weren't an easy sell for the CBS executives. "This was almost like an offense; they couldn't cope with it," said Römer.

After he got voted out by America's Choice, Mega went to a *Big Brother* panel for TV critics, toting copies of the Bible and Robert Greene's self-help book for schemers, *The 48 Laws of Power.* The critics peppered him with questions about recent controversies, including some criticism from New Black Panther leader Khalid Abdul Muhammad, who objected to him giving a white woman a massage on TV. When one columnist asked Mega if white people and Jews were his enemies, CBS senior vice president of communications Chris Ender, who was standing by Mega's side, clutched his heart. Mega responded that he saw anyone who was "evil and unrighteous and against God" as his enemy.

After Mega was voted out, things quieted down in the house, somewhat. Still, no love triangle had emerged, the way Römer expected it to. The Dutch producers tried to create one anyway, by editing together montages that hinted at a competition between virgin Brittany and sex worker Jordan for the heart of jockish Josh—weaving a melodrama from extremely thin material, with a lot of weight placed on two camera shots of Jordan and Josh lying together on a bed, scored to suggest chemistry. Online, where a small but passionate group of nerds had been watching the 24/7 internet live feeds, it was crystal clear that there was nothing going on.

Then Jordan was the second person to be voted out, wrecking that storyline, too. When Jordan first caught sight of an ad for *Big Brother* while watching *Oprah*, she was working at Schiek's Palace Royale, a "gentleman's club" in Minneapolis. She imagined that going into the house might function as a kind of free therapy: If she exposed herself to the world's judgment, she could learn from it. When a CBS psychologist called her the most honest person in the house (the sort of compliment that several reality cast members described getting during psychological testing), Jordan was thrilled.

Later on, she would see it all differently. Either the casting people had missed her psychological issues—among them, a history of trauma—or, more likely, they viewed them as an asset. From her account, Jordan was deep in denial at the time, caught up in grandiose fantasies that she was "the Margaret Mead of strippers." She was also struggling with undiagnosed mental illness, which expressed itself in a hollow identity and wildly shifting, labile emotions—problems that she compensated for by erecting a false persona: "very confident, very opinionated, very antagonistic." In ways she didn't yet understand, she was a reality producer's dream.

The first episode concluded with several beautiful shots of Jordan peering around her bedroom in awe, excited to explore this new setting. But once filming began, her mood crashed. Everything about the *Big Brother* environment felt contrived to Jordan, from the bright colors to the saccharine personalities. She had multiple clashes with other cast members. Shortly before she and Mega were nominated against each other, the two of them bonded. "We don't like them, either," he told her, comfortingly, while she sobbed.

Four weeks into filming, "America's Choice" voted to expel Jordan. She had spent much of the previous week crying, as the cameras ground their gears, making an eerie *nee-nee* sound, as they pivoted to show her in her bunk bed. She sobbed in the Red Room, too, in front of the camera's fixed eye. After she did her live interview with Julie Chen, she was flown to New York to appear on the David Letterman show. That night, at her hotel, Jordan opened up her computer, then began to read the chat rooms. The experience was annihilating.

"Oh my God, the whole country is rejecting me. This is like *millions* of people are rejecting me. And I understand why they reacted that way. I completely do! But man, that was so difficult," she told me. Once the media tour was done, she flew home, where she hid out in her apartment, soaked in shame. CBS had offered no psychological follow-up, but a few weeks later, the producers called her. They wanted to know if she'd be willing to reenter the house, as a late-stage plot twist. She said no, so they found a different hot girl to play the role. "They were just kind of scrambling," Jordan said.

It took Jordan many years to get therapy, which she credits with transforming her life. Maybe she'd misunderstood everything, she thought, looking back; maybe the housemates she viewed as boring were just stable. Or maybe they *were* fake, in ways that she couldn't respond to. She never watched reality shows, which she saw as existentially exploitative. But after we spoke, she decided to watch *The Bachelor.* In the episode she watched, one of the bachelorettes wore a crown and called herself the Queen, a beautiful woman radiating instability. It felt like looking in a mirror. "I'm sure casting selects people like her for the shock-and-awe factor, to give people someone to hate, to stir things up. But they know someone like that can't win the game. She ended up leaving with her tail between her legs, eaten alive."

BY THE TIME THE TWO BIGGEST TROUBLEMAKERS LEFT THE house, the *Big Brother* housemates had absorbed a profound message: If you stood out, you'd be rejected by everyone around you. Talk about sex or politics, flirt or fight, and the TV audience would kick you out. A sludgy groupthink seized the ensemble, defying the best efforts of the producers to spark conflict. Instead, the "hamsters" (as online viewers had nicknamed them) played cards by the pool for hours at a time; they gardened and worked together on their dull, daily tasks; they groomed one another, using Kool-Aid-colored hair dye. They wrote songs about goodness and about not being judged. Any hint of sexual energy or scheming drained away completely.

In a way, the show had become the flip side of *Survivor.* If the Borneo series operated as a surprisingly profound metaphor for cutthroat workplace politics, the Studio City show suggested a *different* type of office, the kind of place where you made bland chitchat all day, terrified of being disliked. Eventually, the production team tried to step in, offering cast members money if they would let Beth—the replacement babe they cast when Jordan turned them down—take their slot. The offer kept going up, reaching $50,000, but every housemate refused to take the bribe. A hideous fetish for solidarity had paralyzed the house.

This logy mood was spiked by heavy waves of paranoia, which were set off by unexpected messages from the outside world. In late July, two mischievous Hollywood screenwriters, who worked nearby, began throwing tennis balls over the walls, attached to fake newspaper clips, including one that suggested that Will Mega was releasing nasty rap lyrics about his housemates, another quoting President Clinton calling the CBS series a disgrace. More unnerving, in late August, an enterprising skywriting pilot began dragging banners above the garden, carrying messages paid for by Jeff Oswald, the spokesman for Media Jammers, a grassroots "culture jamming" group who described themselves as "pranksters with a conscience." The first of these banners read, "Big Brother Is Worse Than You Think: Get Out Now."

These messages inspired two trains of thought. On the one hand, they suggested that the housemates were trapped inside a cruel, exploitative project and that they shouldn't trust their producers, who were lying to them. On the other hand, they suggested that the show was a huge hit, which everyone was talking about—and that they were all massive stars, like Richard Hatch or Rudy Boesch, the instantly recognizable stars of *Survivor,* which had debuted a month before they entered the house. It was enough to send everyone's anxiety level into the stratosphere.

In early September, Media Jammers sent a new set of messages flying overhead: "Losers Talk—Heroes Walk—Together," "There Is Dignity in Leaving," and "It's Bad . . . Take Control . . . Question Julie Chen." The same month, Kaye Mallory, a local schoolteacher, used a megaphone to shout messages over the wall, among them, "If you walk out together, you'll be famous! The ratings are terrible. This will save your dignity!" It's no wonder they didn't accept the bribe and let Beth in: Ms. Megaphone had already warned them not to take it.*

Similar protests had erupted in other countries, but in those places, *Big Brother* was a hit and they were part of the fun. To add to the chaos, Chicken George's family was lobbying viewers to keep him in the house, so a few viewers bought an opposing banner, suggesting that *Big Brother* viewers should vote George out. Whenever planes appeared, the producers would rush the housemates inside, stirring up further paranoia. Desperate, the producers turned the skywriting into a plot on the nightly edited version of the show,

---

* Remarkably, Ms. Megaphone and Oswald also tried to sneak into the crowd for the show's live finale, Oswald successfully. He then managed to shake Paul Römer's hand and congratulate him on an "um, interesting" show. Römer laughed and replied, "It was certainly interesting."

which only made the story feel more confusing for casual viewers. For CBS, it was a disaster. Their prize property, which they'd fought for in an auction, was a laughingstock.

Midway through the season, the show nearly ground to a halt. The way CBS executive Ghen Maynard remembered that Sunday morning, Chicken George, the roofer from Illinois, looked visibly agitated, pacing back and forth, taking short, jerky strides. Then suddenly, George turned to face the cameras. He would be making an announcement at noon, he said. Inside the control room, the CBS crew huddled nervously around the monitor. Their hamster, his eyes bright with mania and his hair dyed Smurf blue, began to speak. Someone shut off the live feeds.

George announced, in grandiose terms—to the housemates and also to everyone at CBS—that he'd solved the puzzle of the show. There was some kind of phrase in the *Big Brother* rule book that had a hidden meaning, he told them; there was a meaningful message on a banner, too; there had been a telling comment that a producer once made in the Red Room. With conspiratorial zeal, George had pulled all of these clues together, then reached a daring conclusion: The secret, hidden goal of the show was for everyone in the *Big Brother* cast to quit, together, and to walk out of the house. If they took this momentous leap, he argued, they would each win a million-dollar prize.

In its way, George's revelation was the natural outcome of the group's stifling culture of niceness: The only way to win was not to play. If the housemates all quit in mutual solidarity, they'd send a message to the world about human decency, about refusing to behave cruelly in order to get money, about refusing to be the pawns of corporate interests. Leaving *Big Brother* would also enable them to build their *own* entertainment brands, George emphasized, rather than serving the needs of CBS. As surreal as the moment was, it could also be seen more sympathetically—as the first legitimate attempt to unionize reality labor.

CBS turned the feeds back on a few minutes in, at which point online viewers watched, in fascination, as the cast began to hash through the question of whether they should walk out the door—a debate that spiraled, in circles, for hours. The group discussed the value of an ethical protest, something that was worth making even if George was wrong about the prize money. "One thing that we have stumbled upon is that we as characters and people are bigger than the show," said Curtis. "The show is about *people*. We *are* those people. It's not about the game show." "Mankind is bigger than the show," Josh responded, solemnly.

While the social psychology scholar in Ghen Maynard was fascinated, the TV executive was flipping out. George was behaving like a cult leader, pulling others into his thrall, even worldly, educated professionals like Cassandra and Curtis, whom Maynard had assumed would be able to resist. Don Wollman, who ran the show's logistics, called in, having been watching the feeds at home. Meanwhile, the Dutch producers were giggling, unconcerned—and when Maynard insisted that they get professional help, arguing that the cast's mental health was at risk, the psychiatrist wasn't concerned, either.

The next day, Römer called Maynard on the phone: *Now* he was worried. The cast had begun digging up the yard, searching for the million dollars. Les Moonves weighed in, too, deputizing the producers to tell the housemates that if they walked out, they'd simply put new cast members in. Studying their expressions, Maynard deduced that Jamie, the ever-smiling beauty queen, was faking her solidarity. Although Römer can't recall the exact details of these events, he knew the game plan: Pull one person aside, then offer them privileges. Once Jamie opened up about her doubts in the Red Room, the mutiny dissolved. Eddie McGee, the wheelchair athlete, told me that he was never actually in on the scheme, adding that his only regret was not encouraging everyone *else* to walk out, so that he could slam the door after them, then win. Maynard remembered it differently: Eddie was as deep in the fog as anyone, he said.

Once it had fizzled out, the *Big Brother* mutiny became easy to dismiss—just another early reality TV clash, like Pat Loud refusing to do a "divorce" scene for Craig Gilbert, or the "pebbles in the pond" debate on *The Real World,* or Richard's accusation that Kelly Wiglesworth ate a Clif Bar in Borneo. But the truth is, George was on to something. Had the cast of *Big Brother* walked out, they would have made history. They would also have been national punchlines, it's true; the genre would surely have rolled forward. But reality TV would have a footnote attached: Mutiny was an option.

As it happens, Chicken George himself doesn't remember the incident this way at all. George told me he never had a meltdown; he doesn't remember any of the conspiracy theories, either, or digging in the garden. He didn't even recall telling his housemates that they could send a message—and when George described the day to me, he did so using the plural. "We were all exhausted. We kind of got tired of having to kick somebody to the curb. The game felt mean."

Either way, he was grateful that nobody listened to him, since it might have killed *Big Brother*—and George, possibly alone among his housemates, loves the show with all his heart. He views his time on CBS as his greatest adventure, an experience that rescued him from his dull life and led him to his job as a car auctioneer, under the name Chicken George. He would've happily continued to work on *Big Brother*, had CBS allowed him to do so. When that idea didn't pan out, George stayed on in California through the summer of 2001, living in an unair-conditioned hangar near Whiteman Airport, helping Blue Yonder Aviation fly banners during the second season of the show, before he finally pulled up stakes and went home to Illinois.

He did appear on an All-Stars season of the series, a few years later, and had a lot of fun meeting people from other seasons. He saw his own castmates as a special breed, however—they were pioneers, George told me, even a kind of second family. Decades later, it still makes him sad that none of them keep in regular touch.

AFTER THAT BURNT PANCAKE OF A TV SEASON, CBS TOSSED THE batter. Römer flew back to Amsterdam. Everyone else got canned, apart from line producer Don Wollman and Julie Chen.* Determined

---

* By now, everyone knew that Chen was involved with her married boss, in the only love triangle to emerge from season 1 of *Big Brother*. From her account in a 2020 oral history of the show, Chen had been forced to take the job: When she tried to turn it down—having been told that it would lock her out of her dream job, working at *60 Minutes*—she was told that it would

to renovate their leaky property, CBS hired a team of skilled producers: the venerable Arnold Shapiro, who was known for the documentary *Scared Straight!*, and his partner, Allison Grodner.

Grodner, a vivacious former child actress, was part of a new
breed of reality producers who'd always worked in the genre. She'd
graduated from film school straight into a Hollywood writer's strike,
then took a job on the CBS docudrama *Rescue 911*. She had watched
the first season of *Big Brother* on the live feeds, finding the raw footage fascinating, in its own way. But it was obvious to her why the
show had failed. For one thing, America clearly had no idea how to
vote—and this round, they wouldn't get the chance. During season 2, the *Big Brother* cast would vote one *another* out, the same way
they did on *Survivor*. (Will Mega told me he considered these the
Mega Rules: Never again would a wild card like him get booted out
first.)

To perform her gut reno, Grodner hired a team of sharp-eyed
American creatives, among them supervising editor Lisa Levenson, a
Prada-clad producer with tabloid chops, whose résumé included
both *General Hospital* and *The Jerry Springer Show*. Joining Levenson were three "show producers," including Jon Kroll, a game show
buff who had been raised in a hippie commune, amid what he described as "naked acid parties, hot tubs, and madness"—a perfect
résumé for the job. The team understood their mission: They were
going to turn *The Brady Bunch* into a loopy, debauched orgy of betrayal and drama, building a soap opera by any means necessary.

During casting, the producers dinged any and all earnest Midwestern kooks. They also rejected anyone who resembled their
tough, likeable first-season winner, disabled blue-collar hunk, Eddie
McGee.* "America's never going to vote out a guy with one leg,"

"technically be assigned to me and if I didn't do it, it could be considered subordination." She
and Moonves got married in 2004, and when, in 2018, the CBS president lost his job after accusations of sexual harassment and assault, Chen continued to host *Big Brother*, changing her on-air
name to "Julie Chen Moonves."

* McGee, who had considered auditioning for *The Real World*, used the prize in the menschiest
possible way: He paid for his parents' mortgage and his brother's tuition. Then he worked at
bars and, in time, built a decent career in scripted television, playing "a veteran in every possible

Kroll told me, bluntly. Instead, they looked for exhibitionists, schemers, and flirts, the kind of players who wanted to work *with* CBS, not rebel against it. From Maynard's account, this new type of casting had its grotty side—he once interviewed a male escort who described his biggest shame as "fucking fat chicks"—but that kind of crudeness could also open the door. When *Big Brother* hopeful Will Kirby met Les Moonves, the CBS president asked him what he'd do if he had a gay housemate—a seeming obsession at CBS casting. Will wisecracked, "I'd fuck him in the ass and make him a sandwich." (In 2020, Kirby told this story to me as a factual anecdote, and then, during fact-checking, insisted that he had been joking. You make the call.)

The new *Big Brother* house had no IKEA-esque bunk beds or chicken coop: Instead, it was a party pad with a hot tub, engineered to emphasize inequality. Some housemates slept on waterbeds; others got army cots. There was a luxurious private suite for one privileged housemate: the newly designated "Head of Household." There were other changes, too: The show ran three days a week, instead of five; viewers paid for the live feeds; and each episode ended in a cliffhanger. Producer Jon Kroll was confident this plan would work, having run a weeklong test, which went exactly as they'd hoped. "I don't know where we found these people, but they hooked up. They got naked, they went crazy, they did all these amazing things, and it just infused us with energy."

The minute the season 2 cast entered the house, the games began. First, the *Big Brother* voice ordered the entire ensemble to cram, Twister-style, into a Buick, in order to win food for the week—and then, when they were inside the car, announced that the last one out would win the Buick. This set off a mad scramble, as some players left the car and others stayed put, with everyone calculating their strategies in a panic, anxious about whether the other people were creating an alliance. As soon as a winner was named, a new contest started: The group was ordered to play a game called "Wheel of

---

war." CBS had sent him a copy of his season on VHS, but he'd never watched it. "I'm not watching that shit," he told me, in a gravelly growl.

First Impressions," in which they labeled one another "Bitchiest," "Hottest," and "Smelliest." The winner became the first "Head of Household," the person whose job it was to nominate two other people for expulsion.

Before the hour was out, there was drama galore—paranoia, scheming, panicky contestants pushed way out of their comfort zones. In fact, the production overshot the mark at first. Ten days in, the housemates were getting hammered, peeing on the walls of the house, and (according to one of the show's story editors, Daniel Shriver) using NyQuil to get high. Then, late one night, Justin, a bartender from Bayonne, New Jersey, started making out in the kitchen with Krista, a single mom from Louisiana. In the control room, the sound had been muted, so it took a minute for the producers to realize what was going on when, out of the blue, Justin brandished a kitchen knife.

"I was like, holy shit! What's he doing? Turn the volume up," said Maynard. Justin had begun mock-threatening Krista, holding the knife to her throat as they flirted, asking her, "Would you get mad if I killed you?"—and then kissing her. Even if Justin meant the threat as a joke, as he would later claim, it was a dark, scary one. The producers removed him from the game, immediately.

This crisis set the online discussion boards on fire with excitement. The previous February, when The Smoking Gun had revealed that Rick Rockwell had an old restraining order for assault, the scandal had destroyed *Who Wants to Marry a Multi-Millionaire?* By July 2001, nobody cared much. When the newspapers unearthed Justin's own old assault conviction, the story came across as ephemeral gossip. When the episode in which Justin held a knife to Krista's throat aired, the show's ratings ticked up.

THE SHIMMERING DARK STAR OF *BIG BROTHER 2* WAS A NEW KIND of player: Will Kirby, who was known to his fans as "Dr. Evil."* A

---

* Will clarified that although "Dr. Evil" was his nickname among viewers, his fellow contestants more frequently called him "Puppet Master" or "Dr. Delicious."

medical intern working brutal shifts in Miami Beach, Will, then twenty-eight, had originally auditioned for *Survivor*, only to learn that *Big Brother* was interested in him instead. Friends and family urged him to turn the offer down, but Will—who had graduated from medical school and been accepted into a JD/MBA program—had an intuition that he was perfectly suited for the reality genre, with his looks, charisma, intelligence, and unusual gift for emotional compartmentalization.

Early on, however, even the self-assured Dr. Evil felt at sea in the CBS house. He cracked jokes in the "Diary Room"—the show's new version of the Red Room—but got no laughs from the loudspeakers, the voice of *Big Brother*. Then, a few sessions in, something clicked. Will had been paying close attention to the "intonation, the cadence" of the *Big Brother* producers, absorbing how rushed they sounded, how eager they were to get the right kinds of quotes. "I'd start talking and they'd go, 'No, not that, not that.' Eventually, they would accidentally train you, because you want that positive reinforcement." While Mega had defied *Big Brother*, hoping to gain control of the game, Will took the opposite approach: He turned himself into the production's biggest ally. "*This is how I help them produce the show.* And subtly, by helping them produce the show, it helps *me*—then I'm in the storylines, I have face time."

It was an approach that, over the next decade, would become the default setting for reality stardom, as players grew increasingly comfortable with the notion of themselves as co-creators of their shows, preparing for a future as a reality celebrity—a concept that only a few early figures, like Lance Loud, had fully embraced. Will didn't mind coming off as a villain, if that image paid off. "We all show each other different aspects of ourselves, you, me, anyone—and if you're only giving them one aspect, that's what they're going to use," he said.

Jon Kroll described Will as the platonic ideal of a reality show cast member. He never complained. He didn't fret about what he'd said, let alone blame CBS for how he might come off when the footage was edited. And to Kroll, Will felt like proof positive that the producers had been right to change the way people voted. During the show's first week, a viewer poll had ranked Will Kirby low enough that had the America's Choice system still existed, he'd likely have been voted out as quickly as Will Mega or Jordan.

Early in the game, Will formed an alliance, "Chilltown," with bar owner Mike "Boogie" Malin and beach volleyball player Shannon, who had quickly become Will's showmance. Chilltown, which was named after an icy room in the house, considered itself the cool crowd, but the name also suggested something else: a clique of bullies. When their housemates united against them, Will kept his game plan nimble—and switched gears. Nominated against his showmance, he egged Shannon on to behave like a creep, which led to her expulsion (grotesquely, she used a housemate's toothbrush to scrub the toilet; the producers made her confess). Once his final ally, Mike, had been voted off the show, Will laid low, to make himself less of a threat. He went on to lose every Head of Household competition for the entire season; he got nominated for expulsion more frequently than anyone else. Still, he never got voted out.

Instead, much like Richard Hatch, he talked nonstop about how awful he was, how evil, how unpopular, the kind of player that no one would vote for when they got to the final two. Then he turned his housemates against one another. "I tell them right to their face, I'm gonna stab you in the back, I'm gonna lie to you. That's what I've been doing and I'm gonna continue to do it," he cheerfully explained in the Diary Room, in an explosive clip that he understood would be shown to his ex-housemates, the people who would be on the final jury.

The result was high drama, every week, just as CBS had hoped. It no longer mattered who got kicked out. "Once the shit disturber goes, the 'floater' steps up and has to play the game," said Kroll. Even the show's crew, who one would imagine would want a break from work, found themselves checking the live feeds from home. To add to the intensity, the top producers were *also* being watched—by Les Moonves, who had his own live feeds, which let him peek into the Diary Room. It was a panopticon within a panopticon, centered around the "camera cross," the hidden spot at the center of the building, from which any crew member could peer into every corner of the house. Grodner would take visitors on tours of the production, including, one morning, George Clooney, who watched the housemates eat breakfast. The housemates, nervously sipping coffee with Dr. Delicious, had no idea Clooney was even there.

The ratings topped twelve million viewers—less than half of the *Survivor: Borneo* ratings, but still an impressive number. Critics reviled *Big Brother,* but no one called it boring anymore—instead, they summed it up as "a torrent of profanity, soft-core sex, petty betrayals, and general mischief." For some crew members, working in the control room was an exciting job, with the bad-boy appeal of working at Chuck Barris's Love Company. Others felt detached, like camera operator Sarah Levy, who marveled at the absurdity of it all, filming Will as he shaved his testicles in the backyard. A few were repulsed by the moral squalor of the environment, including Scott Benton, a low-level story editor who told me, "Every day I wanted to take a shower to wash off the evil of the experience."

Whatever one's perspective, the work was exhausting enough that it filled everyone's thoughts. People slept at work; job boundaries were fuzzy. There was a lot of partying. As story editor Daniel Shriver remembers the overall reality landscape, there were weed people, who were the creative types, and coke people, who cranked out product at a crazy pace. Shriver, who had a prescription for medical marijuana, was the former, smoking up during shift breaks. He had an eclectic background—he'd worked in improv comedy, marketing, and martial arts—and he found that he enjoyed the creative side of the job, which felt like solving a puzzle, hunting for patterns in people's behavior, looking for running jokes and potential montages.

Sometimes, Shriver had the opportunity to build a story intuitively. One day, he noticed that the housemates were joking about the house being evil, unnerved by some ravens on the roof. He decided to embrace that idea, offering them a Ouija board as a prize for a competition, which led to a séance. Now that he had a story about supernatural forces in the house, he needed B-roll to illustrate it, so he promised his crew members a free meal if they could get footage of the ravens. All morning, as the housemates slept, the crew tried to nail the shot—until finally, someone threw blueberry muffins on the roof. One of the muffins ended up falling off the roof into the yard, baffling the roommates, who interpreted it as some kind of sign.

Each day spun around these kinds of surreal, impulsive interactions, a bizarre give-and-take between a cast and crew who never met. In its way, the job *was* a bit like running a haunted house, with the crew playing the ghosts. Scott Benton, bored and sleep-deprived on the overnight shift, found himself taking dares from his colleagues, playing random prerecorded *Big Brother* announcements over the speakers, disorienting the players and making them laugh. He didn't dislike the cast, he told me; it was hard not to feel some tenderness for people you watched all day. But being in the control room felt like being a prison guard—it was tempting to use your power.

Certain cast members were especially vulnerable to this kind of manipulation. Among them was Nicole Nilson Schaffrich, a personal chef who ultimately made it to the final three, along with Dr. Evil and Monica Bailey, a candy store manager from Brooklyn. Will had watched *Survivor* before he auditioned; Monica was a fan of *The Real World*. Nicole was more of a CNN news junkie, but her husband, who was a heavy fan of competitive reality shows, had convinced her that she would be great on television. During the casting process, Nicole had told the psychiatrist everything about her traumatic childhood, not all of which she could remember: Raised as a foster child, she was struggling with the symptoms of PTSD. Just before she opened the house door, a CBS production assistant told her: "You know why we cast you. You're dramatic, outspoken! Go out there and do *that*."

Those secrets turned her into a sitting duck. Nicole had told the psychiatrist that she hated crafts, since she'd never learned to play. One day, *Big Brother* gave the group materials to make foam dolls. To taunt Nicole, Will created a doll that looked just like her, only as a monster, with a cyclops eye and dark pubic hair poking out of the bathing suit. The prank sent her into a tailspin. Unlike Will, Nicole wasn't using the Diary Room to bond with the producers—instead, she was venting, raving into the camera. When she threatened to leave, the *Big Brother* voice would talk her out of it, telling her she'd be a loser, an idea that terrified her. This footage never made it on the air.

On Day 61, those tensions came to a climax in a surreal incident, which took place during one of the show's competitions, out in the garden. At the time, Nicole and her two housemates were all lying on a waterbed together, trying to keep their hands on a house key as part of an endurance contest. Suddenly, a plane with a skywriting banner flew overhead, trailing the message, "N&W IN HOTTUB I'M BETRAYED & HURT—J." The banner had been sent by Nicole's new husband, who, in her absence, had been obsessively trawling the fan forums and reading recaps of the live feeds. When some eagle-eyed Web-watchers glimpsed what they believed was a drunken game of footsie between Nicole and Will, Nicole's husband exploded.

As soon as she saw the banner, Nicole started sobbing. "She lost it. Anyone would," Grodner told me. Desperate to save her marriage, Nicole—who had by then lost her grip on the key and therefore lost the contest—tried to walk out of the house, only to find that the back door was locked. The producers called her into the Diary Room, where executive producer Lisa Levenson, who was one of the team's best interviewers, talked her down.

Eventually, a new banner from Nicole's husband appeared, urging her to stay and compete. She stuck it out, even though she felt increasingly unstable, yet another member of a growing sorority of women who had been crushed by the game, like Sabine and Jordan. In the control room, Benton would watch Nicole rocking, alone in her room; he felt agonized seeing her pain.

IN EARLY SEPTEMBER, GHEN MAYNARD STAYED UP LATE ONE night, putting together notes for a live Tuesday episode. A few hours later, the phone rang, waking him up: It was Maynard's mother, screaming at him to turn on the television. Across the country, the North Tower of the World Trade Center had been hit by a plane.

In a fog, Maynard drove over to CBS. He and Grodner kept on cutting that night's episode until they received word that it wouldn't air. Now they had a bigger problem. The finale was ten days away. According to the official CBS rules, the three finalists weren't allowed to receive any news from the outside world. And yet eerily, Will and Nicole had noticed that planes weren't flying overhead from Burbank Airport. Later on, Will would fly a toy plane around a tower built from Legos, and then crash it into the tower. The way Grodner understood the moment, he was unconsciously struggling to work out what was going on. Over the speakers, she told him to stop.

In Denmark, where Endemol was filming their own season of *Big Brother,* the producers filled the contestants in on the news and showed them footage of the disaster, although they never aired those exchanges. In the Netherlands, they told the housemates as part of the show, only to have them suspect that it was some kind of hoax. Producers also filled in contestants in Belgium, where a relative of one housemate had been in the Towers. In South Africa, they were especially concerned about the safety of their Muslim contestant. (Meanwhile, in Greece, where the show was about to debut, riot police showed up after protesters threw eggs and rocks into the studio, complaining that it eroded people's respect for privacy.)

In the United States, the producers felt torn. According to Maynard, although no one was an aggressive advocate for keeping the news from the housemates, "our rules are our rules—and you kind of go, 'Wouldn't it be fascinating if they're the only three people on the planet who don't know what happened?'" In a 2015 interview, Julie Chen said that she had told Moonves that she wouldn't appear if the housemates stayed in the dark. "And he was like, 'Everyone just calm down, we're not saying we're not going to tell them; we will do what's responsible.'"

In the end, more bad news forced their hand. Monica's cousin, who worked on one of the building's highest floors, was missing. She had died in the crash, although nobody was sure of those details yet—and in the chaos of the moment, all planes were grounded. The producers shut down the live feeds, then called the housemates into the Diary Room. Over the speaker, Grodner read a statement from CBS, explaining, without any specifics, that there had been a terrorist attack on New York and Washington. She kept her voice even, trying to stay cool despite the scary news. "I was expecting a nuclear bomb, at that point, so we handled it the best that we could."

Monica told me that CBS handled the situation well. She spoke with her sister, who urged her to keep playing (there was no way to fly across the country anyway). On September 18, when CBS aired scenes of her getting the news, there were viewers who found the choice exploitative; as Monica herself saw it, there wasn't a better option—and she was proud that under pressure, she had kept her self-control.

Still, the mood was grim. The three finalists continued to play the game, to scheme and undermine one another, playing to the invisible jury that would ultimately select a winner. But at that point, viewers had other things on their minds. Nicole—who had immediately asked the producers if Osama bin Laden was behind the attack—was especially disturbed, horrified that during a global crisis, she was stuck inside a game show. At some point, the producers agreed to let her take anxiety medication. Grodner told me that the contestants were all told they could leave the show if they wanted to.

Scott Benton, the overnight story producer, reached his breaking point. Late one night at his monitor, listening to the final three contestants talk about a horror sci-fi film whose name they couldn't remember, he clicked the microphone on and gave them the answer: "*Event Horizon.*" He no longer cared about the rules. With CBS's permission, he printed out a list of his DVDs so that Nicole, a fellow cineast, could pick one to watch. Over the loudspeakers, they began to bond, talking about some of their favorite films, like *Memento*.

On September 20, two days after the 9/11 episode aired, Will Kirby won *Big Brother 2*. By then, many of the members of the sequestered cast "jury" of his former housemates, including Monica, had come to see Nicole as a basket case, a hysteric, while the self-assured Will came across as a charming schemer who deserved the ultimate prize. The episode, which aired immediately after a televised address from President Bush, got the biggest ratings of the season.

Those final days had changed everyone in the house. Daniel Shriver described it as "the derailment." "I thought, 'What am I doing with my life? *What am I doing with my time on this earth?*'" He continued to work in reality TV jobs, but he wound up devoting his life to his own form of good works: an attempt to organize his fellow reality laborers. Benton left the profession for good—in part because, he acknowledged, no one asked him to stay on. Although he'd only played a minor role in production, he felt guilty enough that he tried to apologize to all of the cast members. Outside the house, he and Nicole became intimate friends, having "trauma-bonded."

Jon Kroll took a job on *The Amazing Race,* then returned to oversee a few more seasons of *Big Brother,* having been promoted to co–executive producer. Like George Verschoor, Kroll wasn't naïve about the show he'd helped turn into a hit. He knew that there were cast members who struggled and crew members who couldn't take it. But what Benton compared to working in a North Korean gulag, Kroll saw as something more like summer camp—a sweaty, intense, but ultimately joyful collaboration, working with hardworking peers, the type who enjoyed being in the trenches and could tolerate a little chaos. He'd built his life in the reality genre, producing both unscripted shows and "legitimate" documentaries, while also exploring a side passion in photography.

Reality was like any other genre, Kroll told me: There was good stuff, there was shoddy stuff, there was everything in between. It was up to each individual to figure out their own ethical guidelines, the places they wouldn't go—for him, that was hidden camera shows. But those choices were what it meant to be an adult. "I was never embarrassed to tell people that I worked for *Amazing Race,* but *Big Brother* was kind of like an embarrassing thing to tell people, at first," Kroll said. "And then I realized, 'What the fuck. I'm doing one of the biggest social experiments in the world, this is fantastic. I'm having a great time doing this show! I'm going to *own* it.' And now I'm just like, I can see how miserable my script friends are—and how few things they've made."

CUE
THE
SUN!

||||||||||||||||||||||||||||||||||||||||||||||||||

2001–2007 (ish)

10

||||||||

THE EXPLOSION

Reality Blows Up—and Becomes an Industry

AT THE TURN OF THE TWENTY-FIRST CENTURY, TIME SPED UP.
For five decades, reality had amounted to a series of tremors—
some minor, some unmissable—cracking the foundations of Hollywood. Now the volcano erupted. In 2000 and 2001 alone, these series
debuted: *The Mole* (the thinking man's *Survivor,* hosted by Anderson Cooper); *Boot Camp* (the military man's *Survivor,* directed by
former *Survivor* director Scott Messick); *Bands on the Run* (the indie
rocker's *Survivor,* on VH1); the wholesome travel competition *The
Amazing Race;* the sleazy marital train wreck *Temptation Island;*
the gonzo prank show *Jackass;* an ambitious murder mystery series
called *Murder in Small Town X;* and both *Fear* (contestants trapped
inside eerie places like abandoned mental hospitals) and *Fear Factor*
(the sadist's *Survivor,* if it were just stunts like the grub-eating challenge and hosted by Joe Rogan). There were gimmicky dating shows,
including *Cheaters, The 5th Wheel, Chains of Love, Dismissed, Elimi-
Date,* and *Shipmates.* There were jazzy talent contests, like the boy
band series *Making the Band,* the HBO/Miramax directing competition *Project Greenlight,* and *Iron Chef USA,* a spin-off of a Japanese
cooking game show. There was *Moolah Beach* (teen *Survivor*), *Scariest Places on Earth* (paranormal reality), *Maximum Exposure* (Fox-

style shockeroo clips), *Spy TV* (*Candid Camera* lite), and the rightly forgotten Fox special *Who Wants to Be a Princess?*, a shoddy *Who Wants to Marry a Multi-Millionaire?* imitator, stripped of the original's skin-crawling dynamism.

In 2002, Fox began to air *American Idol,* a blockbuster talent contest that disrupted the music industry. ABC launched *The Bachelor,* which did the same for heterosexuality. There was also MTV's *Sorority Life* (Kappa Kappa *Real World*); a rat pack of celebreality shows, beginning with *The Osbournes* and the tabloid-tragic *The Anna Nicole Show;* and *Frontier House* (a sincere and often fascinating attempt at historical cosplay, which aired on PBS); as well as *Bachelorettes in Alaska, EX-treme Dating, Meet My Folks* (with lie detector tests!), *Extreme Makeover* (plastic surgery, aerobics, stilettos), *30 Seconds to Fame* (the grandfather of TikTok), *Dog Eat Dog* (another rude twist on *Survivor,* with a crying contest and a "He or She" guessing game), *Monster Garage* (car makeovers), *The Jamie Kennedy Experiment* (B-list *Candid Camera*), *Oblivious* (man-on-the-street *Candid Camera*), *Endurance* (kiddie *Survivor*), *Under One Roof* (real estate *Survivor,* with the winner getting a Fijian beach villa), and *Dog Days,* an Animal Planet show about New York dog owners.

Some of these reality projects were trash, plenty fizzled fast, but a handful—*The Amazing Race, American Idol,* and *The Bachelor,* in particular—became network tentpoles, which would run for decades. Even the failures were cheap write-offs, though. The reality craze had become a bonanza for a set of creative misfits who flowed in from the fringes of Los Angeles, strivers who had been locked out of Hollywood proper. "You had people who were trying to make it in scripting, and couldn't make it, obviously. You certainly had people who were working in the documentary world and were tired of being broke," said Jon Kroll, who was making a good living on *Big Brother* and *The Amazing Race.* There was a subset of ex-military staffers, making a career change; there was an influx of graduates from Emerson College, as well.

Meanwhile, ordinary people were flooding casting agencies, confident they had the stuff to become the next Richard Hatch. There had always been stars who were famous for being themselves—celebrated for their beauty or charisma, not their talent. There was nothing new about spilling your guts in public, either: You could trace that urge back to the romantic poets, or to Freud, or 1970s feminism, or the memoir vogue of the 1990s. But technology was speeding everything up, just after the turn of the century, as if the Web was a truth serum. Every time a free AOL disc frisbeed into someone's mailbox, it felt like an invitation to dial in, then confess, anonymously, to strangers. Mixing the internet with reality TV was the speedball of pop culture.

YOU COULD USE MANY LENSES TO EXAMINE THIS TUMULTUOUS period, but let's begin with a cautionary tale, the story of a producer who created a brilliant reality show, side by side with *Survivor*, then rode the genre's potential to the top, only to crash hard on the brutal shore of what was possible. Unlike most of the gamblers who invented the reality genre, R. J. Cutler had begun his career as a comparative highbrow; he'd gone to Harvard, then worked in theater, alongside director Robert Brustein. Then he pivoted to nonfiction filmmaking, producing the celebrated *The War Room,* a 1993 Oscar-nominated film about the Clinton campaign. By 1999, however, Cutler was starting to get antsy. Documentaries took years to make; they were brutally hard to fund. The dirty secret was that everyone, even the Maysles brothers, needed to find other ways to stay afloat, including advertising.

Television, on the other hand, was bursting with potential, both economic and artistic. During a meeting at ABC, an executive began telling Cutler about seismic shifts in the landscape. There were rumblings of an upcoming writer's strike; an actor's strike was on the horizon, too. Summer ratings were low; cable networks were expanding; the elite pay-cable outlet HBO had been getting buzz for ambitious shows like *The Sopranos* and *Sex and the City.* All of these phenomena threatened the bottom line for the Big Three networks—their ability to roll out mass-appeal, high-rated, ad-friendly shows, on a budget. During a recent corporate retreat, the executive told Cutler, everyone had been looking for a solution—ideally, the kind of show that didn't use writers or actors.

Off the cuff, Cutler pitched an idea for a new nonfiction series—a story about high school students. It was a timely concept: *Beverly Hills 90210* was finishing up its ten-season run on Fox. The executive's eyes bugged out—and he grabbed Cutler's arm and marched him over to another executive's desk, to start shopping the idea around. The same day, Cutler had multiple offers, and in September 1999, Doug Herzog—the executive who bought *The Real World* at MTV in 1993 and who was now working at Fox—ordered thirteen episodes of the new show, *American High*. Cutler was over the moon. After years of grindingly slow film development, he was suddenly in the fast lane.

Inspired by a *Vanity Fair* article about the journalistic fabulist Stephen Glass, Cutler approached Glass's old high school, in Highland Park, near Chicago, using a reference from his old pal George Stephanopoulos. He cut a deal with administrators, donating $100,000 worth of cameras and editing equipment and also offering to teach a class on filmmaking. In the show's early stages, Cutler—who had grown up in Great Neck, a similar high-pressure suburb—was thinking about the dark themes in the Glass article, about the "conflict between ambitions and ethics." By the time the show finished production, however, *American High* had emerged as a deeply humane project, a real-life analogue to the brilliant mid-1990s teen drama *My So-Called Life*. It was full of likeable, layered characters, including an insecure girl and her jock boyfriend, a gay teen coming out to his friends, and a charming trickster with ADHD, on the verge of flunking out.

Cutler's team shot 2,800 hours of footage, which were sifted through by six "loggers," then structured into a narrative by an eight-person story department and six editors. He had hired a set of documentary superstars, among them the director Joan Churchill, who'd shot footage for *An American Family*, as well as Scorsese's longtime collaborator David Tedeschi.

Still, it was the footage the students themselves shot that became the show's calling card, comprising 30 percent of the finished product. Instead of sitting for on-the-fly interviews, they filmed their own confessionals, using handheld video cameras. In one bravura sequence, Morgan Moss, the wiseass student with ADHD, filmed a bitter family argument as it stormed around him, his camera joggling as if he were weaving through a war zone. His mother, off-screen, growled, "Clean your room right now!"; then, Morgan swung the lens to the kitchen table, where his dad was smoking furiously, accusing Morgan of "rotten manners and no respect." There was a brief shot of his brother giving him the finger, then Morgan left the room, as his mom snapped, "Shut that thing off!" He slammed his bedroom door, gazed into the lens for the first time, and deadpanned, with an insouciant shrug, "Like I said, my mom and dad are real pricks."

It was bold stuff—as propulsive as the *American Family* scene of Lance Loud and his mother, Pat, walking through Central Park, only shot as a "selfie," years before that term existed. Cutler kept the pressure low. His teen auteurs could quit, anytime; the cast got to weigh in on edits. Cutler received few notes from Fox. He understood that CBS was simultaneously developing a reality competition called *Survivor*, which had begun filming in Borneo, but to Cutler, some silly game show didn't seem to be related to the show he was making. "We were gigantic snobs . . . vérité agitators," he said, with a laugh.

When *American High* debuted on August 2, 2000, it got ecstatic reviews—and in nearly every one of these raves, Cutler's project was used as a bludgeon against other reality shows. Under the headline "No Rats, No Fakery," Alex Strachan in *The Vancouver Sun* praised the series as "one of the most seminal cinematic documents of human social psychology since Michael Apted's *28 Up*." "It's the realest show out there," Morgan Moss told *Entertainment Weekly*. "'Cause we're not forced to sit on an island. We're not forced to have a shower cam. We don't have to vote people off."

At the lavish premiere party, Sandy Grushow, the president of Fox, threw his arm around Cutler. The next day, he confided to the producer, Fox was going to run a classy silent ad for *American High*, using a black screen scrolling up rave reviews. "Then, at the bottom, the words, '*Season Two coming next year*.'"

It was the last time that Cutler ever spoke to Grushow.

The next morning, Cutler called the Fox automated ratings number, the same one Fleiss and Darnell had obsessed over for years. *American High* had gotten a 5 rating—impressive for 2023, but a series killer in 2000. Fox canceled the series after four episodes, before editing had been completed. As a parting gift, they sent Cutler a silver Tiffany money clip.

Despite getting axed, Cutler was still riding high, particularly since other networks had been calling his production company, Actual Reality Pictures, with offers. PBS agreed to run *American High* the next spring, finding a wider audience. In 2001, the series won the first Emmy award for reality television, under the rubric Outstanding Non-Fiction Program (Reality). Only one element put a damper on the triumph: Morgan, one of the show's standout participants, had landed in legal trouble, having filmed himself having sex with a girl who was two years younger, then shown the tape to his friends.*

Cutler barreled ahead, eager to make more shows in the *American High* tradition: prestige nonfiction, focused on characters rather than competitions, using handheld cameras. By then, he had stopped being a snob about *Survivor*—"a brick house, like watching the NFL!"—but just because he enjoyed the show, that didn't mean it was the type of series he wanted to make. He hoped to keep telling "tiny, tiny stories," to be the HBO of reality television.

Instead, Cutler's options began to narrow. In 2002, in the aftermath of 9/11, Cutler produced *Military Diaries* for VH1, handing cameras to sailors and soldiers and asking them about their musical tastes. The *Los Angeles Times* called the show "funny, poignant, candid," but like *Cops,* it was an ethically tricky production—an invitational series, which was made with, and implicitly for, the military. In 2003, Cutler produced *Freshman Diaries* for Showtime, filming at the University of Texas at Austin—a darker, grittier portrait than *American High*. He also made *The Residents* for the Discovery

---

* Morgan got caught when the girl sought revenge by xeroxing images of him from the sex tape, then pasting them around the Highland Park train station. He took a plea bargain for twenty-four months of probation, with a $1,000 fine and an agreement to appear on the sex offenders' registry.

Channel, a series about the lives of young physicians. Each of these shows lasted for one or two seasons. There was limited demand for "premium nonfiction," Cutler had begun to realize, but a wild thirst for anything that resembled *Survivor.*

Cutler kept on searching for the right format—something genuinely original, a world-rattler. In 2002, he found one. Filmmakers Jay Roach and Tom Lassally had approached Cutler with an outrageous idea, for HBO: *Candidate 2020*, a show that would star a group of seventeen-year-olds who dreamed about being elected president. HBO had aired another political reality show a few years back: *Tanner '88*, an unusual, semi-improvised mockumentary written by Garry Trudeau and directed by Robert Altman, which wove a fake candidate into the real Democratic primary. Roach and Lassally's idea was even more extreme: The filmmakers planned to follow their teen subjects for eighteen more years, until they were eligible to run for high office. It was a bit like Michael Apted's decades-spanning Up series, plus *American High*, swirled into *The War Room*—a slow-burn, emotionally intimate, absurdly far-reaching study of youthful ambition.

For reasons that are likely obvious, this cicadalike production schedule didn't pan out, even at big-pocketed HBO. But FX, a cable network that was in the midst of rebranding, liked the concept, once it had been refocused on a diverse set of adult candidates. That year, the music competition *American Idol* had become the hot new reality show, so FX executive Kevin Reilly suggested that Cutler call his show *American Candidate.* "Our air is so cheap. I can give you an hour a night. You can do anything you want," Reilly told him.

Giddy, Cutler pulled together a think tank of his Washington friends, who devised a truly provocative scheme, featuring an "internet-based shadow political process that would result in a people's candidate." More than just a TV show, *American Candidate* was designed to stoke an actual election, merging documentary and game show elements with then-novel notions of online interactivity, airing every night of the week. The show's contestants would give speeches in front of Mount Rushmore. The finale would air on July 4, 2004, filmed live from the Washington Mall.

Cutler was deep in preproduction when the deal evaporated. Later on, he heard rumors that the Bush White House had called FX, perhaps understandably rattled by this attempt to launch a third-party candidate. Cutler felt heartbroken—although he also admits, looking back, that maybe the idea had some downsides. When Cutler *did* get to produce *American Candidate*, for Showtime, it was a more limited, more conventional competition show, which critics derided as gimmicky and cynical. The winner, evangelical middle school teacher Park Gillespie, had denounced Showtime as "arguably the most godless network on television" on a Focus on the Family website, and then—helped along by a right-wing mailing campaign—won $200,000 and devoted his twenty-minute acceptance speech to endorsing Bush in the real election. (Later on, Gillespie ran a failed race for the House, then worked for Congressman Mick Mulvaney.) During an NPR interview, Cutler was asked how he'd feel if his show ended up producing a nightmare candidate. He wasn't worried: There was no way that any process outside the political world could do any worse than what already existed, he said.

By that time, however, Cutler's confidence was fading. In 2003, in an interview with *Documentary* magazine, he had described the reality genre as still inventing itself, "a toboggan race, twisting and crazy," but he also described pitching comparatively crass ideas, most of which never made it on the air, including *Payback Inc.*, a Comedy Central pilot in which put-upon contestants worked with "an A-Team of pranksters" to get revenge, and *Entrepreneurs,* about wannabe Masters of the Universe. At the time, he was in the midst of completing *The Real Roseanne Show,* a meta-reality show about Roseanne Barr, which was filmed while she made a *different* reality show, about cooking. Cutler would roll out a variety of other programs, among them *Flip That House,* a real estate show for The Learning Channel, in 2005, and *Greatest American Dog,* in 2008, for CBS.

A few years in, Actual Reality merged with the already established Evolution Media, which gave Cutler some freedom to pick and choose his projects—and occasionally, he made a show he was proud of, like the 2005 series *30 Days,* in which documentarian Morgan Spurlock tried on diverse identities (a minimum-wage worker, a devout Muslim) for a month. In 2006, Cutler produced the show *Black. White.*, which had a truly eye-popping premise: A Black and a white family swapped races using elaborate makeup. The makeover was shown during the show's credit sequence, as Ice Cube, Cutler's co-creator, sang the theme song, "Race Card," which had lyrics like "Just cause I'm dressed like I'm straight outta jail/Make mo' money than them white boys at Yale." *Black. White.*, which got reviews that ranged from intrigued to disgusted, won the Emmy for Outstanding Makeup for a Series (Non-Prosthetic).

Cutler stuck it out through *Pretty Wicked,* a 2009 reality competition in which models vied to show their "inner beauty," which he joked to me was actually titled *What's Become of Your Life, R. J.?*—and ultimately he went back to making documentaries, titling his production company This Machine, after the Woody Guthrie quote "This machine kills fascists." His low point had arrived years earlier, back in 2004. That year, an agent persuaded him to collaborate with the star of Mark Burnett's latest hit, a show called *The Apprentice.* He and the real estate mogul Donald Trump were supposed to develop a show based on the board game Monopoly, a project that was a model of corporate synergy, uniting three brands—a high-end documentarian, a fake tycoon, and a game that celebrated capitalism.

For months, Cutler followed Trump around golf courses, sampling terrible clam chowder and getting his arm yanked out of its socket during handshakes. Although the show never got made, the experience stuck with him as a valuable lesson: Not all games were worth winning.

YOU COULD ALSO LOOK AT THE REALITY EXPLOSION THROUGH A wider lens: by peeking into the network C-suites, where every executive had begun frantically panning for the next *Survivor.* Ben Hatta, the son of a famous Japanese wrestler, had moved to Los Angeles in 1998, after ditching a postgraduate art history degree at Columbia to chase show business. He found low-level assistant jobs at first, working at CAA and then at ABC, as the executive assistant to Andrea Wong. Both jobs were in the alternative series and specials department, which at the time was a path that led nowhere—a sleepy backwater, not a power center.

Then, in a blink, everything changed. A week or two into his new job at ABC, the network began airing the glamorously terroristic quiz show *Who Wants to Be a Millionaire*. Michael Davies, the head of the department, left ABC to produce the show, which meant Hatta's boss was suddenly in charge. For a while, ABC built its whole brand around the quiz show, burning out its appeal. The next summer, CBS aired *Survivor*—and at that point, all bets were off. Every network suit seemed to be convinced that game shows were the answer to every problem in the industry—anything with a winner, anything with a massive jackpot, anything that featured real people playing themselves.

Hatta watched from an ABC conference room as Lloyd Braun and Stu Bloomberg lost a frantic auction to buy the *Big Brother* format, muting the phone as the numbers rose and exchanging looks of shock. No one understood what was happening. As each new vogue rolled by—dating shows, celebrity shows, talent shows—the executives around Hatta would wonder out loud when the bubble would burst. "I kept saying, 'No. It's a new genre,'" he said.

Early on, Hatta was present, if only to deliver coffee, for some bizarre pitches, among them a 2000 meeting Wong took with Marlon Brando, who showed up in a tan Members Only jacket to pitch a show about his life, two years before *The Osbournes*. (Brando, who was obsessed with Hatta and his boss's ethnicity, asked him to tell Wong that she was "a beautiful Asian princess.") Ben Affleck and Matt Damon stopped by, pitching an ambitious bounty hunter show called *The Runner*, a reality version of *The Fugitive*, in which all of America would be deputized to hunt down the show's star.

By then, Hatta was getting bored watching people cut deals. From what he could see, the real fun—and maybe the real money—seemed to be on the creative side. When he met Mike Fleiss, who was back on the rise after the fiasco of *Who Wants to Marry a Multi-Millionaire?*, he felt an immediate connection to him. That day, Fleiss had been pitching a format in which the TV audience would control a man's whole life, a little like *The Truman Show*. It never got made, but Hatta jumped ship, becoming Fleiss's assistant, then his development executive, and eventually a field producer on *The Bachelor*.

In the meantime, Mike Darnell was reveling in his power as a tastemaker, now that his pet genre was on top again. During the early aughts, Darnell created several shows with his recognizable stamp, like 2002's *The Glutton Bowl*, in which players gobbled eggs and mayonnaise. For many producers, however, Darnell was viewed less as a creator than as a scavenger, a rip-off artist. The way reality producer Rhett Reese remembered that period, "If you sold an idea to ABC, Fox would turn around and just make the same show so fast that they would beat ABC to the punch. There were no limits." To Darnell, this was just sour grapes. Television had always been about imitation—he just did it better by adding a twist, upping the ante. When *Who Wants to Be a Millionaire* was a hit, Darnell tried a show called *Greed*. Preston Beckman, who was an executive vice president of strategic program planning and research at NBC, and then later at Fox, described these years as "The Wars." By 2005, when two boxing shows debuted, one on Fox and one on NBC, Beckman had lost track: "I think we announced ours first. But, and I'm being 100 percent honest with you, I can't remember if we ripped theirs off. So much was done in secrecy."

At this era's most ridiculous juncture, in January 2002, two near-identical torture game shows debuted simultaneously: ABC's *The Chair*, hosted by John McEnroe, in which players were tied to a chair, placed in a pit, then had their heart rate measured as they took a quiz and were attacked by bees; and Fox's *The Chamber*, hosted by sports radio host Rick Schwartz (who took the job after sports broadcaster Matt Vasgersian quit in disgust*), in which players were tied to a chair, locked inside a chamber, then measured for stress as they took a quiz and were shaken by simulated earthquakes. (There were other tortures, too.) Each network accused the other of theft, but by the end, it was a fight over table scraps. *The Chair* lasted nine episodes, *The Chamber* three—and the legal fight fizzled out as well.

---

* Vasgersian walked out on the first day of rehearsal when he overheard a producer calculating the health ramifications of them flooding the chamber with a swarm of mosquitos.

"We each mounted our shows in, like, ten days," said Andrea Wong, who oversaw *The Chair*. She regarded Darnell less as an enemy than a friendly rival, part of a clique of executives who socialized and shared jokes, even as they undercut one another. To Wong, the battle of the torture game shows just felt like another life lesson: It wasn't worth getting there first if your show was a lemon.

In 2002, Darnell also experienced his own corporate rebrand with *American Idol*. The British show, originally called *Pop Idol*, had begun as a profit machine, one craftily engineered by two music industry Simons: Spice Girls manager Simon Fuller and music manager Simon Cowell. It was constructed entirely of auditions—all killer, no filler. But mainly, it was a music manager's dream, since it was designed to produce a brand-new, super-famous singer each season, a star whose debut album would be owned by Fuller and Cowell. In England, Cowell had become a breakout star himself as one of the show's judges, celebrated for speaking truth to tone-deaf nobodies.

According to Bill Carter's book *Desperate Networks,* U.S. networks were initially resistant to *Pop Idol,* with Fox finally signing on only after Rupert Murdoch's daughter Elisabeth lobbied them to cut the deal. Darnell disputed that account, arguing that he'd always favored the franchise, recognizing that *American Idol* was exactly the kind of upbeat, aspirational franchise the network needed after 9/11. Whether he was pushed or jumped, Darnell suddenly found himself in charge of his first big-box, shiny-floor project, a commercial juggernaut sponsored by Coca-Cola. He found his own angle on the competition, drawn to its unusual blend of tearjerker triumph and *Gong Show*–esque humiliation (or as Darnell put it, "edge and honesty"). Early seasons offered up a bit of both: The show's first winner, Kelly Clarkson, was an unknown twenty-year-old waitress with a husky voice so glorious that she managed to transform the gluey ballad "A Moment Like This" into a #1 hit. Two seasons later, William Hung, a Hong Kong–born engineering student, became a beloved laughingstock for his off-key rendition of "She Bangs." If the audience response to Hung had a racist tinge, he still managed to release three albums and embrace his own anti-fame before retiring to work for the L.A. sheriff's department.

Although *American Idol* was more of a talent contest than a pure reality format, it became the first model of a powerful new subgenre: shows that celebrated artistic skill, from ballroom dancing to fashion design. In the process, it also managed to clear up Darnell's bad-boy rep, sending him along on the path to other mainstream reality hits, overseeing wholesome competition shows like *MasterChef* and *So You Think You Can Dance.*

AFTER THE WORLD TRADE CENTER FELL, PUNDITS PREDICTED that reality programming would surely crumble with it, as *Vanity Fair* editor Graydon Carter (and several others) declared "the end of irony." Strangely, in the aftermath of a major terrorist attack, the newspapers were full of fresh denunciations of the genre, arguing that with the country at war, viewers would surely lose interest in these silly, sadistic entertainments.

Networks struggled to respond to the mood, particularly when it came to a set of travel shows that had already been greenlighted. Some of their choices were purely pragmatic. *Survivor* switched locations, jumping from Jordan to French Polynesia. A cadre of travel shows slated for September got bumped, among them Bunim/Murray's *Love Cruise,* which was originally scheduled to debut on September 11. An ill-starred NBC reality series called *Lost* debuted on September 4 with a premise that suddenly felt sinister: Three blindfolded teams of strangers were dumped in a foreign country, then raced one another to the Statue of Liberty. The most dramatic victim was the Matt Damon/Ben Affleck project *The Runner,* which hemorrhaged millions of dollars for ABC.* *Cannonball Run 2001,* on USA Network, had the good luck to air its finale on September 2.

The winner of this race among race shows was *The Amazing Race,* a project Ghen Maynard had signed immediately after the

* *The Runner* did eventually get produced in 2016, in a far tamer, mostly online variation. Speaking to reality TV blogger Andy Dehnart, former *Survivor* executive producer Craig Piligian described the never-made OG version, nostalgically, as an "unsafely interactive" project. "The runner would have been tackled and tied and drawn—*I got the fucking runner right here! He's tied up in my fuckin' basement, come give me my million dollars.*"

debut of *Survivor*. The co-creation of ad executive Elise Doganieri and her husband, the Dutch-born Bertram van Munster, a former field producer on *Cops, The Amazing Race* had no format at all, at first, just the general idea that eight pairs of players—who could be anyone, from frat brothers to circus partners—would race around the globe. With so little structure, early filming was a logistical nightmare, but by then, a set of polished professionals were available, among them, Brady Connell, the former supervising producer for *Survivor*. A cheerful, hard-driving problem solver, Connell was eager to tackle the project's practical challenges, although one of his plans nearly destroyed it, by accident. Connell, who had lobbied to make the *Survivor* ship sink in the pilot, thought they should have something just as extreme for *The Amazing Race* finale. His original pitch involved the finalists racing to the roof of the World Trade Center, gasping and panting as they ran up the stairs, a sequence culminating with a thrilling helicopter landing.

Connell was disappointed that they wound up filming in Flushing Meadows, Queens, the site of the 1939 World's Fair, instead, when the logistics didn't work out. It turned out to be a lucky break—had his plan worked, the show would surely have been canceled. Even so, the timing was fraught. *The Amazing Race* debuted on September 5, and a week later few viewers were in the mood to watch panicked reality show contestants running through airports. Maynard, who was focused on the crisis on *Big Brother 2*, felt frustrated by the backlash: The way he saw it, *The Amazing Race* and the tragedy had no connection—if anything, the CBS show was a wonderful kind of counterprogramming, a celebration of the interconnectedness of the globe at a moment of trauma and despair.

Although the ratings weren't spectacular, the show got picked up for a second season, just under the wire, and over the years, it easily outpaced much of its competition, distinguished by its beauty, worldliness, and focus on intimate relationships.* By its thirty-fifth season, *The Amazing Race* had become the rare critics' darling of

* Such competition included USA Network's misbegotten *Cannonball Run 2001* and ESPN's *Beg, Borrow & Deal*, in which broke players scrounged for housing and food.

the genre, the sort of series that the whole family could watch together, with its welcoming slogan, "The world is waiting for you."

Several other reality shows were midway through filming when the Towers fell, among them *The Real World: Chicago* and a sweet series about actors called *The It Factor,* both of which edited the disaster into their stories. Even HBO's *Sex and the City* trimmed the Twin Towers from its credits. The tragedy also cast a shadow over a show that had recently aired: an ambitious Fox series called *Murder in Small Town X*. Created by George Verschoor, the series was a murder-mystery story, in which real people competed to solve a murder while interacting with a town full of actors. The winner was Angel Juarbe, Jr., a likeable firefighter from the Bronx. A week after the finale, he died defending the Twin Towers.*

As TV producers scrambled to adjust, one group fully grasped the potential of the reality genre immediately: the U.S. military, which was gearing up for war. In *Time* magazine, James Poniewozik dubbed the rising subgenre "militainment." Among these shows was Cutler's *Military Diaries,* which *The San Francisco Chronicle* described as "a recruiter's godsend." There was also *AFP: American Fighter Pilot* on CBS, a 2002 *Real World*–style treatment of the Air Force, produced by *Top Gun* director Tony Scott; and a year later, ABC's *Profiles from the Front Line,* which *Variety* described, breezily, as "the propaganda hour," produced by *Amazing Race* creator van Munster and his partner Jerry Bruckheimer.

Humanizing instead of analytical, militainment shows emphasized warm stories about the heroism of individual soldiers without providing much context, let alone reportorial skepticism. As Poniewozik put it, the Pentagon had "granted reality producers access with all the reluctance of a five-year-old entertaining a proposal to

---

* The failure of *Murder in Small Town X* devastated Verschoor, who was shooting for a more literary, immersive reality format, inspired by *Twin Peaks* and the movie *Westworld.* He'd transformed Eastport, Maine, into the fictional town "Sunrise," hiring locals as extras and giving the cast daily clues, a system that worked unnervingly well. One night, Verschoor found a contestant hiding under a staircase, waiting for the killer. "I told him, 'Um, it's a game. *I* am the killer. You should go to bed.'" But once he screened it at Fox, he knew the project was doomed. "Everyone went 'Wow . . . *that's* different.'" The network had no idea how to promote it, although Mike Darnell did jokingly suggest planting a real corpse in Times Square.

have ice cream for breakfast." Dick Cheney and Donald Rumsfeld personally okayed access for *Profiles*. Frustrated that reality show-runners were being ushered behind the scenes while they were locked out, ABC News lodged a complaint about van Munster's series to the entertainment division, while a senior news producer at another network griped to the *Los Angeles Times*, "If they're getting access we're not getting, there is something wrong."

On top of these soft-soap narrative treatments of the war, a new set of military-themed competition shows emerged, among them Mark Burnett's first follow-up to *Survivor,* a 2002 USA Network show called *Combat Missions,* starring the grizzled *Survivor* cast-away Rudy Boesch. *Combat Missions,* which debuted in January 2002, split its players into four "squads": Alpha (primarily young Navy SEALs), Bravo (mainly SWAT cops), Charlie (older veterans), and Delta (the "oddballs"). Their challenges included "Meth Lab," a mission against a fictional drug dealer, "Santos Hernandez." Burnett scoffed at the wave of post-9/11 eulogies for reality TV: "This war is perfect timing for *Combat Missions,*" he told reporters.

The show lasted one season. The Delta team included Navy SEAL Scott Helvenston, a fit, blond Captain America type whom Burnett had first met in 1993, as part of another team competing in the Raid Gauloises. A celebrity personal trainer who whipped Demi Moore into shape for *G.I. Jane,* Helvenston was a Zelig of reality shows, showing up as an "alpha-male captain" on the never-aired *Extreme Expeditions: Model Behavior* and on the Fox series *Man vs. Beast,* where he was the only player who won against his assigned animal, beating a chimpanzee in an obstacle course. On *Combat Missions,* Helvenston was a classic reality TV hothead, growling (with bleeps thrown in), "That motherfucker comes near me, man, I'll club him!"

Two years later, however, his life came to a tragic end. Broke, in the wake of a divorce and a failed fitness venture, Helvenston took a three-month, $60,000 freelance gig with the notorious Blackwater Security Company, flying to Iraq for his first experience with real-life combat. Serving with him were two friends from *Combat Missions.* His first week there, Helvenston was murdered in an ambush in Fallujah, then dragged through the streets by a cheering mob and hanged from a bridge across the Euphrates. The grisly images, which were quickly transmitted around the world, set off America's disastrous retaliatory assault on Fallujah. After his death, Burnett described Helvenston as "a true American warrior," and added, "It makes it all seem so much closer. It reminds me of *Black Hawk Down*."

By February 2002, a new set of pundits chimed in. Rather than predicting the death of reality TV, they made a more alarming argument, that instead of being snuffed out by 9/11, the genre had been *strengthened* by the tragedy, which had given it a fresh purpose—as a numbing agent. "Reality TV didn't emerge as compensation for a reality shortage, but as a buffer against the real," argued media scholar Mark Andrejevic in a column called "Reality TV May Be Down but It's Not Out." "The genre offers a reality substitute that has the same flavor as the real thing, but without the disconcerting aftertaste of a call to action—political, social, or otherwise. You don't have to do anything about the reality offered up by reality TV because, as any fan or critic will tell you, it's not really real."

CELEBREALITY LAUNCHED IN MARCH 2002, WITH MTV'S *THE Osbournes*. At the time, Ozzy Osbourne was widely perceived as a washed-up metalhead, the Black Sabbath lead singer who'd bitten the head off a bat. The show transformed him into a classic American TV archetype: a loveable sitcom dad in sweatpants, yelling for his son to fix the remote. Inspired by a 1997 documentary about the family, *Fame and Fortune*, the show centered around Ozzy, a supposedly newly sober addict; his savvy wife, Sharon; and two of their kooky kids, hanging out in a mansion full of devil dolls. It was hardly a model of cinéma vérité realism: Among other things, Ozzy was stoned the entire time they were filming. But for viewers, it felt like a lighthearted goof, with a few touching threads, including Sharon's struggle with cancer. The finale reached 7.2 million viewers.

The Osbournes—and the celebreality that followed, especially *Newlyweds*, which traced the marriage of pop stars Jessica Simpson and Nick Lachey—flipped the premise of reality TV upside down.

Instead of turning ordinary people into stars, they turned stars into ordinary people. For faded luminaries seeking some rejuvenating publicity, there were clear upsides to participating, especially if they got to be the producers of their own shows. A parade of VIPs lined up for this deluxe treatment, among them P. Diddy, Cybill Shepherd, and Liza Minnelli, although few of their projects got off the ground.

One major player did emerge from the celebreality renaissance: Cris Abrego, a former logger (transcriber of dialogue from footage) at Bunim/Murray who was one of the industry's few Latino reality producers. A second-generation Mexican American from suburban El Monte, California, Abrego had faced a series of locked doors when he tried to break into mostly white Hollywood. His big break-through was *The Surreal World*, a 2003 show that had been inspired by an ad for the Lipton product Sizzle & Stir in which Loni Anderson, George Hamilton, Mary Lou Retton, and Mr. T cooked dinner together. When he pitched the idea to Mary-Ellis Bunim, she refused to give Abrego a "created by" credit ("a mistake," Jon Murray said). Abrego changed the title to *The Surreal Life,* then sold it to The WB.

The show's first season featured an artisanal blend of faded stars: grizzled musicians (Vince Neil, MC Hammer), grown-up child stars (Corey Feldman, Emmanuel Lewis), a few veterans of network hits (*90210*'s Gabrielle Carteris and *Baywatch* babe Brande Roderick), and also Jerri Manthey, a recent villain on *Survivor*.

Abrego would go on to create some of the wilder, raunchier, and more diverse shows of the aughts, projects like the 2006 hip-hop dating show *Flavor of Love* (original title: *The Black-chelor*), which starred Flavor Flav of Public Enemy. Abrego sometimes got flak for playing to racial stereotypes, which he found unfair: The way he saw it, he was letting Black and Brown people be as fun, cartoonish, and extreme as anyone else in the genre. Ultimately, Abrego left the creative side of the business, becoming the head of the global conglomerate Endemol Entertainment (later called Banijay), which then bought Bunim/Murray. In a nice bit of irony, Abrego wound up as Jon Murray's boss.

The early celebreality shows were all designed to resemble family sitcoms, a type of comfort TV that felt nostalgic by the early aughts.

The Osbournes was a goth update of Fox's *Married . . . with Children; Newlyweds* was marketed as the new *I Love Lucy;* Abrego's live pitch for *The Surreal Life* was based on shows like *All in the Family.* In 2003, Jon Murray created a reality TV version of *Green Acres,* casting heiress Paris Hilton and her bestie Nicole Richie in *The Simple Life,* a comedy about two spoiled girls forced to clean up chicken poop.

Stars had an advantage over ordinary people who got cast in reality shows: They were used to being public figures. But even if you got the final cut on your project, it didn't guarantee a happy ending. In her touching memoir *Open Book,* pop singer Jessica Simpson described the destabilizing experience of having her marriage fall apart on camera when she was twenty-two years old. At the time, Simpson was a minor pop diva deeply in love with Nick Lachey, a member of the boy band 98 Degrees. When the two got engaged, Simpson's evangelical preacher father—who doubled as her manager—pushed for her to do the MTV reality show, against the wishes of her music company, which thought it would hurt her career. Her dad was right, in the end: *Newlyweds* was incredible PR, melting Simpson's ice-queen image and turning her from a sub-Britney diva into something better, America's sweetest, ditsiest Southern cousin—an intimate type of superstardom. "Reality television knocked famous people off the pedestal," she wrote, creating a fanhood that felt more like friendship, with viewers walking up and hugging her, as if they were sorority sisters.

Early on, Jessica and Nick got used to the crew producing the details of their home lives—arranging for a camping trip, say, or scattering rose petals during a weekend away—but their dialogue wasn't scripted, the way it would be on similar shows a few years later. Instead, the couple were encouraged to riff off their own Ricky-and-Lucy dynamic, with Lachey the chiding, affectionate husband and Simpson his airhead bride. They could say "stop rolling" any time they wanted, but Simpson tried not to. Paradoxically, she found appearing on *Newlyweds more* relaxing than her singing career, since she could wear sweats and no makeup, even fart on camera. Simpson's infamous "bloopers"—like the day she asked if "Chicken of the Sea" meant fish or chicken—were all genuine mistakes. But the experience of making them was liberating: On MTV, she didn't have to be perfect.

That all changed when her marriage started to crumble, a season in. Jessica's career was peaking while Nick's was fading; they were often on the road, living separately. When they were together, there were long silences instead of banter. One day, a PA from the show handed Jessica a tabloid spread, with a headline about Nick partying at a strip club. In a flash, she knew the rules had changed: MTV wanted to film her reaction. It was as if they'd agreed to embed with their own paparazzi.

One day, when Nick and Jessica said "Stop rolling," nothing happened. When Nick asked the crew to leave so that the couple could talk privately, a producer approached him. "If we keep having to stop rolling," he said, "there's no show." The couple said the words simultaneously: "Stop rolling."

With no decent footage available, the producers patched together a sad, fake season finale, resembling a sitcom "clip" show, with happier memories repurposed as flashbacks. The crew felt the loss, too. "In the beginning, it was a very pure show in the sense that Nick and Jessica were in love and the producers hung out with them and we were all like, 'Oh my gosh, she's adorable,'" said an audio technician from *Newlyweds*. "But as you know, if you put any relationship under a magnifying glass, it's going to suffer."

When *Newlyweds* ended, Nick and Jessica tried to save their relationship, but it was too late. "I think we both knew we couldn't blame all our problems on the cameras, but we felt obligated to at least try," wrote Simpson. Even with the crew gone, the eerie feeling that they were being recorded continued to linger. Sometimes, when the couple needed to fight, they would sneak out to a vacant lot near their home, paranoid that the house was still bugged.

ONE PART OF SIMPSON'S LIFE DIDN'T SHOW UP ON *NEWLYWEDS:* her incendiary emotional affair with fellow MTV star Johnny Knoxville, whom she'd met when she played Daisy Duke in the *Dukes of*

Hazzard movie. A Tennessee-born daredevil, the married Knoxville (née P. J. Clapp) was the front man for *Jackass,* a prank show that debuted in 2000. In the tape that sold the show to MTV, he strapped on a cheap bulletproof vest, stuffed it with porn magazines, took a .38, and shot himself in the chest. One year later, the raffish stuntman was sprawled sexily on the cover of *Rolling Stone,* with a wet bull's-eye painted on his chest, wearing jeans and a jockstrap. It was catnip for Simpson, who had a weakness for bad boys—and although the affair led nowhere, it helped blow up her marriage.

Although Knoxville was the handsome face of *Jackass,* the show itself was a deeply collaborative project, dreamed up by a dirtbag fraternity of close friends, who were glued together (sometimes literally) by an ethic of nonstop hazing. Among them was Knoxville's MTV producer Trip Taylor, who, like many of the ensemble members, had grown up in a neglectful, alcoholic family, a background that shaped his ability to tolerate chaos. Taylor, who started out as a carpenter, also had the ideal training for a *Jackass* producer, having just finished up a stint producing *The Tom Green Show,* another influential protoreality series stuffed with pranks and shock comedy segments, like throwing baby dolls at passing cars or putting a severed cow's head in the bed of the Canadian comedian's parents.

Taylor quickly bonded with the *Jackass* team, which included Jeff Tremaine, the editor of the skateboarding magazine *Big Brother;* former Ringling Bros. clown/boundary-pushing lunatic Steve-O; and skateboarder Bam Margera and Bam's own crew, "CKY," or "Camp Kill Yourself." The group's motto was "bros before pros." Their early sketches were hit-and-miss, with rank gags like "street fishing," in which they dangled dollar bills in front of homeless guys. There were edgy updates on *Candid Camera* classics, like one in which Knoxville pulled his car into gas stations, then had a handcuffed man jump out of his trunk, naked and screaming. Still, the show's best pranks weren't on bystanders, but on one another.

In the debut episode of *Jackass,* "Poo Cocktail," Knoxville had his friend squirt him with red pepper spray ("It feels like my eyes have gonorrhea!"), then shock him with a stun gun and a taser, as the two men giggled and screamed. The score was bluesy guitar; the aesthetic was backyard home video, with Knoxville wearing an American flag as a cap. As the clip ended, someone drawled, "You guys want to go watch it on the TV?" There was much more like that, including grocery-cart car crashes, upside-down Porta Potties, and vomited-up live goldfish. For their movies—in which they didn't have to follow MTV's safety standards—they were able to go much further, supergluing their hands to one another's torsos, then ripping them away, covered in chest hair; trapping themselves in a limo filled with bees; and shoving chickens into jockstraps. These stunts were centrally about impressing each other, no matter what the physical cost: In Steve-O's disarming memoir, *Professional Idiot*, he describes stapling the word "Jackass" across his butt cheeks on the first day of filming, then later stapling his scrotum to his leg.

Jackass was half-therapy, half-psychosis, the type of cathartic body horror that viewers either "got" or found repulsive. When interviewers tried to get Knoxville to explain his motives—Was he taming abuse by turning it into a joke? Did these stunts have some kind of spiritual edge?—he shrugged their questions off, telling *Rolling Stone,* "Well, I guess I don't really intellectualize it."

In historical terms, the show was the feral grandson of *Candid Camera,* crossed with *When Animals Attack!,* had the animals been able to film themselves. Like *Cops,* it was a defiantly lo-fi production, filmed on the fly. Trip Taylor got used to running defense with the LAPD as they shot stunts like "Bloody Windshield," another gas station sketch, in which Knoxville coated his car with blood and chicken fat. Another time, the crew "kidnapped" Brad Pitt and nearly got shot by a guard. By the second season, the LAPD had become fans of the show, which "made forgiveness a lot easier," said Taylor. (It also likely helped that the majority of the *Jackass* crew were white.)

Jackass had a secondary motto: "It's not gay if it's on camera." One day, Taylor's wife discovered that a fake *Playgirl* shoot had just been staged in her backyard, with crew member Dave Carnie, aka "oil boy," greasing up cast member Chris Pontius, who wore only a red cowboy hat and a gun belt. "Everything got on the air, except the completion," said Taylor. During a homophobic era, *Jackass* benefited from a perverse logic: Everyone in the show had to be straight, because who else would do something so gay? Taylor took special pride in the day that queer icon John Waters, the director of cult films like *Pink Flamingos,* visited the *Jackass* set and told Knoxville, with awe, "You're sexual terrorists!"

Once in a while someone made a comparison to Buster Keaton, but most critics saw *Jackass* as garbage—and, worse, as dangerous garbage. Although MTV ran a disclaimer,* teen fans *did* try stunts at home, leading to an incident in which a fourteen-year-old got badly burned while imitating "The Human Barbecue," a sketch in which Knoxville had covered himself in steaks and lain on a grill. Senator Joe Lieberman railed against the show, and MTV's Standards and Practices cracked down, banning fire, and also, at one point, vomiting and leaps from more than four feet, as well as "imitatable stunts," a vague category that drove Knoxville crazy, ultimately leading him to quit, in 2002, in order to make movies. The reality was, the show had always been less Buster Keaton and more *Looney Tunes,* a brilliant animated show fueled by a whacked-out, shameless, antiauthority zest. No one got flattened by an anvil on *Jackass,* but they came close.

Steve Unckles got his first job in reality TV on a *Jackass* spin-off, *Viva La Bam,* which starred Bam Margera and his family. Hired as a PA, Unckles got bumped up quickly to a coordinator job, because, he joked, "they just saw that I wasn't super-dumb—and I was lonely and broke." On set in suburban Pennsylvania, Unckles found himself mesmerized by Margera, a brilliantly charismatic performer who was willing to do anything. Unckles dug the show's unique vibe, too, "a funny cartoon, like pro wrestling," and he loved the way they

---

* On the first two episodes, this warning read, "The following show features stunts performed by professionals and/or total idiots. In either case, MTV insists that neither you or any of your dumb little buddies attempt the dangerous crap in this show." By the third, it was upgraded to "The following show features stunts performed by professionals and/or total idiots under very strict control and supervision. MTV and the producers insist that neither you or anyone else attempt to re-create or perform anything you have seen on this show." For especially dangerous stunts, they put a skull and crossbones on the screen.

shot, fast and dirty, with lousy lighting, lending the episodes a funky, distinctive verve.

Ultimately, though, the job wore him down. Their star had bipolar disorder and addictions that were spinning out of control. The crew, like Unckles, was young and working twelve-to-fourteen-hour days. His own pay wasn't bad—$1,600 a week—but there were cast members who were underpaid, and sometimes unpaid. And Chris Raab, who played the crazed character "Raab Himself," kept getting injured, each recovery sinking him deeper into painkiller abuse. Unckles saw legs broken and "a lot worse stuff than that," as the drugs deepened, along with the personal drama. When a backflip went wrong, professional motocross performer Brian Deegan lost a kidney and four pints of blood. There were no EMTs around. Although Deegan sued MTV, he lost—maybe because, according to Unckles, the production had audio of someone telling Deegan, "Don't do this if you don't want to."

For all his affection for the cast and crew, Unckles still feels lingering guilt about his role in those early disasters. "I mean, that wasn't my job, but the thing is, it was *no one's* job. And it needs to be someone's job." In many ways, that era in reality TV felt as if it were taking place in 1910, not the turn of the twenty-first century, he added. "There's no labor laws. No one's looking out! We're all just so desperately looking out for ourselves. And that's not how it should be."

UNCKLES'S EXPERIENCE WASN'T UNUSUAL. AS REALITY SHOWS bubbled up like lava, the genre's undercurrent of exploitation intensified, particularly at more marginal productions, out of the spotlight. Sometimes, the issue was less about safety than abuse. Jude Weng, who worked on *Survivor: Borneo,* told me about a day on *Celebrity Mole* when, after a stunt involving coffins buried in sand didn't pan out, her producer turned bright red, then leaped over an open coffin and tried to choke her. "I'm much bigger than him, so I wasn't even afraid—it was like a kitten scrabbling up me," she joked. Back then, the incident didn't seem worth reporting. "There were no unions, so who am I going to complain to? To HR? There was no HR."

Sometimes, stunts simply went wrong. A contestant on *Dog Eat Dog* sued NBC, claiming a breath-holding challenge gave him brain damage when a bungee-like escape mechanism failed during a breath-holding contest. (He lost the case, seemingly because the contract he'd signed waived any damages.). On Fox's *The Chamber*, one player made it through seven levels of the cold chamber, winning $20,000—then got hypothermia and settled out of court for $100,000 more. During the second season of *Survivor*, which was set in the Australian Outback, a contestant inhaled smoke and then passed out into a fire and had to be airlifted out. Risky stunts weren't new to reality programming. On *That's Incredible!*, participants also got badly hurt—in one case, stuntman Stan Kruml burned his hands to stumps running through a tunnel of fire, an incident that led to a lawsuit, an early "Do Not Try This Yourself" TV warning, and also a switch to airing only previously filmed stunts.

Incidents like these got bad press. They rarely hurt the shows, however—and sometimes they became selling points. After the *Survivor* fire, Burnett told reporters that if his cameraman had dropped his camera to help the contestant who was getting burned, "I would have fired him on the spot." The episode—gorgeously edited, saturated in both danger and glamour—got nominated for an Emmy for Outstanding Picture Editing for Non-Fiction Programming in 2001.

Dan Kornfeld, a reality producer who began his career as a PA on Bunim/Murray shows like *Road Rules*, watched the stakes rise, over the years. When Kornfeld first joined *Road Rules*, in the mid-1990s, it was a sweet show in which young people roamed around the country in a Winnebago, doing low-stakes competitions. In 1998, the show merged with *The Real World*, becoming *Road Rules: All Stars*, which starred former cast members from *The Real World*, including Puck. Then it became *Real World/Road Rules Challenge*, and later *The Challenge*, a more decadent, more aggressive series. By then, Kornfeld was gone—and the cast bore little resemblance to the OG roommates: They were corporate entities with online fanhoods and brand partnerships, like pop stars or athletes.

292 CUE THE SUN!

These shifts weren't always harmful, Kornfeld told me—they were just a question of making a different kind of show, like *WWE Tough Enough*, a 2001 wrestling show he'd worked on. There were all kinds of entertainment. Still, *Tough Enough* stuck to vérité rules, with no interference allowed—a camera assistant nearly got fired for helping a wrestler off the ground. Kornfeld, who would go on to make *Man v. Food,* an extreme-eating show, never got comfortable with staging conflicts, the methods he saw emerge in the aughts.

Like everything else, these shifts were about money. It took months to glean brilliant footage for a reality show, to capture the subtleties of relationships as they emerged, organically. If your cast members already understood who they were supposed to argue with, you could tie a show up in ten days.

FRAUD HAD ALWAYS BEEN A FACTOR IN REALITY FORMATS, broadly defined, on back to Barnum's empire of humbug. But after 2000, the wheels came off the bus—and on some shows, producers took desperate measures. One of the crazier stories involved a bounty hunter series called *Manhunt,* which began as a co-production of UPN and Vince McMahon's World Wrestling Federation.[*] Bob Jaffe, who was best known for the bombastic warrior competition *American Gladiators,* but whose production work harked back to *That's Incredible!,* had been hired to oversee the show. He was handed a four-page prospectus, inspired by the short story "The Most Dangerous Game"—and then the WWF deal fell through. Still, accompanied by his crew members, Jaffe flew down to Hawaii, where they spent six weeks diligently constructing a gargantuan obstacle course, full of snares, in which the cast would race away from bounty hunters carrying paint guns. When filming started, Jaffe hit his own snares, among them, a mysterious problem: The contestants weren't

---

[*] Bounty hunter concepts were hot in 2000: In addition to Damon and Affleck's *The Runner,* a truly wacko pitch called *Danger Island* landed on CBS executive Ghen Maynard's desk, in which real bounty hunters would chase actual ex-cons, supposedly featuring *The Incredible Hulk* star Lou Ferrigno as the host. The show never got close to being made, but it got a lot of press, used as an example of how far reality TV was willing to go.

fighting and scheming, the way they had on *Survivor*. Instead, they were cheering one another on.

Romey Jakobson Glidewell had applied to the show through her half-sister Marki, a casting agent who was having trouble finding people willing to get their heads shaved, one of the show's "punishments." Romey, who was young and newly divorced, felt game for the adventure, so she waved her blond hair around, alluringly, on her audition tape. In Kauai, however, she discovered that the production had made a rookie error: Due to scheduling delays, the cast were left alone together in a hotel for several days. With nothing to do, they promptly bonded, as if they were freshman-year college roommates, infatuated by one another's charm and athleticism, flirting and sharing stories. Then, they got bad news: The prize money had been cut in half, from $500,000 to $250,000. This information triggered a new level of cast solidarity, and one night, as they lounged around in a hotel room, a member of the ensemble suggested an idea: Maybe they should just *split* the pot? Everyone was in.

When filming started, the competition was mysteriously drama free. Sensing disaster, Paramount Network Television president Garry Hart and studio chairman Kerry McCluggage—who had flown in—were determined to stir the pot, using methods that were less like throwing pebbles in the pond than swinging a wrecking ball. During the first competition, producer Christopher Crowe physically tackled a player named Jacqueline Kelly to slow her down; later on, the top brass pressured Jaffe to rig a contest to keep another player they liked in the game. Jaffe said no, but it was a miserable situation—and back in L.A., during editing, things took another dive.

As part of postproduction, Russ Ward—a crew member who was exasperated by Jaffe's choices, like sending cameramen on cast hikes without any producers—was told to dig through the footage, to scrounge up dialogue and plots. He found a jaw-dropping production snafu. Just before the game began, the cast had trained with Navy SEAL Hash Shaalan, who taught them real-life survival skills, like staying silent in the jungle. As a result, the footage of their hikes was entirely silent—just hours and hours of the cast walking in single file and using hand signals. In the end, no one even asked Ward for the edit, so he figured the job was over and left.

Meanwhile, Jaffe's bosses had been demanding that he film *more* footage—a set of scripted confessionals, which would be shot in Los Angeles's Griffith Park, disguised to look like Hawaii. When Jaffe refused to do it, they fired him. Instead, the executives staged those scenes themselves, outfitting the players with bandanas in order to conceal their shaved heads. The cast played along, reluctantly, having been told that if the show didn't air, they'd forfeit their prize money. Eventually, just before the show debuted, the scandal broke: Peter Lance, of the muckraking website The Stingray, wrote an online exposé, complete with paparazzi shots of the fraudulent reshoot.

The *Manhunt* exposé wasn't quite the quiz show scandals, but it was embarrassing. Jacqueline—the first player expelled and the only one who refused to do the fake shoot—filed suit with the FCC (an effort that fizzled, in the wake of 9/11). Paramount put out a clarifying statement, which was initially buried in the closing credits. The show wound up becoming a black mark on everyone's résumé, with the exception of pro wrestler John Cena, who had played one of the show's macho "manhunters." According to several *Manhunt* participants, Cena gamely stayed in character throughout the shoot.

In one sense, *Manhunt* was just another Hollywood footnote—six low-rated reality TV episodes on UPN and out. But it was also a symbol of the darkly comic disarray on the fringes of Hollywood, which is where most shows got made. It was hard to get too outraged about fraud when you were working that hard, for so little money, in an industry that got so little respect. If everyone already assumed that your show was a fake, no matter what you did or how hard you worked, why even bother making it real?

There was one silver lining to *Manhunt:* The cast members kept their promise to one another, with the winner writing everyone else a check. They stayed friends for years, continuing to get together for drinks. It was the first successful reality television union.

III

BY 2002, CASTING A REALITY SHOW HAD BECOME A SCIENCE, down to the thick contracts contestants signed, granting editors total control. There were dedicated hotels near the airport where new casts stayed, so they could go through the gauntlet of interviews and psych tests. "Producers might say, 'I want to see more Black guys. I want to see more gay guys. I want to see more hot girls,'" Jon Kroll said. Although there were a few exceptions—among them the committed gay couple on the first season of *The Amazing Race*—cartoonish stereotypes were the industry default. Swishy gay men got cast for comedy, or sometimes to ignite a clash with a homophobe. Producers would pick one or two Black players, but no more. Each year, the players got cannier about their own brands, their niches—and more aware of the bargain they made by playing themselves.

There was also a natural next step, after the finale aired: a move to Los Angeles. There was even a bar at which reality cast members hung out, a place called Belly Lounge, a seedily luxurious joint that was owned by Mike "Boogie" Malin, one of the Chilltown bullies from *Big Brother 2*.* A reality finale was like college graduation, whether you'd matriculated at Survivor U—the Ivy equivalent, whose players looked down their noses at other shows—or some party school like Temptation Island State. Reality performers roomed together; they dated and networked, hopscotching seasons and franchises.

To earn money, there were a few options. If you were a *Real World* cast member, an agent could book you to speak on college campuses. There were reunions, there were crossover shows, there were All-Star seasons, there were charity events. A few entrepreneurs, like Gervase Peterson from *Survivor*, found that it was a lifestyle that could keep you afloat, for at least a few years.

There was another route into Los Angeles, as well: jumping from the cast into the crew. Colleen Haskell Hampton, who had been em-

---

* A creep, even by reality standards: Among other things, in 2021, Boogie was found guilty of stalking his former *Big Brother* ally Will Kirby.

braced as America's Sweetheart by fans of *Survivor*, was one of the few people to get a unicorn Hollywood opportunity, right away, when she landed the female lead in a Rob Schneider movie comedy, *The Animal*. Haskell had no training as an actress; she felt embarrassed about her reality fame and uncertain about what she should do next. "It's not like Steven Spielberg is calling. And then again—it's fun."

When *The Animal* flopped, Haskell stayed in Los Angeles, taking production jobs on reality shows like *Military Diaries,* with R. J. Cutler. Later, she worked as a logger on *Sorority Life,* at MTV. After the shock of becoming a household name, working behind the scenes felt therapeutic. "I tried to control my past life by working on my future life," she said. Eventually, however, these gigs didn't feel like the right match for her skill set, in part because she felt too protective of the cast. Still, the experience wasn't a bad one—and it helped her come to terms with the genre, including her relationship with her own producers. "You're not their therapist. Everybody is just doing their job," she said.

In the end, Haskell graduated from college and then got an advanced degree. She found a high-up job in corporate strategy, working for a major entertainment company, one you've heard of. As the decades passed, her Gen X shame about her own celebrity—and her old discomfort with "that reality show culture," its tackiness, its tawdriness—started to fade. Colleen now watched reality shows for fun, like many people she knew. "It's embarrassing for me in a different way, because I watch Bravo," she said, laughing.

BY 2003, A NEW PHENOMENON HAD EMERGED: META-REALITY shows, which parodied reality TV—and also *were* reality TV. In a peculiar way, these formats were a sign of the industry's maturity: They were inside jokes, created by insiders. For four decades, there had been scripted satires like Albert Brooks's 1979 *Real Life* (and also Brooks's 1975 *Saturday Night Live* segment "Home Movies," which spoofed *Candid Camera*), Ben Stiller's 1994 *Reality Bites*, Peter Weir's 1998 blockbuster *The Truman Show,* and the 2001 thriller *Series 7: The Contenders,* in which players were handed guns and told to kill or be killed. Way back in 1968, the BBC had aired *The Year of the Sex Olympics,* a stunningly prescient dystopian science fiction fantasy about a future in which a tiny elite controlled the population with sordid game shows. These projects had universally been scathing critiques of the reality TV machine: its sadism, its voyeurism, its commercialism, its queasy blend of phony authenticity and actual exploitation, and especially its cold-eyed producers, willing to manipulate the ordinary people they cast in their projects.

The Joe Schmo Show was different. It was a satire that had been created by reality producers—and it was designed to show that people could behave decently under pressure. The idea had originated in late 2001, when reality producer Paul Wernick and his oldest friend, Rhett Reese, a screenwriter with a background in social psychology, were watching *Big Brother,* a series that Wernick worked on. (A disenchanted refugee from TV news, Wernick had also worked on *The Chair.*) At the time, it was shortly after 9/11; the country was in a grim, sensitive mood. Suddenly, Reese had a revelation: He wanted to make a new type of reality show, one that would celebrate kindness, not cruelty. In the finale, it would reward a nice guy, the kind of person who would make the right choice, every time.

The way Wernick and Reese imagined the project, *The Joe Show,* it would be set behind the scenes of a fake reality series called *The Lap of Luxury.* Only one of the players—the designated "Joe"— would be an actual contestant. Everyone else would be a paid performer, doing a satire of some reality TV archetype, characters that included "The Hutch," a Pucklike troublemaker; Earl, a Rudy-esque geezer; three sexy women (a schemer, a rich bitch, and a Southern virgin); and also Kip, a swishy Puerto Rican gay man. If the scheme paid off, their goodhearted main character would choose loyalty to his best friend over the temptation to join a greedy alliance. In the final episode, he'd learn the truth—and then he'd win $100,000 and become a national hero.

After months of pitching networks but getting no offers, Wernick and Reese cut a deal with Spike TV, the racy cable network for men. They hired Brian Keith Etheridge, a stand-up comic and former classical musician, to help them develop a plot outline and a full set of characters, complete with dialogue. At the suggestion of a Spike executive, Etheridge agreed to play Joe's best friend, on one condition: He'd play the role as himself, under his own name. At Etheridge's urging, they also cast Kristen Wiig, a friend from the improv group the Groundlings, to play a new character: Dr. Pat, a multiply divorced New Age therapist. Etheridge had a crush on Wiig—everyone did, he said. The "fake" director of *The Lap of Luxury* would be played by the real director of *The Joe Show*, Danny Salles. Spike gave the show a ruder title: *The Joe Schmo Show*.

To be their "Joe," the producers found Matt Kennedy Gould, a floppy-haired Penn State graduate, whom they scouted while he was shooting hoops at a gym in Pittsburgh. Matt, who had just dropped out of law school, was a twenty-eight-year-old stoner, living at home with his parents and delivering pizzas. Warm and likeable, he was also a big reality TV fan—and he happily signed up to appear on *The Lap of Luxury*, which guaranteed that he'd win at least $10,000.

The production ran smoothly, at first. During a staged "casting" session, Matt and Etheridge hit it off, creating the key central friendship. The *Joe Schmo* production area was tucked away in a garage on the fictional *Lap of Luxury* set, which let the cast retreat whenever they needed to take a break or get some feedback. Over the course of a rehearsal week, Salles (who didn't learn anyone's real name, so he wouldn't mess up on camera) trained the actors to improvise around Matt, hitting their jokes and plot points, but staying flexible.

Then the actual shoot began—and right away, the plan broke down. Matt wound up spending the first night sleeping in a king-sized bed with both Dr. Pat and Earl, the befuddled geezer. Immediately, he bonded with both characters—especially Earl, whom he viewed as a father figure, in need of his protection. The next day's challenge competition was called "Hands on a High-Priced Hooker"—a Spike-flavored parody of the *Survivor* totem pole challenge. The plan was for Matt to win immunity and a private room. Instead, Matt threw the competition, possibly because he was uncomfortable keeping his hand on the porn actress they'd hired.

Etheridge was alarmed. "It was right then that we realized, 'Oh, fuck, this is a real person,' " he said—since they'd deliberately cast a selfless, openhearted person, he was reflexively empathetic. He built intimate relationships easily, even with the fake people around him. To get the story back on track, the production voted Earl out early, only to have that loss hit Matt hard, to the point of tears. A pattern had developed: Matt stuck up for anyone who was the butt of a joke. He was even kind to the crude, perverted Hutch, played by a gentle actor named David Hornsby, whose whole job was to antagonize him. The script was full of bro-ish humor, with slapstick sequences like Kip wearing water wings and flailing in the pool. These moments felt like bullying to Matt, who would fume at the injustice.

Etheridge, a masterful performer in front of big crowds, felt at sea playing Matt's best friend, a role that consisted of a series of small betrayals. When Matt was asleep, Etheridge told me, the production team would stay up late, arguing about the show's ethics, debating the best way to go forward. Sometimes, the production team cried; a few times, they nearly pulled the plug. Each time, they talked themselves back into the project. "Who knows if we were right or wrong? And, if that's a convenient decision to make, when all of our paychecks relied on it going forward," said Etheridge. (Reese and Wernick told me that the only big debate happened early on, about Earl, and that most nights were focused on planning for the next day.)

In every other way, the shoot was going beautifully. The elimination ceremonies were particularly funny, a perfect parody of formats like *Survivor, Big Brother,* and *The Bachelor.* After each vote, the show's fictional host, who was played, with Probstian pomposity, by Ralph Garman, would smash a symbolic ceramic plate into the fireplace and chant, "Ashes to ashes, dust to dust . . . you are dead to us!" Salles used a special camera jib arm for close-ups, mimicking the syrupy grandeur of Tribal Councils.

A few days in, a new crisis erupted: Matt had developed a crush on the Kristen Wiig character, the eccentric Dr. Pat. To snuff out his feelings, the writers arranged for Dr. Pat to hook up with The Hutch, a tactic that worked (and effectively parodied the convention of the reality TV showmance), but left Matt in a foul mood, feeling at once rejected and confused. Soon after, the cast prepared for another in-house competition, in which they ran into one another while dressed up in big, blow-up sumo suits. The sequence was supposed to be funny, but instead, when Matt ran at Dr. Pat, he hit Wiig so hard she fell backward, smacking her head against the ground. Maybe it was an accident, maybe it was resentment—but either way, Wiig was injured. The actress stayed in character when the ambulance came, but by that point, she was "over" the show, from other castmates' accounts, having lost trust in the producers.

Matt, meanwhile, was overwhelmed by feelings of guilt. To try to compensate for what he'd done, he donated his prize, a vacation, to Dr. Pat. The producers told Etheridge to drop the prepared script: He was now supposed to cheer Matt up instead. It was a strange, disorienting night for everyone: Matt calmed down, but Etheridge could tell that he was confused—why was his low-key, regular-guy friend suddenly acting like a professional stand-up comic?

Finally, the night of the final vote arrived. Just as they'd hoped he would, Matt made the moral choice, choosing loyalty to Etheridge over the chance to join an alliance. When The Hutch was named the winner of *The Lap of Luxury*, Matt clapped, supportively. It was time for the reveal—an electrifying moment for everyone involved in the show. In preparation, Etheridge told the PAs that they should plan for any possible reaction: If Matt punched Etheridge, he said, that was okay, but they should stop him after one punch.

No punches were thrown. Instead, Matt was overwhelmed by shock. His jaw literally dropped. "What is going *onnnn*," he shouted, in a clip that Spike TV would play over and over again in the show's promos. He stared at Etheridge in confusion, seemingly unable to absorb the news. "Are you an *actor*, dude? Hold the phone." Etheridge got teary as he tried to describe the moment. "Presumably, the happy ending was supposed to be *Charlie and the Chocolate Factory—The Wizard of Oz*. It was supposed to be, *You were a terrific person. You're extraordinary!* God, in a world where greed and money and fame at any cost had already deeply taken hold, you're willing to put all of that aside to defend the little guy."

The cast tried to put a positive spin on the outcome. They attempted to bond with Matt, for real this time, staying up all night together in the mansion, drinking and soaking in the Jacuzzi. There was confetti all around; they got free Xboxes. Still, a shadow hung over the whole experience—and three months later, when the show debuted, one review called *The Joe Schmo Show* "the clearest indication that reality TV is truly on its last legs in Hollywood." It seemed as if Reese and Wernick's project might fail, leaving a stink of exploitation in its wake.

Then, the mood shifted. As Spike aired more episodes, the show's ratings rose and critics began to embrace the project, charmed by Matt's warmth and spontaneity. "If only all reality TV was as sweetly goofy as 'The Joe Schmo Show,'" wrote Mike Duffy in the *Detroit Free Press,* marveling that the show has "never come across as cruel or mean-spirited." Some of the crew's crises of conscience had been woven into the storyline, which made their role feel more sympathetic. When Matt did his post-finale media rounds, he came across as largely comfortable with the way that it had all gone down. "I think I found nine new friends," he told *Entertainment Weekly.*

Spike made a 2004 sequel, *Joe Schmo 2*—a parody of *The Bachelor,* using two Joes, a man and a woman—although this time the female Joe caught on, so the producers brought her in on the scheme. Etheridge regretted his work on that show, in part because it messed with people's romantic feelings, something they had tried to avoid during the first production, and in part because it lacked the "magic" they'd found with Matt. But he had found himself in an odd professional position: His most marketable skill, tricking people in reality prank shows, wasn't one he wanted to use. Instead, he ultimately became a sitcom writer, writing scripts for *South Park* and *Mike & Molly.*

In certain ways, Etheridge still felt proud of *The Joe Schmo Show,* which viewers had embraced as a cult favorite, the precursor to prank-show hits like the 2023 series *Jury Duty.* He admired his collaborators, including Wernick and Reese, whom he described as "brilliant" and "good-hearted to the core." But Etheridge also still felt guilty, decades later. Like the *Jackass* ensemble, he had grown up in chaos, surrounded by alcohol and drug abuse. Despite those dark experiences, he described his time working on *Joe Schmo* as "the most emotionally confusing experience of my life." Maybe, he theorized, his family history had prepared him to make this kind of show—or to go into show business in general.

Hornsby was more direct: He wasn't a fan of prank shows, he told me. For him, the key problem with *The Joe Schmo Show* had been consent: Since Matt didn't—and couldn't—know what he was signing up for, the show couldn't, ultimately, be justified, whatever the intent of the people who made it. Like Etheridge, Hornsby praised the show's co-creators, who he said tried to protect Matt, but he described his own memories as "tinged with regret." Although Hornsby never put it to me this way, you could make an argument that *The Joe Schmo Show* was worse, in a certain way, than sleazier shows. After all, was it better to be tricked by kind people or by monsters?

Wernick and Reese, who are working on a reboot of *The Joe Schmo Show*, planned for 2024, reached out to Matt, who declined to speak with me. Etheridge had stayed in contact with him, on and off, over the years, although they'd by now fallen out of touch. But based on interviews Matt has given over the years, his perspective seems to have shifted, more than once. Early on, at his alma mater, Penn State, he spoke enthusiastically about his fifteen minutes of fame: "I'd like to turn mine into fifteen years!" His perspective soured after he moved to Los Angeles. A Spike development deal didn't last; neither did gigs like a 2004 show called *10 Things Every Guy Should Experience* and Bravo's 2005 series *Battle of the Network Reality Stars*. Depressed, Matt retreated to Santa Monica, smoking pot and drinking—and finally, he moved back to Pittsburgh.

In 2008, he told *Entertainment Weekly* that he regretted making *The Joe Schmo Show*. The casting director had found him at a low point, he said, shortly after he'd dropped out of law school. He felt exploited—and the series had just made him feel stupid, in the end.

Back in Pittsburgh, Matt's life stabilized. He got married and sober; he had kids and found a job in the logistics industry. By 2013, he appeared to have come full circle. "You go to therapy and think you're all messed up and you come back to this: *Everybody* is all messed up," he told the *Pittsburgh Post-Gazette*. A decade after the show aired, Matt had come to accept that *The Joe Schmo Show* made viewers happy, that his fans' affection for him was real. In retrospect, he saw the true problem as a personal one, a question of all the underlying "internal issues" that he hadn't wrestled with before agreeing to go on TV. He chose to view those emotions as his own responsibility. "When I came home and did that, my life just blossomed."

THE ROSE

The Bachelor and *Joe Millionaire*

IN FEBRUARY 2000, THREE MONTHS BEFORE *SURVIVOR* DEBUTED on CBS, Mike Fleiss, the disgraced producer of Fox's *Who Wants to Marry a Multi-Millionaire?*, was holed up in Santa Monica, seething. If it wasn't raining every day, it felt that way to him. There was an internal investigation at Fox; he was getting hammered by the tabloid news show *Dateline*. After all that hustle, he was an industry laughingstock.

Worse, he was broke, with two little kids and bills piling up. His Fox deal had been structured so that he got 90 percent of his fee upfront, and then, at the show's end, the final 10 percent. But after Rick Rockwell's criminal background was leaked by The Smoking Gun and Fox canceled future airings, the network disallowed the bulk of his expenses, eliminating not just Fleiss's remaining 10 percent but another $250,000. There were also a few self-inflicted wounds, he admitted, among them the fact that he had scored the special to the Savage Garden song "I Knew I Loved You" without first clearing the rights (with Darnell's encouragement, said Fleiss). The band sued him for $2 million for wrongful use; Fleiss settled for $80,000, all the money he had left. Only Darnell stuck by him, giving Fleiss reality jobs under the table.

Meanwhile, reality TV was entering a wild renaissance. When *Survivor* turned into a blockbuster hit that summer, Fleiss rooted against its success, annoyed that he was a pariah while Mark Burnett was swanning around town, celebrated for making people eat live grubs. By 2001, however, Fleiss had begun rebuilding. He worked on minor reality shows, like *Spy TV,* a *Candid Camera* copycat. He signed a two-year deal with Telepictures, a division of Warner Bros. By then, the chip on his shoulder had become a boulder. Fleiss was determined to create a golden format, something he could shove in the faces of his enemies. In fits of mania, he scribbled down ideas, titles that included *Mail Order Brides, Intervention, Spot Your Former Lover, Social Climber,* and *Ruin Your Life.*

One morning, Fleiss was nursing a fever when he overheard his wife, who was the former president of their high school class, planning a school reunion. "I heard her saying all these names, and I'm like, 'I *hate* all those fucking people.' " Fleiss scribbled down a few notes about a reality show about high school reunions.

Then, still feverish, he hit on a much bigger idea: a romantic game show in which women would compete to find their soulmate. "I just flashed on the whole thing with the roses and, I swear to God, 90 percent of what's on the show today, I saw it in five minutes," Fleiss said. The basic blueprint for *The Bachelor* would never change, from the hometown trips to the fantasy suites. "I had to work on the language: 'Will you accept this rose?' And 'Forgo your individual accommodations.' But I saw the framework."

The Bachelor would become a massive hit, a show that women obsessed over—and Fleiss's ticket back into the reality industry.

FLEISS QUICKLY SOLD HIS FIRST CONCEPT, FOR *HIGH SCHOOL Reunion,* in February 2001, at the youth-oriented network The WB. But when he tried to pitch *The Bachelor,* he hit a few walls. Mike Darnell was busy with a cheating-couples show, *Temptation Island.* Jeff Zucker, at NBC, turned it down, too. But Andrea Wong, at ABC, loved the idea—and when she sent Fleiss's pitch to her boss Lloyd Braun, he emailed back, "This is a home run." Some of Wong's female colleagues at ABC thought the premise sounded sexist, but Wong disagreed. *The Bachelor* had universal appeal: Who hadn't fallen in love and had their heart broken? The format could also be flipped, with many men competing for one woman.

As his co-producer, Fleiss hired Lisa Levenson, who had just completed her triumphant renovation of *Big Brother 2*. Levenson had grown up rich in Scottsdale, Arizona, then studied media at the University of Texas. She had already produced *The Jerry Springer Show* as well as *General Hospital,* for which she won two Emmys. A petite, snub-nosed brunette in Prada, she offered a striking visual contrast to Fleiss, a 6'4" slob who wore flip-flops to network meetings. Levenson loved glitz; Fleiss had begun his career with a clip of a bartender stirring a cocktail with his penis. But like Jon Murray and Mary-Ellis Bunim, the two producers bonded quickly, with a shared taste for tabloid brutality and soap opera twists, a kind of drama that quickly spilled over into their own personal lives. "It was a complicated relationship," said Fleiss, who hasn't spoken to Levenson for more than a decade.

By 2002, reality dating shows were proliferating, in every possible mathematical permutation. On *Dismissed,* you met two dates, then dumped one; on *ElimiDate,* you met four people, then dumped three; on *Chains of Love,* you were chained to multiple dates; and on *The 5th Wheel* (slogan: "Where strangers become friends, friends become lovers, and lovers become bitter, suicidal exes all on the same show"), couples were torn apart by one seductive instigator. There was also the snarky *Blind Date,* which used ironic thought bubbles on the screen. The grandkids of the venerable *Love Connection,* which ran in the 1980s and 1990s, they were all comedy shows about one-off dates with strangers, set at normie venues like Olive Garden.

The Bachelor was different. Instead of focusing on first dates, it told a romantic story that lasted all season, with twenty-five "bachelorettes" who were narrowed down, week by week, as they competed to win the heart of one man. Like *Survivor,* it was simultaneously a soap opera and a game show, with a prank show's intensity. But what really made the show pop was its over-the-top aesthetic, an intoxicating fantasy of heterosexual romance as the ultimate high: first, chemistry; then the sting of rejection or the pageantry of courtship; and finally, the gradual, luxurious buildup toward a magical climax— yet another on-air proposal. Fleiss's first romance show, *Who Wants to Marry a Multi-Millionaire?*, had been a bedazzled Vegas satire of Miss America. *The Bachelor* was a more immersive experience, like being trapped inside an erotic terrarium, lulled by floating rose petals. In a world of tacky, *The Bachelor* was a *fancy* show.

That quality came centrally from Levenson, who, by everyone's account, including Fleiss's, was the person who pioneered the intoxicating quality that she called "zhuzh" (a phrase used on another reality show of the era as well: Bravo's *Queer Eye for the Straight Guy**). Zhuzh, in Levenson's interpretation, was aspirational straight-girl camp: glitter, lots of candles, perfumed pillows and deluxe spa treatments, horseback rides and private jets. It was a modern variation on the gluttonous deluge of consumer goods from *Queen for a Day*, a cavalcade of wish fulfillment. That was Levenson's look, too— and it was the way she carried herself. "She's just a savant," Levenson's former assistant Michael Carroll, who became a producer on the show, told Amy Kaufman in her book *Bachelor Nation*. "She's gorgeous and she wears Prada. She looks the part, so chicks would listen."

As their first bachelor, Levenson and Fleiss cast Alex Michel, a thirty-one-year-old Harvard-educated consultant from Virginia, who had an MBA from Stanford—the pedigreed Gallant to Rick Rockwell's sketchy Goofus. The women, who came from around the country, had been recruited in a variety of ways. There was twenty-eight-year-old Rhonda Rittenhouse, a commercial real estate agent, who had gotten a call at her job in Dallas, seeking potential applicants. There was Trista Rehn, a pediatric physical therapist and former Miami Heat dancer, who had seen a segment on *Extra*. And there was Amanda Marsh, a twenty-four-year-old from Chanute, Kansas, who was having brunch in Santa Monica, during her first

---

* The original term has deeper historical roots, possibly going back to Polari, a secret gay code from the early-twentieth century United Kingdom that originated in the workplace slang of British sailors. *Queer Eye*'s Carson Kressley learned it from Ralph Lauren.

visit to L.A., when a stylish woman approached to ask if she was single. It was producer Katherine Brooks, a fellow Kansan, something that reassured Amanda, as did the revelation that Brooks had appeared on a reality show, playing the spy on *The Mole*—a role that might have pinged someone else's radar. "I thought, 'She doesn't seem like anyone up to anything bad,'" said Amanda.

The show's casting directors were Marki Costello—comedian Lou Costello's granddaughter, whose first job had been with Chuck Barris, back in the mid-1980s—and her partner, Lacey Pemberton. It took a while for them to nail down a bachelor. An early front-runner didn't work out because he had herpes. Then 9/11 happened, throwing the schedule back further. In the end, Alex Michel—who had tried out for *Survivor*—was chosen, although he had to whiten his teeth and go on the Zone diet. When it came to the bachelorettes, ABC was seeking more specific qualities. To help winnow them down, Costello created whiteboards with photos and mini-bios, with bullet points suggesting qualities that might make the women crack—"Daddy's Girl," "Recovering Anorexic," "Just Got Dumped." From Costello's account, Fleiss didn't care as much about those backstories as the other top brass: He just wanted "petite blondes with big tits." (Fleiss denied he cared about cup size, just "beautiful blondes.")

When the women pulled up in their limos for the first day of the shoot, having pregamed on free champagne, they still had only a fuzzy concept of how the show would work. Because there were no Porta Potties, a few of them wound up hiking up their ballgowns and peeing on the side of the road. Inside the house, they were offered more drinks, but no food—and when the food finally arrived (the caterers had been fired, they were told), it was disgusting stuff: white bread with squeeze cheese and pickled cucumber. Unsurprisingly, they got trashed, fast.

The shoot went on for hour after hour, as Alex Michel floated around, alighting on chaise lounges, striking up conversations with groups of women as the producers whispered all around them. By the time they finally filmed the first rose ceremony—the moment the bachelor handed a rose to each woman he wanted to stay, effectively voting the others off the island—it was around 5 A.M. Amanda got the first rose, Rhonda the last. She'd just met Alex, but still, it was an unsettling sensation. "Like, 'I guess I'm chopped liver.' I wasn't used to feeling that way."

Many years later, before she filmed an interview for a *Bachelor* reunion show, the producers asked her not to talk about the drinking. But booze was the crucial ingredient on the first season of *The Bachelor*, the same way it was on other dating shows. Trays of cocktails circulated constantly; the refrigerators were full of refills. Although no one was forced to drink, there was nothing else for them to do: no books, no magazines, no TV. Rhonda remembers Fleiss carrying a tray of margaritas to the pool, then announcing, "I didn't buy this house with a hot tub for you girls to sit around in your sweats." Whenever the drama dried up, he'd send Levenson in to spice things up with some girl talk.

A few days in, the outside world began to fade away. The producers describe this phenomenon as "the bubble," an atmosphere that was intended to focus the women's emotions entirely on the bachelor. They weren't unaware of the cameras; Rhonda remembers her housemates talking about brands like Jif peanut butter, just as Gervase had on *Survivor*, knowing that it would make the footage unairable. Still, they felt perpetually off-balance, particularly during interviews, when they would be asked the same question again and again—often about whether the other girls were there "for the right reasons."

Even before the first rose ceremony, Amanda had offered the producers a juicy sound bite when she mentioned "a sex swing" during what she thought was a pre-interview. Another day, a producer asked Rhonda, "Are you here to make friends?" After a few rounds of questioning, she finally gave them an answer they accepted, "No, I'm not here to make friends, I'm here to meet Alex." It never crossed her mind that the first part of her remark, cut out of context from the rest, would become the modern reality genre's unofficial motto.

On the third night of the shoot, Rhonda didn't get a rose. She found Alex a bit cocky, but the rejection stung anyway. Before she could leave, she was required to do another interview, and the producer began badgering her, all over again, about who was there for "the right reasons"; somehow, he also brought up her grandfather's death (Fleiss told me he didn't know that her grandfather had died). Rhonda melted down. When she held her breath and started to hyperventilate, she caught a glimpse of her producer, making sure that the camera was still running.

For Fleiss, watching from the control room, it was a euphoric moment, not unlike the proposal on *Who Wants to Marry a Multi-Millionaire?*, the one that made him drop to his knees. "When Rhonda Rittenhouse started hyperventilating after the rose ceremony, I'm like, *this thing's working, baby.* . . . And then when we called the paramedics and they came down to see poor Rhonda—hello!" (Rhonda scoffed at Fleiss's description: There *were* no paramedics, she said—maybe there was a doctor, but what they showed on the air was deceptive.) In the final edit, Rhonda came off as a needy stalker. But she felt much angrier, later on, about a different production choice. When she spoke with the show's therapist, they kept the microphones recording—and the show posted that audio on the website, as an "extra." "I blew up and I was ticked off and I didn't handle it well—but I was also a caged rat," she said.

Rhonda's meltdown would become a blueprint in future seasons. Each year, there would be sweet girls, women who were portrayed as being "there for the right reasons"—on an openhearted search for true love. There would also be others: scheming villains, deluded fools, and crazy-eyed stalkers. Costello left after the first season, while her former casting partner stayed on. But in her experience, no one was too off-kilter to cast: "Unstable and pretty? That's gold."

Clashes among the women, which weren't especially common during the first year, would become prized events. But as with Rhonda's panic attack, *any* emotion could be repurposed, edited to look like a response to the bachelor, as opposed to *The Bachelor.* More than anything else, that was the contribution the show made to the genre: It established a bold new level of producer manipulation, forging powerful methods of both production and postproduction, ones that would become the default for many other reality shows.

III

NOT EVERYONE ENDED UP WITH REGRETS ABOUT THEIR TIME IN the house. LaNease Adams, a twenty-three-year-old actress, was one of two Black women in that cast (the other one, Kristina Jenkins, was eliminated during the first rose ceremony). Like many of the women, LaNease had just gone through a bad breakup (with Bill Maher, who refused to commit to her). On the rebound, she fell hard for Alex—and they had the show's first kiss, during a gondola ride in Vegas, a moment that she described in a soft, dreamy voice: "We kissed a few times, every time we went under the bridge. It was spectacular, magical." LaNease made it to the final eight.

From her account, LaNease—who grew up in Los Angeles and had gone to a mostly white college—was naïve about racism, which she thought of as "something from the history books." She'd refused to ask Alex how he felt about interracial dating, when the producers encouraged her to. And for LaNease, much like Sabine on *Big Brother,* while she enjoyed her stay in the house, leaving it was a shock. Her new romance had fizzled; she was living with her parents, broke but famous. To add to the pain, legions of viewers, both Black and white, were attacking her online.

For months, LaNease rarely left the house, obsessively reading the ABC chat boards, riveted by the worst comments, which were often about her kiss; she wrote to a KKK site and pretended that she was an ABC producer, demanding they take down a picture of the kiss. Understandably, she unraveled: She stopped eating, took pills, and eventually, she had a manic break and was institutionalized for a week. It took LaNease a lot of therapy and time to recover, to care less about other people's opinions, she said.

Decades later, however, she remains a loyal supporter of *The Bachelor.* In 2022, she still defended the racial politics of the show, arguing that it was fine for them to cast mostly white women—and also, white women of a certain, narrow type: blond and thin. People had their dating preferences, she told me. "When Flavor Flav did his show, it was mostly Black women," she argued. As for her own traumatic experience, she didn't blame any of it on ABC. "It was just life lessons I'd have had to learn, one way or the other," she said.

IF THE BUBBLE WAS DESIGNED FOR THE CAST, IT CONTAINED THE crew, too. Like the vast majority of reality shows, *The Bachelor* was nonunionized. Everyone worked around the clock, often sleeping near the set—and if you got fired, your contract forbade you from jumping to a competing show. In certain ways, the system operated as if it were a game show within the game show: In *Bachelor Nation*, Scott Jeffress, the show's supervising producer, described peeling off $100 bills, rewarding producers for special achievements, like getting a girl to cry on camera. Levenson handed out Prada handbags to her favorite employees.

There was another factor stirring the chaos on set: Mike Fleiss and Lisa Levenson were having an open—or at least, a not especially well-concealed—affair. The two producers, each of them married (in Levenson's case, to a *Big Brother 2* producer), would sneak off together, although they weren't discreet about it. "All the field producers talked about how much they were screwing around in the limos," said Amanda. Fleiss's right-hand man, Ben Hatta, a development executive on the series, found the situation "embarrassing and disappointing," both because he knew Mike's wife and because he had a lot of respect for Fleiss himself. (Not everyone was aware of the affair: Trista Rehn sounded shocked when I mentioned it.)

Fleiss, who got sober in 2010 (although he still smokes pot these days), described this period to me in rueful terms, spiked with nostalgia. "She was a very important person to me for a long time," he said of Levenson. "I was in a bad marriage. Sexless, loveless marriage. I'm traveling the world with Lisa, making a show about romance, and it was intoxicating." Fleiss described Levenson to me as "a smart, talented person," who had been pivotal to the show's creation. "She brought a female perspective and she wasn't shy about *anything*. I mean, she could brazenly go in and tell somebody to do this or say that—you know, she could cry on command! She's kind of crazy. And *I'm* kind of crazy, so it required that." He paused, then added the obvious: "We were partying heavily." (Levenson didn't return my phone calls or emails.)

During the early seasons of the show, Fleiss was smoking so much pot that he put a towel under the door of his office. He binged on tequila. The cast drank, the crew drank, the managers drank. This behavior was strategic—and to Fleiss, to some extent, it still felt that way, when he looked back. He said, of Levenson, that "she was probably right, that you had to drink with those people to get them to trust you, in those early days. It was probably the right move, in retrospect, as fucked up as that sounds." The money and notoriety were their own high. "Lisa came from a rich family. I came from nothing," said Fleiss. "It was rock star time. And I *love* rock music. I've played in bands my whole life—so I just said, all right, I'm going full Keith Richards on this thing! But she was Richards before I was Richards. She taught me *how* to be Keith Richards."

AS THE SIX-WEEK SHOOT FOR *THE BACHELOR* ELAPSED, AMANDA Marsh and Trista Rehn stayed on, accepting rose after rose. When there were only three contestants left—the third was Shannon Oliver, a stockbroker from Dallas—each finalist was sent on a "hometown" visit, so that Alex could meet their family. By then, both Amanda and Trista had bonded with their respective producers, sharing cocktails and intimate stories. The bubble was working its magic: Both women were falling in love with Alex.

"Our humor was very on point, the chemistry was there," said Amanda. "And so, with enough time and isolation, your mind starts to think, not just 'I want to win this,' out of, like, pride and ego, but . . . '*Oh, he might be the last man on earth.*'" She found herself thinking strategically. Her mother had once said, "Build them up as you tear them down," so she tried to be "happy, bubbly, adventurous, sexual," and she confessed to him that she was falling in love. "When you're drunk, people become more appealing," she added, in a dry tone.

Trista described a similar dynamic, a giddy crush heightened by the isolation. "It was one guy and that's all you're focusing on: no work, no friends, no family, no gym. . . . If I had met him in my real life, I don't know that that would have happened."

The three women were competitors, but they were also companions. Amanda and Shannon would primp for dates together: "We were excited for each other, which is bizarre," Amanda told me. When Shannon won a "princess date," Trista remembered being "so jealous, but in a fun way." Even so, Amanda and Trista never hit it off, with Amanda finding Trista "pretty cold-shouldered."

Camera operator Scott Sandman—yes, the same camera operator who had nearly tanked *Survivor*, when he was fired from the show for slipping Kelly Wiglesworth a Clif Bar—was now working on *The Bachelor*. Sandman can be crude when he talks about women, but he felt unsettled by the show's format, which seemed more alarming than anything he'd seen in Borneo. Producers would goad the girls to humiliate themselves, convincing them that belly dancing would impress Alex. Inside the limo, on the way to a date, they egged Alex Michel on to ask Shannon how many people she'd had sex with, even when she begged them to stop, worried about her grandmother seeing the show, finally using her fingers to show him the number, placing her hand under the camera.

Fleiss took pride in similar "gets." He laughed, remembering the day that he cajoled Shannon to slip out of her robe and get into the hot tub, a process that took two hours. He imitated himself, talking to her. " 'You're on a date in this chalet in Lake Tahoe and there's a hot tub with bubbling champagne right there. Come on. Whatcha doing, girl?' " She tried to negotiate the edit in advance. "She wanted to know if we had cameras in the water."

What Fleiss remembered as a game, Sandman saw as ugly manipulation. But, just as he had during the final days of *Survivor*, he had formed strong opinions about the contestants. Sandman loved Amanda ("a really sweet country girl, like Mary Ann from *Gilligan's Island*, rest in peace") and Shannon (who was doing it for "a lark"), but he disliked Trista, whom he viewed as "a screaming, whining bitch." One night, Trista refused to be filmed when she was packing her bags, then slammed the bag down the stairs, "just bam, bam, bam, bam, bam—just a pouting little girl," he said. Trista doesn't remember the incident, she told me. They were all under huge pressure and sleep-deprived, she pointed out—and also overwhelmed by emotion, by the end of the show. "If I got tense with him, I apologize, twenty years later," she said, then burst out laughing at the absurdity of the situation coming up, after so much time. "The suitcase was probably really heavy and I'm like, 'Dude, you're 180 pounds.'"

Amazingly, just as Sandman had stirred the pot during the first season of *Survivor*, he may have played a role in the finale of *The Bachelor*. Soon after the suitcase incident, he was in the limo with Alex when the bachelor asked him whom he'd choose if he were in his position. "He was saying, 'Okay, you spend more time around these girls than I do. What would *you* do?' And I said, 'Dude, if you pick Trista, you will be the most miserable human being on the planet.'"

In the end, Alex *did* pick Amanda over Trista—although instead of proposing marriage, he suggested that the two of them embark on a serious relationship. Amanda accepted. Years later, she still isn't certain why he chose her, although she says the producers had asked her if she was interested in starring in *The Bachelorette*. She wondered if saying no to the spin-off played a role.

Trista, on the other hand, was completely shocked by Alex choosing Amanda. Although she and Alex hadn't said "I love you," Alex had told her, directly, that he was going to choose her, during their last night together. As the limo drove her away from the show, she looked into the cameras and said softly, "I'm okay, I'm just sad." But she panicked when she realized that she wasn't going to be allowed to speak to Alex, so in the hotel room, she begged the producers to let her make a phone call, to get some closure—which they allowed, as long as they could record it. She remembers him telling her that he'd made a mistake, which only made her spiral further.

Unsurprisingly, the two women became mortal enemies. The way Amanda viewed the situation, she was a girl's girl, warm and sisterly, while Trista was only in it for herself. Amanda and Alex dated for nearly a year, but things soured when, a few months in, she discovered that he'd had sex with Trista during the filming of the season, something the producers never told her. After a bit more post-show drama (Trista showed up at the Kentucky Derby on a day when Amanda and Alex also attended), the first *Bachelor* couple broke up. Alex dropped out of the reality world entirely, working as a financial consultant. He didn't respond to requests for interviews.

What Amanda viewed as a betrayal of the sisterhood, Trista saw differently. From her perspective, Amanda was overreacting to her sexual history with Alex, which was nobody's business. ("He freaking chose her! So how could she be butt-hurt by that?" she said in exasperation.) In the end, Trista would get a different kind of triumph: She became the first star of *The Bachelorette,* the next iteration of the ABC franchise, in which she got to hand out the roses. That season, she fell in love with a poetry-writing fireman named Ryan Sutter, to whom she's still married, with two kids, living in Colorado. In December 2003, ABC aired their elaborate wedding, which required its own tough negotiation. Her agent made sure that Trista—who, like the rest of the cast, hadn't been paid for her reality show appearances—finally made some money, helping pay off the couple's student loans. "This was our nest egg," she said.

Trista and Ryan would appear on other reality shows over the years, including *Dancing with the Stars* and *Fear Factor,* as well as 2014's *Marriage Boot Camp: Reality Stars.* Trista had always felt comfortable in front of the cameras, she told me, a special skill that she understood not everyone had. She knew that she'd gotten off easy, in the context of that era's reality boom: "I felt like I had a good edit. I was lucky that way." She is still friends with Mike Fleiss, whom she called "Mr. Big." Fleiss, for his part, credited Trista heavily for the show's success. "Without her, none of it would have worked. The other girls weren't into it or him—and they weren't quite pretty enough to be on television." A lifelong devotee of Aaron Spelling's church of jiggle TV, Fleiss had always behaved as if he was a beauty contest judge. Before the first season even started, he posted a "Pyramid of Hotness" in his office, with Trista at the top.

After the show aired, Amanda was swamped by reality fame—recognizability without riches. There was some rude press, mocking her sex swing quote, but it faded. She moved back to Kansas, where she retrained as a nurse practitioner, specializing in dermatology; she married a childhood friend, had a daughter, then divorced; she's now engaged to a man she met on Match.com. She's not an enemy of *The Bachelor*, but she's not a fan, either, finding it "hokey." Other than Trista, she's close to her former castmates. And like many early reality stars, she views her season as the only truly authentic one. As artificial as the situation was, the feelings were real. That had always been the dark magic of *The Bachelor*: You could critique its bone-deep sexism, from the Madonna/whore editing to the notion of marriage as a woman's ultimate life goal. The real risk of the show lay deeper, however: It was a butterfly net designed to catch feelings, the precious substance that had always fueled the genre.

After one more season, camera operator Sandman left *The Bachelor*. A gig he took on *Temptation Island* was uglier: He filmed girls when they vomited and passed out; he peeked through slats in their doors; he planted hidden night vision cameras on the beach. Although Sandman had worked on everything from *Survivor* to *Manhunt*, he ended up hating dating shows more than any other type of reality TV—and he was too old to work on these productions, anyway, which were oddly *more* rigorous than adventure competitions. "Leave them for the young kids that don't mind working a twenty-hour day and being shouldered up"—carrying a heavy camera on your shoulder—"waiting for something to happen, which is everyone's worst nightmare." Sandman, who is now in his sixties, stays in good shape, to keep his edge for shoots like *Shark Week*, which felt more socially positive than *The Bachelor*. "I like to see them cry at the end," he said—tears of joy.

The Bachelor would become Fleiss's gold mine. Levenson left after thirteen more seasons, to oversee many other hits, including the culinary competitions *MasterChef* and *Hell's Kitchen*. Fleiss, in contrast, never had another show click. He divorced his first wife, then remarried; in 2019, his pregnant second wife, a former Miss America, accused him of domestic violence and of pressuring her to get an abortion—and then, three months later, the two reconciled. In 2023, he stepped down from *The Bachelor*, after an internal investigation into allegations of racial discrimination. It was just one element within a larger racial reckoning that had engulfed the show, after a season in which they had finally cast a Black bachelor.

Over the years, Fleiss had produced one significant side project: the Hostel horror film franchise, which featured a different brand of torture. He spoke about his television legacy, with a tone of startling contempt. Reality TV had ruined everything, he told me. It helped elect Trump; it corroded people's morals. Like Chuck Barris before him, Fleiss expressed open disdain for his own cast members, all those exhibitionists who no longer had to be cajoled to go wild. When he had first pitched the idea for the show, he said, people didn't understand why someone would kiss another person on camera. "This new generation is just like, 'Why would I ever kiss somebody *off* camera?' That's where they're at," he said.

One person was surprisingly a fan of *The Bachelor:* Rhonda Rittenhouse. After the first season aired, a friend had sent her the VHS tapes, inscribed, "Do not open," a rule that she had honored for years. Decades later, however, the shame is more of a memory. Now she's a member of "Bachelor Nation," the term that fans of the show use for their own bubble. "I think they're great train wrecks," she said, of the newer seasons. Today's contestants just wanted fame, she said—and they were far more self-aware. "Either you have stars in your eyes—or you know what you're getting into. Nobody does it just to do it anymore."

THE FIRST SEASON OF *THE BACHELOR,* SIX EPISODES LONG, DEbuted on March 25, 2002. The finale was a powerful enough ratings contender that ABC scheduled it during April sweeps week, as counterprogramming to *Friends, CSI, Survivor, Will & Grace,* and *ER.* That November, a few months into the show's second season, Fleiss was enjoying a Thanksgiving feast with some of his reality TV peers, among them Andrea Wong and Mike Darnell. During a break in the dinner, Darnell approached Fleiss, privately. He had some bad news. The football game would feature an ad for a new Fox show— and Fleiss wasn't going to like it.

That show was *Joe Millionaire*. Less a rip-off than a warped satire of *The Bachelor, Joe Millionaire*—like *The Joe Schmo Show,* which premiered around the same time—was a prank show disguised as a reality competition. As ever, Darnell had been determined to undermine the latest reality hit, even if it was one created by a close friend, and when his team brainstormed about how to top *The Bachelor,* one of Darnell's employees, Sabrina Ishak, made a simple suggestion: "Why don't we lie to them?" That's just what they did. *Joe Millionaire,* which was set at a French chateau, starred twenty bachelorettes who believed that they were competing to marry a man who had inherited $50 million. In reality, he was a working-class hunk whom producers had taught (barely) to waltz and horseback ride. The show was produced by Rocket Science Laboratories, a company that was co-run by French producer Jean-Michel Michenaud, a former child star who was friends with Mike Darnell. To keep the twist under wraps, the show was code-named *The Big Choice.*

Fleiss was furious, and for a while he wouldn't return any of Darnell's calls, especially after *Joe Millionaire* got higher ratings than *The Bachelor.* (Darnell doesn't remember Fleiss not returning phone calls.) A classic Fox subversion of network earnestness, the show took the greatest strength of *The Bachelor*—its zhuzh, that thick, glittery coating of romantic icing that made it so irresistible for viewers—and then exposed it as something rancid. On *The Bachelor,* love was the ultimate prize. On *Joe Millionaire,* it was bait for the prank, a sick joke that horny men played on greedy women.

As their "Joe," Rocket Science cast Evan Marriott, a construction worker who had the physique and jaw of a Disney prince. Evan, who was making $19,000 a year, was hesitant about the premise, but it was hard to turn down $50,000 and a free trip to France. He also had one local friend in the crew: field producer Matt Antrim, who'd recruited him for Fox. Antrim generally preferred working in casting, but he, too, couldn't turn down a free trip to France. He found his new job surprisingly fun, particularly since, unlike *The Bachelor, Joe Millionaire* turned out to be a luxurious workplace. Antrim, who had a driver and an interpreter, spent days cruising around the Loire Valley, designing grape-stomping dates for the cast. The crew ate duck à l'orange, cooked by a private chef; they stayed in a comfortable hotel. While *The Bachelor* served margaritas, *Joe Millionaire* was awash in fine wine. Antrim remembers his bosses leaving work meetings with their teeth stained red.

From the start, however, there were headaches. A few women caught on to the show's twist right away, suspicious that a rich man knew nothing about his own investments. During one disastrous shoot, a low-flying helicopter buzzed an ancient farmhouse, knocking roof tiles off and wrecking chicken coops, so Antrim ran around town, handing out $10,000 in euros to the injured parties.

Still, the bigger issue was that nothing much was happening, so little that Antrim was confident that the show would be a flop. Only after he flew home did he understand what he'd helped create: a crude but addictive sex comedy, which was built almost entirely through editing. The show's dullest moments were now scored to "womp-womp" musical stings. Little gaffes became huge laughs, like an interview in which a woman explained that she'd love to bathe children in Africa, because "I can't help it, I'm a mercenary person." The format's engine was gleeful humiliation, with the women cleaning up stables and wrestling over ballgowns.

By the finale, the competition was narrowed down to a near-medieval saint/slut morality play, when Evan chose Zora Andrich, a sweet substitute teacher, over Sarah Kozer, a mortgage broker's assistant, who had been portrayed as a scheming tramp. A few episodes in, when tabloids published gossip that Sarah had appeared in bondage films—something that she'd done in order to pay off student loans—it made her look even sluttier, in the show's terms. (Evan had also posed for underwear ads, but no one had much to say about that.)

In what became *Joe Millionaire*'s most notorious moment, Sarah and Evan walked into the woods together. Viewers heard a loud *slurp* sound, audio that was followed by subtitles over a shot of dense foliage: "Uhm / (*smack*) / Uhm / (*slurp*) / Huh Huh Ha He." The obvious implication was that Sarah had given Evan a blow job in the forest, as they tried to evade the cameras. In actuality, the editors had repurposed some of the audio from an earlier day, when Sarah got a massage treatment with one of the other women, during which she'd sighed in pleasure and said, "Do you think it's easier if we lie down?"

Gail Berman, at Fox, acknowledged the deceptive editing later on (sort of—she also blamed them for having walked into the woods)—and in a 2005 article in *Radar,* one of the editors, Daniel Abrams, admitted that the scene had been created "out of whole cloth." The *slurp* had done what it was meant to do: The episode got high ratings and tons of press. Like the faux investigation on *Alien Autopsy,* the ambiguity itself became a selling point, with lack of consent baked into the production model. Maybe the production had used hidden cameras; maybe Sarah had been drunk; maybe the scene had never happened at all—no matter what, in the cultural context of 2003, the joke was on her. The ethical violation itself was the turn-on.

Josh Belson worked as part of the editing team for *Joe Millionaire.* His reality-TV editing experience went back to Fox's *When Animals Attack!,* before the rise of Avid machines, when the work had been physically grueling, a matter of lining up pieces of footage. On shows like *Blind Date,* he'd done some story manipulation, but it was comparatively minor stuff—speeding a sequence up, for instance, or planting small jokes.

Joe Millionaire was an "eye-opening" experience, introducing him to a much more aggressive philosophy, in which editors were auteurs, powerful figures who were allowed to construct a story from scratch. In the edit bay, he learned to create "Frankenbites," using bits of dialogue to form entirely new sentences. The permissiveness felt intoxicating: At last, he was no longer tied to the facts. "Your morals kind of go out the window; they don't really play into it. You're given this new tool! This is going to make our job *so* much easier. . . . By being these evil liars," Belson told me, with a laugh.

Sometimes, the team's edits were more like in-jokes. In an early scene, after Evan popped a champagne cork off a balcony, an editor added the sound of a car crash in the distance, subtle enough that viewers might miss it. "Your goal is to get your teammates to laugh," said Belson. Other edits were blatant. At home, when he watched the final version of the show, Matt Antrim, the field producer, was flabbergasted to see that one woman's angry early rant, which was a re-sponse to her luggage getting lost, had been cut so that it looked like an irrational reaction to being rejected by Evan. She had worn a black shirt in both scenes, which made the edit more difficult to de-tect. "Thank God she had that fit, then," said Belson, when I asked him about the scene. "So we had something to use—to make that exit more powerful, less boring."

Darnell's prank show became a smash hit: Around 23 million people watched each episode, and the finale attracted 40 million viewers, more than the Oscars. The *Chicago Sun-Times*'s Richard Roeper called it "one of the most morally bankrupt shows in the his-tory of television." As Katie Baker summed up the situation, decades later, in *The Ringer, Joe Millionaire* was less a reality competition than it was a short-lived, highly public Ponzi scheme, "a thrilling journey, an ethical morass, and a memorable letdown all in one." It lasted one more season, as *The Next Joe Millionaire*, which was set among European women, then disappeared for two decades. Back in 2003, the finale had aired five days after the finale of *The Bachelor-ette*, starring Trista Rehn, offering two contrasting views of mar-riage: as a triumphant win and a humiliating con.

Like so many before him, Evan Marriott became reality famous. In the aftermath of the show, he had the chance to meet Fox Televi-sion Entertainment Group chairman Sandy Grushow, who shook his hand and told him that he was "part of the Fox family." As Evan told *Vulture* in 2015, "I was happy, not because I thought they were gonna make me Magnum, P.I. But I thought, 'At least if they need someone to sweep up a set, I'll be there.'" Two weeks later, Fox took his lot pass away.

For a while, Evan took advantage of the deluge of media offers—ads, TV specials, speaking engagements—hyped up on a hollow egotism spiked with paranoia, a sensation that lingered after the of-fers stopped coming. "Even though people could have cared less if I got a hamburger or a haircut, I kept thinking, years after the show, 'Somebody's at my window, somebody's taking pictures of me, somebody gives a shit about what I'm wearing today.' I talked myself into this, and some of it was true and some wasn't, but it took me a while to talk myself out of it," he told *Vulture*.

Eventually, Evan went back to his former job, and a few years later, he opened up his own heavy equipment moving company, a development that transformed his life: He felt proud to be doing honest work, at last. Like Mike Fleiss, Evan loathes reality television. "Producers are the sheepherders, and we are the sheep. I do feel like we blazed the trail for all this stuff now, and it is a shame that I sit back now and go, 'God, this is what this all morphed into.' "

NOT EVERYONE SAW DATING OR PRANK SHOWS AS A BLIGHT— and to some people in the industry, they had a wild, even liberatory quality. In 1999, when *Who Wants to Marry a Multi-Millionaire?* aired, Inbal Lessner had found the show hilarious: "I just thought it was so insane. It was like you're watching the *Challenger* take off! It was that kind of moment. Like, something big is going to be attempted. *Humanity will never be the same.*" An Israeli immigrant who had worked on training films for the IDF, Lessner was enrolled in the NYU film program at the time. She studied the Maysles brothers by day, but at night, relaxing with her boyfriend, she watched dating shows like *Temptation Island,* the tawdrier the better. For her, the reality genre felt like a fun cartoon, but also a sharp satirical lens on a phenomenon she she'd never understood: American wedding culture. She'd spent her time in the trenches, having helped edit the footage of Martha Stewart's daughter's wedding, one of many freelance gigs she took to stay afloat.

Lessner lived two blocks from the World Trade Center. After 9/11, traumatized and broke, she moved to Los Angeles. It was a rough time, professionally: Her freelance jobs had dried up and there was no route into scripted TV, where all the editing jobs were unionized. Instead Lessner found work on the 2003 MTV reality competition show *Surf Girls,* then got a "relief pitcher" editing gig on Rocket Science's *The Next Joe Millionaire,* the one with European contestants. Some of these jobs weren't ideal—she got cheated for overtime, among other things—but she was thrilled to be hired as a lead editor on 2004's *My Big Fat Obnoxious Fiance*. It was a big break, a network show with twelve editors and many junior editors, deputized to produce only six episodes.

My Big Fat Obnoxious Fiance starred Catholic school teacher Randi Coy, who knew she was competing in a reality show, but not what kind. To win $500,000 (half for her, half for her family), she and a guy named Steve had to convince their families to take part in a sham wedding, which was just twelve days away, without anyone objecting during the ceremony. What Randi didn't realize was that no other couples were competing—and Steve and his "family" were actually actors, intent on creating comedy and chaos. Meanwhile, her own family had no idea that they were in a reality show at all. They just thought that she was marrying a rude, offensive lout.

Editing for Rocket Science paid well, but it required insanely long hours, and the team, mostly young and childless, grew very close. "It was like the mafia, or like a family," Lessner said. "There were a lot of incestuous relationships. . . . It was like, trauma bonding. We were really into it." Part of that bonding involved repressing any doubts about the show's "Greek tragedy" angle and focusing on the comedy. "You kind of excuse it. You're like, 'Okay. Well, at the end she's going to get half a million dollars, so that's okay, right?'"

My Big Fat Obnoxious Fiance turned into a ratings hit, the most-watched show after the Super Bowl. Lessner understood that Hollywood looked down on the work she did, but the way she saw it, she was part of a team of rebel outsiders, creating crude, unsettling pop art, riding the zeitgeist. In the evenings, the staff would hang out in the office of Jean-Michel Michenaud, drinking pinot grigio; he even had a separate ventilation system, so people could smoke.

A year earlier, *Joe Millionaire* editor Josh Belson had been shocked to create his first Frankenbite, but by 2004, the tool was normalized, although there was still a code of silence around the subject. On *The Next Joe Millionaire*, Lessner helped to clarify the garbled English of the bachelorettes. But, like everyone she worked with, she grew skilled at more creative editing, as well. Once, on *The Bachelorette*, she had to edit together a helicopter date with a man who "could not put a sentence together to save his life," but who had to show excitement, to make the story work. Lessner did it for him: First, she found a clip of him saying "but," a common word. She found another of him saying, "er." Piece by piece, she built a sentence: "I feel butterflies."

Lessner managed to leave the reality industry a few years later, although it wasn't an easy transition: One of her bosses warned her she'd never work again. Over time, she made the jump to "legitimate" work, editing acclaimed documentaries about cults, including *Seduced: Inside the NXIVM Cult* and *Escaping Twin Flames,* as well as powerful feminist films about sexual violence, like *Brave Miss World* and *Victim/Suspect.* Even so, she refused to disavow her early gigs, to scrub her reality history off or pretend that she hadn't enjoyed the job, some of the time. It wasn't that Lessner, who was a feminist, didn't understand the criticism—she'd quit after just one season on *The Bachelorette,* because she found it sexist.

Still, fudging dialogue didn't bother her. "Maybe it's so I can sleep at night, but I'd like to think the people are grateful that I made them sound better." When a colleague sneered at *The Bachelorette,* Lessner shot back that it was the best, most skillful postproduction house in town. Years later, she still remembered the transgressive high of these gigs, the sense of blowing up the culture, exposing its nastiest contradictions, as audiences gawked. It was an idea that she'd absorbed working with Michenaud, who was a fan of Truffaut and Godard, a "French rebel-artist philosopher, a pianist and composer." Had you asked her boss, back then, she told me, he would have defended the work they were doing as its own kind of art, a way of putting a mirror up to America and forcing it to take a good look: "He made us feel like we were part of something very special."

SARAH GERTRUDE SHAPIRO STUDIED FICTION AND FILMMAKING at Sarah Lawrence in the late 1990s. As a senior, she worked as an intern for Killer Films, run by the avant-garde feminist filmmaker Christine Vachon; after graduation, she got an awful job at the Hollywood talent agency ICM. Unlike many of her artistic peers, she had no family money, no safety net; she was proud of her strong work ethic, her ability to tolerate pain and go beyond what was necessary. A friend recommended her to the temperamental photographer David LaChapelle, and although she and her boss hated each other ("David plus a mouthy Jewish broad was just not a great combination"), these jobs working for independent artists shaped her aesthetic. She was a fan of maximalist queer art, equal parts grotesque and gorgeous. She felt at ease with crazy.

Like Lessner, Shapiro had been emotionally shattered in the aftermath of 9/11—and after LaChapelle insisted that she deliver photo negatives to Times Square in the midst of a bomb scare, Shapiro quit, then moved west. In Los Angeles, she found a good job right away, helping produce a TV documentary about high school reunions, which was set in Hawaii. When she got a manila envelope full of paperwork, she signed it without thinking twice.

The show was *High School Reunion*, where she worked side by side with Mike Fleiss's former assistant Ben Hatta. When production ended, she was offered a promotion working on *The Bachelor*, then entering its second season. Shapiro said no, horrified by the show's sexism. Her bosses told her to read her contract, which turned out to be a deal memo, full of language about "unlimited renewable options and perpetuity throughout the known universe." Shapiro, who was twenty-three, had no entertainment lawyer and no idea where to find one. As she understood it, she had no choice: Even if she managed to refuse the job, she'd get blacklisted.

On set, when she first arrived, she played the role of the feminist grouch, wearing a "George Bush, Out of My Uterus" T-shirt. But quickly, something shifted inside her—a change in mindset. Shapiro was good at the job, a natural at playing "the schlubby best friend who hot girls tell shit to." The series tapped a wellspring of internalized misogyny, teaching her to aim it at other women. "I started getting rewarded for it and I started getting money for it—and then I started feeling like it was actually really fucking satisfying! Like: *Destroy* these bitches."

Initially, Shapiro's job was all about organizing the show's zhuzhy dates, which got bigger every season. By the third season, thirty-second ads for *The Bachelor* cost $253,940—a higher rate on average than *The West Wing*—but the key to Shapiro's job, perversely enough, was finagling stuff for free. Like a mini Mark Burnett, Shapiro talked tourist boards into offering up free plane tickets and hotel stays, renovating venues and staging elaborate stunts—in one case, building a full walk-in sandcastle—while offering them no money, just "exposure." In one early triumph, she "sociopathically connected" with the head of tourism in Puerto Rico, a single mom who lost her job when the date became a disaster of Fyre Festival proportions (a long story, involving a water-bound palapa, coconuts, and horses). Shapiro felt grimly exhilarated by these accomplishments—at once ashamed and powerful—but she was also aware of the economic implications of her success: Fleiss and his cronies were becoming millionaires, while the crew was scraping by.

When she got promoted to field producer, Shapiro's job was to produce stories about specific bachelorettes. Because Standards and Practices forbade anyone from writing any of the show's dialogue, the task was all about manipulation, getting people to say and do things without letting them know you were doing it. When Shapiro identified one of the contestants as "an obvious Mountain Lesbian," a jock obsessed with volleyball, the producer spent her days trying to refocus the athlete's competitive edge, to replace her passion for volleyball with a passion for the bachelor, "trying—really trying—to take a rock and turn it into a bird."

The producers understood certain occult truths about human nature, among them that "the worst question is the best question." Shapiro would ask, "So you love dick?" or "So, you're, like, gay?" An irate, defensive response could be spun into sound bites in a way more rational dialogue could not. (At this juncture in our interview, at my rental in Silver Lake, Shapiro asked the question she'd pose if I were a bachelorette: "So, you obviously Airbnb'd this place to fuck a lot of people while you're in L.A.?")

Ben Hatta described the job in similar terms, only he did so with pride. Hatta, too, had sweet-talked vendors into offering free goodies, never mentioning how fast the show's credits would roll by, rendering their contribution invisible. He compared his work with cast members to the movie *Inception,* to "planting seeds," "doing therapy," and also "doing a little puppeteering." Hatta, too, walked me through a typical interaction. "So, when he grabbed you by your hand, I saw your eyes fluttering. Were you getting a little flushed in the face and butterflies?" If the woman replied, "Kind of," he'd urge her on until she echoed his words, making the statement her own. Watching the edited episodes was a thrill. "It was like, '*I got her to say that.*' Those are my words. You created television! . . . You don't have that power in any other genre." What Shapiro understood as sociopathy, Hatta described simply as skilled producing.

Two stories still haunted Shapiro, years later. One was about Jessica Holcomb, a small-town prosecutor who had refused to do an emotional farewell interview. It was 4 A.M., after a five-hour rose ceremony shoot. "I said, 'Jessica, I cannot let you go. I mean it, I'll edit it like you're fucking crazy, because you don't have an exit.'" Jessica wouldn't crack, so Shapiro turned the screws, using her knowledge about the bachelorette's eating disorder. Jessica, a twenty-five-year-old who had gone on the show after her engagement broke up, began sobbing. The editors tied that footage to a shot in which she seemed to claw at the bachelor's shoulder, an edit that made her look like a hysterical stalker, just as Rhonda Rittenhouse once had, after her panic attack in the first season of the show.

On another season, Shapiro worked with a bachelorette she found gorgeous but empty, with "a lizard heart." She knew what her job was: to become the woman's best friend. During a visit to Florida, Shapiro met the woman's likeable, normal family, then found herself puppeteering these civilians, too, cuing the bachelorette's grandmother up to offer to lend her wedding dress.

When her contestant became a finalist, Shapiro had a huge opportunity: the chance to trick her into believing that the bachelor was going to choose her, so that she'd react powerfully when she got dumped, much like Trista Rehn. In retrospect, Shapiro realizes that she should have quit her job. Instead, she poured on the manipulation, "'Oh my God, I'm going to get fired for telling you this.' Like: 'Oh my God, oh my God. It's *you.*'" She helped the bachelorette get into her dress, excited and liquored up. Then, after the woman got dumped, Shapiro drove her around for four hours, using jalapeño peppers to make herself cry, blasting country songs and reaping the meltdown.

These accomplishments earned Shapiro tons of praise. In the control room, her peers would egg her on, whispering into her earpiece, "If she doesn't cry, I'm gonna slap the teeth out of her mouth." It felt like working with prison guards, who justified everything as necessary for the job. But three years into the work, Shapiro broke down. She'd gained a lot of weight by then. She was getting sick all the time. The crew kept getting ear infections from their earpieces, so they scarfed down unprescribed antibiotics, which someone handed out on set. To cope with the hours, they slept in their cars or on set, rarely seeing friends or families. Shapiro, who was queer, had begun sleeping with men as a kind of self-punishment—and also, she felt, because she'd absorbed the most toxic themes of the show, as if exposed to a factory spill.

Finally, Shapiro told her bosses that she was going to drive off a cliff if they didn't let her leave. At first, they took this as another manipulation. "Who poached you?" But eventually they let her go. Shapiro moved to Portland and, for a while, she retreated to farm kale and write folk music. Although she was only twenty-six, she felt ancient. In certain ways, she still felt warmth for her colleagues—her fellow "scrappy fuckers," hard workers with charm, cunning, and resilience under pressure. Reality TV producers were adrenaline junkies; you got no sleep and little money, but you had the chance to play God.

Shapiro found a job in advertising, recruiting one of her former co-workers. Then, she found a new way to play God. In 2013, she wrote and directed *Sequin Raze,* a short film about the night she broke Jessica Holcomb. In 2015, she expanded that into a series for Lifetime called *UnREAL,* an insider's portrait of reality TV, which was set on a dating show called *Everlasting.* In the show, a schlubby spitfire named Rachel, who wears a "This Is What a Feminist Looks Like" T-shirt, is pressured into taking a job on *Everlasting,* then forms a deep bond with Quinn, a brilliant, venal female showrunner fond of Prada purses. Although Quinn is the real visionary behind the show, her male co-creator—a sexist, stoner slob named Chet, a charismatic bully—gets all the credit. Quinn and the married Chet are having a sloppy, not especially discreet affair.

Mike Fleiss told me that he had never watched *UnREAL,* but he didn't like that Shapiro had called him a "populist idiot savant" in an interview. "It's revisionist history for her," he insisted. "She wasn't dragged along. She applied for the job. She begged for the job. She sucked up to Lisa, she got close to Lisa!" He insisted that *The Bachelor* couldn't have forced her to stay. Although Shapiro is legally bound not to talk about the details, she pointed out that in *UnREAL,* Rachel is portrayed as fully responsible for her own worst choices.

Hatta's memory hews closer to Shapiro's, although it's not identical. He described the way shows would lock crew members into a salary rate, committing them to several seasons, which meant several years—and then, when they asked for a raise, would push them to sign on for more seasons. A few years in, Hatta himself didn't ask for a raise, purposely getting "lost in the shuffle." Instead, he snagged a job on *The Amazing Race*—and signed up with a friend at CAA before anyone noticed. "You *can* get out, you've just got to do it, and she didn't," he argued. To Hatta, Shapiro's failure to con her way out of the job explains her negative impression of *The Bachelor.* He, too, made comparisons to prison, only he had a different version of the metaphor: If you didn't escape from shows like *The Bachelor,* he said, "You're stuck in prison and that's your mentality for the rest of your life." Hatta viewed himself as more of an ex-convict. "I got an education, I got some skills, I'm reformed, I'm a better person."

Hatta admired the early episodes of *UnREAL,* which struck him as near-documentary flashbacks to their production room. He admired Shapiro's drive. But he didn't share her interest in industry reform, because the way Hatta saw it, reality TV was inseparable from—and, in fact, defined by—its brutal labor conditions. He considered it "a badge of honor" to have handled those awful hours, the low pay, and the pressure. Hatta, through his own production company, now works on HGTV shows, in "lighthearted" areas, like design and food, avoiding what he described as "headache and heartache shows." In his view, the only sensible way to survive reality TV is to climb upward. "All the money is at the top. All the power's at the top. So I don't care about what's happening here: I'm going *there*."

UnREAL had another admirer, as well: Jessica Holcomb. In an interview with *Cosmopolitan*, Jessica revealed the magic words Shapiro said to get her to break down on *The Bachelor*: " 'You've been very honest about all the girls here being so much prettier than you and skinnier than you and better than you. How does it feel to know that you were right?' " During filming, Jessica had trusted the producers entirely, so when they urged her to be more affectionate to the bachelor, she gave them the footage that looked like "clawing." After the episode aired, she got recognized everywhere. She lost her job; she moved cities; her mother was humiliated. Decades later, however, she had forgiven Shapiro, who she recognized had deep regrets. Like Rhonda Rittenhouse, she had worked hard to move past the shame of the experience, to not let it throw her—to turn it into "a funny story to tell at a party."

When we first spoke, Shapiro was working on a film about the Yazidi women of Kurdistan, although that project eventually fell through. She was married, with a child, and had a bunch of stories in development, all about women's lives. When it came to *The Bachelor*, she was most unsettled by other women's affection for the show. "Why does somebody really, really smart, with an advanced degree, making over $150,000 a year—why are those women obsessed with it, what does it fulfill in them?" she asked me. It wasn't that Shapiro herself was immune to the show's appeal. "There was an atmosphere in the control room on those big nights at the mansion that felt incredibly glamorous," she told me. "It was *fancy*. Like, the actual physicality of the situation was incredibly shitty, shoddy, and hollow. But it was the top-rated show on television."

From her perspective, the show's continued success sent a bleak message: It was a fantasy about liberation through powerlessness. "A part of the allure is that it can really be that simple. If you're skinny enough and pretty enough and you keep your mouth shut, somebody will actually save you, and you don't have to work that hard and it's not all on you and your destiny is not completely in your hands." She was most baffled by the people who were fans of *both UnREAL* and *The Bachelor.* "I was like, 'You guys, it's really bad—it's not, like, funny bad, it's *bad* bad.' To me, it's like eating the heads of babies."

12

||||||

THE WINK
Bravo and the Gentrification of Reality TV

LIKE MARK BURNETT, FENTON BAILEY WAS AN ENGLISH BOY WHO grew up in thrall to American television, although his taste didn't lean toward for *CHiPs* or *Rawhide*. Instead, Bailey was enchanted by the campy 1960s live-action TV version of *Batman*, with its skintight bodysuits and "KAPOW!" captions. When he caught a glimpse of Lance Loud, he was just as fascinated. Here, at last, was a gay man on television, but not used as comic relief or some dour cautionary tale about acceptance, "who wasn't necessarily talking about it, but you just *knew*." To Bailey, Lance was "a beacon of authenticity"—all the realer for his embrace of Warholian artifice.

That glittering beacon drew Bailey to downtown Manhattan, where he studied film at NYU during the early 1980s and bonded with Randy Barbato, who had decamped from New Jersey out of a similar sense of destiny. It was a fantastic time to be gay on the Lower East Side, in his recollection. The two men prioritized nights out at Pyramid Club over classes, partying with drag queens and punk rockers, who occupied overlapping circles. There wasn't much they liked on 1980s network TV, with the exception of *Dynasty*, but late at night, Bailey and Barbato stumbled on something thrilling, a hidden community that had set up shop on the outer regions of the dial: Manhattan public access cable, where anyone could put on a show.

In the wee hours, the obscure Channel 35 aired an anarchic lineup of public access programs, broadcast from society's margins, among them *The Robin Byrd Show,* in which a vivacious, deeply tanned blond vixen in a crocheted bikini frolicked with naked hunks, poking herself in the eye with their soft penises. On *Voyeur Vision,* a husband filmed his wife lounging in bed, as smutty phone calls poured in. On *John's Cabaret,* a piano player took requests from drunks; on *The Mrs. Mouth Show,* the host spoke through an upside-down face scribbled on his chin; and on *The Closet Case Show,* the host, Rick X, seduced listeners with a graphic array of voyeuristic scenarios. Bailey had a special fondness for the eerily pretty Ed Bergman, a hypnotic stud who gazed into the lens of the camera and announced, "You are the light." "It was like *Death in Venice!* And then again, it was like, 'What is going *on?*'"

To Bailey, these programs were punk rock, made by artists who "couldn't play their instruments and made an awful sound, but the energy was so incredible." They were drag, too: a queer art form that turned trash into treasure. Unlike the Hollywood film world—which was both inaccessible and heavily homophobic—these shows felt like a route to a vibrant alternative community, outré and stylish. Before the internet existed, you could just pick up your landline, call the telephone number on the TV screen, and speak, intimately and immediately, to a universe of mysterious, perverted strangers.

This scene became a new home, and in the mid-1980s, Bailey and Barbato formed a queer disco-pop band called The Fabulous Pop Tarts, recording two albums. In 1987, they created *Flaunt It! TV,* a public access show named after an album by new wave band Sigue Sigue Sputnik. On it, they interviewed every downtown notable in their Rolodexes, among them British memoirist Quentin Crisp, gay journalist Michael Musto, and vaginal punk-magician Sticky Vicky. In 1991, Bailey and Barbato founded World of Wonder, their film production company. Their goal was to make documentaries about their passions, starting with *Manhattan Cable.* In the series, which aired on Britain's Channel 4, they edited together the best bits of the public cable shows, then interspersed them with their own footage.

To make money, Barbato spent his days at an ad agency, while Bailey worked as a film editor, helping to cut together industrial films for the Wall Street firm Drexel Burnham (he also used the edit bay to cut videos for the Pop Tarts). One of Bailey's bosses was *The Real World* pioneer Alan Cohn, the same film editor who had invented the Bunim/Murray show's distinctive look, with its sly musical gags and saturated, absurdist zooms. Bailey considered Cohn "a filmmaking dynamo," but when the MTV series debuted in 1992, it wasn't quite to his taste: too "douchey," and a little too constructed. "I thought it was really significant, but I didn't think it was really *good*," he said.

World of Wonder would be more gonzo, he hoped, a wavy mirror reflecting the taboo, tabloid phenomena in the news, from the anarchy of the helicopters hovering over the O. J. Simpson car chase to televangelist Tammy Faye Bakker. If there were cameras everywhere, that struck him as a liberatory sign, a democratization of the media. "It was the fetish of the time," he said, comparing the era (positively) to the sleek dystopia in the movie *Blade Runner*.

The Fabulous Pop Tarts had already stumbled upon the man they saw as their artistic soulmate, back in the 1980s, in an appropriately cinematic way: During a visit to Atlanta, their car's headlights hit on RuPaul Andre Charles, who was pasting up photos of himself that read "RuPaul Is Everything." A Black drag queen from San Diego, RuPaul was a public access star, who appeared on an anarchic program called *The American Music Show*. A mistress of high style, his outfits exemplified the punk-drag approach that the Pop Tarts adored: a mohawk, a loincloth, a crop top, thigh-high wading boots, and football shoulder pads made of trash cans, say. The three men bonded, recognizing one another as "devotees of the church of Warhol."

For the next decade, Bailey and Barbato struggled to elevate RuPaul's career, certain that he was fated for stardom. RuPaul became a host on *Manhattan Cable*. In 1993, his pop single "Supermodel (You Better Work)" became a dance-club hit, celebrated by Kurt Cobain at the MTV Video Music Awards. In 1994, he got a contract with MAC Cosmetics. In 1996, he hosted a talk show, *The RuPaul Show*, which World of Wonder produced in collaboration with branding whiz kid Lauren Zalaznick, who was then a senior vice president at VH1. These bursts of pop-culture success were satisfying but insufficient achievements, in Bailey's eyes. He saw RuPaul not as a novelty act but as a huge, resonant icon like Oprah Winfrey, "a self-aware diva who was able to combine outrage with sweetness and spirituality." For many years, Bailey had imagined a different type of television show, an outrageous drag queen beauty pageant, all glitter and camp, the Trojan horse that could carry queer punk into the mainstream.

No one was willing to produce that show, however. When they pitched the concept to Stephen Chao at Fox, the creator of *America's Most Wanted* sneered at them—and although Chao was nastier than most, he wasn't alone. Gay men had been prominent players in reality TV from the start, from Lance Loud to Pedro Zamora and Richard Hatch. A striking proportion of early reality producers were gay men, among them *Survivor* creator Charlie Parsons, Bunim/Murray's Jon Murray, and Doug Ross at Evolution, as well as Mark Itkin, the top reality TV agent in Hollywood. Perhaps gay men were more attuned to the tensions between behavior and performance; maybe they were more willing to innovate, as outsiders.

Still, gay representation only went so far—a character here and there, in mostly straight ensembles. Bailey dreamed of something more transgressive: queer aesthetics treated not as a side dish, but as the main course. It would take him many years to reach that promised land, as the culture gradually shifted around him, clearing the space for RuPaul to make his dazzling entrance.

IN 1981, WHEN DAVID COLLINS, THE FUTURE CREATOR OF *QUEER Eye for the Straight Guy*, was fourteen years old, he ran away from home. The high-achieving football star, class president son of evangelical Christians in Cincinnati, Ohio, Collins had, for once, broken the rules: He'd cut class to smoke pot at the zoo with his boyfriend. When the school cracked down, suspending him and barring him from a choral trip to Europe, Collins was furious. The two boys packed up, then flew to Manhattan, carrying several thousand dollars—and even after his friend returned home, Collins stayed on. Amazingly, the teenager managed to rent and decorate a studio apartment at the Belvedere Hotel. He finagled a job at The Yale Club bar; he modeled for boys' clothing catalogues. Months later, Collins's family finally tracked him down and convinced him to come back to Ohio, but it was a burst of defiance many gay men during that homophobic era might identify with, even if few of them would go quite so far—a brazen makeover, whatever the risks.

After that dramatic detour, Collins started over. He went to Ohio University, and then, at twenty-one, he met his partner, Michael Williams, who was thirty-one, on the set of Jodie Foster's movie *Little Man Tate*. The couple co-founded Scout, a Boston location-scouting company, working on films like *Legally Blonde*. But after 9/11, when their overseas contracts were faltering, they began toying with an unusual idea: a reality television show. It wasn't exactly a natural match for their highbrow social circle, which included Collins's close friend David Metzler, who was straight; they were indie-movie buffs and art aficionados, not *Survivor* fans. Their experience with the reality genre had been limited to producing *First Person,* an Errol Morris interview series that aired in 2000 on the cable arts network Bravo, a highbrow platform dedicated to opera, ballet, and Cirque du Soleil.

Then one fall night in 2001, the friends attended an artist's open-studio night. The way Collins tells the story, just as they walked into the loft, a scene erupted: A woman was berating her husband, telling him he should be more like the stylish gay men around them. It was an ugly scene. "Out of the blue, the skies parted, a light came down in the corner of the room," Collins told me. Three men, champagne flutes in hand, strode over. They began to fuss with the man's hair, to tell him that he had enormous potential. They urged his wife to be more positive. Collins turned to Williams and said, "Did you see that? That was queer eye for the straight guy." Williams shot back, "That's our show."

There's another version of this origin story, one that Collins's old friend Peter Fisher told journalist Michael Joseph Gross in 2004, when *Queer Eye for the Straight Guy* was at the height of its buzz.

According to Fisher, the show's eureka moment was slightly less idealistic. "There was this really good-lookin' straight guy and this not so good-lookin' girl, and Dave said, 'Some gay guy should dress him up, and get him a better girl.' That's where the idea really came from." Whatever the truth, these mirror-image stories capture the complexity of *Queer Eye for the Straight Guy*. In one version, gay male creativity is a superpower, healing the world and building bridges. In the other, it's realpolitik, an awareness of how to "trade up." The magic of *Queer Eye* was how seamlessly it merged both themes and, in the process, sparked another makeover: renovating Bravo itself, turning the channel into a magnet for queer reality programming.

To pitch their concept to the networks, the Scout team designed a parody version of *Esquire,* Williams's favorite men's magazine. The cover was a slovenly "before" shot of their office manager, clutching some Dunkin' Donuts Munchkins. Inside was a manifesto about straight male style, a breakdown of the show's format, and some slick black-and-white portraits of the "Fab Five," with Williams and the team posing with wine bottles and hair dryers. Each expert represented a different section of *Esquire*: Fashion, Grooming, Interior Design, Culture, and Food and Wine. They had mini-profiles, complete with nicknames ("The Hammer"), turn-ons (shag carpet), turn-offs (bare walls), and takes on what was hot (Michael Chabon, Moroccan design) and not (goatees, silver and black). This unagented pitch got no immediate response from VH1 and other networks, so they went to Bravo, where they already had a relationship with one of the executives, Frances Berwick. The show was an odd match for Bravo, with its high-art shows and older viewers, but Berwick agreed to fund a pilot. In 2002, Scout started filming.

The first culture expert was James Hannaham, a Yale graduate and theater performer who wrote for *The Village Voice* (and, full disclosure, a personal friend). When Hannaham showed up for his audition, he recognized every other Black gay artist in the green room—he was there to resolve a "diversity crisis," he understood, like Janel Scarborough on the pilot of *The Real World*. Still, Hannaham was drawn to the production's warm atmosphere, particularly the easy bond between the gay Collins and the straight Metzler, whom everyone called "The Daves." Hannaham was paid $2,000—a good chunk of change—and he had fun invading the home of a straight guy in Boston, critiquing the man's CDs and his bookcases, recommending that he replace his musty copy of Ayn Rand with Zadie Smith's *White Teeth*.

His fellow Fab Fivers included Ted Allen, an elegantly square culture writer for *Esquire*, and Carson Kressley, an effervescent stylist for Ralph Lauren. When these two quick-witted naturals stayed on, while he and the other two cast members got cut, Hannaham wasn't too shocked—although he did wonder if he had been too butch for the show's notion of queerness, especially Black queerness. Collins and Williams disputed that, chalking up their decision to the focus group, who had bridled at his comparison of Billy Joel to iceberg lettuce.* Still, Hannaham's recasting was only the beginning of *Queer Eye*'s struggles with the role of the culture guy, always the most undefined aspect of the show.

At first, the *Queer Eye* pilot looked like it would never get picked up. Then, more than six months later, a corporate earthquake hit: NBC had bought Bravo—and Berwick talked NBC president Jeff Gaspin into giving the defunct show another look. Suddenly, the stakes were sky-high, as was the marketing budget. In 2003, Scout Productions filmed around a dozen more episodes, incorporating three new cast members: Kyan Douglas for grooming; Thom Filicia for design; and Blair Boone—who was, like Hannaham, a Black artist with highbrow tastes—as the culture guy. Two episodes later, Boone, too, was out.† On the recommendation of Gaspin, who had just seen the off-Broadway musical *Zanna, Don't!*, the show's creators hired that musical's star, twenty-three-year-old Jai Rodriguez, whom Collins described to me as "a beautiful Brown boy and a musical theater queen."

Recasting aside, the filming went reasonably smoothly, with the Fab Five revamping the grooming habits of an expansive variety of

---

* A riff on a John Waters joke that ultimately got back to Billy Joel himself, who responded, good-naturedly, that he *liked* iceberg lettuce.
† Boone sued the show for breach of contract, reaching a settlement.

straight men, who ranged from a Greek fitness instructor with Fabio hair to a gruff Staten Island transit cop, along with one *Queer Eye* crew member, recruited in a crunch. Each episode took four days to film. On the first day, the Fab Five would pull up in a black SUV and analyze their subject's "dossier," like Charlie's Angels. Then they'd do the weekly "ambush"—tearing through each man's home, tossing out zingers, rotten produce, and bad shampoo. The next two days were occupied by shopping and spa treatments, cooking lessons and home design, whatever the story required.

There were a few contrivances involved—Thom Filicia didn't actually design a room in three hours—but *Queer Eye* was a genuinely unscripted project, driven by the chatterbox eloquence of its freewheeling ensemble. The Fab Five burned a toupee on a barbecue grill; they broke into a game of Twister on an ugly shower curtain. On the last day of filming, they would shower their subject with praise, then coach him on how to host some major event. A few weeks later, they would film a series of "loft" segments, in which the group gathered on sofas, sipping cocktails, to watch each straight man's "graduation" on the TV, as if they were urbane gods, toasting mere mortals. To the show's director of photography Michael Pearlman—whose background was in Dogme film but who had once taken a paycheck job on a cruel prank show—it all felt like a pleasant change of pace: a reality show that was all about empowerment, rather than humiliation.

In the first *Queer Eye* episode that aired, the team made over a shy artist named Brian "Butch" Schepel, boiling Butch's jockstrap. Carson taught him to combine denims; Thom painted his walls red; Jai designed promo cards for his business; and Ted tutored him on how to make mini pizzas. Finally, Kyan chopped off Butch's lank blond ponytail, then donated it to the charity Locks of Love. In the final scene, Butch hosted his first art exhibit as the Fab Five watched, delighted, at home. "Cheers, queers!" said Ted, clinking neon-bright cocktails.

Carson Kressley became the show's breakout star, tossing out bon mots like Paul Lynde on *Hollywood Squares*. In the opening episode, he told Butch, "There's a little gay boy in Indonesia who would *kill* for that hair. His name is Terry!" He mock-flirted with the men, in banter that sometimes bordered on a roast. Not everything aged well: The group called themselves "The Faggoty Fab Five"; they used slang like "retarded" and called a chubby belly a "jelly dough-nut." But despite the zingers, the tone was heartwarming. Men would cry when they got their hair cut, opening up about their inse-curities. In one episode, when a Port Authority security guard admit-ted that he was nervous "in his skivvies, next to a gay guy" in a tanning booth, Kyan gently talked him down, rather than call him out. For Carson—who was wary of straight men, having experi-enced his share of bullying—the experience was an eye-opener, of-fering him "a sweetness and a kinship," he told me.

During the ambush, the crew would stumble on objects, like porn, pot, and sex toys, they couldn't show on TV; one time, it was "snug fit" condoms. When the production unearthed a problem that was truly dark, like hoarder-level filth or family dysfunction, they addressed it privately. "They weren't salivating hyenas," said Pearl-man, who was convinced that the show was on to something big when he watched the straight crew members after work, drinking beer and debating collar choices.

Kelly Korzan, an early *Queer Eye* editor, had worked on only one other reality show before, the comparatively sincere PBS series *Fron-tier House*. The Bravo job was quicker-paced, but equally satisfying. There was no need for any Frankenbites, with so many authentic quips available, especially from Carson. The trickiest scene to edit—the frenetic ambush—was also the most fun to put together. Sifting through the rich footage, she could see something subversive in the mix: the rare show in which gay men saved the day while straight men wept.

NBC GAVE *QUEER EYE* A MASSIVE PROMOTIONAL BLITZ, WITH planes dragging banners reading "Queer Eye Is Coming" over local beaches. The Brooklyn Bridge got shut down to film a music video in which the Fab Five got stuck in traffic, because the whole city was desperate to get to their party. To the thump of Canadian duo Widelife's "All Things (Just Keep Getting Better)," sung by Simone

Denny, the cast strutted toward Manhattan, boogying through bodegas and beauty parlors to the swanky Fez club below Time Cafe. After several attempts to nail the move, Ted Allen sliced the cork off a champagne bottle with a saber, delivering a perfect telegenic smirk.

A thirty-seven-year-old Midwesterner, Ted luxuriated in the glamour of the video shoot, sure it was a bubble about to pop. Instead, NBC's gamble paid off, vaulting the Fab Five into fame, with more than 1.16 million people tuning in for the premiere. In *Entertainment Weekly,* Carina Chocano called it "a full-scale humanitarian relief mission: Queers Without Borders." In the gay magazine *The Advocate,* a critic mused, "Who would have thought that throw pillows and chocolate mousse could be among the most powerful weapons of social change?" The Fab Five were guests on *The Tonight Show* and *Oprah,* posed for the cover of *Entertainment Weekly,* and, in 2004, won the Outstanding Reality Program Emmy. Their program was such a mainstream hit that at the White House Correspondents' Association dinner, President George W. Bush joked about the Fab Five making over Attorney General John Ashcroft. "We were jealous," said World of Wonder's Fenton Bailey, who had always wanted to launch this sort of project—a queer hit for the whole world, not a cult sensation.

There was criticism, too. Some gay observers saw the show as minstrelsy. Others viewed it as greasy consumerism, an attempt to make straight men as insecure as straight women already were. At the Television Critics Association Awards show, when Carson was asked whether the program reinforced stereotypes, he shot back, "There's not one flight attendant or florist on this show!" In Ted's view, the criticism was simply off target. In a pop-culture environment that treated gay hairdressers and designers as swishy jokes, *Queer Eye* elevated them, celebrating them as skilled artisans. Even better, it portrayed gay men's lives as so enviable that anyone, of any sexuality, would want to emulate them.

In 2003, the word "queer" was still an insult—or, to a smaller set of people, an academic term ("queer theory") or a radical political label, as in the activist group Queer Nation, a spin-off of ACT UP. Collins viewed it as a crucial element of the title, however—and it was never in any danger of being censored by NBC. (There was a more picayune linguistic debate: Collins preferred *The Queer Eye for the Straight Guy,* which didn't fit in *TV Guide.*)

There was one area of sensitivity, however. Amazingly, up until the show aired, three of its cast members weren't quite out to their families. Ted Allen, who had had a steady partner since his twenties, hadn't ever talked about the fact that he was gay with his parents. Raised Methodist in Indiana, he wasn't an especially political person. (Although, as he put it to me wryly, he "felt very strongly that people should stop being mean to us.") He begged The Daves to change the title, but Collins stuck to his guns. If "queer" was scary, that was a *good* thing, he argued. In the end, Ted's mother (who wound up being enormously supportive) called the program "QE."

Carson Kressley also wasn't out. "Which is insane, right? Many people were shocked by that—but if you knew Carson's family, you understood," said Collins. "He was very much 'the good boy.'" A sophisticated globe-trotter in the workplace, Carson had grown up in a small, conservative town in Pennsylvania, in a family of horsey WASPs, within whose universe he was *already* famous, as a member of the U.S. Saddle Seat World Cup Team. Still, like Ted, he had avoided the subject of his sexuality. "I hadn't been that brave," he told me. The week before *TV Guide* put him on the cover, Carson spoke with his parents. Later on, his mother called him up in excitement—her beauty parlor friends had seen the premiere. The show wound up being a blessing, by placing his sexuality in a celebratory context, inseparable from his stardom.

When it first aired, *Queer Eye* was paired with another Bravo show, *Boy Meets Boy.* Like *Queer Eye, Boy Meets Boy* had been created by a gay reality producer, Evolution's Doug Ross. But although the series was marketed as a gay spin on *The Bachelor,* it had more in common with *Joe Millionaire:* Half of the contestants were straight men, pretending to be gay for the prize money. Contractually, no one was allowed to do anything more than kiss. When, late in the filming, the bachelor, James Getzlaff, learned the gimmick, neither he nor his gal pal Andra reacted well. In the media, Ross liked to pitch the show as a social experiment—at last, straight men would learn what it was like to be in the closet! NBC president Jeff Gaspin was more candid: He would never have green-lit a gay dating show without that nasty twist, which provided a lure for the straight audience.

Collins found the show "icky." Like *Playing It Straight*, a similar series on Fox, it was fueled by gay panic, not gay pride. It ended after one season, a shadow remnant of the *Queer Eye* era.

THE OTHER *QUEER EYE* CAST MEMBER WHO WASN'T FULLY OUT to his mother was Jai Rodriguez. Jai, the third culture guy to get cast, had played the drag queen Angel in *Rent;* he'd also starred in the campy fantasia *Zanna, Don't!*, a musical about a world in which gay people are the norm. But although he was out in Manhattan, he was more guarded when he visited his family on Long Island. Raised by a fundamentalist Christian mother, Jai had been cut off from pop culture, and when he first saw Pedro Zamora on *The Real World,* a decade after his season aired, he felt mainly dread. Yes, Pedro was a gay Latino man, like him—but he had also died of AIDS, just as Jai's aunt had when he was sixteen. It was too frightening to be inspiring.

Jai was intrigued by the word "queer," which a *Rent* cast member used to refer to himself. But as a late addition to the cast, he was suffering from a heavy dose of imposter syndrome, in part because he'd been encouraged by the casting director to fluff up his résumé, to claim that he was twenty-six and a college graduate. The tactic got his foot in the door, but it also intensified Jai's sense of himself as an outsider—the youngest cast member, the one person of color, and the only one from a blue-collar background. His role was also the least defined, less a skill set than a blurry notion of "good taste," a concept the show's creators hadn't thought about deeply.

During filming, Jai felt inspired by Carson's confidence, his freewheeling, bravura aura of authenticity. But after the show blew up, his mood sank, as he brooded about his position on the show. *Queer Eye*'s slogan was "Style. Taste. Class," but although the Fab Five might dress a Latino cop from Queens up to look like a WASPy Manhattan lawyer, they'd never do the reverse. As well-intentioned as his bosses were, they weren't thinking about these issues. When a *MADtv* sketch portrayed Jai as expendable, the joke stung.

The second season was tough for everyone. The ratings tanked. The cast was fighting to renegotiate their pay. NBC aired nonstop marathons; under pressure to churn out endless episodes, the show's quality dropped. That included the quality of the products that were integrated into the show, like Lucky Brand jeans or a Domain settee. To simplify the system, David Collins had teamed up with Tina Elmo, the brand manager for *Sex and the City*. Still, the show's standards had degraded—and by 2007, Collins said, "We'd put Crest Whitestrips in the story, whether anyone needed them or not." That year, *Queer Eye* got canceled.

Some *Queer Eye* cast members would become stars of reality TV, most notably, Ted Allen, who became the much-adored host of the cooking show *Chopped,* which debuted on the Food Network in 2009. Others, like Thom Filicia, went back to their former professions. Jai's options felt more limited. At one meeting, an agent sniffed that he was "never going to be the new Antonio Banderas." By the time Collins and Williams rebooted the show as *Queer Eye* (with no more "straight guy") for Netflix in 2018, using a new cast, Jai had become one of their viewers, seeking a bit of inspiration. The updated version of *Queer Eye* was far more racially diverse, and also openly emotional. It was more attentive to the role of people's identities; not everyone who got made over was straight or a guy. Karamo Brown, the latest culture guy, had a defined role: He was a life coach, reaching out to men full of self-doubt, in segments that were about self-esteem and mental health, not just style. Watching the episodes, Jai felt wistful. He was proud that he'd blazed a trail, but he could have used that kind of support.

WHEN LAUREN ZALAZNICK GOT HIRED BY BRAVO IN 2004, THE network had one big hit: *Queer Eye for the Straight Guy*. Everything else in her portfolio or already in development looked like a grab bag, from *Celebrity Poker Showdown* to James Lipton's *Inside the*

Actors Studio. There was nothing especially urbane in the mix, or gay, or aimed at women—nothing that matched Zalaznick's own persnickety taste. An avatar of Gen X chic with a crisp gray bob and nerd glasses, she was a whiz at branding, having helped design the credit sequence for MTV's *The Real World.* She'd produced several celebrated indie movies, among them *Kids, Safe,* and *Swoon,* and she'd overseen the renovation of two other cable networks, turning MTV's stodgy sister network into the sleek VH1, then revamping Trio, a niche arts network. Bravo was another fixer-upper.

In summer 2004, Zalaznick declared her mission statement: Bravo would now use *Queer Eye* as its blueprint. Her tiny staff, which included a mouthy former news producer named Andy Cohen, was deputized to seek out programs they would drop into five programming "buckets": Fashion, Design, Food and Wine, Culture, and Grooming. These shows would be aimed at a niche demographic, which was dominated by gay men and their female friends ("the Wills and the Graces"), a new kind of viewer, whom Bravo general manager Frances Berwick nicknamed "the affluencers." This group adored shopping and living the good life, but they also preferred something else in their TV, a certain artifice—irony, camp, the queer tilt of both *Batman* and Lance Loud. They loved "the wink."

Zalaznick had faith that the affluencers would spread the good news about Bravo through word of mouth, instead of ordinary marketing—an idea that led to a new logo for the network, showing a voice bubble like the ones in cartoons. Unlike other cable channels—like Lifetime, "Television for Women"—Zalaznick wanted the new Bravo to feel warm, but also exclusive, a club for people who were in on the joke. Their new slogan was "Watch What Happens."

Only one show in development matched this plan: *Project Runway,* a format that had a tangled development history. The show had originally begun as a spin-off of HBO's *Project Greenlight,* a talent contest for movie directors, a show that had been co-created, in 2001, by Eli Holzman, a former Harvey Weinstein assistant who ran Miramax's fledgling TV studio. *Project Greenlight,* which was made in partnership with Ben Affleck and Matt Damon, was a critic's darling, but even its own producers knew that as a reality format, it had a fatal flaw: It was a competitive game show with zero suspense, since the winner was announced up front. Holzman, who knew nothing about reality TV, had created the show primarily to sell movie tickets, just like *American Idol* sold albums. That idea turned out to be a non-starter, since the films *Project Greenlight* winners directed were duds.

Project Runway had more sinister roots, which went back to Weinstein's insistence that Miramax make a reality show about fashion models, based on *Model Apartment,* a pitch by a German model named Daniela Unruh. Holzman found that concept tacky (everyone, including Donald Trump, was pitching model shows) so he suggested an alternative: a *Project Greenlight* spin-off about fashion designers. Because he knew nothing about fashion, Holzman joined forces with the supermodel Heidi Klum, as well as her managers, Desiree Gruber and Jane Cha—and after Bravo bought the idea, they hired Dan Cutforth and Jane Lipsitz from Magical Elves, who had worked on VH1's indie-music competition *Bands on the Run.* It was an odd, sprawling collaboration, bringing together Miramax cineastes, VH1 reality-TV experts, and New York fashionistas, members of a cloistered universe that would rather be caught dead than watch a show like *Survivor.*

This team came up with a clever format, one that was far more suspenseful than *Project Greenlight.* Each week, the designers got a new challenge, like designing a little black dress or a postal-worker uniform—and then, one designer was eliminated during a runway competition, overseen by fashion world judges. To serve as experts, they recruited the gilded preppie designer Michael Kors, *Elle* magazine fashion director Nina Garcia, and *Sex and the City* costume designer Patricia Field. In the end, the winner, who was determined after a final challenge set during New York Fashion Week, got $100,000 to launch a full fashion line.

By then, there already was a successful reality show about fashion models—Tyra Banks's *America's Next Top Model,* on UPN—but Weinstein was determined to feature models anyway, so Holzman grudgingly included a "vestigial" element, in which each designer picked one model to work with. Rewatching the first season, the model scenes feel oddly garish, only sketchily connected to the main narrative, with strange montages of the young women half-naked, their breasts blurred out—the one indicator that there was anything shadowy behind the scenes. It would be years before the truth came out, which was that Weinstein had been using *Project Runway* as a hunting ground, starting with his harassment of Daniela Unruh. In 2020, in a Manhattan courtroom, Weinstein was toppled by a *Project Runway* production assistant named Miriam Haleyi, whose brave testimony helped sentence him to prison for thirty-nine years.

For viewers who embraced the Bravo fashion show back in 2004, those crimes felt unimaginable. In fact, *Project Runway* struck many of the cable network's viewers as a rare blast of sunshine, one of the first reality shows to celebrate skill and craftsmanship. With its cast of unknown designers working hard to make beautiful things, it also managed to be sweetly gay-positive simply because it was set in a world where gay men held sway. This aura was heightened by the show's secret ingredient: its host, Tim Gunn, a snowy-haired fashion professor from Parsons School of Design. Like the Fab Five, Gunn was a beacon for gay representation: a soft-spoken, egoless educator with a generous vision of fashion's function in the world.

There were other gay men on the show, as well. For Jay McCarroll—a mouthy Alexander McQueen–loving iconoclast from rural Lehman Township, Pennsylvania, who had been recruited from a New York arts competition—the Bravo production felt like a Hail Mary pass, a last chance to break into an elite industry that was closed to punk eccentrics like him. A longtime reality TV aficionado, Jay had a special place in his heart for gay cast members, particularly Pedro Zamora on *The Real World*. He'd auditioned for the role on *Queer Eye* that Carson Kressley was cast in. Yet despite his years studying the genre, Jay was still thrown off-kilter when the cameras began to follow him around, low on sleep and cut off from the world. There was a lot he loved about the experience, even so: He bonded with the producers, treating his interviews as a wonderful form of therapy—it was a chance to speak his mind, at last.

That season, everybody winged it a little, including Tim Gunn, who had to be warned not to thread a contestant's bobbin lest he violate game show rules. One challenge was originally set at the local drugstore chain Duane Reade, and when it fell through, producers scrambled to switch it to a supermarket. There, the contestants were handed $50, with an hour to shop and a midnight deadline to complete an outfit. To everyone's surprise, this gimmicky moment led to a great design: a delicate gown made of corn husks, built by a young designer named Austin Scarlett. With no refrigeration, his dress nearly wilted, but it won the first round.

Jay McCarroll told me that his own memories had long since been displaced by the edited version of the show. But he remembered that he briefly considered making a dress out of eggshells, before coming to his senses. If *Project Runway* had turned out to be more of a goof than a high-fashion competition, McCarroll didn't mind—and when he won the final competition, he was thrilled. After the series aired, he felt deeply grateful for his positive edit: He'd said some "pretty evil things" about the other contestants during those "therapy" sessions, none of which got aired.

When filming was completed, Zalaznick was certain that *Project Runway* would be a hit. It was everything that she had been striving for: a "premium and aspirational" series, layered with Bravo-friendly winks—ideal viewing for the affluencers, who would surely spread the word. Instead, the first episode tanked. "It was the single worst-rated show on Bravo in a decade. Worse than all of the bad ballet and opera!" said Zalaznick, still annoyed. The third episode did worse. By Christmas, she was worried: If *Project Runway* flopped, so would Bravo. Zalaznick began to deliberately overschedule the show, running marathons throughout Christmas—until finally, the ratings perked up. It was an easy climb from there, in the press and in ad sales.

Without consciously intending to do so, *Project Runway* went a step beyond *Queer Eye*. While *Queer Eye* had celebrated gay men, it wasn't aimed at a gay audience—the main characters were the straight men, after all, the ones who grew and changed. On *Project Runway,* on the other hand, the queer artists, like Scarlett and McCarroll, along with the sweetly uptight host, were the show's charming and complicated protagonists, portrayed as craftsmen and visionaries. "Nobody *had* to be gay on that show—it's just that the milieu in which they were working was so gay," said James Hanna-ham, the original *Queer Eye* culture guy, who became a fan of *Project Runway*. In season 2, the Bravo series included seven racially diverse gay male contestants—clowns, heroes, and villains, arguing and flirting and working together. In season 4, Christian Siriano, a twenty-one-year-old with a Quentin Crisp wit, was the grand winner.

Jay McCarroll's win could have led to a similar ascent. It didn't—for reasons that were tied back to Miramax. One day, McCarroll was having drinks at the Oyster Bar in Manhattan with Tim Gunn, bonding over the intense experience the two men had just been through. McCarroll's grand prize consisted of several elements: $100,000, a Banana Republic mentorship, and the right to create a new clothing line, to debut during Fashion Week. When he and Gunn read through his contract together, however, they stumbled across a troubling clause, one that was even more onerous than the contract for *American Idol*, which gave the profits from the winner's first album to the show's creators. On *Project Runway*, the winner was required to give Miramax 10 percent of their intellectual property—not just for that fashion line, but in perpetuity. According to an interview Gunn gave on a podcast in 2023, he advised McCarroll to push back on the clause, which McCarroll did—turning down the money, the mentorship, and the Fashion Week debut. Gunn himself pushed for his bosses to change the contract, and for many years, they lied to him, claiming they had altered the policy. Eventually Gunn—who wasn't himself paid as talent during his first two seasons—found out about these lies, and after sixteen seasons, he left *Project Runway* in disgust, along with Heidi Klum; the two of them then created their own series, *Making the Cut*.

McCarroll wasn't allowed to talk about the settlement he'd struck with Miramax—"I can only just shrug my shoulder," he said, in a playful tone, when we spoke over the phone. But his resistance was a welcome bit of pushback to a genre that had always exploited the same people it made stars.

ZALAZNICK HAD ONE OTHER BIG GAMBIT THAT YEAR: *BLOW OUT,* which had been programmed into the Grooming bucket. A celebration of the glamorous career of Los Angeles stylist-to-the-stars Jonathan Antin, the show was produced by Allison Grodner and Arnold Shapiro, fresh off *Big Brother 2.* More wealth-worshipping than *Queer Eye for the Straight Guy* or *Project Runway,* the show gleamed with over-the-top lifestyle porn, starting with the credits, a vertiginous montage of Rodeo Drive, gold cards, brooding stylists, and Revlon products, all treated as interchangeable consumer items.

If *Project Runway* was effortlessly gay, *Blow Out* was neurotically straight. Jonathan, a sex pest with Dick Tracy cheekbones, spent most of his time hitting on employees and barking at contractors. In theory, the series was a workplace drama, as well as an homage to the 1970s Warren Beatty satire *Shampoo,* but it wound up as more of a trial run for a new subgenre, the soft-scripted reality soap opera, driven by hilariously low-pressure conflicts. Should Jonathan decorate with white bowls or black ones? Give lesser starlet Kate Bosworth an emergency trim? As they debated the solutions to these non-problems, everyone in the ensemble spoke in air quotes, as if they were at a party where they were determined to be overheard. It was a dramatic mode that was new in 2004, but would dominate Bravo by 2006.

One TV critic described Jonathan as "so extraordinarily vain and self-conscious that he's impossible to root for," while another complained, "You'd have to troll the Great Barrier Reef to find a bigger eel." After the finale aired, however, Christopher Kelly wrote a piece that smartly reframed the new show as a fresh flavor of camp, "the *Citizen Kane* of reality television," a uniquely effective lens on its subject's megalomania. Had *Blow Out* been an earnest documentary about a handsy boss who yelled a lot, it might have been unwatchable. Instead, its resolute phoniness made it irresistible, letting viewers "luxuriate in Antin's blood-sporting, dismiss it as mere entertainment and finally even sympathize with it a bit, too."

Together, *Project Runway* and *Blow Out* would come to define the Bravo brand: the glamorous talent contest and sleek, aspirational real-life soap opera, each of them layered with irony like a seven-layer dip. In 2008, in *The New York Times Magazine,* Susan Dominus described Zalaznick's impact on the cable network in class terms. She had effectively gentrified the sketchy neighborhood of reality programming, with all those basic bachelorettes and bug-eating contests, transforming it into a newly marketable landscape, one that felt "boutique and chic," a glimmering Tribeca of the mind. "The formula may be lowbrow—attractive people pitted against one another, ruthless eliminations—but the content is, if not exactly highbrow, then certainly high-style," wrote Dominus.

As with gentrification in urban neighborhoods, this process happened in stages: first the stylish gay men, then the rich white women who loved to shop. Bravo would continue to feature competition shows like *Project Runway* (among them a popular cooking competition called *Top Chef*). But the *Blow Out* model was the one that ultimately triumphed, with the workplace element burned away like crème brûlée. A new slate of shows was about to emerge, beginning with a blockbuster franchise that would make the Bravo neighborhood newly unrecognizable, starring a different kind of ensemble: the sort of women who might hire a designer or a chef, but never dream of sewing or cooking themselves.

SCOTT DUNLOP WAS A "SERIAL ENTREPRENEUR" LIVING IN COTO de Caza, a gated community in Orange County, California, when he decided to pitch a TV show making fun of his neighbors. *Behind the Gates* was inspired by a few other projects: the Oscar-winning film *American Beauty,* a prestige drama about rich, empty suburbanites, and the HBO show *Curb Your Enthusiasm,* a prestige comedy about rich, empty Angelenos. Dunlop's own version was designed to be more like *Curb,* an improvisational docusatire, aimed at local families he found riveting, including cliques like "The Tennis Bitches," who played sets with his wife. His early focus was on Jeana Keough, a brash, vivacious former *Playboy* Playmate/ZZ Top muse who was married to a retired baseball star, and whose teenagers went to school with his own kids. "You guys are like Ozzy Osbourne, without the drugs!" he told Jeana—a compliment, sort of.

Dunlop filmed a sizzle reel for his project, full of loose, *Curb*-like sketches, in which his neighbors played versions of themselves, vamping by their pools. Bravo executives Shari Levine and Andy Cohen, who had been promoted to vice president, liked the concept, but not the stagy, raw quality of the footage, in which the characters broke the fourth wall. After a few rounds of development, Cohen wanted to drop it. By then, however, failure was not an option: *Queer Eye* had started tanking in the ratings and the Orange County series had turned into Bravo's biggest bet.

Aiming for something more like ABC's glossy prime-time soap opera *Desperate Housewives,* Levine hired Dave Rupel, a veteran soap opera writer. The season was refocused on five women whose mega-mansion lives matched the Bravo brand. Along the way, the cable network changed the show's title to *The Real Housewives* (*Behind the Gates* sounded like "a docuseries about Auschwitz or gardening," Dunlop acknowledged). Then, at Lauren Zalaznick's insistence, it became *The Real Housewives of Orange County*— a double shout-out to *Desperate Housewives* and the teen show *The O.C.* Andy Cohen hated the title's clunkiness, but Zalaznick could smell a franchise, with a *Housewives* in every city. In the promotional photos, the cast coyly held oranges, just as the *Desperate Housewives* cast had held apples: two brands of sweet temptation, filmed in the same Edenic setting where Craig Gilbert had filmed Pat Loud, the original desperate housewife, way back in 1971.

The Real Housewives of Orange County began with glamour shots of sunlit mansions and blond MILFs playing tennis, while, in voiceover, the women made declarations like "Image is everything in my world!"—taglines that had been inspired by housewife Vicki Gunvalson's sudden exclamation, "I don't want to get old!" There were a few hair-raising bits, among them Jeana's explanation that "My husband and his mother picked me out of his girlfriends, thinking that I had the right build for their genetics." Still, despite their shameless superficiality, the stars could be oddly relatable, funny, and frank. They dished about their breast implants and spoiled kids and, in later seasons, about their divorces and bankruptcies. While

The Real World started over every year, *The Real Housewives* kept documenting the same ensembles.

Rupel, who had written for *General Hospital,* had clear ideas of what a soap opera required: tears, sex, and emotion, plus "hunky shirtless men." The first season, however, he struggled to get the cast to trust him. When Kimberly Bryant, the only actual stay-at-home mother (the others worked in jobs like real estate; one didn't have kids), had a skin cancer scare, she stonewalled the crew, refusing to let them film her while she waited for the results. Frustrated, Rupel deputized two female producers to film Kimberly privately, to help her "get the 'I am woman' thing out of her system." When Kimberly had finished venting about getting good news and feeling fine, the producers followed Rupel's instructions, asking her to imagine getting bad news about her cancer. She immediately burst into tears, sobbing and opening up about her fear of dying and leaving her children alone. Once Rupel edited in some B-roll of his star and her daughter, he had the soapy emotion he needed: vulnerability instead of stoicism.

The hunky-men issue required its own negotiation. Although the crew had no trouble getting Slade, the preening fiancé of the youngest housewife, to go topless, that wasn't enough eye candy for Andy Cohen, who was prone to sending excitable, no-caps emails to Rupel, a fellow gay man, about which cast members he found hot, both male and female. Rupel deputized two female producers to convince Shane Keough, Jeana's eighteen-year-old son, to show some skin: "It took a lot of cajoling, but he finally washed his car shirtless," Rupel told me proudly. (He wouldn't have done this had Shane been under eighteen, he clarified.)

Shane, who is now in his thirties and selling real estate, didn't remember that exact moment, he said—there had been too many of those experiences, drinking from red cups, showing off with his friends, as cameras circled and producers whispered. He knew that he had come across as a spoiled jackass on the air, which wasn't exactly wrong, he told me. But he was also a teenager. The worst scenes, like him cursing at his mother, had been pulled out of context, after the producers had deliberately set him up to get him to lose his cool.

In certain ways, Shane struck me as a modern version of Grant Loud, someone he had never heard of. He had been another cute California teen boy, filmed as he partied with his friends, showing off but also kind of clueless about how it would look on TV. The difference was that Shane's parents, a Playmate and a baseball star, had raised him to *expect* fame, from early on—he had nearly been cast in a Tim Allen movie as a kid, and the whole family went on regular auditions. He didn't remember anyone convincing him to take his shirt off—he took his shirt off all the time, so maybe he had just thought the carwash idea was cheesy. But Hollywood was just like that, he emphasized. Trying to act as an adult had been much more of a mind-fuck. "You think you're confident until someone says get down to your tighty-whities in front of fifty people," he said, wryly. He'd tried to learn to be less suggestible. By now, *The Real Housewives* was mostly just an icebreaker: "I'm sorry your wife made you watch this!"

IN 2007, BUNIM/MURRAY, THE CREATORS OF *THE REAL WORLD*, launched their own series about wealthy divas: *Keeping Up with the Kardashians,* a celebreality show about the Kardashian–Jenner blended family, focused on daughters Kourtney, Kim, and Khloé and their savvy "momager" Kris. When the show debuted, on the star-obsessed, Bravo-esque E! network, Kim Kardashian, who was the daughter of the late celebrity lawyer Robert Kardashian, was less famous than she was fame-adjacent. She was a professional closet organizer who had appeared on Paris Hilton's Fox show *The Simple Life*; she had dated the divorced *Newlyweds* star Nick Lachey; and she was a tabloid star, in the wake of a leaked sex tape. The E! series turned her into an icon and an entrepreneur, specializing in products like lip plumpers and waist trainers. With an augmented ass that became as recognizable as the Nike swish, Kim was a magnet for cultural contempt—and also, a role model for young women.

For many observers, *The Real Housewives* and *KUWTK* would come to define not just channels like Bravo or E!, but reality TV itself. These weren't shaky-cam documentary experiments, capturing (or even pretending to capture) authentic, unpredictable human behavior. Instead, they proudly foregrounded their own artificiality, by casting women who already saw themselves as public figures. For these women, femininity functioned as a form of vaudeville, or maybe a type of drag performance: Every emotion and desire was outlined in neon, so that it could seen from space. Because both of these shows debuted shortly before the economy crashed, in 2008, they also worked as a convenient outlet for class rage, aimed at the 1 percent. Instead of taking shots at the invisible, interchangeable businessmen who had wrecked the economy with subprime mortgages, the culture could fixate on their symbolic trophy wives, ultravisible peacocks flashing their gold cards and Pilates abs on Bravo.

Just as Zalaznick had dreamed, *The Real Housewives* soon had franchises in cities that included New York, Beverly Hills, Washington, D.C., Atlanta, New Jersey, and Salt Lake City, each with its own distinctive flavor. The *KUWTK* empire spun off its own universe of shows (and beauty products, websites, video games, etc.). The economics varied widely: The Kardashians ran their show, while the Housewives did not—and although Dunlop couldn't talk specifics, he noted, "There's a lot of litigation across the *Housewife* spectrum." But in time, the cast members had grown savvier about how their behavior could pay off with a personal brand. Splash wine in a frenemy's face now, flack a specialty perfume later on.

There were no gay male housewives or Kardashians. In fact, early on, Bravo had dropped a gay character from *Behind the Gates,* former R & B singer André Stevens-Thomas, the head of the local homeowners association. Still, both shows were catnip for gay men. This audience even had its own representative, embedded within the network: Andy Cohen, who had morphed from an executive superfan to the host of every reunion show. Cohen had begun his career at CBS News, interning alongside future *Big Brother* host Julie Chen Moonves. He had been a fan of the reality genre going back to the original *The Real World,* and even then, he had crushes. "I was deeply in love with Eric, but I just thought he was so dumb," he told me, laughing. As the host of *Watch What Happens Live with Andy Cohen,* he became the human embodiment of Bravo's voice-balloon logo, asking the stars nosy questions over cocktails. As far as he was concerned, his workplace was reality television—and also, one of the rare institutions that had survived the changes in the television industry. "The only network that matters anymore is Bravo," he said.

Lauren Zalaznick ran Bravo until 2013, when she left NBC and pivoted to digital media. Like many reality pioneers, she recognized that her legacy was a divisive one: There had always been a gulf between viewers who grasped the "anthropological heft" of these shows and those who definitely did not. To her, however, anyone who sniffed at her shows was blinded by snobbery: For Zalaznick and Scott Dunlop, the one review that truly got the show was a piece written back in 2007, by former VH1 president Michael Hirschorn. In *The Atlantic,* Hirschorn had made the best case for the value of a set of shows the world dismissed as disposable. Maybe the Bravo lineup lacked the "visual panache" of prestige cable, Hirschorn wrote. But shows like *The Real Housewives* reflected something authentic, if you knew what to look for. They were mirrors of the bleakness of supposed privilege, reflecting themes that scripted drama had never captured, a fractured world in which "financial anxieties, fraying families, and fear of aging leave inhabitants grasping for meaning and happiness as they steer their Escalades across Southern California's perfectly buffed, featureless landscape."

BAILEY AND BARBATO—THE FORMER FABULOUS POP TARTS—HAD watched the Bravo brand emerge from a distance, shimmering and intoxicating, an oasis for a certain type of viewer. As with *The Real World,* back in the early 1990s, the Bravo franchises were never a perfect match for their sensibility. They were more sleek than gonzo, a bit less than punk. But they swung open a door.

In 2008, World of Wonder was finally able to produce *RuPaul's Drag Race,* the radical project they had been pitching, in one form or another, without success, since the 1980s. Bravo passed on it; so did

E!. Instead, their series wound up debuting on a shoestring budget on Logo, a gay-themed sister channel to VH1, before jumping to VH1 and ultimately to MTV. By the time the show finally aired, Obama had been elected president, a development that felt, for quite a while, like a harbinger of a permanent change, into a rainbow-tinted era of inclusivity.

In the Obama era, *RuPaul's Drag Race* was no longer an exception. In fact, there were so many queer hits on the cable schedule, his show set out to satirize them. On its ticky-tacky, low-budget stage, RuPaul Andre Charles, in a man's suit and elegant black glasses, searched for "America's Next Drag Superstar." A slate of unknown drag queens battled it out during mini challenges (a sexy car wash) and maxi challenges ("Channeling Oprah"), and then participated in a bravura lip-synch competition. The loser was determined using a system called "C.U.N.T.": Charisma, Uniqueness, Nerve, and Talent. The show's funky, sharp-elbowed sensibility might once have fit in only on Manhattan public access cable, but by the late aughts, it was able to ripple out to a broader audience, especially online. Like a sharp performer at a ballroom house, RuPaul expanded on and "read" the Bravo brand, a prank call coming from inside the building.

RuPaul's Drag Race also put the spotlight on a new demographic of contestant: Black and Brown sissies and queens, many of them from poor backgrounds, the inverse of Bravo's "aspirational" focus on wealth. These performers spoke frankly about the complexities of their identities; when queer culture began to shift over the years, the show moved with it, dropping rubrics like "Female or She-Male?" It embraced trans performers, and in 2021, featured a cisgender woman and a straight man.

By the early aughts, Fenton Bailey was already an elder statesman of reality TV. He would always be a defender of the genre, delighted to see it finally let its queer roots grow out. That didn't mean Bailey loved every reality program, however—and there was one series, in particular, that struck him as downright dangerous. Back in the go-go '80s, when Bailey was putting together industrial propaganda films for Drexel Burnham, he'd written a note to Donald Trump, the man behind *The Art of the Deal*, to ask if the real estate tycoon had any interest in making some kind of documentary. Trump's assistant Norma Foerderer wrote back, to explain that her boss had no interest in going on television. Apparently, he'd changed his mind.

13

||||||

THE JOB

The Apprentice and the End of Reality Innocence

ON A COLD SPRING DAY IN MAY 2002, THE FOURTH SEASON OF *Survivor* filmed its reunion special, live, in Central Park. For the occasion, Wollman Rink had been turned into an Orientalist wonderland, with a flame pit, torches, and totem poles, as well as a group of half-naked "natives" playing the bongos. The reunion's exuberant host, Rosie O'Donnell, kicked off the festivities with an off-key parody of the theme from *Gilligan's Island*. At the end of the show, O'Donnell blindfolded that season's castaways, urged them to eat gummy worms—and then tossed them the car keys to a cherry-red Saturn Vue, shouting out, "Saturn rules! . . . Thank you, CBS, and thank you, Saturn!"

In the bleachers were a few Borneo castaways, among them Gretchen Cordy and Joel Klug, who shivered under silver Mylar blankets, which were eventually snatched away because the crinkling interfered with the audio. Seated nearby was Donald Trump, along with his then-girlfriend Melania Knauss. Watching Trump shake hands with excited fans, Gretchen felt baffled: She'd grown up in New York, and from her perspective, the real estate magnate was a tabloid joke, a washed-up, bankrupt fraud, reduced to parodying his own image on 1990s sitcoms. Wollman Rink, which Trump had renovated in 1986, was his only success story.

Fellow castaway Joel had a different reaction. He felt mesmerized by the sight of Trump—and later that night, at the *Survivor* after-party, he found himself standing on a second-floor VIP balcony, peering up at an intimate interaction between Trump and Mark Burnett. The two men were leaning against the railing of a higher, more exclusive balcony, with their heads close together, seemingly deep in an intimate dialogue. "It was like watching the temptation of the devil," Joel said, although he didn't specify which was which.

The next February, Burnett and Trump met at Trump Tower. Within weeks, they'd signed a deal to make *The Apprentice*, for NBC, a competitive reality show in which Trump would play the same role that he'd played in Wollman Rink: the universally beloved New York real estate tycoon, legendary for his business prowess. In the press for the show, which debuted on January 8, 2004, Burnett often described the origins of the idea as tracing back to late 2002, when he'd watched carnivorous ants swarm an animal carcass in the Amazon. "Just like ants, people on the whole are industrious but will also pick your bones clean, given half a chance," Burnett wrote in his 2005 memoir, *Jump In!* He decided to create a city *Survivor*, set among urban predators. He also wanted to work closer to home: One of his sons had told him, on the phone, "Daddy, I don't remember what you look like."

Burnett told a less colorful story in court, in 2005, after he was sued by Mark Bethea, a businessman who claimed Burnett had ripped off a reality format called *CEO*, starring Donald Trump, which he'd registered with the Writers Guild of America West in 2000. Under oath, Burnett described a more quotidian inspiration: *Trouble at the Top*, a BBC documentary about corporate clashes, which he'd watched in a hotel room with his then-girlfriend. In the end, a federal judge ruled that *CEO* and *The Apprentice* weren't all that similar, other than starring Donald Trump. When Bethea threatened to sue again, in California in 2006, the two reached a confidential settlement.

From the account of British producer Duncan Gray, the format for *The Apprentice* was still barely embryonic as of 2003, when Burnett pitched it to ABC, where Gray had recently been hired. It was Gray's first big American pitch meeting, and although Gray had complicated feelings about Burnett—the man who got all the credit for the *Survivor* format Gray had helped create—he knew that Burnett was reputed to be a master pitchman. He was surprised at how lackluster the presentation was: no pitch deck, no props, and Trump wasn't with him. When Burnett was asked to describe potential challenges, he waved the question away, saying that they'd sort out all the specifics later.

After Burnett left, ABC Entertainment president Lloyd Braun polled his staff. One executive thought a show about work sounded boring. Another executive thought Donald Trump was too off-putting to be a host. There were questions about the budget, too. Gray spoke last, eager to show off for his new colleagues: "And I go, well, look—if *American Idol* is the West Coast dream, then this is the East Coast dream. This is *Working Girl!*" Despite Burnett's wobbly pitch, it was a kickass concept. That was the end of Gray's high-flying American television career, as he remembers it. Afterward, his boss told him to never pull that kind of stunt again. Three months later, when Braun reassigned Gray to work on Jimmy Kimmel's show, he learned his own *Apprentice*-like lesson: Never contradict your boss in front of *their* boss.

Although ABC ultimately put in a low bid, NBC wound up buying the show. It "caught my fancy right away," said then-CEO Jeff Zucker in an interview with the Television Academy, bragging that he had a better understanding of "the power of The Donald . . . the magnitude of The Donald" than his L.A. colleagues. The truth was, however the sales process went down, *The Apprentice* was a blue-chip concept. It managed to unite the two most successful reality models of the era—twisty, scheming team competitions like *Survivor* and talent contests like *American Idol*—and then added a shameless capitalistic twist. It was the first reality show to treat corporate marketing itself as a creative act, a form of self-expression as joyful as ballroom dancing.

In early 2003, Mark Burnett hired game show producer Ted

Smith, handed him the *Survive!* pitch book, then deputized him to create "the biggest job interview in the world," starring Donald Trump. Smith—who was originally hired by Burnett to work on a different show, *Destination Space*, which got grounded after the Columbia space shuttle tragedy—quickly read all of Trump's books. Then he wrote a five-page prospectus, outlining the format: two teams, a set of challenges, and then a dramatic boardroom sequence in which Trump, accompanied by two trusted aides, would interrogate the losing team and pick one player to fire. The way Smith envisioned it, each episode would end with a dazzling celebration of Trump Tower, as Trump walked the two potential losers out to the building's rotunda, put them into the glass elevators, and then, theatrically, pressed the up or the down button, consigning them to "the suite" or "the street."

Burnett and his partner Conrad Riggs hired a war room to hammer out the details further. When Darryl Silver, a producer who'd been working in Eastern Europe, got frog-marched into one of these sessions, he found veterans like *Survivor* bigwig Jay Bienstock mid-brainstorm. Silver had already signed an NDA—a prerequisite to even learn the show's premise—and he struggled to soak up the chatter, frantically scribbling phrases like "CBS heartland trail pk audience." He jotted down a list of potential challenges, which included "Grace Under Pressure," "Brown Nose Your Boss," and the very Trumpian "Avoiding Corp Tax Challenge."

The first idea Silver pitched was less cynical, however: a competition to sell the most lemonade to New York pedestrians. This childlike, universal task, which wasn't tied to any particular brand of lemonade, would become the center of the first episode. It was symbolic of the aspect of *The Apprentice* that was truly clever, and in its way, even idealistic, centered on a fantasy vision of capitalism as a meritocratic game, a joyful sport open to anyone—Mark Burnett's vision of America. In the world of *The Apprentice*, your colleagues had arrived in New York from all over the country, from every class and educational background, and half of them were women. Any of them could win the top prize, with enough gumption and hard work.

The problem was what the show was selling. In the show's credits, Donald Trump swooped over the Manhattan skyline in his private helicopter, to the seductive thump of the '70s O'Jays classic "For the Love of Money"—"Moneymoneymoneymoney! Money!" There were shots of Trump Tower, Trump Casinos, the Trump jet, and Trump himself, looking sleek, serious and in control. In ways that no one yet imagined, Trump was about to become Burnett's most effective product placement yet.

THE APPRENTICE WAS FILMED ON THE FOURTH FLOOR OF TRUMP Tower, in a fake boardroom set with no windows and dramatic, shadowy lighting. The doors, which seemed to lead into an office, led instead into the space where the cast slept. Trump worked on the twenty-fifth floor of the building, so each day, he'd take the elevator downstairs to film his scenes, then head back up when he was done. His sketchy reputation had preceded him. Kelly Van Patter, who was in charge of design on the first five seasons of both *Survivor* and *The Apprentice,* had been told to get the furniture for free, which turned out to be an impossible task in New York: Every company she approached turned her down flat, since Trump was a notorious deadbeat. She wound up signing small out-of-town vendors, who received DVDs of the show, a nice note, and the chance to say their work was featured on *The Apprentice.*

The original plan had been to pit "street smarts" against "book smarts," but when those categories proved too hard to define, the producers divided the teams by sex instead. The men named their team "Versacorp"; the women, "Protégé." The cast members included Troy McClain, a high school graduate from Idaho whose senior yearbook quote had been "Donald Trump, I'm coming"; Kwame Jackson, a Harvard graduate from Goldman Sachs; Sam Solovey, a real estate flipper from Washington, D.C.; Ereka Vetrini, a senior marketing manager from New York; Omarosa Manigault, a Howard University graduate who had worked for the Clinton administration; Amelia (Amy) Henry, a spunky blond Texan marketer; and Bill Rancic, a middle-class entrepreneur from Chicago. Most of them were "regular cats trying to make it," as audio operator Richard Velazquez put it to me—they weren't actors pretending to be businesspeople. Many had earned MBAs; a few had impressive résumés.

That didn't mean they were unaware of the cameras—or the politics of casting. Sam Solovey knew he'd been cast as a stereotype, "the swarthy little guy who uses his hands when he talks," then paired with a roommate, Troy McClain, who'd never met anyone Jewish. Troy was just as self-aware: One day, Sam found a crib sheet sticking out of his new friend's bag, a list of country-boy phrases like "happier than a puppy with two peters." Troy told me that the list was his way of prepping to be a public figure: "You're like, 'Okay, well, I'm going to add to my narrative.'"

Bill Pruitt was the last producer who was hired to work on *The Apprentice,* fresh off his Emmy-winning work on *The Amazing Race.* A USC-trained, Coen-brothers-worshipping cinema buff, Pruitt had switched to reality production after 9/11, when some movie funding fell through. His early jobs had been sordid ones, filming drunk girls on MTV's *Sorority Life,* and, even worse, on Fox's *Paradise Hotel,* where a "grim detachment" ruled the day. "Mike Darnell would call down to the bosses and go 'Make them fuck, make them do stuff.' You felt like you were poking the lion in the cage to perform. It was sad. They're just staring back at you like, 'What do you want?'" Pruitt said. Then he'd landed his big break, on *The Amazing Race*— and by the time he got hired on *The Apprentice,* he was riding high, able to negotiate a good deal by playing the two jobs against each other. It was another solid opportunity: a network show with a clever format, working with top-flight producers like Bienstock, the cream of the post-*Survivor* industry.

His workdays were intense and all-encompassing: Pruitt directed teams of camera operators and audio technicians, helped to organize "tasks," and traced each team's dramas, their clashes and private moments, looking for stories. He was present for the boardroom sequences, as well. Like *Survivor, The Apprentice* had an inner circle, a group of top producers who interacted with Trump himself. The first time they met, Pruitt found Trump "very charismatic, very aloof in a movie star sort of way, playing the part and not altogether

unpleasant—just the titan that we wanted him to be." He had no illusions about Trump's history, but as Joel Klug had discovered, you
couldn't look away from him.

Trump could be collegial, too, particularly with the largely Black
and Latino crew, schmoozing at the crafts table, scooping up M&M's,
and asking, 'Who should I fire?'" German Abarca, a cameraman,
remembers "shooting the shit with him about the Yankees." That
first season, Trump wasn't sure the show would be a hit and he was
often distracted, said Pruitt. "It was like handling Marlon Brando on
Apocalypse Now, trying to organize his schedule."

Still, the show itself was going smoothly. The cast had great, telegenic personalities, and the competitive format, like that of *Survivor*
and *The Amazing Race,* produced solid stories. Each week, one team
would lose their challenge (for the first four challenges, the men lost),
and then meet Trump in the boardroom, where he—along with his
two deputies, the snowy-haired geezer George Ross and Carolyn
Kepcher, a deadpan blonde who ran Trump's golf course—asked
them questions. The first to get booted was David Gould, an MBA
from Stern Business School. He hadn't done anything wrong during
the challenge, so no one expected Trump to fire him. "We didn't even
have good footage on the guy," producer Jamie Canniffe told me,
with a laugh. "We were like, 'How are we going to make this story?'"

Stranger yet, Trump didn't merely say, "You're fired," he made a
gesture as he did so, pinching his fingers together, then jabbing the
air—they called it "the cobra." In the control room, there was a
murmur of shock. "It felt like he had just shot the guy," said Pruitt.

PRUITT'S FONDEST MEMORIES WEREN'T ABOUT TRUMP—THEY
were about coming up with cool, movielike sequences for the show,
creative improvisations that were their own kind of game. During
the tenth episode, after the teams were shuffled then split again,
Pruitt was having lunch in Central Park with another producer when
he got a panicked call: A task had fallen through. The two producers
grabbed separate pedicabs and raced to Midtown—and when they

arrived at Trump Tower, the room lit up. Marketing pedicabs would be a perfect replacement task.

Although Trump, who hated the rickshaw-like vehicles, nearly killed the idea, the producers assigned it anyway, and as the two teams began pedaling downtown, Pruitt had an idea, calling up a helicopter pilot who was on his way back from New Jersey, then asking him to try to capture some B-roll. "Freaking guy flies down and gets a shot as they're pedaling in formation down 5th Avenue like a wedge," Pruitt said, still aglow at the score.

A great story sometimes trumped strict accuracy. When her team brainstormed ways to make money off pedicabs, Texas marketer Amy Henry had an idea: They should sell ads on the sides of the pedicabs, like NASCAR cars. The way Pruitt remembered that interaction, the cameras didn't catch Amy saying it—and by the time they had started recording, Bill Rancic was backing Amy up, saying, "That's a great idea. We can put advertising on the rickshaw." Later on, when Pruitt knew that Bill was going to be the grand-prize winner, he crafted the episode to make the ads look like Bill's idea. This was the nature of the job, he said. They needed to include foreshadowing, in order to justify Bill's ultimate success, and there was no point in feeling guilty about it. "It just made sense, storytelling-wise."

Some participants "got" reality TV–making better than others. Like Richard Hatch and Dr. Evil before her, Omarosa Manigault embraced the role of troublemaker from the start. "You know how sharks bump and then they attack? She would bump a character—and Ereka was, for some reason, her target throughout the season—and then get Ereka in a spin-up, and then she would attack her," said Pruitt. German Abarca, who filmed many of Omarosa's fights, spoke about her with spooked awe. "She was hard-core. She wouldn't give in to anybody. Even Trump."

Other participants were less self-aware. Sam Solovey had applied for the show on a whim, then bribed his way up the enormous audition line, using this bit of mischief in order to stand out as a contestant. After he got cast, he read all of Trump's books—and although

Sam cringed, looking back on it, at the time, he had swallowed Trump's mythology whole, viewing the tycoon not as a fraud or a bully but as a fellow underdog. He fixated on small details about Trump's life, like the fact that Trump's father wore a hairpiece, like his own father. He hoped that Trump would find him just as relatable.

Instead, after a brief moment in the sun—Sam featured prominently in the lemonade stand task—he broke down, exhausted. Like Rhonda Rittenhouse on *The Bachelor,* Sam had offered up a perfect comedy clip to the editors, a bug-eyed moment of shock after he got fired. Sam became the show's clown, a sycophant who was one notch more obsessed with Trump than the rest of the Trump-loving cast. In the press, he was a good sport, embracing the jester's role—and during the show's live finale, he carried a briefcase of cash, a visual joke about him bribing Trump. It doubled as product integration: Without talking to NBC about his plans, Sam had cut his own side deal with Samsonite, who let him keep the briefcase.

Product integration was a sticky subject for the show in the first season, when major sponsors were wary of the untried format. Ted Smith, who was now a producer, did manage to nail down one significant partnership, with a private jet company called Marquis Jet, for which the women's team whipped up a "heavy testosterone" ad campaign, using aviation photos that resembled erections. During the majority of the season, however, the producers were forced to build their tasks around the only brand that they didn't have to cut a deal with: the Trump Organization. Contestants sold Trump apartments; they hawked Trump's decrepit casinos. When a team won, they got a ride in Trump's helicopter. Out of desperation, they even flacked Trump Ice, a branded bottled water whose label Kelly Van Patter found hilariously paradoxical: It showed Trump glaring in front of flame-red curtains, like a tacky devil.

In one way, this was a marketing failure: *The Apprentice* wasn't pulling in fat deals, which had always been Burnett's specialty. But it was also, perversely, a creative success for the series, since it left more room for goofy, likeable tasks, things like a scavenger hunt and a flea market challenge. Several challenges were pegged to New York settings, like Sotheby's or the Times Square Planet Hollywood restaurant. Smith felt especially proud of a New York art world challenge, in which each team worked with an emerging artist, flacking paintings like *The Hollowed Pussy*, an image of a taxidermized cat. That week, Omarosa was the one who got the boot, when Trump told her it was impossible to sell a product she didn't believe in.

Like all game shows, *The Apprentice* was regulated by the FCC. Before each boardroom scene, the inner circle, which included showrunner Jay Bienstock and producers Pruitt, Jamie Canniffe, Seth Cohen, and Katherine Walker, would meet with Trump in order to fill him in on how the players had been doing, since he hadn't been around for the shoot. No one was allowed to tell Trump whom to fire—and none of the boardroom scenes were scripted. But when Pruitt and his peers summarized the challenges, they tried to be as useful as possible, offering "two lights": a pair of contestants worthy of getting kicked off. These meetings were recorded, Pruitt told me: Bienstock had cannily decided to keep audio records in case the production was ever investigated as a game show. (Canniffe and Walker didn't remember them being recorded.)

Many weeks, Trump simply ignored this information, just as he had when he fired David Gould and shot him the cobra. He worked off gut reactions, instead. Sometimes, he'd simply lose his temper midway through interrogating a candidate, then say, "You're fired!" You could view this tendency two ways: On the one hand, Trump was firing people who didn't deserve to be fired. On the other hand, he had an undeniable instinct for lively TV, and for keeping everyone, including his producers, off-kilter. Trump could be crude in these scenes, reliably gross about the female contestants (Walker remembered him referring to one woman as "the one with big implants" and to Omarosa simply as "the Black chick"), and sometimes cruel. But his willingness to talk off the cuff made the boardroom sessions, which took many hours to film, pop— the dialogue felt persistently lively, darkly funny, and unpredictable. When Trump pushed for the show to make them longer, NBC agreed.

Pruitt was frustrated, initially. "I remember thinking, 'This blowhard. We're devoting more screen time to him?' What about our well-crafted stories? The way we make it seem like they're winning and they're actually going to lose? I *love* that stuff."

The longer the shoot went on, the more Pruitt saw glimmers of Trump's private self. During one meeting near Trump's golf course in Briarcliff Manor, Trump bragged, "Do you like this house? Melania doesn't even know about this house." It certainly sounded to Pruitt as if Trump were bragging about a private sex shack, although he couldn't know for certain. "In these tiny intimate gatherings, we would be privy to some of Trump's candor, for lack of a better term, and treat it as a—" Pruitt stumbled as he tried to explain the blend of emotions he felt. "But we would be observing."

Then, just before the final boardroom sequence, something ugly happened—and just as quickly, it got repressed. By then, there were no teams left, just two finalists: Kwame Jackson, the Black Harvard grad who had worked at Goldman Sachs, and Bill Rancic, the white Chicago entrepreneur. Each of these men had been deputized to organize a major event: Kwame was told to oversee a Jessica Simpson concert at Trump's Taj Mahal hotel, in Atlantic City, while Bill managed a celebrity tournament at Trump's golf course. The winner would receive a job with Trump, with a $250,000 yearly salary and the opportunity to develop his new Chicago hotel.

At one meeting, the inner circle, along with Trump's two deputies, Kepcher and Ross, began to discuss the players. As usual, they sketched out the options for Trump, debating which person he might fire and why. The way Pruitt remembered it, the mood leaned toward Kwame, who had delivered a fantastic concert, working hard to overcome significant obstacles—among them, the fact that he had been backstabbed by Omarosa, who was allowed back into the game by the producers after she was "fired." Bill's event had gone smoothly, but it was an easier task and he hadn't contributed as much. Even Trump's deputy judge Carolyn Kepcher, who ran the golf course, struck Pruitt as impressed by Kwame.

Then Trump spoke up. "Yeah, but would America really buy a nigger winning?" he said, to no one in particular. For Pruitt, the shock of the moment had been dreamlike, surreal: "I remember where I was looking, I remember what I was seeing, certainly what I was hearing. . . . Coughing, stammering, Carolyn's face flushed. . . . And then there was that nervous laughter. Not *compliance* by any means, but it's like, 'Next!,' like—'Skip that!'" No one said anything in response: "I think someone came in strategically with another question."

In Allen Salkin and Aaron Short's book *The Method to the Madness*, Kepcher denied this story, telling him, "I assure you if I heard the N-word being used I would remember, and I'd be disgusted. I do not remember such an incident." (Then she tried to take the email off the record.) Jamie Canniffe told me Trump had never used "language like that" in his presence; he said he didn't have a clear memory of this meeting, because there had been so many of them. Katherine Walker said she wasn't there for the meeting, the way Pruitt remembered (she'd produced only the first half of the episode, she said). But she backed Pruitt's story up: She had heard about Trump using the slur to refer to Kwame shortly after it happened, though she wasn't sure who had told her. She'd never heard him use that word before; she felt upset, especially on behalf of Kwame, for whom she had tremendous respect.

None of the other people who were present responded to inquiries. But one person who wasn't present that day did remember Trump saying something similar: In his memoir, *Disloyal*, Michael Cohen, Trump's former lawyer, who was often on set in his role as the co-president of Trump's TV production company, described a conversation with Trump, which took place four years after the finale, at the launch of the Trump International Hotel and Tower in Chicago. That night, Trump, who was reminiscing about his decision to choose Rancic, had told Cohen, "There was no way I was going to let this Black fag win."

Pruitt had heard Trump make plenty of crass remarks about women's bodies, but he'd never heard any racial slurs. He would think about the disturbing exchange many times, as the years passed. Maybe Trump had been trying to shock them, he thought; maybe he just felt freer in their private circle, after so many weeks together. "I don't know. But the intimacy of it all gave him the feeling that he could say what he did and think that none of us would think otherwise—or do anything about it. And in some respects, he was right."

CLAIRE SCANLON, WHO WORKED AS AN EDITOR ON *THE APPRENTICE*, had been taking gigs in reality TV since she'd left graduate school, eager to pay down her student debt. She'd had some satisfying jobs, making high-end documentaries for PBS, but in between, she also worked on Darnell's cheap, tawdry clip shows at Fox, sifting through crime footage that was so violent it gave her nightmares. *The Apprentice,* in contrast, felt like an opportunity to make something both cool and popular. Unfortunately, Scanlon's first stab at cutting the pilot, which she made "hectic and frenetic," to mimic the energy of downtown Manhattan, seemed to spook her boss, Jay Bienstock. Scanlon got bumped to night work.

Ultimately, Scanlon's lively early cut helped launch the show's distinctive style, which leapt from screwball-fast scenes of the contestants, running around a brightly lit Manhattan, to those eerie boardroom exchanges, which were striped by shadows, with long pauses and rhythmic music, as if they had been transmitted from some anteroom in Hell. And even after her demotion, Scanlon kept volunteering for extra shifts, eager to redeem herself. Because Trump made so many impulsive choices, a lot of the job involved producers and editors brainstorming together, trying to make his firings logical, then architecting in foreshadowing, by whatever means necessary. In the raw footage, Trump struck her as "dumb as bricks." He had screwed up so many scenes, the season wound up slathered with "ADR"—automated dialogue replacement—which meant rerecording Trump's dialogue, then editing it in as voiceovers.

When Scanlon screened the footage for the finale, it was obvious to her that Kwame Jackson deserved to win. She'd never seen the brainstorm that Pruitt described to me; she never heard Trump use a racial epithet, either, in any of the footage. But in her original cut of the boardroom discussion, Scanlon included a line from Trump in which he mused, "The optics would be great if I hired a Black man to run this. So I know it looks good, if I do." Her bosses asked her to remove that line. "They said, 'We can't show that to anybody.'" She dutifully trimmed the exchange out.

Scanlon would go on to edit two more seasons of *The Apprentice,* then got fired, two weeks before Christmas, after a male editor came back from paternity leave. By then, the spell of working on a glossy hit had worn off. Over the next decade, Scanlon would make the leap from reality TV to scripted series, from editing to directing. She'd built a successful career in shows she was proud of, like NBC's *The Office,* with a specialty in cool, female-friendly sitcoms like *The Mindy Project* and *Abbott Elementary.* When she looked back, *The Apprentice* struck her as grimy and corrupt. Why had she been so eager to please, she wondered. So desperate to fit in? The show's culture had been sexist at its core, a place where even powerful women spoke crudely about other women's bodies; and of course, it had had an awful outcome, selling Trump to voters. "Why did I want to be there? Who cares if it's popular, if it's a horrible show."

THE APPRENTICE DEBUTED ON JANUARY 8, 2004, TO DECENT RATings and mocking reviews. "Are you dumbstruck with amazement, even envy? Or are you seized by an urge to burst out laughing at this spectacle?" wrote Frazier Moore of the scene in which Trump invited the winners of the lemonade stand contest to his Louis Quatorze–themed apartment, bragging to them that it was a place he brought presidents and kings. "You will see, hear, think, dream, imagine, and vomit the name Trump," wrote Bob Longino, grading the show a C+.

A few weeks in, with *The Apprentice* getting walloped by *American Idol,* NBC switched it over to the "must-see" Thursday lineup. Only then did the show become a hit—and once the ratings rose, the coverage shifted. *Newsweek* put *The Apprentice* on the cover, praising Trump as "in a strange way, down to earth" and "as paternal as he is stern." If there had ever been any notion of switching hosts after the first season, it was gone. Now that the show was a hit, heavyweight sponsors stepped up to purchase lucrative product-integration deals, including Pepsi, Microsoft, and Procter & Gamble. By 2005, the cost to plug your product on *The Apprentice* had jumped to $2 million, with the profits split between Burnett and Trump, an extension of the sweet deal that Burnett had struck with CBS for *Survivor.*

Daley Haggar was an aspiring comedy writer from Texas, new to Los Angeles, when she took a low-level job on the tasks team. By season 2, there were no more lemonade stands. Instead, her job was mainly about brands, about creating a task—like, say, creating a new flavor of ice cream—then finding a company (in this case, Ciao Bella) to pay to play. The task-building part was fun, but the deal-making could feel "skeezy," particularly if the product itself was no good, like a gross vanilla-mint toothpaste from Procter & Gamble. Mark Burnett—who was spinning many plates that year, including producing a short-lived sitcom called *Commando Nanny,* based on his life—stopped by now and then, to offer the room far-out suggestions, like, "I have a vision of a blimp!" (In season 3, there was a Goodyear challenge.)

David Eilenberg, who had written for game shows like *The Weakest Link,* worked with Haggar; after the show ended, he would climb the ladder, working for Burnett and then Roku. Eilenberg saw things through a businessman's lens: To him, placing products on *The Apprentice* was just another form of creativity, part of the show's "spirit of experimentation." Viewers weren't being tricked, he insisted. By the mid-aughts, everyone understood that if Pepsi got mentioned, that meant Pepsi had paid the bill for the episode. It was elitist to argue otherwise, like saying the viewers were dumb.

When the tasks were fully developed, Haggar's team flew to New York to work on the filming, and over the next two seasons, her job kept expanding. At first, she monitored the contestants for cheating. Later on, she wrote Trump's cue cards, for various interstitial sequences, clarifying the story for viewers. Scripted dialogue didn't work for Trump, so Haggar's job was to nudge him to say positive things about the sponsors, boring but crucial facts that were contractually required. "They'd be like, 'Whatever you do, Trump has to say that Domino's pizza was founded in 1967 by Bob Domino!'" she joked. Trump would ignore these demands, refuse to do retakes, and then leave the set. "He wanted to go play golf or do Trump things. . . . And then of course, I'd get a call from Domino's: 'He didn't say the thing about Bob Domino!'"

Through her earphones, Haggar could hear all the on-set banter, which meant hearing Trump say "everything you'd expect"—sexist remarks, particularly, including nonstop commentary about the female contestants' bodies. During the second season, he griped that the women weren't hot enough, but when, the next season, the team cast a hottie, Haggar, with depressing intuition, knew that Trump would find her insufficiently hot. She was right: As soon as the female contestants left a meeting with him, she could hear him "yelling at the casting people and the producers, 'Come on, what's up with this chick! I said, "Get *hot chicks*"'—like, that whole deal."

The crew laughed this stuff off. Behind the scenes, it was a given that this was who Trump was, a sexist braggart who made piggish demands. "He seemed very harmless at the time, and I was not impressed," said Sarah Levy, a camera operator. Levy, who started working in season 2, dug the job itself, "leapfrogging" around Manhattan, chasing the action and collecting "beautiful B-roll." She rarely interacted with Trump—"unless you were rich, powerful, or beautiful, you were invisible to him"—although she knew he'd hit on one of her fellow camera operators, who was more his type.

Art director Van Patter repeatedly saw Trump say "horrible" things, openly, including asking the male contestants, "Hey, so, what do you think about her boobs? Would you love to fuck her?" The producers would yell "cut" and go talk with him privately, but no one stopped it. Noel Casler, who worked as a "talent wrangler" on the *Celebrity Apprentice* live finales, beginning in 2008—and who, after Trump was elected president, embraced a new role as an anti-Trump gadfly on Twitter—talked to me about some of Trump's more egregious acts, including taking Adderall backstage and making sleazy remarks about his daughter Ivanka, revelations Casler used as material in his stand-up act, daring Trump to sue. Audio operator Richard Velazquez backed Casler up on these allegations. "I can't say if he saw this guy sniffing Adderall. I can't say that, but I can say that Noel's not a big liar."

Few people took Trump's behavior seriously, at the time. To its crew, *The Apprentice* was self-evidently a rude comedy, a show that was as satirical, in its own way, as *Joe Millionaire*. It was always a shock whenever they spoke to the contestants, many of whom truly admired Trump and saw him as a professional and personal role model.

The hours were long; the pay was low. Haggar saw crew members snort coke to make it through the night. So yes, there were down-sides. But she could also see that this was how things were shaking out in her industry, around the turn of the twenty-first century. Haggar and her boyfriend, both aspiring comedy writers, didn't watch a lot of sitcoms, but they did watch *Survivor*, which felt more surprising, and in its way, more experimental, than anything else on network TV. The successful comedy writers she knew were complacent babies, a smug clique of white guys lounging at their pools. At Hollywood parties, when peers would curse her out—"all the writers and the wannabe writers: 'You're ruining everything!'"—Haggar refused to apologize for making a living. In fact, had Trump's career ended there, she would have been proud to have played a role. "Too bad it turned into a *Black Mirror* episode."

IN 2004, THE YEAR *THE APPRENTICE* DEBUTED, PATRIC VERRONE, a writer for the animated series *Futurama*, was the secretary treasurer of the Writers Guild of America West, part of a cadre of radicals who called for more aggressive tactics, including swelling the union's ranks by showing solidarity with writers from game shows and animated shows. Reality workers were a harder sell, he knew. The way most WGA writers saw it, the genre was the enemy—a wedge networks used to resist union demands, first in 1988, when the WGA struck for twenty-two weeks, and then again in 2001. If reality laborers suffered, maybe they deserved to.

Even so, there were reality crew members who were eager to join the cause. Among them was Daniel Shriver, who'd worked in various positions on shows that included *Manhunt* and *Big Brother 2*—he was the crew member who'd built a story around the *Big Brother* house being haunted, complete with a Ouija board. Around 2003, when Shriver was working on the show *Renovate My Family*, he heard a rumor from a fellow improv comic that the WGA might start organizing reality laborers. It felt like a dream come true: a small way to make the world a better place.

Shriver joined the WGA reality organizing committee, which found egregious code violations everywhere they looked, from time cards that simply read "WORKED," no matter how long the hours, to empty titles, which were often handed out in lieu of decent treatment. Sleep-deprived workers were forced to drive for hours to get home, risking their lives. Many people, among them Shriver himself, had struggled with on-set abuse, including sexual harassment. Reality workers tended to be young, single, and childless, without the advantages of their scripted-TV peers, like family money or connections. But mostly, they'd been trained to view nightmarish workplace conditions as normal, to take pride in simply surviving their jobs. Verrone called them "the Invincibles of the turn of the century."

In late 2005, after Verrone was elected president of WGA West, he promoted David Young, a veteran needleworker organizer, to be the executive director of the union's organizing unit. Young launched a set of aggressive protests, which were designed to draw attention to the reality industry. *The Apprentice* was a particularly juicy target: It was a network hit that explicitly celebrated firing people, workplace bullying, and corporate greed. In September 2005, when *The Apprentice* aired a short-lived spin-off starring Martha Stewart, protesters picketed an *Ad Age* conference, dressed as Trump and Stewart, their outfits plastered in brand names. They crashed a network panel at the Waldorf-Astoria and a panel of reality TV producers in Beverly Hills; they leafleted the Museum of Television & Radio. Kristen Parks, who worked for Burnett Productions, remembered her team ducking labor protests at Trump Tower. "We had to deal with every lunatic that wants to screw up the show," she said. To avoid any disruption, *The Apprentice* wound up printing out two call sheets, one as a decoy.

The WGA's complaints were two-pronged. On the one hand, they wanted better hours, pay, and benefits. On the other hand, they were protesting product integration. WGA writers shouldn't be forced to write ad copy, they argued—and if they *did* write it, they should get a cut. On a site called productinvasion.com, the group listed lurid examples, like an *Apprentice* episode in which the players gushed about a flop *Jumanji* spin-off called *Zathura*. They held a "Frankenbite contest," asking editors to send in patched-together dialogue. The only effort that went viral, however, was a goofy interactive page that took aim at Donald Trump himself. Earlier that year, Burger King had put out an interactive ad called "Subservient Chicken," in which customers bossed around a man in a chicken suit. The union's version, "Subservient Donald Trump," let you boss an animated Trump around, forcing him to scrub tables or play air guitar.

In May 2005, Verrone held a big meeting for people who worked in alternative TV genres, including animation and reality. Around four hundred people showed up—an impressive turnout, since everyone who attended risked getting fired or blacklisted. Ultimately, though, the meeting got heated. Some reality workers expressed doubts about describing themselves as "writers"; others were worried that pushing for better pay would kill the genre entirely.

Charles Kramer, a preditor who had worked on *The Osbournes,* was a strong advocate of organizing reality laborers, but he had been working on the issue from a different angle, helping organize editors with Local 700, the Editors Guild, a chapter of the International Alliance of Theatrical Stage Employees. When Verrone opened the floor, Kramer stood up to confront him. The WGA was working in bad faith, he argued. They wanted to swell the WGA's numbers to help increase their negotiating power, but they had no intention of following through and fighting for their rights. "Real" writers—scripted writers, that is—would never stand in solidarity with field producers from *The Bachelor.* Then Kramer stormed out.

In the end, the skeptics were proven right. In 2006, an early "vanguard" strike on *America's Next Top Model* fizzled, fast, when twelve workers got fired. (Dave Rupel, the showrunner for *The Real Housewives,* hired two of them, worried they'd be blacklisted.) Still, the efforts continued: In December 2007, at a rainy-day rally outside *American Idol* producer Fremantle Media, Tenacious D performed, and picketers carried signs reading "Unscripted? Yeah, write." Kai Bowe, one of the vanguard strikers who had been fired from *America's Next Top Model,* told the crowd, "If you are a writer or a producer in reality, the Writers Guild is your union. It's that simple." Verrone, who was acting as the day's MC, promised picketers that they'd be in the new contract, describing reality labor as, among other things, crucial leverage for the future, if WGA writers hoped to prevent "an army of non-guild writers" from taking over.

Instead, the WGA wound up dropping improved conditions for reality workers from their list of demands, shortly after contract negotiations started. *Big Brother* producer Jon Kroll, who supported the cause but was wary of the union's promises, felt disgusted. "Like, if you're going to do it, do it—but don't get a bunch of people to risk their jobs and then sacrifice them."

Verrone, who had remained active in the WGA through the 2023 strike, had had an impressive career as both an animator and a labor agitator. He had regrets, when he looked back on that difficult year. But he also argued that there was ultimately little the WGA could do, when it came to resolving the problem of reality labor: The cultural divide was too powerful in the end. Scripted writers might strike for digital rights, but not for healthcare for Daniel Shriver.

For Shriver, the failure was crushing. He had stuck his neck out for years, speaking to journalists about industry secrets like Frankenbites. He'd helped publicize a documentary about Hollywood work conditions called *Who Needs Sleep?*, even though it didn't mention reality. He'd become the lead plaintiff in a lawsuit against Rocket Science, which was filed in 2005 with the help of the WGA's lawyers. Ultimately, though, Rocket Science filed for bankruptcy, likely in order to avoid paying damages. Then, it changed its name.

Over the years, some organizing efforts did pay off, particularly on the bigger, more profitable reality TV franchises. In 2011, *American Idol* "flipped," unionizing with IATSE. In 2014, Mark Burnett postproduction employees won a union contract, and in 2023, postproduction workers on *The Amazing Race* unionized, as well.

But most reality TV jobs remained nonunion, fly-by-night gigs without any protections or any health benefits—a tradition that went back all the way to the audience participation era. In an interview on the WGA's Reality Unite website, *M*A*S*H* creator Larry Gelbart described the situation as an ancient scam, one that felt familiar from his early work in radio. Comedy stars wanted it to look as if they'd made up their own dialogue; employers didn't pony up for medical care, or anything at all. "Pensions? What pensions?

There were no pensions." Witnessing the exploitation of reality labor sixty years later "makes me feel very much as though this is where I came in," said Gelbart.

Inbal Lessner, who had made a good living working as an editor at Rocket Science, had attended that early WGA meeting in order to show support for her less well-compensated colleagues, but she found that many of her peers took "a Republican approach" to their labor: They thought that it was their job to cover health insurance and retirement, to figure it all out. Years later, at forty, with two kids, Lessner knew how much she'd lost. "I want those benefits," she said.

People close to power often shared this "Republican" attitude. Among them was Kristen Parks, Mark Burnett's reality coordinator, who had been paid around $700 a week when she helped cast *Survivor*, working seven days a week. Even when she got promoted, her salary never topped $70,000. Eventually, Parks burned out—and now, she was selling high-end real estate in Los Angeles. Parks had nothing but glowing praise for Burnett, whom she idolized as a genius—he could have been president himself, she told me. (She also liked Trump a lot.) Like Chuck Barris's loyal employees, way back in the 1970s, Parks had many nostalgic memories of her "nuts and fun" daredevil years, traveling the globe, living off wasabi peas and Diet Coke, sticking Post-it notes on her alarm clock to remind her where she was.

When it came to unionization, however, she rooted for management. "They went on strike and reality ate their lunch," Parks told me, with relish, looking back on the genre's triumph at the turn of the millennium. We were a few weeks into the 2023 WGA strike when we spoke, so she added, "And now they're going to do it again." It's not that she didn't have sympathy for low-paid workers, having been one—but in her view, reality television was a nonunion genre by definition. "I don't know that it's ever gonna change," she told me. She used the term "snowglobing" to refer to certain types of jobs, the ones that had defined her youth. "Your life looks really awesome to everyone else, until someone shakes it really hard. And then you're like, Whoa! Everything is flying around! How do I get out of here?"

For Shriver, life took a steeper dive. When the WGA effort failed, he got blackballed—a producer friend warned him that he was likely on a list of "don't-hires." Step by step, he slipped below the poverty line, a situation intensified by problems in his personal life, among them a messy custody battle. By the time we spoke, Shriver's efforts to get health insurance for his peers struck him as deeply ironic: At sixty, he was about to get a hip replacement, using low-quality state-provided insurance, while living off food stamps and using hotel vouchers for housing. In a dark mood, he told me that rather than using him as a source, I'd write his obituary.

When I asked why he was still open to taking reality TV jobs, Shriver said that he didn't have a lot of options. "It sucks to be the tip of the spear," he told me—and he knew he wasn't likely to find work in the industry. But he also made the joke Patric Verrone had made, the one that *everyone* in Hollywood makes, eventually. In it, a man has a job sweeping up elephant shit in the circus. It's a grueling, humiliating gig, impossible to do without getting dirty, with long hours and low pay. But when someone asks him why he doesn't just quit, he blows up: "What—and leave show business?"

IN 2004, EARLY IN THE SECOND SEASON OF *THE APPRENTICE,* Trump and Mark Burnett spoke on a panel at the Museum of Television & Radio. Surreally enough, the moderator was Billy Bush, the *Access Hollywood* host who would, one year later, wind up on a hot mic with Trump, talking about what stars could get away with. During the panel, Trump hunched forward, hands clasped, his mood sour. He griped about losing the Emmy to *The Amazing Race* ("this piece of crap"); he groaned about the HBO version of *Angels in America* winning prizes (out of loyalty to Roy Cohn, maybe?); he mocked his critics in cruel, personal terms ("this fat slob Joy Behar"). The ratings for *The Apprentice* were dropping, but you'd never know it to hear him talk.

Burnett, on the other hand, seemed cool and confident. Wearing jeans and a necklace made of shells from Borneo, he cheerfully batted away Bush's surprisingly tough questions—Had Burnett softened Trump's more abrasive qualities for the screen? Was reality TV a fad? Was it cruel?—and steered the discussion, always, toward praise for Trump. With a smile, Burnett described his star as "a real American maverick tycoon," who "will say whatever he wants," a hero like "the men who built the old West." He explained that America had become a global leader "because of guys like Donald, who create jobs and a tax base that can support the entire planet." Burnett described *The Apprentice* itself as a love letter to his adopted country, a show about "what makes America great."

Over the next six seasons of *The Apprentice*, Trump's on-air persona grew harsher. He recast his sycophantic deputies with his sycophantic children. The producers experimented with fresh show structures, taking another run at "book smarts" versus "street smarts." (Trump had always wanted to do a "race war" season, but it never happened.) Still, the ratings dropped. In 2007, after the show had been pulled from the schedule—then revived, months later—Burnett agreed to split the product integration fee three ways, among himself, Trump, and NBC. An impending writers strike helped convince Ben Silverman, the new NBC president, to keep Burnett's failing show going, by repackaging it as *The Celebrity Apprentice*.

During this period, Trump—who had, way back in 1990, licensed a syndicated game show called *Trump Card*—produced a few short-lived reality shows without Burnett's involvement, all of them about models being trained to behave better. The first was MTV's *Pageant Place*, then *The Girls of Hedsor Hall* (originally called *Lady or a Tramp*), featuring a former Miss USA, Tara Conner, whom Trump had "saved" after she nearly lost her crown for underage partying. When Rosie O'Donnell called Trump a sexist hypocrite, he did a media tour sneering that Rosie was fat and ugly, insinuating that she wanted to screw Tara Conner. That buoyant day at Wollman Rink, when O'Donnell and Trump worked together to help boost *Survivor*, was ancient history.

In 2008, Burnett and Trump launched *The Celebrity Appren-*

tice, which featured faded stars, plus a few corrupt politicians, like Rod Blagojevich. Instead of doing business challenges, the quasi-celebrities competed to raise money for charities. It was a slippery setup, one that bore a certain resemblance to the Trump Foundation, another enterprise that had been designed to make a deadbeat look like a philanthropist.

Finally, in August 2015, NBC fired Trump. That year, he had launched his presidential campaign, gliding down the Trump Tower escalator, then delivering an angry speech in which he called Mexican immigrants rapists. At the time, that kind of rhetoric crossed the line for NBC. But seemingly every day that followed, that invisible line would be nudged, and then crossed, again and again, until it was hard to remember what people once considered unacceptable.

When Trump was elected president, some of the people who had worked on *The Apprentice* felt responsible, even (and based on my interviews, especially) those low on the call sheet. Camera operator Sarah Levy lamented that they had "created this false view of him." Former audio technician Richard Velazquez told me, "It kills me, because we created this jerk. We assisted him with his plans. It's our fault." Velazquez, who'd grown up in the projects on the Lower East Side, got along fine with Trump, back when he was filming him in his helicopter. He'd never heard him make racist remarks. "He's not stupid, he's from New York, man. There's levels to this shit. He's not going to run around shouting the N-word in productions. But if he feels a certain kind of way about a guy? I wouldn't put it past him." Still, Velazquez, who ultimately worked his way up in the reality industry, becoming an executive producer, had always understood exactly whom he was working for: a "mobbed-up deadbeat," an "entitled prickazoid."

For others, however, the cognitive dissonance never entirely dissolved. Yes, Trump was a phony-baloney, deep in debt, who was playing a cartoon version of himself. But that was the whole *point* of the reality genre: It was a guilty pleasure, grounded in what Trump (or really, his ghostwriter Tony Schwartz) had called, in *The Art of the Deal,* "truthful hyperbole." Trump was "great TV, because he had no filter," said Jamie Canniffe, who had started as a low-level producer in season 1, then rose through the ranks to become *The Apprentice* showrunner through season 6. Canniffe was happy to talk about the show, but he waved away all questions about politics: *The Apprentice* was made as entertainment, he emphasized. "We made him seem like a superhero. But that was our job—to protect our host. And the bigger and more successful he was in the show, the better the show was, because the higher the stakes were for people who wanted to work for him, and that all connected."

Producer Ted Smith, who continued to work for Mark Burnett, was certain that Trump would lose the election after he insulted John McCain, and then, after the *Access Hollywood* tape—he was confident he'd lose all the way through Election Day. Even if Trump wasn't his "cup of tea," Smith said, that didn't mean he wasn't proud of *The Apprentice*. To him, Mark Burnett was a modern Willy Wonka, which he meant as high praise: He was the ultimate marketer.

That was the taboo truth about *The Apprentice*, in the end—the quality that made it more impressive, not less. Anyone could rebrand a mediocre businessman, some small-timer in need of a glow-up. But taking a failed tycoon who was a heavily in hock and too risky for almost any bank to lend to, a crude, impulsive, bigoted, multiply-bankrupt ignoramus, a sexual predator so reckless he openly harassed women on his show, then finding a way to make him look attractive enough to elect as the president of the United States? That was a coup, even if no one could brag about it.

As Trump's political career heated up, one member of the *Apprentice* cast spoke out: Kwame Jackson. During the first season, Kwame had been the rare cast member who wasn't especially impressed by Trump—and was under no illusion about his own casting, either. When a fraternity buddy of Kwame's had read a casting notice on the Wharton alumni list, he had called Mark Burnett Productions directly, to let them know that he and Kwame—Black graduates of Wharton and Harvard, working at J.P. Morgan and Goldman Sachs—were available. When they met with casting director Rob LaPlante, they joked that only one of them could get cast, due to the one-Black-guy rule that was common knowledge.

Like Trump himself, Kwame viewed *The Apprentice* as a branding platform, a potential route to a career a bit sexier than Wall Street, maybe entrepreneurship or television itself. Handsome and deep-voiced, Kwame came across well on the air; he avoided creating too much drama until that final round, when he had his showdown with Omarosa, the only other Black contestant. He didn't feel cheated or blame Bill for how things had ended. But he had always known that race would play a role, in the form of "tribalism." He knew how Trump—and other white men—thought, unconsciously or consciously: "Bill Rancic looks like me, talks like me, *reminds* me of me."

In April 2016, early in the primaries, Kwame became the first contestant to speak out publicly against Trump, who had been attacking Obama with the "birtherist" libel for half a decade. Although contestants from every season of *The Apprentice* and *The Celebrity Apprentice* were invited to the press conference, which was called by season 4 winner Randal Pinkett, only four showed up: Kwame; Tara Dowdell, from season 3; Randal Pinkett; and Marshawn Evans Daniels, also from season 4, who appeared on video. All four were Black—and no one else from Kwame's season participated.

"This is no time to be silent," Kwame told journalists, invoking the need to speak "loudly at the precipice of fascism" and arguing, "Let us choose Kennedy over Kardashian-ism each and every time." Kwame made several more polished appearances on CNN and Fox, arguing, with calm clarity, that Trump was not merely a bad candidate, but a danger to the country. "You have a chance to step into the void," Kwame told me. "And when you let that moment pass, you regret it forever."

He had no question about who was responsible for Trump's rise: Mark Burnett, whom he described as a coward for having never spoken out. Several of his own cast members, including his friend Troy McClain, had also supported Trump. "They made their choices, too," said Kwame.

TRUMP'S TIME IN OFFICE WOULD BE STUDDED BY REALITY TV stunts, ultratheatrical, half-fake, half-real spectacles, beginning with that choreographed glide down the escalator. There was the live televised cabinet meeting, in which Mike Pence and Reince Priebus slavishly praised their boss, as if they were in the *Apprentice* boardroom. There was the time he tried to stage a Supreme Court choice as a race between two finalists. Trump even hired Omarosa to work for the administration, although that worked out as well for him as it had for Kwame.

For Mike Fleiss, the creator of *The Bachelor,* Trump's rise felt like an indelible stain on the genre, exposing something existentially rotten in the industry. "All that talk about the decline of Western civilization and the sign of the apocalypse? It turned out to be true," he said. Like Kwame, he blamed Mark Burnett, who he believed had used Donald Trump as an avatar for his own ambitions. After all, who would be the better candidate for president: Trump, a bankrupt has-been with no self-control, or Burnett, a man who actually understood the Art of the Deal? An immigrant couldn't run for president, so becoming a kingmaker would have to suffice.

Fenton Bailey, the co-creator of *RuPaul's Drag Race,* argued that the opposite was true. "It incenses me to see people say that Trump was a reality TV president," he told me. "No, he wasn't. Here's the thing about Trump. Trump is someone who has proven himself, again and again, to be able to corrupt *everything* he touches." The way Bailey saw it, Trump ruined reality TV, not the other way around. Yes, *The Apprentice* had taken Trump's failed casinos— "The Taj Mahal, which smelled of rotting carpet and manky old sheet rock," he sniffed—and made them look glamorous. Yes, Burnett was a hypocrite, a loud-and-proud Christian who propped up a sinner. But the genre itself wasn't the problem. Trump had left a stain on real estate, Twitter, and democracy as well.

A few years into *The Apprentice,* Bill Pruitt left the show that he helped create, disenchanted by seeing it evolve into "a forty-minute-long commercial." He began to sign up "for any show that had 'Deadliest' in the title," traveling all over the globe. Pruitt filmed seafaring shows; he worked on high-octane athletic competitions. Eventually, he settled into making food reality shows, a stable, lucrative berth. Pruitt knew that he had been a lucky man, having put his kids through college working in the genre, making shows that viewers loved.

Despite it all, Pruitt took pride in *The Apprentice*. Two things could be true at the same time. Like Velazquez, he had no trouble acknowledging that the show elected Trump. "We propped that guy up at season one, like nobody's business. His empire was crumbling." Like Kwame, he had spoken up in the press, one of the only producers to do so. When the "pussy tape" leaked, a month before the election, Pruitt tweeted, spontaneously, that there were worse tapes—tapes that Burnett controlled. (Burnett's representative responded that MGM controlled the *Apprentice* material, not Burnett. She also called the idea that Burnett was politically influential "COMPLETELY FALSE": "Burnett's star left the show, and his show was canceled. He had a star who was interested in politics. Would have been better for Burnett had he not run so he could keep the show on the air.")

Over the years, Pruitt had patiently given quotes to journalists, feeling morally obligated to tell people what he knew, NDA or no. Yet Pruitt, like Bailey, believed that it was wrong to blame reality television for what had happened with Trump—or to lump the two together. *The New York Times* had helped elect Trump, he pointed out. Rupert Murdoch and Fox had done it, too. The publishers of *The Art of the Deal* (which are also the publishers of this book) were responsible, and so were CNN, the WWE, and the leaders of the Christian Right. Everyone ignored the danger Trump posed to the country, because he was too good for business. Pruitt's genre was more than its worst moments, he argued: Sometimes it was glorious and sometimes it was ugly, but it was ultimately too rich—and too mesmerizing—to dismiss. The people who made it shouldn't be dismissed, either. "People work just as hard to make shows that they sell their souls for," Pruitt told me.

EPILOGUE
Fake It Till You Make It

YOU CAN'T ALWAYS TELL THAT SOMETHING HAS CHANGED—OR that it's changed you—until it's over. Critics had written off reality programming as a fad back in the 1940s, when mouthy civilians first shook up the economics of radio; and in the 1970s, during the flare-ups over *An American Family* and *The Gong Show;* and then again in the 1990s, when Fox and MTV set out to disrupt the major networks. They were sure the genre was toast after *Who Wants to Marry a Multi-Millionaire?,* and double-sure after 9/11. But in the end, all of our faces got stuck that way.

When did the beginning end? Maybe around 2004, when *The Apprentice* turned product integration into a variety show talent, no different from ballroom dancing or fashion design. Or maybe the pivot was 2006, after the rise of *The Real Housewives,* around the time that cast members began to identify as influencers, viewing themselves as performers and collaborators, brand representatives, rather than subjects, of the shows they appeared in. By then, the reality industry was no longer an experiment. The short-lived WGA attempt to organize unscripted workers had tanked. Nearly two decades later, when WGA and SAG-AFTRA went on strike in 2023, the conditions of reality laborers barely came up in the media, and although a few crew members were unionized, the cultural divide between the unscripted and unscripted worlds remained a chasm.

Even so, reality production had solidified into its own distinct profession, with its own craft, traditions, mentors, and university classes, taught by industry veterans. If you made your living as a field producer or an editor for a reality series, you might still get the stink eye at some Hollywood party, but there were other parties to dance at. If you were lucky, talented, or brutal enough to scramble up over the other crabs in the reality barrel—often with the imprimatur of a powerful executive producer like Mark Burnett, a global company like Endemol Shine, or an institution that taught an established house style, like Bunim/Murray or Bravo—there was big money to be made.

Reality veterans had developed a defiant pride in their craft. "Reality is such a great training ground. You learn so many skills and you do more jobs than they'll let you in the scripted world," said camera operator Sarah Levy, who had jumped from work on shows like *Big Brother* to scripted series like *Parks and Recreation*. She'd seen her share of the ugly stuff—while filming the show *Wife Swap*, she'd watched a deeply devout woman get goaded into a breakdown—but she'd worked on emotionally powerful shows, too, projects that were stages for rich, empathetic portraits of human behavior. Not every reality show was the same, any more than every drama or sitcom was the same. She no longer hid her work history—and she thought there was a lot that "scripted" people could learn from people who worked on the other side, if they wanted to listen.

Richard Velazquez, who had risen from audio to co–executive producer on *The Apprentice*, then went on to become a director and producer, making adventure reality series like *Alaskan Bush People*, felt the same way. "Here's what's funny, we're like the wild, wild west, the dregs—and they look down their nose at us. But we'll do shit that they can't accomplish. Meaning, I'll show up with a crew to a location I've never been at and get that shit lit and shot, and show a pretty dope story with some really nice movement. They need three months to plan two pages! We don't need that."

Even when the culture looked down on reality shows, it was saturated with their influence, and often in direct dialogue with them. Each year, scripted satires of the genre became more scathing and surgical, in the hands of brilliant creators like Nathan Fielder, Tim Robbins, and Sacha Baron Cohen, who nailed the self-delusion and manipulations of the job, on both sides of the camera. Just as *The Office* had been inspired by early British reality TV, the best modern comedies were allergic reactions to reality's cultural dominance, including the transcendent HBO series *The Comeback* and the brilliant British comedy *I Hate Suzie,* in which Billie Piper played a reality star devoured by her own craving for the spotlight. Reality TV was too important a subject for satire to ignore.

But most people who worked in the reality business didn't feel like they had to justify their craft anymore. They were building fun, satisfying mass entertainments, shows that viewers adored and understood. As more than one crew member told me, everyone had their own line—the thing they wouldn't do. (For a surprising number of them, that was dating shows.) But reality television wasn't the only job where that was true.

REALITY CASTS HAD CHANGED, TOO. FOR MORE THAN HALF A century, the crucial ingredient of reality shows had been naïveté. People who signed up for these programs trusted producers, viewing them as friends, mentors, and even psychologists. They skimmed the fine print and asked few questions—and for a long time, it was hard to know *what* to ask, anyway. On-set boundaries were weak, on purpose, because intimacy was the best way to get people to open up.

That had always been the dark, resonant paradox of the reality genre: The less ethical a show was, the more authentic the footage it captured. The more trusting (or drunk or exhausted) the participants were, the more likely it was that they'd ultimately crack, releasing a flood of feeling that couldn't be faked. This was most obvious on prank shows back to *Candid Camera,* but if you looked at things from a certain angle, *all* reality shows looked like prank shows.

In the wake of *Survivor,* that naïveté began to dissolve. There had always been a few stars, like Pedro Zamora and Will Kirby, who saw themselves as full collaborative partners in the shows they starred in, working with producers and directors to shape their narrative. Now those pioneers were role models. Anyone who moved into the *Big Brother* house or auditioned for Bravo understood that if they cried or picked a fight, they'd get screen time; they could be savvy about embracing a villain edit or sparking a showmance, leaning into the genre's clichés instead of resisting them. Sometimes, cast members set out to fake their way into fame, but often they were seeking a unique emotional high. On a reality show, you had the chance to fall in love with a stranger or confront the limits of your physical strength, witnessed by a global audience. For many people, doing this kind of television wasn't a naïve misstep at all—it was a conscious choice to participate in an extreme sport, one whose risks they embraced.

That didn't mean no one got hurt. Casting departments still regularly picked people who were too innocent or too unstable to understand the implications of that contract, which forbade you from complaining about Frankenbites, not to mention more insidious mistreatment. Decades into the genre's maturity, a few cast members had begun pushing back, including the *Real Housewives* star Bethenny Frankel, an unlikely Norma Rae, as well as stars of shows like *Love Is Blind* and *Below Deck,* who had begun speaking up about on-set abuse. A small but growing subset of activists had a long-term vision: to blow up the most outrageous parts of the standard contract, which were surely illegal—and one day, to set up guardrails on set, to get reality stars decent pay and more humane treatment.

Still, many contestants had a clear-eyed awareness of the bargain they had struck. This made the shows phonier, but also more fair. (They bought their tickets, they knew what they were getting into. I say, let 'em crash.) Members of this new breed were, arguably, better prepared to handle "reality fame," which was often their goal in auditioning in the first place. Facebook launched in 2004, YouTube in 2005, Twitter in 2006. When the iPhone debuted in 2007—a reality studio tucked in your back pocket—a new breed of self-promoters emerged, canny about the long game. Even if their worst moment got played on a loop, they understood there were ways to capitalize on that, by transubstantiating from a civilian into a brand, a magnet for partnerships.

It had been a long time since Lance Loud, during his final interview with the Raymonds, described the pride he took in not ever having sold out, refusing to sell a dance bar in the Valley the rights to his name, unwilling to barter away "whatever little magic" his time on *An American Family* had produced. For a generation raised by Kim Kardashian, that attitude was as foreign as punk rock.

THE BIGGEST CHANGE, HOWEVER, WASN'T IN THE PEOPLE WHO made reality shows or the people who starred in them. It was in the people who watched them.

For half a century, viewers had giggled at *Candid Camera*, been unsettled by *An American Family*, and hooted and howled at *Cops*. They'd been charmed by the *Real World* kids and snickered at *Who Wants to Marry a Multi-Millionaire?* They weren't fans of reality TV, though—that was a category that didn't exist yet. They were more like rubberneckers, riveted by the latest train wreck.

By the early aughts, that was no longer true. A new audience, which had grown up watching these franchises, had fully embraced the genre, *as* a genre, without expecting it to be something it wasn't. Sometimes these fans favored one format, following *Survivor* the way baseball fans followed the Yankees, obsessing over statistics and bios. Sometimes they were students of a niche subgenre, like cooking contests; sometimes they identified with a giddy sorority, like the Bravoholics or Bachelor Nation, worshipping their favorites and tearing them to bits, often at the same time. Online or off, these viewers threw themselves into spirited and sometimes surprisingly profound arguments about shows the world considered irredeemably shallow. For them, reality had become a shared language, a way to talk about who they were and what they valued, what was fair and what was authentic, a debate conducted in in-jokes and memes, podcasts and charticles, through group text and office talk. Like all gossip, it was a coded way to talk about politics, large and small.

You could see a glimpse of this kind of viewer in *The Truman Show,* in brief scenes that were sliced into Truman's own story: a bald man watching TV in a bathtub; two elderly women wearing bathrobes, on their sofa; two waitresses serving throngs of fans in a Truman-themed bar. Their homes were full of Truman merchandise, even a scribbled crayon portrait of Truman pinned to the wall of a frazzled mother's kitchen. Fans this devoted weren't especially concerned about exposing the magic trick—that wasn't *their* code. If something on a reality show looked fake, well, that was part of the fun, since they were in on it. If something looked genuine, that was wonderful, too.

For these viewers, there was no controversy—any qualms about the medium had faded, long ago. The most successful reality show had it all: a titillating flash of the authentic, framed by the dark glitter of the fake, like a dash of salt in dark chocolate. No taste was harder to resist.

||||||

ACKNOWLEDGMENTS

I'd just begun the research for this book when Covid hit, in March 2020—and then I spiked a fever after taking a red-eye from Los Angeles, just after talking to John Langley about *Cops*. For more than a year, as I did interviews over the phone and via Zoom, I was dealing with the confusing symptoms of long Covid (which receded gradually after the Moderna shot, thank God). So while I would already be grateful to my husband, Clive, I particularly appreciate his support back when I was taking two mysterious naps a day and worried that my brain had turned to Swiss cheese. A loving, funny presence, brilliant brainstormer, and sharp structural thinker, he helped me untangle the Funt section, sat with me in a hotel courtyard full of rats when I struggled with the intro, and did tech support after Scrivener crashed; without him, this book would not exist. So if you have any problems with it, blame Clive.

I also want to thank Laura Miller, who read several chapters in early draft form, but, more important, let me rant to her about the Barris '70s and every detail of the obscure British show *Living in the Past*, often when she was recovering from hip surgery, as if we were in some inverted version of Stephen King's *Misery*.

My editor, Ben Greenberg, was a wonderfully patient listener as I worked out the problems with early drafts, which took a while—and I'm particularly grateful to him for helping to come up with the genius concept for the cover, and also for adding the exclamation point. Deep thanks as well to my excellent agent, Suzanne Gluck, for her savvy guidance in the confusing world of publishing and for championing and believing in this book. I also owe a major debt of gratitude to Courtney Hodell, who pinpointed a crucial structural issue, inspiring me to rethink the book's chronology and several key themes.

Major thank-yous to A. O. Scott, Daniel Zalewski, Ariel Levy, Andrew Marantz, Alex Barasch, and Bob Kolker, who gave me invaluable feedback on early chapter drafts, as well as to James Poniewozik and Michelle Goldberg, who generously read a late draft of the whole book. Thank you to Ron Simon and the Paley Center for Media, for help with research, and to the Beinecke Rare Book and Manuscript Library at Yale, for access to the Lance Loud archives. I'm grateful as well to David Remnick, a great boss, for his support and inspiration during this protracted process.

Deep thanks to the many friends who helped me think this subject through, often over drinks, including Selina Alko, Christine Connor, Jelani Cobb, Vinson Cunningham, Kirsten Danis, Brooke Gladstone, Dave Gutman, Karen Hill, Anna Holmes, Fred Kaplan, Larissa MacFarquhar, Sasha Nemecek, Ellen Umansky, Michael Schulman, Rachel Syme, Jordan Thomas, my fabulous sister-in-law Carlye Adler, and the Office Hours drinks crew, among them, Josh Furst, James Hannaham, Jeanne Heifetz, Arlene Keizer, Jonathan Lethem, Christopher Molanphy, J. T. Price, Martha Southgate, and Bill Tipper. Thank you as well to Michael Chabon and Ayelet Waldman, for giving me key advice in the nick of time. And to my wonderful sons, Gabriel and Zev, who let me read unbaked passages out loud.

My fact-checkers for this book, Jane Bua, Sean Lavery, Parker Henry, and Rachel Stone, are an amazing, rigorous, and thoughtful crew. They went above and beyond in trying to nail down the details of this much-disputed story, including issues where sources disagreed about what happened. If there are mistakes in the book, they're mine, not theirs.

Thank you to the fantastic staff at Random House, including the great copy chief Loren Noveck, copyeditor Liz Carbonell, proofreader Diana D'Abruzzo, and PDF rabbi Leila Tejani; as well as Michelle Jasmine and Michael Hoak, publicity and marketing whizzes, for helping get this sucker out into the world.

Finally, a huge thank-you to all of the book's sources for their candor. I hope I've done a decent job representing the genre, in its many contradictory shadings, and that this book helps viewers understand the value of your labor, on both sides of the camera—and how much you deserve to be compensated and protected in the workplace.

‖‖‖‖

BIBLIOGRAPHY

The majority of this book is based on in-depth interviews I did with more than three hundred sources, including network executives, show creators, executive producers, field producers, editors, preditors, camera operators, audio technicians, production assistants, psychologists, casting directors, and cast members—the vast labor base that has helped build the reality genre over seven decades. These generous sources are mostly named in the text, although I also spoke to several people off the record, to confirm or clarify stories. I also relied on the magnificent database of the Television Academy's "The Interviews" site, a jaw-dropping resource for anyone interested in early television history.

In addition, I used the following resources, which range from academic monographs to dishy memoirs, along with online oral histories, newspaper criticism, podcasts, and fan sites. Some books are listed under one chapter, but helped to inform other chapters as well. At the end, I've included a broader list of books on reality TV that I used for context, insight, or to challenge my ideas, but which didn't fit directly into any particular chapter.

INTRODUCTION: BETTER WRITE THAT ONE FAST

Meyrowitz, Joshua. *No Sense of Place: The Impact of Electronic Media on Social Behavior* (New York: Oxford University Press, 1986).
Sanneh, Kelefa. "The Reality Principle: The Rise and Rise of a Television Genre." *New Yorker,* May 9, 2011.

CHAPTER 1: THE REVEAL

Television Academy interviews

Charlie Andrews, Bob Banner, Allan Burns, Sonny Fox, Marge Greene, Bill Klages, Arnie Kogen, Charles Lisanby, Barney McNulty, Bertram van Munster, Bernie Orenstein, Joan Rivers, Arthur Schneider, Saul Turtel-taub

Books and journals

Blake, Howard. "An Apologia from the Man Who Produced the Worst Program in TV History." In *American Broadcasting: A Source Book on the History of Radio and Television,* edited by Lawrence W. Lichty and Malachi C. Topping (New York: Hastings House, 1975).

Cassidy, Marsha F. "The Cinderella Makeover: *Glamour Girl,* Television Misery Shows, and 1950s Femininity." In *The Great American Makeover: Television, History, Nation,* edited by Dana Heller (New York: Palgrave Macmillan, 2006).

———. *What Women Watched: Daytime Television in the 1950s* (Austin: University of Texas Press, 2005).

Cox, Jim. *The Great Radio Audience Participation Shows: Seventeen Programs from the 1940s and 1950s* (Jefferson, N.C.: McFarland, 2001).

Crosby, John. *Out of the Blue: A Book About Radio and Television* (New York: Simon & Schuster, 1952).

Dunning, John. *On the Air: The Encyclopedia of Old-Time Radio* (New York: Oxford University Press, 1998).

Funt, Allen. *Eavesdropper at Large: Adventures in Human Nature with "Candid Mike" and "Candid Camera"* (New York: Vanguard Press, 1952).

Funt, Allen, with Philip Reed. *Candidly, Allen Funt: A Million Smiles Later* (New York: Barricade Books, 1994).

Funt, Peter. *Self-Amused: A Tell-Some Memoir* (Jefferson Bay Books, 2021).

Hilmes, Michele. *Only Connect: A Cultural History of Broadcasting in the United States.* 3rd ed. (Boston: Wadsworth Cengage Learning, 2011).

Kisseloff, Jeff. *The Box: An Oral History of Television, 1920–1961* (New York: Viking Penguin, 1995).

McCarthy, Anna. "'Stanley Milgram, Allen Funt, and Me': Postwar Social Science and the 'First Wave' of Reality TV." In *Reality TV: Remaking Television Culture,* edited by Susan Murray and Laurie Ouellette (New York: NYU Press, 2009).

Meyrowitz, Joshua. "We Liked to Watch: Television as Progenitor of the Surveillance Society." *The Annals of the American Academy of Political and Social Science* 625 (September 2009).

Murray, Joan. *The News* (New York: McGraw-Hill, 1968).

Nadis, Fred. "Citizen Funt: Surveillance as Cold War Entertainment." In *The Tube Has Spoken: Reality TV and History,* edited by Julie Anne Taddeo and Ken Dvorak (Lexington: The University Press of Kentucky, 2010).

Riesman, David, with Nathan Glazer and Reuel Denney. *The Lonely Crowd: A Study of the Changing American Character* (New Haven: Yale University Press, 1950).

Rivers, Joan, with Richard Meryman. *Enter Talking* (New York: Delacorte Press, 1986).

Scheiner, Georganne. "Would You Like to Be Queen for a Day? Finding a Working Class Voice in American Television of the 1950s." *Historical Journal of Film, Radio and Television* 23, no. 4 (2003).

Slate, Sam J., and Joe Cook. *It Sounds Impossible* (New York: Macmillan, 1963).

Stern, Richard. *Golk* (Chicago: University of Chicago Press, 1987).

Tyrrell, Lou. *The Flying Phone Booth: My 3 Years Behind the Candid Camera* (New York: MBLT Marketing, Inc., 2011).

Watts, Amber. "*Queen for a Day:* Remaking Consumer Culture, One Woman at a Time." In *The Great American Makeover: Television, History, Nation,* edited by Dana Heller (New York: Palgrave Macmillan, 2006).

Periodicals and other sources

Barry, Ellen. "Trump's Love Affair with the Royal Family Dates Back to His Mother." *New York Times,* June 3, 2019.

The Best of Allen Funt's Candid Mike, vol. 1, Kermit Schafer Productions Bloopers label manufactured by RCA Custom, 1955, vinyl.

"'Candid Microphone' ABC's New Tape Recorded Show Radio's Most Novel and Amusing Program." *Audio Record* 3, no. 10 (November 1947).

Crosby, John. "Radio in Review: The First Year." *East Liverpool Review,* May 6, 1947.

——. "Radio in Review: '49 Model John J. Anthony." *Ottawa Journal,* February 26, 1949.

——. "Radio in Review: Misery Programs Are Peep Shows." *Oakland Tribune,* September 7, 1946.

Fritz, Jose. "The Goodwill Hour." Arcane Radio Trivia, October 6, 2009, tenwatts.blogspot.com/2009/10/goodwill-hour.html.

Giaimo, Cara. "How Candid Camera Spied on Muscovites at the Height of the Cold War." Atlas Obscura, December 8, 2015.

Hartwell, Dickson. "The Gadfly of Radio." *St. Louis Post-Dispatch,* October 5, 1950.

"Host John Crosby Has 18 Million Followers." *South Bend Tribune,* November 2, 1957.

"John J. Anthony Is Dead at 68; Radio's Marital Problem Solver." *New York Times,* July 18, 1970.

"Last Frontier of Privacy Falls to the Microphone." *Berkshire Eagle,* August 4, 1947.

Major, Jack. "Jack Treats 'Em All Like Queens: But Some Act Like Nuts." *Akron Beacon Journal,* May 19, 1963.

Meegan, Jean. "Radio's Problem: Too Much from Too Many: Critics Scream, Actors Howl, but Audience Participation Shows Go On and On and On." *Tampa Bay Times,* July 21, 1946.

Stewart, R. W. "Can't You Take a Practical Joke? 'The Candid Microphone' Eavesdrops on the Unsuspecting." *New York Times,* November 23, 1947.

Torre, Marie. "TV-Radio" (Jack Bailey profile). *Bangor Daily News,* March 10, 1960.

"Tribute to John J. Anthony." *Golden Days of Radio* podcast, September 10, 2018.

Yowp, Don. "Human Misery Is on the Air!" Tralfaz, February 28, 2018, tralfaz.blogspot.com/2018/02/human-misery-is-on-air.html.

CHAPTER 2: THE GONG

Television Academy interviews

Chuck Barris, Milton Delugg, Phyllis Diller, Bob Eubanks, Jamie Farr, Leonard Goldberg, Wink Martindale, Al Michaels, E. Roger Muir, Gary Owens, Fred Silverman

Books and journals

Baber, David. *Television Game Show Hosts: Biographies of 32 Stars* (Jefferson, N.C.: McFarland & Company, 2008).

Bailey, Blake. *Philip Roth: The Biography* (New York: W. W. Norton & Company, 2021).

Barris, Chuck. *Confessions of a Dangerous Mind: An Unauthorized Autobiography* (New York: St. Martin's Press, 1984).

——. *Della: A Memoir of My Daughter* (New York: Simon & Schuster, 2010).

——. *The Game Show King: A Confession* (New York: Carroll & Graf, 1993).

——. *You and Me, Babe* (New York: Carroll & Graf, 1974).

Buffington, Stephanie. *The Love Company* (Parker, Colo.: Outskirts Press, 2016).

Hadleigh, Boze. *Game Show Confidential: The Story of an American Obsession* (Essex, Conn.: Lyons Press, 2023).

Trow, George W. S. *Within the Context of No Context* (New York: Atlantic Monthly Press, 1997).

Wagman, Fredrica. *Playing House: A Novel.* 35th anniversary edition (Hanover, N.H.: Steerforth Press, 2008).

Periodicals and other sources

Andrews, Peter. "The Hating Game." *Saturday Review,* March 29, 1980.

Baltake, Joe. "No Good 'Stuff' in Gong Movie." *Philadelphia Daily News,* May 27, 1980.

Barthel, Joan. "King of TV Gamesmanship." *Life,* October 10, 1969.

Bowles, Jerry. "How to Be Your Own Best Seller: Authoroid Chuck Barris Engages His Ego in a Grand Promotion." *Esquire,* December 1974.

Breznican, Anthony. "CIA Hitman or Practical Joker?" Associated Press, January 5, 2003.

Carrion, Christian. "RIP Chuck Barris." Buzzerblog, March 22, 2017, buzzerblog.com/2017/03/22/rip-chuck-barris/.

"The Gong Show." *TV Guide,* April 15, 1978.

Harris, Harry. "Two Morning Game Programs Bow on ABC." *Philadelphia Inquirer,* December 21, 1965.

Hill, Michael. "The Good Guys Finish First for a Change." Baltimore *Evening Sun,* December 24, 1979.

Holston, Noel. "NBC Plans Amateur Show." Orlando *Sentinel Star,* May 3, 1976.

Kelly, Erin. "The Horrifying Story of Rodney Alcala, the Serial Killer Who Won 'The Dating Game' During His Murder Spree." allthatsinteresting.com /rodney-alcala-dating-game-killer, July 26, 2021.

Koehler, Joseph M. "Blind Date." *Billboard,* July 17, 1943.

"A Look at the Gong Show in 3-D." *Grand Prairie Daily News,* August 1, 1967.

Lowry, Cynthia. "No Brain Games for Chuck Barris." Associated Press, May 21, 1967.

———. "Things Change Rapidly for Chuck Barris on Networks." *El Dorado Daily News,* May 23, 1967.

Mathews, Jack. "Buddy Granoff: Women and TV." *Detroit Free Press,* December 21, 1979.

Mikkelson, David. "Fact Check: Up the Butt, Bob." Snopes, October 11, 2002.

Petersen, Clarence. "Chuck Barris Is a Very 'Game' Fellow." *Chicago Tribune,* August 31, 1972.

Polak, Maralyn Lois. "Interview: Mrs. Wagman Talks About Her Strangely Sexy Novel of Love, Incest and Suicide." *Philadelphia Inquirer,* July 7, 1974.

———. "Jaye P. Morgan: She Couldn't Keep Her Shirt On." *Philadelphia Inquirer,* March 13, 1983.

"A Popsicle Act Gets Gong Show in Trouble." *Chicago Sun-Times,* September 21, 1977.

Stoner, Carroll. "To Remember Pain Is Honest and Brave." *Philadelphia Inquirer,* July 29, 1973.

"3's a Crowd." Chuck Barris Wiki, chuckbarris.fandom.com/wiki/3%27s_A_Crowd.

CHAPTER 3: THE BETRAYAL

Television Academy interviews
James Day, Alan and Susan Raymond

Books and journals
Day, James. *The Vanishing Vision: The Inside Story of Public Television* (Oakland, Calif.: University of California Press, 1995).

Ephron, Nora. "No, but I Read the Book." In *Crazy Salad and Scribble Scribble: Some Things About Women and Notes on the Media* (New York: Vintage Books, 2012).

Goulart, Ron. *An American Family* (New York: Warner Paperback Library, 1973).

Holmes, Su. "The Television Audience Cannot Be Expected to Bear Too Much Reality: *The Family* and Reality TV." In *The Tube Has Spoken: Reality TV and History,* edited by Julie Anne Taddeo and Ken Dvorak (Lexington: University Press of Kentucky, 2010).

Killen, Andreas. *1973 Nervous Breakdown: Watergate, Warhol, and the Birth of Post-Sixties America* (New York: Bloomsbury, 2006).

Loud, Pat. *Lance Out Loud* (New York: Glitterati Incorporated, 2012).

Loud, Pat, with Nora Johnson. *Pat Loud: A Woman's Story* (New York: Coward, McCann & Geoghegan, 1974).

Ruoff, Jeffrey. *An American Family: A Televised Life* (Minneapolis: University of Minnesota Press, 2002).

Rupert, Laurie, and Sayanti Ganguly Puckett. "Disillusionment, Divorce, and the Destruction of the American Dream: *An American Family* and the Rise of Reality TV." In *The Tube Has Spoken: Reality TV and History,* edited by Julie Anne Taddeo and Ken Dvorak (Lexington: University Press of Kentucky, 2010).

Wilkes, Paul. *Six American Families: An Insider's Look into the Families Seen on National Television* (Office of Communication, United Church of Christ, 1977).

Wilkman, Jon. *Screening Reality: How Documentary Filmmakers Reimagined America* (New York: Bloomsbury, 2020).

Periodicals and other sources

Alexander, Shana. "The Silence of the Louds." *Newsweek,* March 12, 1973.

Farber, Jim. "Lance Loud Was an Early Reality Star. He Was Also a Gay Punk Pioneer." *New York Times,* May 31, 2021.

Gilbert, Craig. "Reflections on 'An American Family.'" *Studies in Visual Communication* 8, no. 1 (Winter 1982).

Hamerow, Eleanor. Personal video interview with Adam Nadler.

Holley, Tim. "Producer Bares Soul in Tale of Filming 'American Family,'" *Bridgeport Post,* February 18, 1973.

"Lance: His Life & Legacy—Lance & Andy Warhol." PBS, 2002, pbs.org /lanceloud/lance/warhol.html.

Maynard, Fredelle. "An American Family: The Crack in the Mirror." *Image* (WNET), January 1973.

Miller, Merle. "Dear Pat, Bill, Lance, Delilah, Grant, Kevin and Michele: I Loved You." *Esquire,* May 1, 1973.

"Nora Ephron Discusses Feminism and Her Book 'Crazy Salad,'" Studs Terkel Radio Archive, broadcast July 28, 1975.

O'Connor, John J. "TV: Arguments over 'An American Family' Are Smothering Its Contents." *New York Times,* January 22, 1973.

——. "TV: C.B.S. Views an American Family's Discontent." *New York Times,* November 24, 1971.

Rich, Frank. "Cinema: True Fakery." *Time,* March 5, 1979.

Roiphe, Anne. "'An American Family': Things Are Keen but Could Be Keener." *New York Times,* February 18, 1973.

Seligsohn, Leo. "Live-In TV Crew Paints Close-Up Family Portrait." *Press & Sun-Bulletin,* January 11, 1973.

Smith, Cecil. "Family Portrait on PBS a Hit." *Newport News Daily Press,* January 26, 1973.

——. "Super Home Movies? No, in Reality It's 'An American Family.'" *Los Angeles Times,* January 7, 1973.

Wagner, Joyce. "Camera Starkly Reveals an American Family." *Kansas City Times,* January 10, 1973.

Winer, Laurie. "Reality Replay." *New Yorker,* April 18, 2011.

CHAPTER 4: THE CLIP

Television Academy interviews
John Langley, Bertram van Munster

Books and journals
Banks, Miranda J. *The Writers: A History of American Screenwriters and Their Guild* (New Brunswick, N.J.: Rutgers University Press, 2015).
Davis, Sean Michael. *Shoot to Thrill! The Life and Times of a Reality TV Cameraman* (Self-published, 2019).
Schlatter, George, with Jon Macks. *Still Laughing: A Life in Comedy* (Los Angeles: Unnamed Press/Rare Bird 2023).

Periodicals and other sources
AFV: America, This Is You! podcast, 2021.
"Attorneys Eyeing Legal Action Against Rivera's Program." *Los Angeles Times,* December 12, 1986.
Battaglio, Stephen. "Even in the Age of YouTube, 'America's Funniest Home Videos' Is Still an ABC Hit." *Los Angeles Times,* July 18, 2017.
Bunce, Alan. "Fox's 'Cops' Has the Right Beat." *Los Angeles Times,* February 16, 1992.
Caps, Johnny. "The Flashback Interview: Shawn Weatherly." Pop Geeks, November 5, 2019, popgeeks.com/the-flashback-interview-shawn-weatherly.
Cerone, Daniel. "'Cops' Hits Streets of L.A." *Los Angeles Times,* May 21, 1994.
Corry, John. "'OceanQuest': Afloat in Suspended Disbelief." *New York Times,* August 18, 1985.
Deeb, Gary. "Real Disputes: Staff, Co-Hosts of NBC's Top-Rated Show May Look Happy, but Many Are Inwardly Seething." *Kansas City Star TV & Radio,* February 13, 1982.
Dorschner, John. "The Nick of Time . . . and Newsweek, and Geraldo, and Nightline . . . The Making of an American Sheriff." *Miami Herald,* August 5, 1990.
Hill, Michael E. "Taking the Plunge: Former Miss Universe Relishes Underwater Challenge of 'Oceanquest.'" *Orlando Sentinel,* August 25, 1985.
Itzkoff, Dave. "Like the 10 O'Clock News, 'Cops' Endures." *New York Times,* September 9, 2007.
"Jack, Be Nimble!" *Time,* March 15, 1954.
Jones, J. R. "How Dragnet Became a PR Coup for Law Enforcement: The Story of the Long-Running Cop Show, Jack Webb, and the LAPD." *Chicago Reader,* August 24, 2017.

Joseph, Greg. "In 'Sweeps,' We Get Not Exactly the News." *Arizona Republic,* May 9, 1990.

Kahn, Joseph P. " 'Vice' Was Nice, but 'Cops' Is Tops." *Boston Globe,* January 7, 1989.

O'Connor, John J. " 'Cops' Camera Shows the Real Thing." *New York Times,* January 7, 1989.

Okeson, Sarah. "From on the Screen to on the Scene: Producer to Be Broward Deputy." *Miami Herald,* December 6, 1986.

"Oprah Was Told It Would Be 'Impossible' to Beat Phil Donahue." 2003, oprah.com/own-oprahshow/oprah-was-told-it-would-be-impossible-to-beat-phil-donahue-video.

Quah, Nicholas. " 'Running from Cops' Is Already One of the Year's Best Podcasts." *Vulture,* May 17, 2019.

Reeves, Michael. "A Superstar Grows in Englewood, N.J." *Philadelphia Inquirer,* August 8, 1978.

Rosenberg, Howard. "Is There No Control of Rivera's Kind of 'Journalism'?" *Sacramento Bee,* December 6, 1986.

Schwartz, Tony. "George Schlatter Finds the Fun in TV." *New York Times,* May 6, 1982.

Shine, Jacqui. " 'Dragnet' Was Straight Up LAPD Propaganda, on National TV for Years." Timeline, June 20, 2017.

Stelloh, Tim. "Bad Boys: How 'Cops' Became the Most Polarizing Reality TV Show in America." The Marshall Project, January 22, 2018.

Taberski, Dan. *Running from Cops* podcast, Pineapple Street Media and Topic Studios, 2019.

Williams, Mike. "Broward's TV Cops Get Bad Guys, Good Ratings." *Miami Herald,* January 11, 1989.

Winfrey, Oprah. "Oprah Talks to Phil Donahue." O, September 22, 2002.

CHAPTER 5: THE HOUSE

Television Academy interviews
Tom Freston, Jonathan Murray

Books and journals

Johnson, Hillary, and Nancy Rommelmann. *MTV's The Real Real World* (New York: MTV, 1995).

Kennedy. *The Kennedy Chronicles: The Golden Age of MTV Through Rose-Colored Glasses* (New York: Thomas Dunne Books, 2013).

Patane, Joe. *Livin' in Joe's World: Unauthorized, Uncut, and Unreal!* (New York: Harper Perennial, 1998).

Powell, Kevin. *The Education of Kevin Powell: A Boy's Journey into Manhood* (New York: Atria, 2015).

Tannenbaum, Rob, and Craig Marks. *I Want My MTV: The Uncensored Story of the Music Video Revolution* (New York: Plume, 2011).

Winick, Judd. *Pedro and Me: Friendship, Loss, and What I Learned* (New York: Henry Holt and Company, 2000).

Periodicals and other sources

Blake, Meredith. "He Was Half of 'The Most Famous Argument' in Reality-TV History. Time Proved Him Right." *Los Angeles Times*, April 9, 2021.

———. "'The Real World' Made 'Julie from Alabama' a Star. The Spotlight Wasn't What She Hoped." *Los Angeles Times*, March 8, 2021.

Cerone, Daniel. "MTV's Sort-of Real 'World': Cable: For Its Docu-Soap Series, the Network Put Seven Young People Together 'To See What Might Happen.'" *Los Angeles Times*, May 28, 1992.

Kleinfield, N. R. "Barefoot in the Loft: A Real New York Story." *New York Times*, March 22, 1992.

Nussbaum, Emily. "The Woman Who Gave Birth to Reality TV." *New York Times*, February 22, 2004.

O'Connor, John J. "'The Real World,' According to MTV." *New York Times*, July 9, 1992.

Shales, Tom. "'Real World': MTV's Ego Trap." *Washington Post*, May 27, 1992.

CHAPTER 6: THE CON

Books and journals

Harris, Neil. *Humbug: The Art of P. T. Barnum* (Boston: Little, Brown, 1973).

Manseau, Peter. *The Apparitionists: A Tale of Phantoms, Fraud, Photography, and the Man Who Captured Lincoln's Ghost* (Boston: Houghton Mifflin Harcourt, 2017).

Rockwell, Rick. *"What Was I Thinking?" The Truth About Reality TV and Modern Media* (Self-published, 2002).

Wilson, Robert. *Barnum: An American Life* (New York: Simon & Schuster, 2019).

Zook, Kristal Brent. *Color by Fox: The Fox Network and the Revolution in Black Television* (New York: Oxford University Press, 1999).

Periodicals and other sources

" 'Alien Autopsy' Rebroadcast Tonight." *Clarion-Ledger*, September 4, 1995.

Bianculli, David. "Best Bets." *Fort Worth Star-Telegram*, November 25, 1995.

"A Celebration of Greed: 'Who Wants to Marry a Multimillionaire?' Sent a Message of Hypocrisy to Voters Asked to Outlaw Same-Sex Marriages." *San Francisco Examiner*, February 18, 2000.

Chonin, Neva. "Looks Like Splitsville Already for TV Couple / Millionaire Groom Says She's Gone Home to Mom." *SFGate*, February 23, 2000.

"Darva Conger and Rick Rockwell Reunite." ABC News, February 21, 2001.

Goodman, Tim. "Reality, TV Make Strange Bedfellows." *Angelo Standard-Times*, March 2, 2000.

Jopson, John. "Re: Additional Insight on the Alien Autopsy." Correspondence, January 15, 1999, web.archive.org/web/20091217194004/http://www.dirtypoetfilms.com/JcJarchives/Alien_Autopsy.html.

Kuczynski, Alex, and Bill Carter. "Fox's Point Man for Perversity; 'World's Scariest Programmer,' Starring Mike Darnell as Himself." *New York Times*, February 26, 2000.

Kushman, Rick. "Mild-Mannered Mayhem: He's the Man Behind 'When Good Pets Go Bad.' But Fox's Mike Darnell Is Still Just a Kid at Heart." *Sacramento Bee*, April 27, 1999.

Lagerfeld, Nathalie. "How an Alien Autopsy Hoax Captured the World's Imagination for a Decade." *Time*, June 24, 2016.

Lowry, Brian. "Networks Seek Twist to Reality." *Cincinnati Enquirer*, December 21, 1999.

——. "Visionaries, for Better or Worse." *Los Angeles Times*, November 3, 2002.

Mazo, Ellen, Sally Kalson, and Mackenzie Carpenter. "Who Wants to Marry Rick Rockwell? A Millionaire from O'Hara Became TV Network's Catch of the Day." *Pittsburgh Post-Gazette*, February 20, 2000.

"Noah's Ark TV Report a Hoax." *Wichita Eagle*, November 3, 1993.

Vanderbilt, Tom. "When Animals Attack, Cars Crash and Stunts Go Bad." *New York Times Magazine*, December 6, 1998.

Weinstein, Steve. "A Bikini Strategy to String Viewers Along." *Los Angeles Times*, February 11, 1988.

"What the Groom Never Got to See." *Newsday*, June 29, 2000.

Wittstock, Melinda. "How TV Crossed Taste Barrier: The Hidden Past of the Groom on Who Wants to Marry a Millionaire Has Sparked a Backlash Against Voyeur Programming." *Guardian*, March 4, 2000.

Zurawik, Dave. "Stand By for a Season of Sleaze." *Baltimore Sun*, January 24, 1999.

CHAPTER 7: THE GAME

Television Academy interviews
Mark Burnett, Don Roy King, Les Moonves, Jonathan Murray, Jeff Probst

Books and journals
Burnett, Dianne. *The Road to Reality: Voted off the Island! . . . My Journey as a Real-Life* Survivor (Sacramento, Calif.: Agape Media, 2012).
Burnett, Mark. *Jump In! Even If You Don't Know How to Swim* (New York: Ballantine Books, 2005).
Carter, Bill. *Desperate Networks* (New York: Broadway Books, 2006).
Dugard, Martin. *Surviving the Toughest Race on Earth* (New York: McGraw Hill, 1998).
Percival, John. *Living in the Past* (London: British Broadcasting Corporation, 1980).
Street-Porter, Janet. *Baggage: My Childhood* (London: Headline, 2004).
——. *Fall Out: A Memoir of Friends Made and Friends Unmade* (London: Headline, 2006).

Periodicals and other sources
Addley, Esther. "Sinisa's Story." *Guardian,* July 26, 2002.
"Ancient Life Tough on Feet, British Family Finds." *Daily Reporter,* December 17, 1977.
Apple, R. W., Jr. "Five Couples Live in Lifestyle of 2,200 Years Ago." *New York Times,* March 2, 1978.
Ault, Alicia. "Turning a Camera, Stress and the Wild into a Sudden Hit." *New York Times,* July 23, 2000.
Balf, Todd, with Martin Dugard. "Endurance: Team American What?" *Outside Magazine,* February 1995.
Branigan, Tania. "The Guardian Profile: Janet Street-Porter." *Guardian,* November 19, 2004.
Brooks, Richard. "Tough Street Talking." *Observer,* September 25, 1988.
Brown, Maggie. "Smiles and Chaos as Programme Focuses on Launch: Channel 4's Big Breakfast Starts Next Week with Paula Yates and Bob Geldof the Attractions." *Independent,* September 22, 1992.
Carter, Bill. "Survival of the Pushiest." *New York Times Magazine,* January 28, 2001.
Chao, Stephen. "Mark Burnett on How to Become the Biggest Producer in Prime Time Television." Wonder How To, April 20, 2011.
Edwardes, Charlotte. "Survivor Game Show Based on Public School." *Telegraph,* June 3, 2001.

Haldane, David. "Endurance Race Started Badly, Ended Worse." *Los Angeles Times,* April 4, 1993.

Hogan, Michael. "'Our Presenter Got Kidnapped by German Pornographers'—How We Made The Word." *Guardian,* November 7, 2022.

Hooper, Mark. "'We Wanted to Hack Your Television!'—How Yoof TV Changed the World." *Guardian,* May 14, 2019.

"Interview: Annabel Croft Recalls Loneliness of Tennis Tour." *Scotsman,* June 17, 2017.

Keefe, Patrick Radden. "How Mark Burnett Resurrected Donald Trump as an Icon of American Success." *New Yorker,* December 27, 2018.

Markman, Jon D. "The Ultimate Race." *Los Angeles Times,* February 24, 1991.

Tosches, Rich. "From the Mountains, to the Desert, to the Sea . . . Quintet Finds Southland Perfect as Training Site for Race Across Oman." *Los Angeles Times,* August 13, 1992.

CHAPTER 8: THE ISLAND

Television Academy interviews
Mark Burnett, Les Moonves

Books and journals

Burnett, Mark, with Martin Dugard. *Survivor: The Ultimate Game* (New York: TV Books, 2000).

Lance, Peter. *The Stingray: Lethal Tactics of the Sole Survivor* (Cinema 21 Books, 2000).

Tisdale, Sallie. *The Lie About the Truck: Survivor, Reality TV, and the Endless Gaze* (New York: Gallery Books, 2021).

Periodicals and other sources

Carlozo, Lou. "This Is the Tale of Our Castaways; They're Here for a Long, Long Time." *Chicago Tribune,* May 2, 2001.

Holmes, Martin. "Birth of a Phenomenon—An Oral History of Survivor: Borneo." Inside Survivor, May 29, 2020, insidesurvivor.com/birth-of-a-phenomenon-an-oral-history-of-survivor-borneo-43932.

"Jeff Probst." *The Producer's Guide: Todd Garner & Hollywood's Elite* podcast, September 13, 2018.

Keck, William. "Networks Wedded Firmly to Reality-Show Concept." *Los Angeles Times,* June 27, 2000.

McDonald, Brook. "Survivor's Imperial Aesthetic and the American Guise of Innocence." BA American Studies Thesis at University of Sydney, October 2017.

Reinstein, Mara. "Through Two Decades and 40 Seasons, the Tribal Council Remains the Heart of 'Survivor,'" *The Ringer,* May 12, 2020.

Richard, Ianic Roy. "The Forgotten Legend of Susan Hawk." A Tribe of One, August 26, 2020.

——. "The Stacey Stillman Case: A Deep Dive." A Tribe of One, August 18, 2017.

Ross, Dalton. "Jeff Probst Says CBS Diversity Pledge 'Forever Changed *Survivor.*'" *Entertainment Weekly,* September 21, 2022.

"'Survivor' Winner Hatch Cleared of Abuse Charge." *Washington Post,* August 29, 2000.

CHAPTER 9: THE FEED

Television Academy interviews
Julian Gomez

Books and journals

Bazalgette, Peter. *Billion Dollar Game: How Three Men Risked It All and Changed the Face of Television* (London: Time Warner Books, 2005).

Wendel, Sabine. *Big Sister: Alles Wat Je Zou Moeten Weten om te Overleven als Realityster* (Self-published, 2020).

Wilson, Pam. "Jamming Big Brother: Webcasting, Audience Intervention, and Narrative Activism." In *Reality TV: Remaking Television Culture,* edited by Susan Murray and Laurie Ouellette (New York: NYU Press, 2004).

Periodicals and other sources

Barfbag. "Aerial Assault: The History of Banner Planes Over the Big Brother House." YouTube, April 24, 2022.

Bell, Nick. "Major Men." *TBI: Television Business International,* April 1994.

"Big Brother Gang Won't Budge—Even for $50,000." ABC News, September 7, 2000.

Brockes, Emma. "Last Man Standing: Bart Spring In't Veld Has Some Advice for the Brits Who'll Be Filmed 24 Hours a Day for a New TV Programme." *Guardian,* July 11, 2000.

Carter, Gary. "Learning to Kiss." TEDxAmsterdam, November 20, 2009.

Carter, Meg. "From the Man Who Gave You Big Brother: Couples in Chains!" *Independent,* September 5, 2000.

"CBS Rechecking Background of 'Big Brother' Participant." *New York Times,* July 15, 2000.

Fletcher, Martin. "Big Brother Stole My Life." *Times,* September 5, 2008.

Hunt, Stacey Wilson. "Mark Burnett, Julie Chen, Nigel Lythgoe and Reality A-List on Racist Contestants, Caitlyn Jenner and the Wrath of Leslie Moonves." *Hollywood Reporter,* June 22, 2015.

Nickell, Kelly. "In Holland, 'Big Brother' Is Watching—and So Are the Dutch." Associated Press, October 28, 1999.

Strachan, Alex. "Serving God and Big Brother." *Vancouver Sun,* July 29, 2000.

Wilkes, Neil. "Big Brother US: Justin Evicted for Knife Threat." Digital Spy, July 12, 2001.

CHAPTER 10: THE EXPLOSION

Television Academy interviews

Mike Darnell, Tom Freston, Barry Manilow, Don Ohlmeyer, Hector Ramirez

Books and journals

Abrego, Cris, with Mim Eichler Rivas. *Make It Reality: Create Your Opportunity. Own Your Success* (New York: Celebra, 2016).

Andrejevic, Mark. *Reality TV: The Work of Being Watched* (Lanham, Md.: Rowman & Littlefield, 2004).

Gillan, Jennifer. "From Ozzie Nelson to Ozzy Osbourne: The Genesis and Development of the Reality (Star) Sitcom." In *Understanding Reality Television,* edited by Su Holmes and Deborah Jermyn (New York: Routledge, 2004).

Glover, Stephen "Steve-O," with David Peisner. *Professional Idiot: A Memoir* (New York: Hyperion, 2011).

Pozner, Jennifer L. *Reality Bites Back: The Troubling Truth About Guilty Pleasure TV* (Berkeley, Calif.: Seal Press, 2010).

Simpson, Jessica, with Kevin Carr O'Leary. *Open Book* (New York: Dey Street, 2020).

Periodicals and other sources

Andrejevic, Mark. "Reality TV May Be Down, but It's Not Out." *Newsday,* February 5, 2002.

Armstrong, Jennifer. "Nick and Jessica on Being Married . . . with Cameras." *Entertainment Weekly,* January 9, 2004.

Baah, Nana. "'Like Shooting a Wildlife Doc': The Oral History of 'The Osbournes.'" *Vice,* March 3, 2022.

Bonin, Liane. "Meet Joe's Schmo, Matt Gould. The Reality TV Star Says He Knew Something Was Fishy on His Fake Show." *Entertainment Weekly,* October 28, 2003.

Braxton, Greg. "Is It Really That Black & White?" *Los Angeles Times,* March 4, 2006.

"Copycat Behavior Causes Concern for Viewers of MTV's 'Jackass.'" *Orlando Sentinel,* February 6, 2001.

Deggans, Eric. "Changing Reality TV." *Tampa Bay Times,* January 7, 2002.

Dehnart, Andy. "Amazing Race Behind the Scenes: An Oral History of CBS's First Race Around the World." Reality Blurred, September 3, 2021.

De Moraes, Lisa. "'Reality' TV Is Marching to the Military's Tune." *Washington Post,* March 18, 2002.

Duffy, Mike. "Show's a Joke, but 'Joe' Isn't." *Detroit Free Press,* October 26, 2003.

Eakin, Marah. "America's Favorite Dysfunctional Family: The Oral History of 'The Osbournes.'" *The Ringer,* March 3, 2022.

Epstein, Andrew. "Stunters of '81: Jumping into Court." *Los Angeles Times,* August 9, 1981.

Essex, David. "Actual Reality: A Day in the Life of R. J. Cutler." *Documentary,* November 1, 2003.

Gallo, Phil. "Profiles from the Front Line." *Variety,* February 26, 2003.

Hedegaard, Erik. "Johnny Knoxville: The King of Pain." *Rolling Stone,* February 1, 2001.

Hofmiester, Sallie. "'Manhunt' Exec Alleges TV Show Was 'Falsified.'" *Los Angeles Times,* August 16, 2001.

James, Meg. "How a Kid from El Monte Became One of Hollywood's Few Latino Executives." *Los Angeles Times,* August 17, 2022.

Jensen, Elizabeth. "'Reality' TV Eagerly Marches Off to War." *Los Angeles Times,* February 22, 2002.

Kohanik, Eric. "Fine Tuning: Joe Schmo 2 Finale Helps Define Silliness of Reality." *Windsor Star,* August 9, 2004.

Lawrence, Jerry. "Child Porn Case Ends in Plea." *Chicago Tribune,* November 22, 2001.

Liner, Elaine. "With Skupin Out of the Picture, 'Survivor' Tribes Set to Merge." *Blade,* March 7, 2001.

Liptak, Adam. "Growing Rowdier, TV Reality Shows Are Attracting Suits." *New York Times,* January 7, 2003.

Lowry, Brian. "American Candidate." *Variety,* July 29, 2004.

"'Manhunt' Generates Controversy but Not Ratings." *Pacific Business News,* August 21, 2001.

Mills, Marja, Allan Johnson, and Gary Dretzka. "Cameras Roll on 14 Teen 'Survivors.'" *Chicago Tribune,* July 30, 2000.

Moore, Frazier. "A Reality President in 2004? Filmmaker Has High Hopes for Series 'American Candidate.'" Associated Press, August 21, 2003.

O'Hare, Kate. "Showtime Scours the Nation for an 'American Candidate.'" *Zap2It,* August 1, 2004.

Owen, Rob. "Tuned In from Hollywood: 2 Pittsburgh 'Schmoes' Advise Current Player." *Pittsburgh Post-Gazette,* January 8, 2013.

Paulsen, Wade. "'Combat Missions' Star Scott Helvenston Among 4 Dead in Ambush in Fallujah, Iraq." Reality TV World, April 2, 2004.

Perera, Andrea "Mom Mourns Her Fallen Son." *Orlando Sentinel,* April 2, 2004.

Poniewozik, James. "Mediawatch: That's Militainment! The War on Terror Gets the Cops Treatment. Evil Axis, Evil Axis, What You Gonna Do?" *Time,* March 4, 2002.

Randall, Eric. "The 'Death of Irony,' and Its Many Reincarnations: An Investigation into Just Who Declared Irony Dead in the Wake of 9/11/2001." *Atlantic,* September 9, 2011.

"Reality Contestant Passes Out During Stunt." Reality TV World, March 28, 2002.

"The Real Reality: What Former Stars from 'Flavor of Love,' 'My Super Sweet 16,' and More Were Thinking When They Signed On." *Entertainment Weekly,* August 1, 2008.

Robins, Wayne. "That's Reality!—As the TV Networks See It." *Newsday,* March 22, 1981.

Schoch, Deborah, Julie Tamaki, and Monte Morin. "Death Came Brutally to a Man Who 'Never Quit.'" *Los Angeles Times,* April 3, 2004.

SurvivinDawg. "Combat Missions—Episode 13 Summary." Reality TV World, April 17, 2002.

Susnjara, Bob. "'American High' Subjects Charged with Making Sex Video with Minor." *Daily Herald,* July 28, 2001.

Weiss, Tara. "Reality TV Programs May Lose Viewers." Gannett, October 20, 2001.

Williams, Kam. "Black Man Reflects on Being White for Five Weeks." African American Literature Book Club, aalbc.com/reviews/brian_sparks.htm.

——. "Primetime Primary." *On the Media,* NPR, January 30, 2004.

CHAPTER 11: THE ROSE

Books and journals

Hilton, Paris. *Paris: The Memoir* (New York: Dey Street Books, 2023).

Kaufman, Amy. *Bachelor Nation: Inside the World of America's Favorite Guilty Pleasure* (New York: Dutton, 2018).

Sutter, Trista. *Happily Ever After: The Life-Changing Power of a Grateful Heart* (Boston: Da Capo Press, 2013).

Periodicals and other sources

Adams, LaNease, as told to Lindsay Geller. " 'The Bachelor's' LaNease Adams: 'I Was Depressed After Racist Backlash from Alex Michel's Season.' " *Women's Health*, July 6, 2020.

Baker, Katie. " 'Joe Millionaire' Turned Reality TV into the Super Bowl. Then It Vanished." *The Ringer*, May 1, 2020.

Dehnart, Andy. "Evan Says Joe Millionaire Was 'Fake' and 'Staged'; Fox Used Sound Effects." Reality Blurred, January 27, 2004.

Greco, Patti. "An Ex-*Bachelor* Contestant Remembers Being Humiliated by the Creator of *UnREAL*." *Cosmopolitan*, June 29, 2016.

Herzog, Kenny. "Joe's Dirt: The Man Formerly Known as *Joe Millionaire* on Why Reality Bites." *Vulture*, September 21, 2015.

Highfill, Samantha. " 'Joe Millionaire' Star Evan Marriott Has Resurfaced 12 Years Later." *Entertainment Weekly*, March 20, 2015.

Holloway, Daniel. "Unscripted Exec Lisa Levenson Joins Wilshire Studios." *Variety*, October 24, 2018.

"LaNease Adams Recalls Having the First-Ever Bachelor Kiss." Carrie's Chronicles, August 2, 2020.

Lowry, Brian. "Fox Hands Rivals a 'Wedding' Present." *Los Angeles Times*, February 24, 2000.

———. "Probe Absolves 'Multi-Millionaire?,' Fox Says." *Los Angeles Times*, April 13, 2000.

Max, D. T. "Confessional." *New Yorker*, June 13, 2016.

Page, Shelley. "Pride, Prejudice, a Load of Manure: Joe Millionaire Borrows a Page from Jane Austen." *Ottawa Citizen*, February 15, 2003.

Petrozzello, Donna. "The New 'Joe Millionaire': Fox Aims for Ratings Success a Second Time Around." New York *Daily News*, October 27, 2003.

Seal, Mark. "Reality Kings." *Vanity Fair*, July 2003.

Starr, Michael. "Love Triangle Backfires on Bachelor No. 1." *New York Post*, January 10, 2003.

CHAPTER 12: THE WINK

Television Academy interviews

RuPaul Charles, Andy Cohen, Patricia Field, Jonathan Murray, Lauren Zalaznick, Jeff Zucker

Books and journals

Bailey, Fenton. *ScreenAge: How TV Shaped Our Reality from Tammy Faye to RuPaul's Drag Race* (London: Ebury Press, 2022).

Cohen, Andy. *Most Talkative: Stories from the Front Lines of Pop Culture* (New York: Henry Holt and Company, 2012).

Gunn, Tim, with Ada Calhoun. *Gunn's Golden Rules: Life's Little Lessons for Making It Work* (New York: Gallery Books, 2010).

Miller, Toby. "Metrosexuality: See the Bright Light of Commodification Shine! Watch Yanqui Masculinity Made Over!" In *The Great American Makeover: Television, History, Nation,* edited by Dana Heller (New York: Palgrave Macmillan, 2006).

Moylan, Brian. *The Housewives: The Real Story Behind the Real Housewives* (New York: Flatiron Books, 2021).

Quinn, Dave. *Not All Diamonds and Rosé* (New York: Macmillan, 2021).

Weber, Brenda R. *Makeover TV: Selfhood, Citizenship, and Celebrity* (Durham, N.C.: Duke University Press, 2009).

Periodicals and other sources

Allen, Ted. "*Queer Eye* Was Not 'Minstrelsy.'" *Slate,* July 9, 2015.

Barker, Olivia. "Regular Guys Cast Jaded Eyes at Metrosexual Trend." *USA Today,* January 25, 2004.

Bauder, David. "Bravo Television Launches a Reality Dating Series for Gay Men." Associated Press, June 4, 2003.

Brennan, Matt. "TV Mentor Tim Gunn Is Freaked Out Too: 'Every Night at 7 O'Clock I Burst into Tears.'" *Los Angeles Times,* April 16, 2020.

Bruce, Leslie. "'Fashion Is Not for Sissies': An Oral History of 'Project Runway's' First 10 Years." *Hollywood Reporter,* August 16, 2012.

Dominus, Susan. "The Affluencer." *New York Times Magazine,* October 30, 2008.

Eades, Mark. "Producer Gets Real About the Real Housewives." *Orange County Register,* January 10, 2007.

Francescani, Chris. "Mimi Haleyi Details Sexual Assault Allegation in Harvey Weinstein Trial Testimony." ABC News, January 27, 2020.

Giltz, Michael. "Queer Eye Confidential." *Advocate,* August 18, 2003.

Goodykoontz, Bill. "'Blow Out' Fizzles, Thanks to Star." *Arizona Republic,* June 7, 2004.

Gross, Michael Joseph. "Flying High." *Boston Globe,* November 28, 2004.

Kelly, Christopher. "Haute Coiffeur: 'Blow Out' Braids Gripping Hair-Salon Melodrama with Raw Ambition and Gives Jonathan Antin's Star Power a Chance to Shine." *Fort Worth Star-Telegram,* July 16, 2004.

"Low Pay for the Queer Guys." The Smoking Gun, September 11, 2003.

Nichols, James Michael. "After Dark: Randy Barbato & Fenton Bailey, AKA The Fabulous Pop Tarts." *Huffington Post,* July 27, 2014.

"Tim Gunn at Home in New York City." *Really Famous with Kara Mayer Robinson,* YouTube, May 1, 2023.

CHAPTER 13: THE JOB

Television Academy interviews
Mark Burnett, Marilu Henner, Jeff Zucker

Books and journals
Cohen, Michael. *Disloyal: A Memoir; The True Story of the Former Personal Attorney to Donald J. Trump* (New York: Skyhorse Publishing, 2020).
DeVolld, Troy. *Reality TV: An Insider's Guide to TV's Hottest Market* (Studio City, Calif.: Michael Wiese Productions, 2016).
Gold, Kym, with Sharon Soboil. *Gold Standard: How to Rock the World and Run an Empire* (New York: Skyhorse Publishing, 2015).
Kepcher, Carolyn, with Stephen Fenichell. *Carolyn 101: Business Lessons from* The Apprentice's *Straight Shooter* (New York: Fireside, 2004).
Poniewozik, James. *Audience of One: Donald Trump, Television, and the Fracturing of America* (New York: Liveright, 2019).
Salkin, Allen, and Aaron Short. *The Method to the Madness: Donald Trump's Ascent as Told by Those Who Were Hired, Fired, Inspired—and Inaugurated* (New York: All Points Books, 2019).

Periodicals and other sources
"America's Top Union Fight." August 15, 2006, d-day.blogspot.com/search?q =top+union+fight.
"ANTM Staff Goes on Strike: 'Top Model' Staffers Want New Deal. Striking Producers Hope to Win WGA Recognition, Benefits." CNN, August 8, 2006.
Dagostino, Mark, and Brian Orloff. "Rosie Slams Trump, The Donald Fires Back." *People,* December 20, 2006.
Durkin, J. D. "Ex-*Apprentice* Stars Slam Trump's Presidential Bid: 'Let Us Choose Kennedy Over Kardashian-ism.'" *Mediaite,* April 15, 2016.
Elber, Lynn. "Picket Line, Not Catwalk, at 'Top Model.'" Associated Press, August 10, 2006.
"Ex-'Apprentice' Contestant Slams Trump." CNN, April 15, 2016.
"IATSE Makes 3-Year Deal with 'American Idol' and 'America's Got Talent' Producer Fremantle." *Deadline,* July 26, 2011.
Keegan, Rebecca. "The Anger, Passion and Scorched-Earth Strategy of the Man in the Middle of the Hollywood Writers' War." *Hollywood Reporter,* June 5, 2019.

Longino, Bob. "'The Donald' Overwhelms All in 'Apprentice.'" *Atlanta Journal-Constitution,* January 8, 2004.

Moore, Frazier. "Donald Trump Is the Prize on 'The Apprentice.'" Associated Press, January 10, 2004.

"'Next Top Model' Writers Want Union Status." UPI, July 21, 2006.

Patten, Dominic. "'Survivor' Editors Ratify IATSE Contract with Mark Burnett Company." *Deadline,* August 21, 2014.

Schiller, Gail. "'Apprentice' Lures Sponsors Despite Ratings Slide." Reuters, December 5, 2007.

Stanley, T. L. "Writers Guild Protests TV Product Placements: T.I. Disrupts Ad Age Madison & Vine Advertising Week Session." *Ad Age,* September 27, 2005.

"The Ultimate Rollback: An Interview with Larry Gelbart." www.reality united.com, August 22, 2006 (via Wayback Machine).

Verrier, Richard. "Writers Guild's Confrontational Approach Getting Mixed Reviews." *Los Angeles Times,* December 20, 2005.

"The WGA Gets Real: The March on Fremantle." *Variety,* December 7, 2007.

EPILOGUE: FAKE IT TILL YOU MAKE IT

Pomerantsev, Peter. *Nothing Is True and Everything Is Possible: The Surreal Heart of the New Russia* (New York: Public Affairs, 2014).

Warhol, Andy. *The Philosophy of Andy Warhol (From A to B and Back Again)* (New York: Harvest, 1975).

OTHER BOOKS ON REALITY TV

Sam Brenton and Reuben Cohen, *Shooting People: Adventures in Reality TV* (New York: Verso, 2003); Clay Calvert, *Voyeur Nation: Media, Privacy, and Peering in Modern Culture* (Boulder, Colo.: Westview Press, 2000); Anna David, ed., *Reality Matters: 19 Writers Come Clean About the Shows We Can't Stop Watching* (New York: Itbooks, 2010); June Deery, *Reality TV* (Cambridge, U.K.: Polity Press, 2015); Michael Essany, *Reality Check: The Business and Art of Producing Reality TV* (New York: Focal Press, 2008); Richard M. Huff, *Reality Television* (Westport, Conn.: Praeger Publishers, 2006); Danielle J. Lindemann, *True Story: What Reality TV Says About Us* (New York: Farrar, Straus and Giroux, 2022); Lucas Mann, *Captive Audience: On Love and Reality TV* (New York: Vintage, 2018); Laurie Ouellette and James Hay, *Better Living Through Reality TV* (Malden, Mass.: Blackwell Publishing, 2008).

INDEX

A. L. Alexander's Goodwill Court, 6–7
Abarca, German, 366, 367
Abdul-Jabbar, Kareem, 94
Abrams, Daniel, 321
Abrego, Cris, 284
Actual Reality, 272, 274
Adams, LaNease, 311–12
Addley, Esther, 182
The Adventures of Ozzie and Harriet, 10
The Advocate, 214, 342
Affleck, Ben, 276, 346
African Americans, 295
  The Apprentice, 364, 367, 369, 370,
    371, 384–85
  The Bachelor, 311, 317–18
  Big Brother, 234
  Black. White., 275
  Cops, 104, 105, 106–7, 109
  The Dating Game, 33
  The Police Tapes, 100, 102
  Queen for a Day, 11
  Queer Eye, 338, 339
  The Real World, 118, 128, 129, 130
  RuPaul, 335–36, 357–58
  Survivor, 191, 197, 224, 225

Aftonbladet, 182–83
Age of the Voluntary Amateur, 20
Alcala, Rodney, 44
Alexander, Jason, 156
Alexander, Shana, 69, 72
Alien Autopsy, 151–53, 154
Allen, Ted, 339, 340, 342, 343, 345
Alli, Baron Waheed, 177
Altman, Robert, 273
The Amazing Race, 267, 279–81, 330,
  379
American Bandstand, 30
American Candidate, 273–74
American Families, 117
"An American Family" (Roiphe), 67–68
An American Family
  airport scene, 79–80
  Bill and Pat's divorce, 56, 57–60, 63–64
  Bill as single man, 56–57
  credit sequence of, 64–65
  critics' response to, 66, 67–69, 71–73,
    84
  "disappearance" of, 73
  editing of, 61–62
  episodes of, 57, 62–63

An American Family (cont'd):
  filming of, 53–55, 60
  genesis of, 50, 51
  Gilbert's introduction to, 63–64
  influence of, 73–75
  Lance and Pat as stars of, 54–55
  Murray and, 115, 117
  popularity of, 65, 68
  production process, 55–56
  Raymonds' ethical line, 59
  as third iteration of reality TV, 49
  WNET/13's marketing of, 65–66
An American Family Revisited, 75–76
American High, 270–72
American Idol, 268, 278, 279, 373,
  379
American Vice, 95–97
America's Funniest Home Videos, 89,
  90–92
America's Most Wanted, 98, 159
America's Next Top Model, 347, 378
Andersen, B. B., 195, 199
Andrejevic, Mark, 283
Andrews, Peter, 46–47
Andrich, Zora, 320
Anthony, John J., 4, 6
Antin, Jonathan, 351
Antrim, Matt, 319, 320, 321–22
"An Apologia from the Man Who
  Produced the Worst Program in
  History" (Blake), 8–9
"applause-o-meter," 9
The Apprentice
  casting of, 364–65
  credits, 364
  editing of, 372
  episodes of, 363, 366, 368–69
  filming of, 364
  format of, 362
  genesis of, 361
  product integration, 368, 373–74,
    377–78, 388
  production crew issues, 375–76
  ratings and reviews of, 373, 381, 382
  replacement of Trump's dialogue, 372

  sexism and racism, 370, 371, 372–73,
    374–75
  Trump's personality change on, 382
  as ultimate in marketing, 384
  as uniting two successful reality
    models, 362
  as WGA unionization target, 377
Apted, Michael, 114–15
art, defining, xix
The Atlantic, 357
Atlas Obscura, 22
audience participation programs, 5–7, 12
  See also specific shows
"Ayatollah of Trasherola," 24
  See also Barris, Chuck

The Bachelor
  ability to catch true feelings, 317
  alcohol and, 309, 313
  blueprint, 305, 306, 310
  casting, 307–8, 311, 313
  debut of, 268
  genesis of, 305
  Levenson and, 306–7
  obtaining freebies for, 327–28
  producer manipulation in, 310, 314
  production crew, 308, 312, 330
  relationships between women in cast,
    314, 315–16, 317
  rose ceremonies, 308–9
  Shapiro and, 326–27, 328–29
  strengths of, 319
  success of, 318, 327, 331–32
The Bachelorette, 315, 316, 322, 324–25
Bachelor Nation (Kaufman), 307, 312
"Bachelor Nation," 318
Bailey, Fenton, 333–34, 335–36, 342,
  358–59, 386
Bailey, Jack, 8, 9–10
Bailey, Monica, 259, 261–62
Bain, Bob, 150–51
Baker, Katie, 322
Balkey, Richard S., 166
Ball, Lucille, 10
Baltake, Joe, 46

Baltazzi, Maria, 199

Barbato, Randy, 333–34, 335–36, 357

Barbour, John, 41

Barbour, Malcolm, 93

Barefoot, Brian, 221

Barnum, P. T., 154

Barris, Chuck

  basic facts about, xvi, 29–30, 34, 38, 39, 42, 47–48

  criticism of shows of, 40

  fall of, 46–48

  The Gong Show and, xvi, 40, 42, 44–45

  Metzger and, 42–43

  The Newlywed Game and, 34–37, 42

  as portrayed in movie, 48

  situationalism approach and, 209

  See also *The Dating Game*

Barris Bandits, 38

Barris, Della, 44, 46

Barthiel, Joan, 33, 34

Basil, Toni, 94

Bassi, Leo, 241

Beane, Billy, 155

Bearde, Chris, 40

Bear Pond (Weber), 113, 125

Beckman, Preston, 277

Been, Dirk

  basic facts about, 197, 210

  Burnett and, 226, 227–28, 229

  casting of, 194

  Klug and, 229

  lawsuit against *Survivor,* 225

  Stacey Stillman and, 225, 226–27

  voted off, 208, 227

Before They Were Stars, 160

Behind the Dog Tag, 14

Behind the Gates, 352, 353–55

Below Deck, 391

Belson, Josh, 321, 322, 324

Benton, Scott, 258, 259, 260, 262, 263

Berg, Gertrude, 10

Bergman, Ed, 334

The Berkshire Evening Eagle, 19

Berman, Gail, 321

Berry, Frank, 106

Berwick, Frances, 338, 339

Bethea, Mark, 361

Bianculli, David, 152

Bienstock, Jay, 199, 363, 369, 372

The Big Breakfast, 177

Big Brother

  cast, 239–41

  as cinéma vérité, 238

  debut of, 237–38

  development of, 235–37

  editing of, 238

  franchises, 241–42

  live streaming of, 234, 238

  popularity of, 238–39

Big Brother U.S.

  absence of love triangle, 244, 246

  attempts to make interesting, 248

  bidding for, 242, 276

  casting of, 243

  cast mutiny, 250–51, 252

  cast voted out, 245, 246, 248

  changes in season two, 253, 254

  culture of niceness, 248, 250

  debut, 243–44

  final days of, 262–63

  Will "Dr. Evil" Kirby, 255–57

  9/11/2001 and, 260–62

  problems, 242–43

  reaction to, 244–45, 248–50, 258, 262

  Paul Römer and, 242

  supernatural forces storyline, 258–59

  work pace, 258, 259

Black. White., 275

Blake, Howard, 8–9

Blasband, Becky, 123, 131–33

Blind Date, 31, 306, 321

  See also *The Dating Game*

Bloomberg, Stu, 178, 276

Blow Out, 351–52

Boesch, Rudy

  after *Survivor,* 229

  casting of, 194

  characteristics of, 196

  Combat Missions and, 282

  description of, on *Survivor,* 171

Boesch, Rudy (cont'd):
  Eco-Challenge and, 226, 228
  Hatch and, 196, 208
  Survivor reunion, 224
Boland, Murray, 173
Boone, Blair, 339
Boot Camp, 231
The Boston Globe, 101
Boswell, George "Chicken George," 243,
  244, 249, 250, 251, 252
Bouza, Anthony, 100
Bowe, Kai, 378
Boy Meets Boy, 343–44
Bråkenhielm, Anna, 182
Brando, Marlon, 276
Braun, Jonathon, 221
Braun, Lloyd, 276, 305, 362
Bravo brand, 351–52, 357
Breaking the Magician's Code, 155–56,
  158, 163
Bride and Groom, 5, 162–63
Briggs, Chris, 164
British reality TV, 162, 172–74, 177
  See also specific shows
Brokaw, Tom, 167
"The Broken Family," 69
Brooklyn Eagle Quiz on Current Events, 5
Brooks, Albert, 74–75
Brown, Karamo, 345
Bruckheimer, Jerry, 281
Brustein, Robert, 269
Bryant, Kimberly, 354
Buffington, Stephanie, 38–39
Buis, Greg, 194, 208, 211, 215–16, 229
Bunce, Alan, 105
Bunim, Mary-Ellis
  death of, 145
  Faraldo and, 125–26, 127
  importance of, xvi
  Keeping Up with the Kardashians and,
    355
  Love Cruise and, 279
  Murray and, 116
  The Real World, 113, 121, 141
  shows after The Real World, 144–45

situationalism approach and, 209
  St. Mark's Place and, 117
Burnett, Dianne, 185, 186, 208
Burnett, Mark
  The Apprentice and, 361, 362, 363,
    373, 374
  basic facts about, 172, 184–88
  Been and, 226, 227–28, 228–29
  The Celebrity Apprentice, 382–83
  characteristics of, 188–89, 199, 203
  Combat Missions and, 282, 283
  Corrao and, 190
  Eco-Challenge versions, 188–89
  as kingmaker, 386
  Moonves and, 191–92
  "on the fly" interviews and, 205
  on panel at Museum of Television &
    Radio, 381, 382
  Parsons and, 190
  on Pulau Tiga, 201, 214
  The Real World and, 188
  Survive! and, 180, 181
  Survivor and, 207, 225, 226, 291
  on Tribal Council, 207–8
  unionization and, 379
Bush, Billy, 381
Bush, George W., 342
butods, 202–3
But What If the Dream Comes True,
  61, 62

Cacciatore, Ron "Chicken," 101
Canada, Linda, 101, 103
Canby, Vincent, 60
Candidate 2020, 273
Candid Camera
  Candid Microphone and, xv, 12, 16–18
  critics on, 18–20, 23–25
  "elevator stunt," 21, 23
  episodes, 21–22
  first iteration of, 20–21
  as first prank show, 12–13
  lack of anonymity of subjects, 23
  as old-fashioned fun, 27
  "the reveal" on, 25

"Smile! You're on *Candid Camera*"
and, 25, 26
sociologists and, 22, 23
in Soviet Union, 22
success of, 22, 23
Candidly, Allen Funt (Funt), 14, 27,
28
Candid Microphone, xv, 12, 16–18
Canniffe, Jamie, 366, 369, 371, 383–84
Cannonball Run 2001, 279
Carnie, Dave, 288
Carrey, Jim, xvii–xviii
Carroll, Michael, 307
Carson, Michael, 186
Carter, Bill, 191–92, 278
Carter, Gary
basic facts about, 235
Big Brother and, 236, 240, 241–42
Expedition: Robinson and, 183
Survive! and, 181, 182
Carter, Graydon, 279
Casler, Noel, 375
Cassidy, Marsha F., 9
Cavett, Dick, 67, 68
"celebreality" TV, 144, 283–85
See also specific shows
The Celebrity Apprentice, 382–83
Celebrity Boxing, 169
Celebrity Mole, 290–91
Cena, John, 293, 294
Cha, Jane, 347
The Chair, 277
The Challenge, 144–45, 291
The Chamber, 277, 291
Chao, Stephen, 97, 98, 105, 159–60, 336
Charles, RuPaul Andre, 335–36, 357–58
Chavez, Manuel, 97
Chen, Julie, 243, 252–53, 261
The Chicago Sun-Times, 322
"Chicken George," 243, 249, 250, 251,
252
Childress, Helen, 140
Chocano, Carina, 342
Christopher, Sonja, 195, 199, 208, 210,
213–14

Chuck Barris Productions, 31, 33–34,
37, 38, 47
"Chuckie Baby." *See* Barris, Chuck
Churchill, Joan, 57, 270
cinéma vérité
An American Family and, 57, 62
Big Brother, 238
Cops as, 105
Raymonds and, 53, 62
reality TV as commercial, xv
The Real World as, 135–36, 137
self-awareness of reality TV's subjects
and, 141
theory about best material, 55
Cinema Verite, 78–79
Clark, Dick, 30
Clarkson, Kelly, 278
"clip shows," 155
The Closet Case Show, 334
Cocaine Blues, 93–94
Cohen, Andy, 346, 353, 354, 356–57
Cohen, Michael, 371
Cohn, Alan, 118, 119–20, 135–36, 141, 335
Collingwood, Chris, 127
Collins, David, 336–37, 339, 342, 343,
344, 345
Collins, Dorothy, 22
Collins, William "Will Mega," 243,
244–46, 247, 256
Color of Change, 106
Combat Missions, 282–83
Comeau, Andre, 123, 140
Commando Nanny, 374
Confessions of a Dangerous Mind
(Barris), 47
Confessions of a Dangerous Mind
(movie), 48
Conger, Darva, 163–65, 168–70
Connell, Brady, 197, 280
Conner, Tara, 382
Cook, Joe, 4
Cops
accused of racism, 102, 105, 106–7
cancellations of, 106–7
critics' response to, 101–2, 105

Cops (cont'd):
  examples of episodes of, 103, 104–5
  as "an existential variety show," 104
  forerunners to, 98, 99–100
  formula used by, 101
  genesis of, 95
  importance of, 98, 108
  pilot, 100–101
  police departments and, 105–6
  as prank show, 101
  premiere of, 89
  success of, 93, 105
  The Truman Show and, xvii
Cordy, Gretchen, 106, 194, 208, 210,
    216, 360
Cornett, Leanza, 163
Corrao, Lauren
  American Families pilot and, 117
  Burnett and, 189–90
  on interference from producers,
    126–27
  The Real World and, 121, 142
  Survivor and, 178
Corry, John, 87
Cosmopolitan, 331
Costello, Marki, 308, 310
Cowell, Simon, 278
Coy, Randi, 324
"Critics Scream, Actors Howl, but
    Audience Participation Shows Go On
    and On and On" (Meegan), 7
Croft, Annabel, 174
Crosby, John, 5–6, 19–20
Crowe, Christopher, 293
Cutforth, Dan, 179, 180, 181, 347
Cutler, R. J., 269–75

Daily News, 67, 245
Damon, Matt, 276, 346
Daniels, Marshawn Evans, 385
Darnell, Mike
  Alien Autopsy: Fact or Fiction,
    151–53, 154
  The Bachelor and, 305
  basic facts about, xvi, 147–48, 149

Boot Camp, 231
Breaking the Magician's Code, 155–56,
    158
  business model of, 152, 155, 156, 157
  Diller and, 149–50
  extreme-sports shows, 156
  Fleiss and, 158, 160, 161–62, 168, 304
  flops by, 277
  as Fox's "head of specials," 150–58
  importance of, 157, 158
  Joe Millionaire and, 319, 322
  journalists and, 156–57
  Life After Reruns, 149, 160
  as producer-provocateur, 365
  *Who Wants to Marry a Multi-
    Millionaire?,* 162, 163–69
  *The World's Meanest People Caught
    on Tape,* 160–61
  See also American Idol; Survivor
Darva's House, 169
Dateline, 169
The Dating Game
  Alcala on, 44
  Blind Date and, 31
  Delilah Loud on, 70
  described, 32, 33
  The Gong Show and, 42
  spin-offs, 37
  success of, 33
  timing of, 31, 33
dating shows, 306
  See also specific shows
The David Susskind Show, 73–74
Davies, Michael, 178, 190, 191, 276
Davis, Sean Michael, 105
Day, James, 50
daytime talk shows, 88–89
"Dear Pat, Bill, Lance, Delilah, Grant,
    Kevin and Michele" (Miller), 72–73
Debin, Jonathan, 32, 38
Deeb, Gary, 40
Deegan, Brian, 290
Dehnart, Andy, 279
Dejonge, Trixie, 39, 41
Dektyar, Oskar, 135

Della (Barris), 48
Delugg, Milton, 42
de Mol, John, Jr., 234–36, 238, 242
Desperate Networks (Bill Carter), 191–92, 278
Detroit Free Press, 301
Di Bona, Vin, 90
The Dick Cavett Show, 67, 68
Diller, Barry, 98, 101, 149–50
"dirty documentary" genre, xv
Disloyal (Cohen), 371
Dizzy, 118
documentaries, xv, 268, 269, 273
Documentary magazine, 274
Doganieri, Elise, 280
Dog Eat Dog, 291
The $1.98 Beauty Show, 37
Dominus, Susan, 352
Donahue, Phil, 88
Douglas, Kyan, 339, 340
Dowdell, Tara, 385
Downey, Robert, 46
Dragnet, 98, 99
Drew, Robert, 53
Duffy, Mike, 301
Dugard, Martin, 186
Dunlop, Scott, 352, 356, 357

Eamee, 118
Eavesdropper at Large (Funt), 15, 18
Eco-Challenge, 188–89, 204, 225, 228
Eco-Challenge Lifestyles, 187
Edwards, Antoinette, 60
Edwards, Billy, 60
Edwards, Bogart, 60
"An 18-Year-Old Looks Back on Life" (Joyce Maynard), 72
Eilenberg, David, 374
Einhorn, Randall, 204–6, 231–32
Elmo, Tina, 345
Elphick, Helen, 176
emotainment, 234
Encounters, 150
Endemol Entertainment, 182, 235–41, 284

Ender, Chris, 246
Entertainment Weekly, 138, 271, 301, 302, 342
Enter Talking (Rivers), 27
Ephron, Nora, 71
Escape! Because Accidents Happen, 157
Esquire magazine, 40, 70, 72, 338–39
Etheridge, Brian Keith, 297–99, 300, 301, 302
The Etiquette Game, 37
Eubanks, Bob, 35–37, 43
European reality TV, 162, 172–74, 177
Evolution Media, 242, 274
Expedition: Robinson, 182–84
extreme-sports shows, 156
Eye on L.A., 148–49

The Fabulous Pop Tarts, 334
Face International, 185
The Family Game, 37
Faraldo, Danielle
    Bunim and, 126, 127
    Korpi and, 123
    The Real World and, 113–14, 121–22, 125–26, 141
Farr, Jamie, 41
Fawcett, Farah, 33
Feist, John Russell, 198, 199, 212, 219–20
Field, Patricia, 347
Fields, Kim, 94
Filicia, Thom, 339, 340, 345
Film Comment, 56, 83
First Person, 337
Fisher, Peter, 337–38
Flagg, Fannie, 23
Flagler, J. M., 24
Fleiss, Mike
    after *The Bachelor,* 317–18
    after *Who Wants to Marry a Multi-Millionaire?,* 304
    The Bachelor and, 310, 314, 317
    biography of, 158–59, 312, 313
    Chao and, 160

Fleiss, Mike (*cont'd*):
  Darnell and, 158, 160, 161–62, 168, 304
  Hatta and, 276–77
  High School Reunion and, 305
  Joe Millionaire and, 319
  Levenson and, 306, 312–13
  Nash and, 160
  on reality TV, 318
  Rehn and, 316
  on Sarah Shapiro, 330
  Shocking Behavior Caught on Tape,
    161
  on Trump's presidency, 386
  Who Wants to Marry a Multi-
    Millionaire?, 162, 163–69
  The World's Meanest People Caught
    on Tape, 160–61
Flip That House, 274
The Flying Phone Booth (Tyrell), 27–28
Foerderer, Norma, 359
Foley, Sean, 221
Fort Worth Star-Telegram, 152
Fowler, Karen, 243
Fox, Rob, 125
Fox, Sonny, 17
Fox TV, xiii, 97–98, 151–53, 154, 157,
  162, 163
Frakes, Jonathan, 151–52
Francis, Arlene, 31
Frankel, Bethenny, 391
"Frankenbites," 321, 341, 379, 391
Freshman Diaries, 272
Fuentes, Daisy, 90
Fugelsang, John, 90
Fuller, Simon, 278
The Funny Money Man, 13
Funt, Allen
  biography of, 13–14, 21, 26–27
  Candid Camera, 12–13
  Candid Microphone, xv, 12, 16–18
  characteristics of, xvi, 13, 24–25, 27,
    28, 29
  critics' loathing of, 23–24
  emotional state of audiences and
    participants and, 25–26

"hidden microphone" shows, 14–16
  Joan Rivers and, 23, 27–28
  situationalism approach and, 209
  Totally Hidden Video and, 158
Fun TV with Kato-chan and Ken-chan,
  90
Fusil, Gérard, 185, 187

The Game Game, 37
The Game Show King (Barris), 44–45
game shows, 8–12, 49
  See also specific shows
Games People Play, 86
Gandolfini, James, 78–79
Garcia, Nina, 347
Gardner, Heather B., 113, 123, 128,
  130–31, 140–41
Garman, Ralph, 299
Garofalo, Janeane, 139–40
Gascon, David, 106
Gaspin, Jack, 339, 344
Gates, Daryl, 106
The Gay Byrne Show, 173
Gelbart, Larry, 379–80
Geldof, Bob, 177
"Gene Gene the Dancing Machine," 41
Getzlaff, James, 343
Giaimo, Cara, 22
Giddings, Al, 86–87
Gilbert, Craig
  Cinema Verite and détente with Louds,
    79
  editing of *An American Family,* 61–62
  filming of *An American Family,* 55, 56,
    57, 58
  financing of *An American Family,* 56
  idea for *An American Family,* 50–51
  introduction to *An American Family,*
    63–64
  on Loud's participation in *An*
    American Family, 65
  misgivings about *An American Family,*
    69
  Pat Loud on, 83–84
  Raymonds on, 78–79

Roiphe on, 68
situationalism approach and, 209
Gillespie, Park, 274
Gillett, Peter, 174
Gillott, Jacky, 176
Glass, Frankie, 179
Glass, Stephen, 270
Glidewell, Romey Jakobson, 293
The Glutton Bowl, 277
Godfrey, Arthur, 21
Gold, Kym, 185
Goldberg, Leonard, 34
The Golden Cage, 236
Golk (Stern), 24
The Gong Show, xvi, 40–43, 44–45
The Gong Show Movie, 46
Goodman, Tim, 170
The Good Will Hour, 6
Goodwin, Tommy, 53
Gordan, Howard, 150
Gould, David, 366, 369
Gould, Matt Kennedy, 298, 299–300,
   301, 302–3
Grandstaff, Tracy, 118–19, 121, 132
Granoff, Budd, 30, 45
Gray, Duncan, 177, 179, 180, 181, 209,
   362
Gray, Ramona, 194, 196, 210, 219–20,
   224–25
Greatest American Dog, 274
Greed, 38, 277
Greenebaum, Gary, 106
The Gripe Booth, 14
Grodner, Allison, 253, 258, 260–62, 351
Gross, Michael Joseph, 337–38
Gruber, Desiree, 347
Grushow, Sandy, 157, 166–68, 271–72,
   322
Guardian, 182
Gumbel, Bryant, 224
Gunn, Tim, 348, 350

Haggar, Daley, 373–74, 375–76
Haleyi, Miriam, 348
Hall, Arsenio, 98

Hamburger, Philip, 23–24
Hamerow, Ellie, 61
Hampton, Colleen Haskell, 295–96
Hannaham, James, 338–39, 349–50
Hanser, David, 61
Harris, Ed, xvii, xviii
Hart, Garry, 293
Haskell, Colleen
   after *Survivor,* 229–30, 295–96
   basic facts about, 197, 210, 216
   Buis and, 208
   casting of, 194
   Survivor reunion, 224
Hasselhoff, David, 94
Hatch, Richard
   after *Survivor,* 230
   as antihero, 213
   basic facts about, 196, 212, 223
   Boesch and, 196, 208
   casting of, 196
   description of, on *Survivor,* 171
   final tribal council, 219, 220
   fishing equipment won by, 211–12
   food crisis precipitated by, 217–19
   gambit by, to remain, 208–9
   sexuality of, 196, 208–9, 213
   Survivor reunion, 224
   as understanding *Survivor* as game of
      manipulation, 209–10
"The Hating Game" (Andrews), 46–47
Hatta, Ben, 275–77, 312–13, 326,
   327–28, 330–31
Hawk, Sue
   after *Survivor,* 229, 230
   casting of, 194, 196
   description of, on *Survivor,* 171
   final tribal council, 219–20
   Survivor reunion, 224
   Wiglesworth and, 209
Heartburn (Ephron), 71
Helvenston, Scott, 282–83
Hemond, Susan, 186, 187
Henry, Amelia (Amy), 364, 367
Herzog, Doug, 118, 270
Hewland, Jane, 172–73

Hiatt, Lincoln, 179
hidden-camera stunt, invention of, 13
High School Reunion, 305, 325–27
Hill, Michael, 48
Hilton, Paris, 285
Hirschorn, Michael, 357
Hoffman, Kristian, 70
Holcomb, Jessica, 328, 329, 331
Holliday, George, 106
Holmes, Beth, 193
Holston, Noel, 40
Holzman, Eli, 346, 347
homosexuality
    An American Family, 67, 68, 333
    Baily and Barbato, 333–34
    Boy Meets Boy, 343–44
    Channel 35 and, 334
    early gay reality producers, 336
    Jackass, 288–89
    media homophobia, 68, 72
    Project Runway and, 348, 349–50
    reality TV and, xviii, 173
    The Real World, 133–35, 138
    Survivor and, 196, 213–14
    on TV during Obama years, 358
    use of word "queer," 342–43
    See also Queer Eye for the Straight Guy
Hornsby, David, 299, 302
host as provocateur, 15–16
Houston, Whitney, 94
How's Your Mother-in-Law?, 37
Humphreys, John, 152–53
Hung, William, 278

I Hate Suzie, 390
Image, 65
"invitational show," 102
Ishak, Sabrina, 319
Itkin, Mark, 116, 144, 159, 336
It's in the Book, Bob! (Eubanks), 36–37
It Sounds Impossible (Slate and Cook), 4

Jackass, 287–89
Jackson, Kwame, 364, 370, 372, 384–85

Jackson, La Toya, 94
Jackson, Michael, 33
Jaffe, Bob, 292–93, 294
Jail, 108
Jeffress, Scott, 312
Jenkins, Kristina, 311
The Jerry Springer Show, 88
Joe Millionaire, 319–23
The Joe Schmo Show, 297–303
John's Cabaret, 334
Johnson, Arte, 41
Johnson, Nora, 71
Jones, Jim, 118, 119, 139–40
Jopson, John, 153–54
Jordan, Jean, 243, 246–48
Joslin, Elliot, 21
Juarbe, Angel, Jr., 281
Jump In! (Mark Burnett), 188, 361

Kahl, Kelly, 191–92
Kampf, Philip, 173, 174
The Kansas City Times, 66
Kardashian, Kim, 355, 356
Kasem, Casey, 94
Kaufman, Amy, 307, 312
Keach, Stacy, 94
Keck, William, 231
Keeping Up with the Kardashians, 144, 355–56
Kelly, Christopher, 351
Kelly, Jacqueline, 293, 294
Kenniff, Sean, 194–95, 196, 197, 208, 211, 218, 229
Keough, Jeana, 352, 353
Keough, Shane, 354–55
Kepcher, Carolyn, 366, 370, 371
Kern, Jamie, 243, 251
Kin, Curtis, 243
King, Allan, 50, 60
King, Rodney, 106
Kirby, Will "Dr. Evil," 254, 255–57, 259, 262, 391
Kirchner, Frances, 39
Kirhoffer, John, 199
Kiss and Make Up, 5

Kiviat, Robert, 150–51, 152, 153
Klug, Joel
    after *Survivor*, 229
    basic facts about, 195–96, 197, 210,
        214
    Been and, 229
    on eating live grubs, 202
    reunion show, 360
    Stacey Stillman and, 225
    on Trump, 361
Klug, Rob, 118
Klum, Heidi, 347, 350
Knauss, Melania, 360
Knievel, Robbie, 156
Knoxville, Johnny, 286–87
Kornfeld, Dan, 291–92
Korpi, Norman, 123, 133–35
Kors, Michael, 347
Korzan, Kelly, 341
Kozer, Sarah, 320–21
Kramer, Charles, 378
Kressley, Carson, 339, 340–41, 343
Kroll, Jon, 253–54, 256, 257, 263, 268,
        295, 379
Kroll, Lester, 4
Kruml, Stan, 291
Kuralt, Charles, 61
Kushman, Rick, 156

Lachey, Nick, 283, 285–86, 355
Ladies' Home Journal, 70
Ladizinsky, Ivan, 221–22
Lake, Ricki, 88
Lance, Peter, 223, 226, 294
*Lance Loud! A Death in An American
    Family,* 76–77
Lane, Diane, 78–79
Lange, Jim, 32, 44
Langley, John
    *American Vice: The Doping of a
        Nation,* 95–97
    biography of, 93, 108–9
    characteristics of, 92–93, 107–8
    Cocaine Blues, 93–94
    "Stop the Madness," 94–95

Wurms and, 102–3
    See also Cops
Langley, Morgan, 108
Langston, Murray, 41
LaPlante, Rob, 384
Lardner, John, 24
Larry King Live, 169
Lassally, Tom, 273
Lasser, Louise, 73–74
Laughter Therapy, 28
Law and Order, 99–100, 102
Lear, Norman, 37–38, 73–74
Lessner, Inbal, 323–25, 380
Lester, Susan, 51, 84
Levak, Richard, 194
Levenson, Lisa
    The Bachelor and, 306–7, 312, 317
    Big Brother and, 253, 260
    Fleiss and, 306, 312–13
    importance of, xvi
Levine, Shari, 353
Levy, Lyn, 30
Levy, Sarah, 375, 383, 389
Lewin, Kurt, 13
Lewis, Jenna, 195, 197, 206, 229–30
Lewis, Richard, 21–22
Lieberman, Joe, 289
Life After Reruns, 149, 160
Life magazine, 33, 34
Lim, Terence, 206, 207, 227
Lipsitz, Jane, 347
Live PD, 107
Living in the Past (Percival), 176
Living in the Past (television program),
    175–76
The Lonely Crowd (Riesman), 22
Longino, Bob, 373
Los Angeles Times, 51, 66, 69, 97, 105,
    106, 186, 187, 231, 272, 282
Lost, 279
Loud family
    after *An American Family Revisited,*
        76–78, 80–83, 84
    after final episode of *An American
        Family,* 70–71

Loud family (*cont'd*):
airport scene, 79–80
An American Family Revisited, 75–76
attempt to explain selves to American public, 66–67, 71–72
Bill and Pat's divorce, 56, 57–60, 63–64
Bill as single man, 56–57
critics' response to, 66, 67–69, 71–73, 84
described, 51–52
fan mail to, 68
filming of, 52, 53–55, 59, 60
hours of film shot of, 61
rewatching of *An American Family* by, 81
sibling relationships, 80–81
"The Love Company," 33–34, 38, 39, 258
The Love Company (Buffington), 39
Love Cruise, 279
Love Is Blind, 391
Love Letters, 234–35

Maas, James, 22
Mack, Ted, 41
Major Bowes' Original Amateur Hour, 40–41
Making the Band, 144
Making the Cut, 350
Malin, Mike "Boogie," 257
Mallory, Kaye, 249
Manhattan Cable, 334
Manhunt, 292–94
Manigault, Omarosa, 364, 367, 369, 370, 385, 386
Mann, Don, 189
man-on-the-street radio programs, 5–7
Margaret Mead's New Guinea Journal, 51
Margera, Bam, 287, 289
Marquis Chimps, 33
A Married Couple, 50, 60
Marriott, Evan, 319, 320–21, 322–23
Marsh, Amanda, 307–8, 309, 312, 313, 314, 315–17
Martin, Steve, 33

Mary Hartman, Mary Hartman, 73–74
Masterson, John, 87
Maynard, Fredelle, 65, 71–72
Maynard, Ghen
The Amazing Race and, 279–80
Big Brother and, 242, 250, 251, 255, 260–61
biography of, 190–91
Survivor and, 191–92, 195, 222
Maynard, Joyce, 72
McCarroll, Jay, 348, 349, 350
McClain, Troy, 364, 365, 385
McCluggage, Kerry, 293
McEnroe, John, 277
McGee, Eddie, 243, 251, 253–54
McLuhan, Marshall, xix
Mead, Margaret, 66, 74
Mecklenberg, Al, 57
Meegan, Jean, 7
Messick, Scott, 194, 199, 205–6, 208, 231
The Method to the Madness (Salkin and Short), 371
Metzger, Ellen, 39
Metzger, Mike, 32, 42–43
Metzler, David, 337, 339
Miami Herald, 103
Michel, Alex, 307, 308, 311, 314, 315–16
Michenaud, Jean-Michel, 319, 324, 325
Milgram, Stanley, 23
"militainment," 281–83
Military Diaries, 272
Miller, Merle, 72–73
Mills, Fernando, 203
"misery shows" on radio, 6
Mister Candid Camera, 25–26
"The Modern Thumb Screw" (Crosby), 6
Money Talks, 26–27
Moonves, Les, 190
Big Brother and, 242, 244, 257
Survivor and, 191–92, 195, 196
Survivor reunion and, 223
Moore, Frazier, 373
Morgan, Jaye P., 41, 43
Morgan, Raymond R., 8
Moss, Morgan, 271, 272

The Mrs. Mouth Show, 334
Muir, E. Roger, 34
Mumler, William H., 154
Murder In Small Town X, 281
Murdoch, Anna, 159, 160
Murdoch, Rupert, 88, 101
Murray, Jon, 113
  An American Family and, 115, 117
  biography of, 114–16
  Bunim and, 116
  friendship between Oliver and
    Gardner, 128
  importance of, xvi, 145–46
  Keeping Up with the Kardashians and,
    355
  Love Cruise and, 279
  Oliver and, 122–23
  The Real World and, 113, 121, 124,
    137, 141
  sexuality of, 133–34
  shows after *The Real World,* 144–45
  The Simple Life and, 285
  situationalism approach and, 209
Musto, Michael, 135
My Big Fat Obnoxious Fiance, 324
The Mystery of Al Capone's Vaults, 95,
  149

Nash, Bruce, 157, 158, 160
Navarro, Nick, 101
NBC Nightly News, 167
Nelson, Harriet, 10
Network 7, 162, 172–74
The Newlywed Game, 34–37, 42
Newlyweds, 283, 285–86
Newsweek, 69, 222, 373
The New Treasure Hunt, 40
The New Yorker, 23–24
New York Herald Tribune, 5
New York magazine, 71
The New York Times, 60, 61, 66, 85, 86,
  87, 102, 137–38, 156–57, 166, 189
The New York Times Magazine, 67–68,
  72, 352
The Next Joe Millionaire, 322, 323, 324

Nicholson, Robert "Nick," 34
Nies, Eric, 113, 123
9/11/2001, 260–62, 279, 281
"No Rats, No Fakery" (Strachan), 271
Now It Can Be Told, 150

O'Brien, Simon, 174
OceanQuest, 86–87
" 'OceanQuest' " (Corry), 87
O'Connor, John J., 66, 102, 137–38
O'Donnell, Rosie, 360, 382
The Office, 232
Ohlmeyer, Don, 157
Oliver, Julie
  day job at Viacom, 139
  Gardner and, 128
  on Korpi's sexuality, 134
  Murray and, 122–23
  Powell and, 129–31
  The Real World and, 113, 135–36
Oliver, Shannon, 313, 314
Ondrusek, Gene, 194, 200, 224
Open Book (Simpson), 285
Oppenheimer, Jess, 45
The Original Good Will Hour, 4
The Osbournes, 283–84, 285
Oswald, Jeff, 249
Oui magazine, 70
Owens, Peter "Babylon," 201

Paley, William, 30
The Paranormal Borderline, 153
paranormal series, 150–54
The Parent Game, 37
Parker, William H., 99
Parks, Kristen, 189, 377, 380–81
Parsons, Charlie
  background of, 172, 173
  The Big Breakfast, 177
  Big Brother and, 242
  Burnett and, 190
  "Castaway" and, 174
  Davies and, 178
  Survivor and, 174–75, 178, 180–81,
    223

Parsons, Charlie (cont'd):
  Survivor in Britain and, 178
  The Word, 177
Pat Loud (Pat Loud and Nora Johnson),
  71
Pearlman, Michael, 340
Pemberton, Lacey, 308
People Are Funny, 5
People magazine, 87, 103, 170
The People's Court, 6, 87
Percival, John, 175–76
Peterson, Gervase
  after Survivor, 229
  basic facts about, 197, 214
  as Black contestant, 214
  casting of, 194
  final tribal council, 220
  racial politics of Survivor, 224–25
  Survivor reunion, 224
Petros, Brittany, 243, 246
Phillips, Irna, 10
Pilafian, Peter, 57
Piligian, Craig
  characteristics of, 199, 203
  The Runner and, 279
  Survivor and, 195, 201, 207, 214
Pinkett, Randal, 385
Pittsburgh Post-Gazette, 165,
  302–3
Planet 24, 177, 182
Playboy, 169
PM, 19
The Police Tapes, 75, 100, 102
Pollard, Phil, 17
Polone, Gavin, 78
Poniewozik, James, xvi, 281–82
Pontius, Chris, 288
Pop Idol, 278
Povicj, Maury, 88
Powell, Kevin, 123, 128, 129–31
prank shows, 12–13, 101
  See also specific shows
predictors, role of, xvii
Pretty Wicked, 275
Prisoners Out of Control, 157

Probst, Jeff
  Buis and, 215–16
  characteristics of, 207
  Expedition: Robinson and, 183–84
  hiring of, 199
  as host, 206–7
  on producers' hoped for winner, 225
  Survivor and, 197, 233
Prochilo, Doug, 191
producer-provocateurs, 13, 15–16, 210,
  314, 320, 365
product integration, 368, 373–74,
  377–78
Professional Idiot (Steve O), 288
Project Greenlight, 346–47
Project Runway
  cast's contracts, 350
  as defining Bravo brand, 351–52
  episodes, 347–49
  genesis of, 346, 347
  homosexuality and, 348, 349–50
  ratings, 349
  as reality show to celebrate skill and
    craftsmanship, 348
protoreality shows, 6, 88
  See also specific shows
Pruitt, Bill, 365–67, 369–70, 371, 386–87
public access cable TV, 87–88
Pulau Tiga. See Survivor

Queen for a Day, 8–12, 87
Queer Eye for the Straight Guy
  casting, 338–39
  criticism of, 342
  culture guy, 339
  filming of, 340–41
  genesis of, 337–38
  homosexuality of cast, 343, 344–45,
    349
  promotion of, 341–42
  slogan, 344
  success of, 342

Raab, Chris, 290
Raadgever, Martijn, 237

racism
  Cops, 102, 105, 107
  The Real World and, 128–30
  Survivor, 224–25
  of Trump, 370–71
Radar, 321
radio
  calls from listeners, 3
  forerunners of reality TV on, xv
  "hidden microphone" shows, 14–16
  Kroll/Anthony, 4
  man-on-the-street programs, 5–7
  "misery shows," 6
  postwar era programs, 3
  quiz shows, 4
  talk, 3–4
"Raid Gauloises," 185–87
Rainey, David "Puck," 142, 143
Raisbeck, Robert, 8
Rancic, Bill, 364, 367, 370, 385
Raphael, Sally Jessy, 88
Raymond, Alan and Susan
  An American Family and, 51, 53–56,
    57, 59
  An American Family Revisited, 75–76
  Cinema Verite and, 78–79
  *Lance Loud! A Death in An American
    Family,* 76–77
  last interview with Lance Loud, 77–78
  Pat Loud on, 83
  The Police Tapes, 75, 100, 102
Reagan, Nancy, 94
*The Real Housewives of Orange
  County,* 353–55, 356, 357
Reality Bites, 139–40, 296
reality TV
  appeal of, xv
  attempt to change terms naming, xiv
  audiences, 392–93
  authenticity of, 13, 15–16, 210, 314,
    320, 357, 365
  British, 162, 172–74, 177
  casts, 138–39, 140, 295, 390–91
  characteristics of ideal shows, 162
  "the confessional," 142

  credulous cynicism of, 154
  as documentaries, xv, 273
  end of, 388
  fake videos for, 161
  genres, 8–13, 49–50
  gentrification of, 352
  as guilty pleasure, 383
  labor conditions, 330–31
  mindset of industry producing, xvii
  mockumentary sitcoms and, 232–33
  9/11/2001 and, 260–62, 279, 281
  "original sin" of, 119
  producers and stars of early, xvi
  programming in 1980s, 85, 86–87
  on public access cable TV, 87–88
  radio forerunners of, xv
  self-awareness of subjects and
    authenticity of footage, 141
  series debuting in 2000 and 2002,
    267–68
  situationalism approach, 209
  as social experiment, xvi, 263
  Survivor and supposed death of, 170
  teenagers as directors and stars of
    own, xiv
"Reality TV May Be Down but It's Not
  Out" (Andrejevic), 283
Real Life, 74–75, 118, 296
real-life soap opera, 49–50, 73
  See also specific shows
Real People, 85, 86
The Real Roseanne Show, 274
The Real World
  bonding between crew and cast, 124
  Burnett and, 188
  as cinéma vérité, 135–36, 137
  credit sequence, 137
  critics' response to, 137–38, 141
  debut of, xv
  distinctive look of, 335
  diversity and casting, 128, 129, 130, 338
  editing of, 135–36
  episode with photo of Eric naked,
    113–14, 125–26
  filming of, 113, 124

The Real World (cont'd):
  first season of, 136–37
  fling between Richmond and Blasband, 131, 132
  fling between Richmond and Grandstaff, 132
  Hedonism II resort in Jamaica, 131–32, 133
  "he said/she said" conflict on, 129
  homosexuality on, 133–35, 138
  importance of, 114
  movie satire of, 139–40
  pilot, 118–20
  popularity of, 138
  problem of lack of drama, 124–25
  Rodney King beating and, 128–29, 130
  second season, 141
  set, 123–24
  staff, 121
  The Truman Show and, xvii
  Zamora and, xviii, 135
The Real World: Los Angeles, 141
The Real World: Road Rules, 144
The Real World: San Francisco, 142–43
The Real World/Road Rules Challenge, 144–45, 291
Rebuttal, 5
Reese, Rhett, 277, 297, 302
"Reflections on 'An American Family,'" (Gilbert), 69
Rehn, Trista, 307, 312, 313–15, 316
Reid, Tim, 94
Reilly, Kevin, 273
Reisfeld, Peter, 118–19
The Residents, 272–73
Richie, Nicole, 285
Richmond, Bill, 124, 125, 131–32
Riesman, David, 22
Riggs, Conrad, 191, 363
The Ringer (Baker), 322
Rittenhouse, Rhonda, 307, 309–10, 318
Rivera, Geraldo, 95–97, 149, 150
Rivers, Joan, 23, 27–28, 98
Roach, Jay, 273
Road Rules, 291

Road Rules: All Stars, 291
Robbins, Tim, 78–79
The Robin Byrd Show, 334
Robinson, 183
Rocket Science Laboratories, 319, 323, 324
Rockwell, Rick, 163, 164, 165, 166, 167, 168, 169, 255
Rockwell, Sam, 48
Rodriguez, Jai, 339, 340, 344–45
Roeper, Richard, 322
Roiphe, Anne, 67–68, 72, 84
Rolling Stone, 166, 287
Römer, Bart, 235
Römer, Paul
  Big Brother in U.S. and, 242, 244, 246, 251
  development of *Big Brother,* 235, 236, 237
Rosenberg, Howard, 91, 97
Ross, Doug, 343–44
Ross, George, 366, 370
Ross, Paul, 177
Roswell, 152
Roth, Peter, 155
Rouse, Terry, 97
The Runner, 276, 279
Runner's World, 186
Running from Cops podcast, 105, 107
RuPaul's Drag Race, 357–58
The RuPaul Show, 335–36
Rupel, Dave, 353, 354
Ryan, Gerry, 173–74

The Sacramento Bee, 156
Saget, Bob, 90–92
Salkin, Allen, 371
Salles, Danny, 298, 299
Sandman, Scott, 217, 218–19, 314–15, 317
San Francisco Examiner, 166
Santilli, Ray, 151, 152, 153
Sassa, Scott, 157
The Saturday Review, 46–47

Savija, Sinisa, 182–83
Scanlon, Claire, 371–73
Scarborough, Janel, 118, 338
Schaffrich, Nicole Nilson, 259–60, 262
Scheiner, Georganne, 10–11
Schepel, Brian "Butch," 340
Schlatter, George, 85–86
Schlesinger, Adam, 127
Scholtze, Patrick, 235
Schwartz, Rick, 277
Schwarzenegger, Arnold, 94
Scott, Nelson, 96, 97
Scott, Tony, 281
Screw magazine, 70
Sears, Mike, 189, 193
Sequin Raze, 329
Series 7: The Contenders, 297
Shaalan, Hash, 293
Shales, Tom, 138
Shapiro, Arnold, 253, 351
Shapiro, Sarah Gertrude, 325–27,
    328–29, 330, 331–32
Sheets, Tom, 161
Shelly, Tom, 199, 201, 222
Shoot to Thrill (Davis), 105
Short, Aaron, 371
Shriver, Daniel, 258–59, 262–3, 376, 379,
    381
Sightings, 150
Silver, Darryl, 363
Silverman, Fred, 45
Simon, Ron, 79
The Simple Life, 144, 285
Simpson, Jessica, 283, 285–86
Sims, Howard "Sandman," 40
Siriano, Christian, 350
situationalism approach, 209
60 Minutes, 40
Slate, Sam J., 4
Slep, Al, 17
"Smile! You're on *Candid Camera,*" 25,
    26
Smith, Cecil, 66
Smith, Ted, 362–63, 368, 369, 384
The Smoking Gun website, 166–67, 168

"snowglobing," 380
Solovey, Sam, 364, 365, 367–68
Souza, Josh, 243, 246
Space Jump, 157
Spillman, Lynne, 193, 195
Spin magazine, 141
sponsors
    Burnett's use of, 186, 189
    fear of alienating, 155
    homosexuality and, 134
    reality TV stars' salaries and, 139
    Survivor and, 192
Spurlock, Morgan, 274–75
St. Mark's Place, 117
Standard-Times (San Angelo), 170
Steele, Diane, 165
Stern, Howard, 158
Stern, Richard, 24
Stevens-Thomas, André, 356
Steve O, 288
Stewart, Martha, 377
Stiller, Ben, 139–40
Stillman, Stacey, 195, 208, 210, 223,
    225–29
Stojanovich, Paul, 157
"Stop the Madness," 94–95
Strachan, Alex, 271
Street-Porter, Janet, 172–73
Strike It Rich, 8
stunt problems, 291
The Surreal Life, 284
Survive!, xiii, 178–81, 189–90
Survivor
    after 9/11, 279
    arrival on island, 197–98
    Burnett and Piligian during, 201
    cast after, 229–30
    casting, 193–96
    cast voted off, 199, 206, 208, 211, 216,
        225, 226–27
    as "catnip" to sponsors, 192
    conditions on island, 198–99, 200–201
    conflicts between crew and cast, 215
    cost of, 192
    crew after, 231–32

Survivor (cont'd):
    development of, 174–75
    eating live grubs, 202–3
    editing, 220–22
    Einhorn and, 204–5
    evolution of, 233
    as *Expedition: Robinson,*
        182–84
    fake island mythology, 206
    field producers' power, 201–2
    filming of, 204–6, 207, 208,
        210–11
    final tribal council, 219–20
    food crises, 216–19
    format of, 171
    as game of manipulation, 209–10
    homosexuality and, 196
    importance of, 171
    lawsuit, 225–29
    main characters of, 171
    Ghen Maynard and, 191–92
    moral dimension of, 197
    plots of, 208–9, 221
    production crew, 193, 194, 199–200,
        203, 227
    production problems, 201
    racial politics of, 224–25
    reunions, 223–24, 360–61
    second season in Australia, 291
    signature line of, 207
    situationalism approach of, 209
    success of, 222–23, 305
    Wicker Man event, 205
    See also Survive!
The Survivor Company, 192
Susskind, David, 27
Sutter, Ryan, 216

Taberski, Dan, 107
Taggart-Ratcliffe, Millee, 145
talk radio, 3–4
Tanner '88, 273
Tarses, Jamie, 178
Taxicab Confessions, 162
Taylor, Rip, 37

Taylor, Trip, 287, 288, 289
"Team American Pride," 186–87
Tedeschi, David, 270
Television Business International,
    235
Temptation Island, 317
Terkelsen, Brian, 187
Terry, John, 57
That Girl, 31
That's Incredible!, 86
That's My Line, 86
The Times United Kingdom, 241
30 Days, 274–75
This Machine, 275
Thomas, Jay, 163
Thompson, Mark, 155, 156, 166
"The Threat to Democratic Capitalism
    Posed by Modern Culture" (Chao),
    159–60
3's a Crowd, 45–46
Three on a Date (Buffington), 39
Time magazine, 99, 281
Totally Hidden Video, 27, 158
Tremaine, Jeff, 287
The Triumph of Christy Brown, 51
Trow, George W. S., 45–46
Trudeau, Gary, 273
The Truman Show, xvii–xviii, 296,
    393
Trump, Donald
    before *The Apprentice,* 360–61
    Bailey and, 358–59, 386
    The Celebrity Apprentice, 382–83
    characteristics of, 364, 365–66, 369–70,
        375, 382
    Cutler and, 275
    election of 2016, 383, 385
    fired by NBC, 383
    Fleiss on, 386
    on panel at Museum of Television &
        Radio, 381–82
    presidency of, 386, 387
    Queen for a Day and, 9
    racism of, 370–71
    reality shows produced by, 382

sexism of, 374–75
See also The Apprentice
Truth or Consequences (radio program),
    5, 13
TV Guide, 41
Tyrell, Lou, 27–28

Unckles, Steve, 289–90
unionization, 89–90, 376–77, 378–81,
    388–90
"The Unknown Comic," 41
"The Unknown Hussy," 41
UnREAL, 329–30, 331
Unruh, Daniela, 347, 348
"unscripted programming," xiv
Up series, 115

The Vancouver Sun, 271
Vanderbilt, Tom, 156–57
Vanity Fair, 270, 279
van Munster, Bertram, 105, 280, 281
Van Patter, Kelly, 199, 206, 220, 364, 368,
    375
Vasgersian, Matt, 277
Velazquez, Richard, 365, 375, 383
Verrone, Patric, 376, 377, 378–79
Verschoor, George
    after *The Real World,* 144
    on Faraldo, 125, 126, 127
    Murder In Small Town X and, 281
    The Real World and, 122, 131–32, 142
    Survive! and, 179
Vetrini, Ereka, 364
Video Music Awards, 138
The Village Voice, 168
Viva La Bam, 289–90
Voyeur Vision, 334

Wacht, Adam, 118
Wagner, Joyce, 66
Waldon, Cassandra, 243, 245, 251
Walker, Katherine, 369, 371
Wallace, Mike, 40
Wapner, Joseph, 87
Ward, Burt, 149

Ward, Russ, 293
The Washington Post, 41, 91, 138
*Watch What Happens Live with Andy
    Cohen,* 357
Waters, John, 289
Wayans, Keenen Ivory, 190
Weatherly, Shawn, 86–87
Webb, Jack, 98–99
Weber, Bruce, 113
Wecht, Cyril, 151
Weinstein, Harvey, 346, 347, 348
Welcome Travelers, 5
Weng, Jude, 202, 203–4, 231, 290–91
Wernick, Paul, 297, 302
What Do You Say to a Naked Lady?,
    26
What Was I Thinking? (Rockwell), 169
What Women Watched (Cassidy), 9
Who Wants to Be a Millionaire?, 162,
    276
*Who Wants to Marry a Multi-
    Millionaire?,* 162, 163–69, 255,
    323
Wiglesworth, Kelly, 194
    after *Survivor,* 230
    basic facts about, 201, 208, 211
    final tribal council, 219
    food crises and, 217–18
    relations with cast members, 209
Wiig, Kristen, 298
Willard, Fred, 86
Williams, Michael, 337, 338
Williams, Montel, 88
Williams, Willie, 106
Williamson, Dud, 8
Winfrey, Oprah, 88
Winston, Stan, 151
Wiseman, Frederick, 99–100
"Within the Context of No-Context"
    (Trow), 45–46
Wollman, Don, 251, 252
women
    Barris's shows as hating, 47
    as comic relief, 10
    creators of early television, 10

women (*cont'd*):
  feminism and, 31, 45
  The Original Good Will Hour and, 4
  The People Pickers and, 30
  Queen for a Day and, 8–11
  stay-at-home mothers glamorized on
    television, 10
  Trump's sexism, 374–75
Wong, Andrea, 191, 276, 278, 305–6
The Word, 177
World of Wonder, 334, 335–36, 357
World's Biggest Bitches, 161, 170
*World's Greatest Hoaxes: Secrets Finally
  Revealed,* 152, 153–54
*The World's Meanest People Caught on
  Tape,* 160–61
World's Most Amazing Videos, 157
*The World's Most Embarrassing
  Throw-up Moments,* 157
World's Scariest Police Chases, 155
"Would You Like to Be Queen for a
  Day?"(Scheiner), 10–11
Writers Guild of America (WGA),
  89–90, 376–77, 378–80, 381, 388

writers of reality TV, 89–90, 376–81,
  388–90
Wurms, Jerry, 101, 102–3

The X-Files, 150, 152

The Year of the Sex Olympics, 297
You and Me, Babe (Barris), 40, 47
Young, David, 377

Zalaznick, Lauren
  Blow Out and, 351
  legacy of, 352, 357
  Project Runway and, 345–46, 349
  *The Real Housewives of Orange
    County* and, 353
  The Real World and, 137
  The RuPaul Show and, 336
Zamora, Pedro, xviii, 135, 142, 143, 144,
  344, 391
"zhuzh," 307
Zimbardo, Philip, 23
Zucker, Jeff, 305, 362
Zwerin, Charlotte, 61

ABOUT THE AUTHOR

EMILY NUSSBAUM has written for *The New Yorker* since
2011. She is the winner of the 2016 Pulitzer Prize for
criticism and the 2014 National Magazine Award for
Columns and Commentary. Previously, she was the
TV critic and editor of the Culture Pages for *New York*
magazine, where she created the Approval Matrix. She is
also the author of *I Like to Watch,* which was a finalist
for the PEN/Diamonstein-Spielvogel Award for the Art
of the Essay. She lives in Brooklyn with her husband,
Clive Thompson, and their two children.

emilynussbaum.com

ABOUT THE TYPE

This book was set in Sabon, a typeface designed by
the well-known German typographer Jan Tschichold
(1902–74). Sabon's design is based upon the original
letter forms of sixteenth-century French type designer
Claude Garamond and was created specifically to
be used for three sources: foundry type for hand
composition, Linotype, and Monotype. Tschichold
named his typeface for the famous Frankfurt typefounder
Jacques Sabon (c. 1520–80).